Palgrave Studies in the Enlightenment, Romanticism and Cultures of Print

General Editors: **Professor Anne K. Mellor** and **Professor Clifford Siskin**

Editorial Board: **Isobel Armstrong**, Birkbeck; **John Bender**, Stanford; **Alan Bewell**, Toronto; **Peter de Bolla**, Cambridge; **Robert Miles**, Stirling; **Claudia L. Johnson**, Princeton; **Saree Makdisi**, UCLA; **Felicity Nussbaum**, UCLA; **Mary Poovey**, NYU; **Janet Todd**, Glasgow

Palgrave Studies in the Enlightenment, Romanticism and Cultures of Print will feature work that does not fit comfortably within established boundaries – whether between periods or between disciplines. Uniquely, it will combine efforts to engage the power and materiality of print with explorations of gender, race, and class. By attending as well to intersections of literature with the visual arts, medicine, law, and science, the series will enable a large-scale rethinking of the origins of modernity.

Titles include:

Scott Black
OF ESSAYS AND READING IN EARLY MODERN BRITAIN

Claire Brock
THE FEMINIZATION OF FAME, 1750–1830

Brycchan Carey
BRITISH ABOLITIONISM AND THE RHETORIC OF SENSIBILITY
Writing, sentiment, and slavery, 1760–1807

E. J. Clery
THE FEMINIZATION DEBATE IN 18TH-CENTURY ENGLAND
Literature, Commerce and Luxury

Adriana Craciun
BRITISH WOMEN WRITERS AND THE FRENCH REVOLUTION
Citizens of the World

Peter de Bolla, Nigel Leask and David Simpson (*editors*)
LAND, NATION AND CULTURE, 1740–1840
Thinking the Republic of Taste

Ian Haywood
BLOODY ROMANTICISM
Spectacular Violence and the Politics of Representation, 1776–1832

Anthony S. Jarrells
BRITAIN'S BLOODLESS REVOLUTIONS
1688 and the Romantic Reform of Literature

Mary Waters
BRITISH WOMEN WRITERS AND THE PROFESSION OF LITERARY
CRITICISM, 1789–1832

Palgrave Studies in the Enlightenment, Romanticism and Cultures of Print
Series Standing Order ISBN 1–4039–3408–8 hardback 1–4039–3409–6 paperback
(outside North America only)

You can receive future titles in this series as they are published by placing a standing
order. Please contact your bookseller or, in case of difficulty, write to us at the address
below with your name and address, the title of the series and the ISBN quoted above.

Customer Services Department, Macmillan Distribution Ltd, Houndmills, Basingstoke,
Hampshire RG21 6XS, England

Bloody Romanticism

Spectacular Violence and the Politics of Representation, 1776–1832

Ian Haywood

First published 2006 by
PALGRAVE MACMILLAN
Houndmills, Basingstoke, Hampshire RG21 6XS and
175 Fifth Avenue, New York, N.Y. 10010
Companies and representatives throughout the world

PALGRAVE MACMILLAN is the global academic imprint of the Palgrave
Macmillan division of St. Martin's Press, LLC and of Palgrave Macmillan Ltd.
Macmillan® is a registered trademark in the United States, United Kingdom
and other countries. Palgrave is a registered trademark in the European
Union and other countries.

ISBN-13: 978–1–4039–4282–1 hardback
ISBN-10: 1–4039–4282–X hardback

This book is printed on paper suitable for recycling and made from fully
managed and sustained forest sources.

A catalogue record for this book is available from the British Library.

A catalog record for this book is available from the Library of Congress.

10   9   8   7   6   5   4   3   2   1
15   14   13   12   11   10   09   08   07   06

Transferred to digital printing in 2007.

To my family

Contents

List of Illustrations

Acknowledgements

This book would not have been written without the support of the Arts and Humanities Research Council, who granted me a Research Leave Award for 2005–06. I would like to express my gratitude to the AHRC and to Roehampton University for supporting my application to this scheme. The editorial team at Palgrave were enthusiastic about the project from the beginning, and particular thanks are due to Paula Kennedy and Anne Mellor. Special thanks to Anne Janowitz for her unflagging support for my intellectual endeavours. Timothy Fulford generously allowed me to read chapters of his book *Romantic Indians* in advance of its publication. Finally, thanks to staff and students at the following universities who have listened to me speak on this topic and who provided valuable feedback. In Britain: the universities of Warwick, Birmingham, Glasgow and Oxford; outside of Britain: the Gorky Literary Institute, Moscow; Plovdiv University, Bulgaria; and Trinity College, Dublin.

List of Abbreviations

LWF   Helen Maria Williams, *Letters Written in France*, Neil Fraistat and Susan S. Lanser, eds (Ontario: Broadview, 2001)

LFF   Helen Maria Williams, *Letters from France; Containing a Great Variety of Original Information Concerning the Most Important Events that have Occurred in that Country in the Years 1790, 1791, 1792, and 1793*, 2 vols (Dublin: J Chambers, 1794)

LCS   Helen Maria Williams, *Letters Containing a Sketch of the Politics of France From the Thirty-First of May 1793, till the Twenty-Eighth of July 1794, and of the Scenes which have passed in the prisons of Paris*, 2 vols (G. G. and J. Robinson, 1795)

SAE   *Slavery, Abolition and Emancipation: Writings in the British Romantic Period*, General eds Peter J. Kitson and Debbie Lee, 8 vols (Pickering and Chatto, 1999)

TEE   *Travels, Explorations and Empires: Writings from the Era of Imperial Expansion 1770–1835*, General eds Tim Fulford and Peter J. Kitson, 4 vols (Pickering and Chatto, 2001)

Introduction: Romantic Agonies

> When an enlightened age and nation signalizes itself by a deed, becoming none but barbarians and fanatics, Philosophy itself is even induced to doubt whether human nature will ever emerge from the pettishness and imbecility of its childhood.
>
> (P. B. Shelley, 'A Letter to Lord Ellenborough', 1812)[1]

It is March 1802. Dorothy and William Wordsworth spend the morning at Dove cottage reading a draft of William's poem 'The Butterfly'. In the afternoon a stranger knocks on the door asking for alms. The man is a 'faint and pale' sailor who is on his way to London to testify against his former captain, the master of a slave ship. The captain's crimes are succinctly reported in Dorothy's journal: 'one Man had been killed a Boy to put to lodge with the pigs and was half eaten, one Boy set to watch in the hot sun until he dropped down dead'. The sailor is determined to expose the atrocities: 'O he's a Rascal, Sir, he ought to be put in the papers!' The sailor also reveals that he 'had been cast away in North America and had travelled 30 days among the Indians where he had been well treated', and that he has persistently evaded press-ganging: 'he would rather be in hell than be pressed'. The next day, Wordsworth composes another poem 'The Emigrant Mother'.[2]

Here, in miniature, is the Romantic landscape of spectacular violence. In this brief encounter, Dove Cottage becomes the canvas for the atrocious global violence of imperial Britain. The sailor's much-travelled 'pale' body is a material signifier of the horrors of the slave trade and the depredations of European warfare. The figure of the sailor is a nexus of these two colossal institutions of violence, a carrier of the experience of global atrocities who brings these narratives back to the British fireside.[3] But the Dove Cottage sailor is also a radical, resistant voice, a representative of the need to expose and shame these institutions 'in the papers'. It is the 'press' which will pressure public opinion and find justice for the original 'pressing' of vulnerable bodies (according to the *OED*, the first use of the word 'press' to signify the

1

newspapers was in 1797, coincidentally the same year as the British naval mutinies). In one sense, the sailor personifies the progressive movement of history, as the British slave trade was to be abolished just five years later. But the sailor could not have known that Dove Cottage was a crucible of Romantic literature, a site of the production of 'the papers' of a new literary sensibility. Notice that his visit is chronologically and textually bracketed by two Romantic poems: the first, a seemingly innocuous nature poem; the second, a topical response to the ongoing war with Napoleonic France. The two poems represent a defining tension within Romantic poetry between retreat and engagement, between a subjective contemplation of nature and the need to intervene more overtly in the violent reality of history. But there are other challenges and illuminations in the sailor's confession. His foray into the American wilderness explodes the stereotype of the 'savage' American Indian, and the sailor's defiance of press-ganging evokes the radical power of the eighteenth-century English 'mob'. This forgotten peace protestor, a classic Romantic vagrant and wanderer, embodies a spectrum of ultra-violent historical forces in Romantic history and culture.

Given the prevalence of hyperbolic violence in the Romantic public sphere, it is surprising that a dedicated study of this topic has not yet been written. The rationale of *Bloody Romanticism* is therefore relatively simple: British Romanticism was historically concurrent with a series of catastrophically violent events – slavery and the slave trade, the American revolution, the French revolution, the Irish rebellion, and a series of industrial and political riots. In all these areas, the reading public was bombarded with a vast number of representations of extreme violence, yet this cultural landscape has not yet been fully integrated into our mapping and understanding of Romanticism. There has been no attempt to bring these different areas of conflict together and to study their shared and interactive discursive practices. One explanation for the lack of scholarly research in this field may be the fact that the critical issues which arise from a detached contemplation of this historical landscape are discomforting: How do we take account of the impact of these events on the Romantic imagination and the production of Romantic-period literature? Is the notion of 'bloody' Romanticism itself extreme? What is the appropriate critical language for analysing representations of extreme violence and for weighing up the effectiveness of a text, both in its own right and relative to other texts? It is of course impossible to answer these questions fully in a book of this length, but the argument of *Bloody Romanticism* is relatively straightforward if intentionally provocative. My thesis is that a new set of tropes needs to be introduced into our understanding of Romantic literature and culture. These tropes centre on the historical reality of what I am calling 'spectacular' violence. This punning phrase is designed to capture two defining aspects of the violence under discussion: its visual nature, extreme scale and public impact; and its sensational mode of representation. The word 'sensational' also carries two senses: first there is the modern cluster of meanings – dramatic, exciting, visceral, superlative – and secondly there is the eighteenth-century derivation from sensationalism: an appeal to the senses, sensibility and the sublime. I will show that the reason that spectacular violence became an important discourse in the Romantic period is not simply that the subject matter was politically controversial. In order for the Romantic period to develop an unprecedented self-awareness about the depravities of public violence, and in order for the radical critique of cyclical State violence to be disseminated throughout the public sphere, spectacular violence had to become a major cultural force. After all, atrocities and appalling violence have taken place throughout human history (and continue to the present day, though their representation is heavily screened by corporate media) and it is not my premise that the Romantic period was necessarily more violent than previous epochs. Even if this could be proved by some objective measure (for example, as will be clear already from the Dove Cottage incident, the Napoleonic wars affected most families in Britain), this would not in itself make Romantic-period violence 'spectacular' in my sense of the word. In order for violence to become spectacular, there had to be a high degree of cultural investment in the deployment of specific tools of representation. The emergence or foregrounding of a new cultural discourse is generally the result of a combination of 'external' and 'internal' factors: the 'external' factors are the determining forces of historical change, the 'internal' factors are the resources which art and literature utilize to meet these challenges. I have already outlined the significant historical events which produced an engaged response from Romantic writers and print culture, so let me move on to a brief discussion of the spectacularization of the Romantic representation of violence.

Put briefly and baldly, I will argue that spectacular violence was a vital and indelible component of those two foundational discourses of Romanticism: sensibility and the sublime. The affective power of both of these discourses was based on the reaction of a spectator to a suffering body (and for the purposes of this book, the body is human). More accurately, the affective gaze of both sensibility and the sublime was theorized as deriving from a dramatic confrontation of three bodies or subject positions: one in a situation of power, one in a situation of distress and a third body (the spectator, viewer or reader) observing the other two. Moreover, the aesthetic dynamic of this triangular vignette was primarily visual: both power and sympathy flowed from the sight of the abject body. In a very obvious sense, this moment of suffering was a 'spectacle', a staged and framed display of violence which was designed to carry a highly charged emotional and moral message. There was much overlap between sensibility and the sublime in providing guidelines for the 'correct' representation of suffering and explaining the controversial pleasure which could be derived from witnessing someone else's extreme suffering. I will look at the issue of exploitative spectatorship in a moment, but the key point is that spectacular violence was an integral component of the foundational eighteenth-century construction of sensibility. Put another way, spectacular violence was the violent extreme of the representation of suffering; it subjected the conventions of sensibility to a sublime degree of pressure, and in order to flourish, it required the development of some new tools of representation (in particular, a technique I have called 'hyperbolic realism', an attempt to take the scene of suffering to the limit point of what can be represented). But at its core, spectacular violence retained the basic structure of the bloody vignette, and it is this scene, subject to a wide variety of modifications and imaginative transpositions, which *Bloody Romanticism* follows through different spheres of national and global conflict. The bloody vignette was an extreme form of the vignette of suffering which was such a fundamental scene in late-eighteenth-century sentimental and Romantic literature, particularly when such writing engaged directly with political themes. But the bloody vignette cannot be pinned down to a particular ideological viewpoint, as it was a highly mobile trope which was readily appropriated by warring political factions and even self-divided Romantic writers.

The argument of *Bloody Romanticism* is that spectacular violence needs to be regarded as one of the tributary discursive streams which nourished the Romantic literary imagination. As the following chapters will show, Romantic readers were inundated with bloody vignettes: the imagination was the vehicle which transported the reader into a world of violence which was both remote and intimate. Like the Dove Cottage incident, spectacular violence brought the excesses of imperial violence and suffering into the heart of British culture. There was a shared concern in propaganda, reportage and literature to 'imagine' extreme violence and to make it relevant to the reader or viewer by utilizing the bloody vignette. The sheer volume of material covered in my five chapters should constitute clear evidence that Romantic readers were prodigious consumers of spectacular violence, and it is high time that this fact, and its impact on Romantic studies, was recognized. Spectacular violence released into Romantic culture a new repertoire of tropes of violation, but, as we shall see, it also equipped the reader with the means to contextualize and critique that violence. It is this dual purpose and effect which makes the study of spectacular violence so essential.

Apart from Ronald Paulson's seminal book *Representations of Revolution (1789–1820)* (1983), it is only in recent studies of Romantic literature and slavery that the theme of spectacular violence has been closely studied and probed. In particular, Marcus Wood's two books on slavery, *Blind Memory: Visual Representations of Slavery in England and America 1780–1865* (2000) and *Slavery, Empathy and Pornography* (2002), conduct a wide-ranging and illuminating investigation into what Wood regards as an almost complete failure of the Romantic imagination to humanize the figure of the slave.[4] Wood attributes this failure to an ingrained flaw in the aesthetics of sensibility, a strategic weakness which allowed the slave's suffering to be 'appropriated' by the viewer or reader. I regard this approach as challenging but too reductive. As I will show in a moment, vignettes of violence were not organized around a binary opposition of self and Other. On the contrary, spectacular violence provided a variety of shifting subject positions for the reader, and this specular dynamic made the relations of power between victim, perpetrator and spectator complex and challenging. But I also want to question Wood's assumption that most representations of slave violence constituted a degrading form of voyeurism. It is indisputably the case that anti-slavery writing contributed to the abolition of the slave trade in 1807 by raising consciousness about the atrocious treatment of slaves, and it seems perverse to cast this achievement as a monstrous act of (covert or explicit) cultural and ideological perversion. Moreover, as *Bloody Romanticism* will show, anti-slavery was not unique in its production of violent spectacle, and there are significant discursive continuities between slavery and other spheres of violent conflict which are not usually regarded as fatally undermined by an 'appropriation' of suffering. In each of these areas, it is my contention that spectacular violence is a manifestation of abusive power rebounding on itself, a process which Sartre, commenting on Fanon's *The Wretched of the Earth*, called the 'boomerang' effect.[5]

Historically, the common factor between these arenas of violence, and the crimson thread which ties them together, was the onward march of British capitalism and imperial power. This was seen clearly by Edmund Burke. As Luke Gibbons has observed, Burke's theories of sublime Terror were a 'set of diagnostic tools to probe the dark side of enlightenment, particularly as it was used to justify colonial expansion, religious bigotry, or political repression'.[6] Burke wanted to turn the Terror of violent spectacle against its perpetrators, 'emphasising the true horror that underpinned the colonial sublime' (4). This required a focus on compelling individual cases or vignettes of 'sublime' cruelty, a mode of representation which generated both 'sympathy' for and indignation at the fate of the victim. Burke derived this methodology from the new cult of sensibility, an aesthetic and cultural force which was to have such a profound effect on Romanticism. It is surely no coincidence that Burke produced *A Philosophical Enquiry into the Origin of Our Ideas of the Sublime and Beautiful* (1757) in the same decade that saw the publication of other key theoretical texts of sensibility: David Hume's *An Enquiry Concerning the Principles of Morals* (1751) and Adam Smith's *The Theory of Moral Sentiments* (1759). Hume and Smith make clear that the essence of sensibility is the sympathetic response of the spectator to a scene of suffering: in Hume's words, 'No man is absolutely indifferent' to the 'misery of others'.[7] The representational foundation of the operation of the sentimental moral faculty is therefore a spectacle of distress: as Janet Todd comments, both writers stressed 'the specular nature of sympathy'.[8] Significantly, both Hume and Smith use examples of extreme cruelty to prove their case, a point of overlap with Burke's theories of sublime Terror. Hume introduces the figure of a tyrannical landowner, 'a man, who had enslaved provinces, depopulated cities, and made the field and scaffold stream with human blood' (221). Hume's response to this figure is meant to be exemplary: he is 'struck with horror at the prospect of so much misery', but he also feels the 'strongest antipathy against the author' (221). Smith is even more sensational. He illustrates his theory of moral sentiments by alluding to a victim of torture:

> Though our brother is upon the rack . . . we place ourselves in his situation, we conceive ourselves enduring all the same torments, we enter as it were into his body, and become in some measure the same person with him, and thence form some idea of his sensations.[9]

This viewing position is not, as Marcus Wood argues, an invitation for the spectator to 'fantasize his/her own fictions of torture',[10] but a mode of identification which is simultaneously or interchangeably sympathetic and analytical. Smith is clear that the 'attentive spectator' must be adept at both 'changing places in fancy with the sufferer' (2: 203) and remaining 'impartial' (2: 219). In this way, both sensibility and rationality are operative. Burke also required aesthetic safeguards: 'When danger or pain press too nearly, they are incapable of giving any delight, and are simply terrible; but at certain distances, and with certain modifications, they may be, and they are delightful.'[11] The contention in *Bloody Romanticism* is that the 'certain distances' and 'certain modifications' which Burke requires are in fact in-built features of most spectacular violence. This distancing effect arises from the foregrounding of the violent gaze, the inclusion of one or more spectator figures within the violent vignette. This configuration of multiple points of view gives the reader or viewer a range of subject positions, and breaks down the binary opposition of self and Other which is implied in the simplistic viewer–victim model. Josephine McDonagh has noted a similar use of 'the triangle of violator, victim and spectator' in eighteenth-century vignettes of infanticide, and this complex aesthetic produces an 'intricate network of identifications' for the reader, who usually becomes the fourth player in the scene.[12]

The bloody vignette is a dynamic system of competing gazes and visual collisions. It is also a micro-narrative, and like other narratives it can be probed for its subtexts, symbols and cultural resonances. For example, when Burke states that danger and pain must not 'press too nearly', he is almost certainly punning on the word 'press' to evoke a form of torture which had just been practised spectacularly on Damiens, the 'late unfortunate regicide in France', whom Burke cites as an exemplary instance of the sublime power of the 'emotion of distress' (79). The execution of Damiens, who was torn apart by horses in front of the cream of French society, became a *cause célèbre* of *ancien régime* barbarism. Voltaire included a thinly veiled version of the execution in *Candide*, and the incident was cited by Thomas Paine as a touch-stone of the evils of 'kingcraft'. But most students of Romanticism are likely to know about Damiens from the fact that his execution is used to open Foucault's *Discipline and Punish* (1975). For Foucault, Damiens marks the beginning of the end of 'punishment as a spectacle'. During the Romantic period, the 'great transformation of the years 1760–1840', Foucault argues that the inflicting of pain in public was replaced by the panoptic regulation of the modern prison system; social control replaced brutal repression.[13] Foucault qualifies his historical schema by noting some exceptions to his rule, and he cites the exhibitionist use of the guillotine during the French revolution. But, as *Bloody Romanticism* will show, Foucault's thesis is inadequate when the global violence of imperial Europe is taken into account. Foucault's theory also underestimates the extent to which 'punishment as a spectacle' was the subject of a rigorous political critique at the time. Radicals and reformers realized that public torture and execution was a contradictory phenomenon: a ritual of political and class oppression which both exalted and undermined State power. For the penal reformer Cesare Beccaria, writing in 1764, public execution was the worst possible role model of governance, an 'example of savagery'.[14] By the 1790s, Thomas Paine was able to link Damiens to the popular justice of the French revolution. Paine, like many radicals, believed that Terror was a form of behaviour which the people learned from their masters: 'They learn it from the governments they live under, and retaliate the punishments they have been accustomed to behold.' The decapitation of Foulon after the storming of the Bastille, argues Paine, is an echo of the dismemberment of Damiens:

> The effect of those cruel spectacles exhibited to the populace, is to destroy tenderness, or excite revenge; and by the base and false idea of governing men by terror, instead of reason, they become precedents. It is over the lowest class of mankind that government by terror is intended to operate, and it is on them that it operates to the worst effect. They have sense enough to feel they are the objects aimed at; and they inflict in their turn the examples of terror they have been instructed to practise.[15]

For Paine, only a non-violent revolution and a voluntary abdication of power by the ruling classes could break this cycle.

This brief account of the *Bloody Romanticism*'s scholarly rationale will hopefully have explained my use of the term 'spectacular violence'. The phrase is designed to capture two defining aspects of the violence under discussion: its extreme scale and public impact, and its sensational mode of representation. I have also coined the subsidiary term 'hyperbolic realism' in order to identify a central, contradictory quality in much of the writing studied in this book: the tension between mimetic authenticity and mimetic ineffability. Marcus Wood addresses this issue by posing the question, 'is there a rhetoric for the description of atrocity beyond that of inventory?'[16] This impossible dilemma means that, for Wood, all writers and artists have to make 'compromises' between the two mimetic extremes of denotation (the inventory) and sublime incredulity (16). Rather than adopt a deficit model of 'compromise', however, my notion of hyperbolic realism incorporates ineffability as one of the rhetorical devices which writers used to dramatize the 'evil' nature of their material. This does not mean that the 'inventory' was not important, as many texts looked at in the following chapters will show. Nor does this mean a diminution in the sheer mimetic power of realism: 'pressing' the experience of violence into the public sphere. By the late eighteenth century, writers who wanted to portray spectacular violence were in an advantageous position, being able to draw on the achievements of both novelistic verisimilitude and the discourse of on-the-spot reportage, which was a hallmark of the construction of 'news' in the press.

In each of the areas of conflict studied in this book, I have tried to show that the wider Romantic print culture was not merely a pretext for Romantic literary texts, but a significant cultural force in which many key tropes were circulated and consolidated. This explains my decision to prioritize those writers who commanded a significant popular following. No doubt it would have been possible to have taken a more orthodox New Historicist approach, and to have excavated the repressed or displaced violent 'unconscious' of a large number of canonical Romantic texts, but, with a few exceptions, I leave that work to other scholars.

The organization of the chapters is based on both chronology and impact, though I am not trying to construct a coherent genealogy or metanarrative. I have begun with slavery as I believe that the colossal volume of anti-slavery propaganda published from the 1780s onwards placed spectacular violence firmly on the cultural landscape. The French revolution was obviously another prodigious source of violent imagery and narratives, and it seemed sensible to place the Irish rebellion directly after its French inspiration. The chapters on America and the Romantic mob begin by rewinding the historical clock, but the themes of these two chapters provide a nice contrast of remoteness and closeness in relation to the subject position of the Romantic reader.

Chapter 1 looks at the function of spectacular violence in representations of slavery. As Peter Kitson and Debbie Lee note, the geographical remoteness of slavery made the British reading public's experience of slavery dependent on representation: slavery was in this sense a 'written institution'.[17] Despite the vast amount of literature and propaganda generated by the anti-slavery campaign, it is only quite recently that the influence of slavery on Romanticism has begun to concern scholars. Lee expresses her initial reluctance to subject Romantic poets to this perspective: 'To put the Romantic imagination in close proximity to the horrifying details of slavery seemed plain wrong', a comment which, interestingly and unintentionally, reproduces the sensational ambience of much anti-slavery writing.[18] I study the 'horrifying details of slavery' in a wide range of genres including poetry, tracts, fiction, lectures and black life-writing. I include slave rebellions in the Caribbean and America, as these are literal and discursive moments of extreme resistance in which slave power holds up a mirror to colonial barbarism.

Another of Lee's points, that Romanticism is 'grounded in the historical specificity of the transatlantic trade' (29–30), reveals the limitations of an exclusive focus on just one source of 'horrifying details'. The Romantic imagination is also 'in close proximity' to several other sources of sublime violence, the most conspicuous of which is the French revolution, the topic of Chapter 2. As Simon Schama declares, 'in some depressingly unavoidable sense, violence *was* the revolution itself'.[19] The pioneering study in this field, as already mentioned, is Paulson's *Representations of Revolution*. Paulson shows convincingly that the French revolution was an unprecedented cultural event which generated compelling tropes of political, intellectual, social and sexual transgression, a whole new cultural pathology of revolutionary iconography. Though my study is obviously indebted to Paulson's book, I give more weight to what I call higher journalism, notably works by Cobbett and Helen Maria Williams, both of whom Paulson neglects. I also take issue with Mary Favret's claim that during the war against France, 'publicity raised a paper shield – a shield of newspaper reports, pamphlets, songs and poems – against the destructive violence of war'.[20] As Betty T. Bennett has observed, 'every hireling scribbler' was writing poems about the war, and Simon Bainbridge prefers to see such texts as 'paper bullets' which highlighted rather than concealed the carnage of war.[21]

By comparison with slavery and the French revolution, the topic of the Irish rebellion of 1798 (Chapter 3) has been almost totally absent from Romantic studies. This is not the place for an extended discussion of the reasons for this neglect, but I hope I have made a reasonable attempt to put this remarkable event on the literary-historical map. I begin by looking at the ways in which contemporary reportage seized on rebel massacres in order to construct the rebellion as a sectarian outrage rather than a republican revolution. I then look at literary representations of the rebellion in Romantic fiction: Edgeworth and the 'national tale', Maturin and the Gothic, and Michael Banim and the historical novel. I finish the chapter by proposing that Scott's novel *Old Mortality* can be read as an allegory of the Irish rebellion.

Chapter 4 focuses on the violence associated with American Indians, a theme which has increasingly begun to interest scholars,[22] though I am careful to locate this violence in the wider framework of colonial conflict stretching back to the Spanish 'conquest'. The focus of the chapter is on two infamous atrocities: the Fort William Henry massacre of 1757 and the murder of Jane McCrea in 1777. I consider the reasons for the notoriety of these incidents and examine their significance for political debates, propaganda, captivity narratives, epic poetry and early American fiction, most notably Fenimore Cooper's *Last of the Mohicans*.

In Chapter 5, spectacular violence comes 'home' to the mother country. The theme of this chapter is what I call the spectacular mob, a potent cultural stereotype which emerges in the Gordon riots and continues its anarchic destruction into the nineteenth century. I look at significant literary interventions into this process, including anti-Jacobin satire, Byron's defence of the Luddites and Scott's novel about popular justice, *Heart of Mid-Lothian*.

It is, perhaps, no coincidence that the conventional chronological bound-aries of Romanticism – 1776 (the American revolutionary war) or 1789 (the French revolution) to 1832 (the Reform Bill) – also define moments of spec-tacular violence. Yet until quite recently, Romantic literature's imaginative investment in violence was regarded by scholars as restricted almost entirely to the Gothic novel. As Mario Praz observed in *Romantic Agony*, 'The majority of writers in this period did not seem to have realized the nature of their predilection for cruel and terrifying spectacles.'[23] Now that the definition of Romanticism has broadened and deepened, the full extent of the period's 'predilection for cruel and terrifying spectacles' can begin to be revealed and explored. The contention of *Bloody Romanticism* is that spectacular violence had the power to turn the 'atrocities of democracy' into one of the defining political and cultural problems of the Romantic period.[24]

1
'Beneath the Bloody Scourge Laid Bare the Man': Slavery and Violence

'Distressed captives'

The deluge of anti-slavery propaganda which hit the British public sphere in the late eighteenth century placed spectacular violence firmly on the cultural landscape. Graphic descriptions of slave atrocities were regarded as a powerful cultural tool for critiquing European 'civilised' values. In order to point the finger of blame squarely at the European slave trade, anti-slavery writers developed a highly effective and influential repertoire of bloody vignettes which charted the slave's journey from captivity to enslavement, from Africa to the plantation, from freedom to abjection. The aim of these representations was to make clear that violence was not only essential to the slave system, but that the system also encouraged and condoned extreme violence. The system also bred its own nemesis in the form of slave rebellion, at which point the white body replaced the black body as the subject of violation. But the central thrust of these representations was not just a damning portrait of the reality of the slave system (in which the facts would speak for themselves) but the conversion of the slave into an archetypal victim who was the responsibility of the reader. It was necessary to do more than remind the reader that slaves were British property. The reader had to be made to feel the injustice of the crime and to be inspired to take action. To make this impact, writers had to mobilize the resources of spectacular violence: hyperbolic realism, sentimentality, the sublime and a whole repertoire of extraordinarily bloody crimes. As we shall see, some Romantic authors expressed strong reservations about the sensationalism of the displaying of the tortured slave body, but the bloody vignette remained a cornerstone of representations of slavery throughout the period. Slavery was the guilty conscience of Romanticism, and it is significant that emancipation was also exactly coterminous with the Reform Bill, an event which conventionally marks the closure of the Romantic period. The challenge which the anti-slavery movement posed for late-eighteenth-century print culture was made clear by the Abbé Raynal:

> imaginary distresses draw tears from our eyes, both in the silent retirement of the closet, and especially at the theatre. It is only the fatal destiny of the Negroes which doth not concern us. They are tyrannized, mutilated, burnt, and put to death, and yet we listen to these accounts coolly and without emotion.[1]

Clearly, if the reader was not to remain 'coolly' complacent about the immolation of slaves, there was a need for a change of register to awaken the senses and mobilize the conscience. Sensibility had to be pushed towards the sublime: the sentimental discourse of tearful 'imaginary distresses' could not capture the violent excesses of slave oppression, the 'tyranny' of the absolute abuse of absolute power. The horrors of slavery had to be brought closer to the reader. As Bishop Wakefield observed in 1784, the European treatment of slaves was an 'unrelenting spirit of barbarity, inconceivable to all but the spectators of it'.[2] The moral imperative was to turn readers into proxy 'spectators', but this would be a shocking and disconcerting experience. Brycchan Carey has observed that, for many respectable Britons at this time, 'the realisation that, in the case of slavery, a major branch of the national trade was engaged in systematic torture and violence may well have produced psychologically deep-seated feelings of shame and repugnance'.[3] As Josephine McDonagh has noted, the 'spectacle' of slavery 'becomes something like a mirror, reflecting back to the European the true horror he inflicts'.[4] The 'scopic possibilities of the violence and inequality' of slavery became, in Markman Ellis's phrase, the 'bad sublime' of the Enlightenment.[5]

The strategic transition from the discourse of sentiment to that of sensationalism is built into the paradigmatic slave narrative which was constructed by the abolitionist movement. This was organized around a central rupture from an idealized African origin (a place of sentiment) to an infernal European subjection (a place of sublime horror in which the teleology of the plantation is a grim and grisly travesty of the pastoral peace of Africa). The shift can be seen as early as the 1760s in the pioneering abolitionist writings of Antony Benezet. In *A Caution and Warning to Great Britain and Her Colonies* (1767), Benezet presents Africa as a georgic paradise, a place of 'industrious, humane, sociable people' and 'fruitful' industry (35). The 'tender attachments' of African slaves are 'broken by this cruel separation'. There is a conventional sentimental focus on disrupted family affections, 'some parent or wife, who had not opportunity of mingling tears in a parting embrace' (38).[6] The abject condition of the slaves is summed up as 'distressed captives', a phrase which hovers on the boundary of both sentimentality (distress) and sensation (captivity), and a trope which will be endlessly recycled in literature and political debate during the Romantic period: for example, one only has to think of the Gothic novel and the regicidal controversies of the 1790s. The trope is also performing additional ideological work in transferring the idea of captivity from the white to the black sufferer. As Linda Colley has shown in her book *Captives*, the white slavery of Barbary pirates, a huge cultural embarrassment to Europeans, was conveniently erased by the rapid emergence of transatlantic chattel slavery as synonymous with slavery itself.[7]

At the point of embarkation on slave ships, Benezet's Africans are 'stripped naked and strictly examined by the European surgeons, both men and women, without the least distinction or modesty', before being branded. This is a much less comfortable subject position for white 'men and women' than 'mingling' tears with the 'distressed' African families. There is potentially an awkward parallel between the medico-pornographic gaze of the surgeons and that of the disinterested reader who is also assessing this scene for its political and moral import. Perhaps the textual 'caution and warning' lies in the lesson to be learned from this uneasy contiguity. Once Benezet promises that divine vengeance will strike the European 'thieves and murderers' (49), a safer distance between perpetrator and reader has been opened up again – presumably, the reader's conscience is more alert and prepared for a 'cautious' response to the next atrocity.

In *Some Historical Account of Guinea* (1771), Benezet also makes clear that in order to make the 'distant sufferings' of Africans (54) 'sensibly affect [the] heart' of the reader (61), he will show that Africans have 'the same natural affections' as Europeans (63). In a radical application of the theory of sensibility, this manoeuvre brings the reader and the slave into close proximity as fellow, feeling human beings, though it is often a violent encounter which illustrates this 'natural affection' most conspicuously by contrasting it with inhumane, institutionalized heartlessness. Another early abolitionist text, John Wesley's *Thoughts Upon Slavery* (1774), exposes the insensible gaze of the slave-owning class, giving the humane reader little choice but to empathize with the violated slave:

> When you saw the flowing eyes, the heaving breasts, or the bleeding sides and tortured limbs of your fellow-creatures, was you a stone or a brute? Did you look upon them with the eyes of a tiger? When you squeezed the agonising creatures down in the ship, or when you threw their poor mangled remains into the sea, had you no relenting? (95)

Again, there is a movement here from conventional sentimentalism ('flowing eyes' 'heaving breasts') and Christian martyrology ('bleeding sides') to sensational violence (the throwing of 'poor mangled remains' into the sea is surely a reference to the infamous case of the *Zong* (1781), that touchstone of legalized barbarity in which over a hundred sick slaves were thrown into the sea on the captain's orders in order to make an insurance claim). To vicariously experience or imagine such 'agonies', to imaginatively mingle tears with the victim, was not to 'appropriate' the slave's suffering (in Marcus Wood's terms) but to demonstrate a basic (nominally Christian) humanity lacking in the pro-slavery 'brute'.[8] Coleridge's fierce criticism of indulgent sensibility, as we shall see, was directed at its failure to promote action, not its ability to generate sympathy or tragic pleasure.

Thomas Clarkson's 'Tragical scenes'

With the founding of the Society for Effecting the Abolition of the Slave Trade in 1787, the anti-slavery campaign rapidly gathered momentum and embarked on a massive propaganda campaign. The foregrounding of spectacular violence in this torrent of print can be measured by looking at one of the abolitionist movement's most influential tracts, Thomas Clarkson's *An Essay on the Slavery and Commerce of the Human Species* (1788). According to Peter Kitson, Clarkson's tract 'informed his audience of the horrors of slavery in a way that no other writer had so far done'.[9] In Clarkson's narrative, each stage of the slave's journey is marked by numerous 'tragical scenes' of atrocious violence (*SAE*, 2: 57). Following Benezet, the slave story begins with an unashamedly sentimental depiction of Africa. Clarkson admits that this scenario owes as much to literary artifice as it does to fact. In order to close the gap between the reader and African, Clarkson imagines how Africa 'might not have unreasonably be presumed to have been presented to my view, had I actually been there' (*SAE*, 2: 39). As an imaginary on-the-spot reporter, he then interviews a 'melancholy' and 'intelligent' African (*SAE*, 2: 40), a sentimental figure who weeps copiously while describing his kidnapping, but who also expresses rage and condemnation: 'What is *Christianity*, but a system of *murder* and *oppression*?' (ibid.). His tears are met with his oppressors' dry eyes, but Clarkson gives the scene a sensational twist. Not only are these Christian captors 'unable to be moved', they are actively sadistic and 'even smile, while they are torturing' (*SAE*, 2: 43). Though Clarkson, the interpolated interlocutor, denies that these 'infidels' and 'monsters' are true Christians, he has to face the African's charge that Christian Europe is responsible for making Africa 'a scene of blood and desolation' (*SAE*, 2: 44). Clarkson replies to the African that if only the 'cries and groans' of slaves could reach the 'generous Englishman at home', they would 'pierce his heart, as they have already pierced your own. He would sympathise with you in your distress. He would be enraged at the tyranny of his countrymen, and resist their tyranny' (ibid.). This is a powerful application of sensibility, but at this point in the exchange there is a theatrical disruption: 'a shriek unusually loud, accompanied with a dreadful rattling of chains, interrupted the discourse' (ibid.). Almost on cue, this irruption of violent reality into the dialogue is a melodramatic example of those very 'cries and groans' which Clarkson wants the reader back in England to hear. The reader is, presumably, 'pierced' by this pain, just as the slave, and the narrative, has also been pierced by it.

There is another telling moment of dramatic narrative interruption at the next stage in the slave's progress, the infamous middle passage. One of the most horrific and graphic scenes in this section of the narrative is an account of a seaman ordered to dispose of a sick female slave by throwing her into the sea, a theme which recalls in miniature the scandal of the *Zong*.[10] The scene also anticipates the persecuted, guilt-laden sailors of Southey and Coleridge's poetry. As the sailor takes the unconscious woman in his arms in a travesty of a romantic embrace, she 'opened her eyes, shewing, in the most expressive manner, that she was yet alive' (*SAE*, 2: 46–7). This startles the sailor, who 'hesitated for a moment'. As Wesley put it, 'when you threw their poor mangled remains into the sea, had you no relenting?' The dramatic pause is the sailor's chance to regain and 'express' his humanity, just as the slave woman, to heighten the moral charge of the scene, has been momentarily restored to life. But the sailor is so terrified of disloyalty to his 'barbarian' captain – a familiar monstrous figure in slave texts – that he beats the woman and drowns her, an unthinkable act according to the rules of sensibility, and the point at which, presumably, the reader parts company with both the 'poor' sailor and his victim.

The dehumanizing regime of the middle passage is painted with thick brush strokes. The slave quarters are full of the 'blood and mucus of the intestines' (*SAE*, 2: 51). Clarkson shows that all attempts by the slaves to exert any control over their bodily destiny – through forms of self-harm such as suicide by drowning or hunger strikes, or through attempts to find a means to escape, or violent resistance – are met with fierce retaliation. The punishment for a male slave accused of being the ringleader of a planned uprising is to tie him up and stretch him perpendicular so that he is fully exposed: 'In this situation every licentiousness, that wanton barbarity could suggest, was permitted to be practised upon him' (*SAE*, 2: 52). One reading of this scene might be that it provides a voyeuristic, even homoerotic, fantasy, but this ignores the fact that a figure of tyrannical power is present within the vignette, and the reader is highly unlikely to identify with this perpetrator of atrocity. Indeed, the reader is as just as likely to remember Adam Smith's dictum that an extreme 'imaginary resentment' at injustice can lead to 'an immediate and instinctive approbation of the sacred and necessary law of retaliation'.[11] In other words, fantasies of vengeance and defiance rather than abjection and domination may have been a powerful appeal of the slave atrocity. For Clarkson and other writers, slave uprisings during the middle passage were motivated by honourable motives which put the European masters to shame. Thomas Day and John Bicknell's poem *The Dying Negro, A Poetical Epistle* (1773), for example, imagined a successful insurrection on a slave ship. The leader of the revolt takes a heroically defiant stand in a manner reminiscent of Milton's Satan:

> And may these fiends, who now exulting view
> The horrors of my fortune, feel them too! (*SAE*, 4: 22)

As 'Afric triumphs', the imaginative scope is widened to an apocalyptic vision of the collapse of European empires, 'their flaming cities crash around' (*SAE*, 4: 23). Clarkson's reportage is more restrained, but one of his rebel slaves is presented as chivalric: 'he looked upon the people of the ship as robbers, as despoilers of families, and himself as a deeply injured man' (*SAE*, 2: 48). A rising does take place but the slaves are 'mangled' by gunshot. As Claude Rawson has shown, the use of gunpowder against the vulnerable native body was a hallmark of European colonial domination.[12] But the defiant slave of the middle passage is also a reminder of the sublime, avenging, righteous terror of full-scale plantation rebellion, the most extreme counter-narrative of European imperial hegemony.

Clarkson presents plantation life as a continuation not an amelioration of violent rule. This system was, to borrow a phrase from a later pamphlet by James Stephens, 'cart-whip government',[13] and its systemic brutalities were to be the principal target of the emancipation campaign. It was particularly important for abolitionists to debunk plantocratic, paternalistic myths about happy, contented slaves enduring a benevolently despotic regime of work discipline. For Clarkson, a plantation is an autocratic culture of absolute power dependent on innumerable 'acts of inferior, though shocking, barbarity' and generating a 'turn for wanton cruelty' on the part of the masters (*SAE*, 2: 65). Clarkson could have been influenced by Montesquieu's description of the typical slave master: 'fierce, hasty, severe, choleric, voluptuous, and cruel'.[14] The corrupting effect of slavery on the enslaver is most conspicuously shown in cruelty and sadism: 'Any thing that passion could seize, and convert into an instrument of punishment, has been used' (*SAE*, 2: 68). The drive for 'contriving modes of torture' (*SAE*, 2: 65) reaches levels of Gothic ingenuity such as roasting runaway slaves in 'iron coffins' (ibid.). But Clarkson reveals that, despite this regime, the essence of slave mentality is not resignation or Foucauldian docility but hatred: 'they are perpetually at war in their hearts with their oppressors, and are continually cherishing the seeds of revenge' (*SAE*, 2: 71). Clarkson is prepared to risk fuelling European paranoia about slave disloyalty in order to hammer home the point that violent rule breeds a violent response. In this regard, his analysis meshes with a wider radical analysis of the imitative, cyclical and carnivalesque violence of revolutions and popular justice. In terms of the timing of the *Essay*, his words could not have been more prophetic: within a year, the Bastille had fallen, and within three years the first successful slave revolution began in San Domingo.

Clarkson concludes the *Essay* by returning to the essential paradox of representations of slavery, the incredible reality of the violent Terror which is routinely and systematically administered and yet is also beyond the pale: 'there is no species of cruelty, that is recorded to have been exercised upon these wretched people, so enormous that it may not be *readily believed*' (*SAE*, 2: 73, original emphasis). Print culture is therefore caught in a double bind:

it is the medium of 'recorded' fact, but it also has to communicate the 'enormous' violation of the codes of civilized behaviour. Hence Clarkson's use of a sensationalized sentimentalism which begins with a familiar literary convention (distressed pastoral virtue) but quickly gives way to a repertoire of sublime horror. Like other writers, Clarkson defends his use of hyperbolic language on mimetic grounds, as the only appropriate register for conveying the nightmare reality of slavery. Without this *frisson*, there is the danger that the reader will become desensitized to atrocity. For Clarkson it is the latter mentality which defines the slaveowners: the figural converse of abolitionist sensationalism is pro-slavery litotes, where those who are 'trained up to scenes of cruelty from [the] cradle... represent that treatment as mild, at which we, who have never been used to see them, should absolutely shudder' (*SAE*, 2: 65n.). Yet, a strict Aristotelian line would require an impossibly exhaustive inclusiveness and an overexposure to dehumanizing actions which could be counterproductive. Most writers had to negotiate this tension between mechanical repetitiveness and the effective, exemplary vignette. In one direction, the tendency of purely denotative realism was towards the catalogue (Clarkson's submission to the parliamentary enquiry into slavery in 1788 would be the best example of this); in the other direction, the push was towards a more limited number of extended, set-piece spectacles, which often formed the climax of a narrative strand. Understandably, few authors believed that the statistical catalogue would be as effective as narrative in moving the general public. Narrative could convey the violence which defined the horrors of slavery at every stage of the slave's 'progress' from violated pastoral innocence to unstable subjection. The violent tableau became a conventional highlight of representations of slavery across a whole range of genres: pamphlet polemic, poetry, the public lecture, the slave autobiography, history and memoir, and reportage. The sentimental elevation of slave suffering went hand in hand with the European violation of the slave body. Scenes of hyperbolic violence became cultural shorthand for the evils of slavery.

'Not a subject for declamation': John Newton, Olaudah Equiano and the middle passage

The abolitionist focus on violence applied particularly to the horrors of the middle passage, that most iconic phase of slave experience which the sensational *Zong* scandal of 1781 had brought to the attention of the reading public. The 1788 parliamentary commission into the slave trade, to which Clarkson submitted a huge amount of evidence, called the middle passage 'that intermediate stage of tenfold misery', a description which conveys the rapidly escalating horrors of the slave's journey into captivity.[15] The slave ship became a theatre of violent display, a cross between a floating prison and a torture chamber, a microcosm of the 'bad sublime'. Moreover, it was the place where the crucial transition from Africa to slavery took place, where the slave became an object and a commodity. Recent criticism by Henry Louis Gates Jr. and Marcus Wood has attacked the 'myth' of the middle passage for its 'erasure' of Africa and its dehumanizing image of the slave as 'a tabula rasa of consciousness'.[16] But as the following analysis will show, accounts of the middle passage did more than merely 'stimulate notions of guilt and culpability on the part of an educated English audience'.[17] Dehumanization is a theme not an affect of spectacular violence. The aim of the 'myth' of the middle passage was to expose the extreme inhumanity of the trade in human flesh. It is worth a reminder that the average profit for a slaving ship was 9 per cent per journey: the escalating horrors of the middle passage went hand in hand with the conversion of the human cargo into escalating profits.[18] The central rhetorical effect of the middle-passage is therefore to fuse together commodification and violence. Nor is it the case that the slave is uniformly a 'cultural absentee', a 'blank page for white guilt to inscribe'.[19] As we shall see, representations of the middle passage also incorporate fantasies of slave resistance and rebellion.

In John Newton's *Thoughts on the African Slave Trade*, which also appeared in 1788, that 'annus horribilis' of early Romantic period slave texts, the scopic and moral emphasis is on the sexual degradation of the slave cargo. Newton was a reformed ex-slaver who had given evidence to Clarkson. His account therefore carried the authority of an eyewitness, though he makes clear (whether true or not) that he did not participate in the atrocities. Possibly motivated by the desire to exorcise the demons of his previous career, Newton depicts an excessively sadistic regime on board the ship. The captain administers punishments such as floggings and the use of the thumbscrew, but his manner of executing slaves is the key detail, as he 'studied, with no small attention, how to make death as excruciating to them as possible. For my reader's sake, I suppress the recital of particulars' (*SAE*, 2: 93). This reticence, a component of hyperbolic realism's dramatic repertoire of rhetorical effects, does not prevent Newton squeezing out one further 'particular' in which a sailor throws a slave's baby overboard to stop it crying (*SAE*, 2: 94). This is a classic example of what Moira Ferguson calls the 'denatalization' of the slave woman's body.[20] As we shall see, this particular method of disempowerment reaches a spectacular apotheosis when it is appropriated by rebellious slaves and turned back on their former rulers. In Newton's narrative, the discarding of the slave child signifies the literal and symbolic transfer of the slave woman's body from African culture to European ownership. The rape of slave women, which Newton also focuses on, can therefore be interpreted politically as a ritualization of abjection,[21] and not simply a perk of the job for a sex-starved crew:

When the Women and Girls are taken on board a ship, naked, trembling, terrified, perhaps almost exhausted with cold, fatigue and hunger, they are often exposed to the wanton rudeness of white Savages. The poor creatures cannot understand the language they hear, but the looks and manner of the speakers are sufficiently intelligible. In imagination, the prey is divided, upon the spot, and only reserved till opportunity offers. Where resistance, or refusal, would be utterly in vain, even the solicitation of consent is seldom thought of. But I forbear – This is not a subject for declamation. (*SAE*, 2: 96)

Once again, the limit point of representation is reached, but not before the vignette has established the inverted roles of 'white Savages' and black 'prey'. In order to refute the myth that slaves are insensible to suffering, Newton insists that these victims are capable of 'modesty, and even delicacy, which would not disgrace an English woman' (*SAE*, 2: 97). He then goads the pro-slavery lobby by asking sardonically how these 'facts' might be received by the 'wives and daughters of this happy land' (ibid.). The complexly gendered, violent gaze of this scene provides the enlightened female reader with a dynamic interchange between a sympathetic identification with the victim and a moral mission to change the views of her monstrously 'happy' peers. Like many writers in the slavery debate, Newton mobilizes the stereotype of women as the natural arbiters of sensibility, but by universalizing this quality his aim is to outflank his male opponents and expose double standards: the respect that men claim to accord to women's 'modesty' and 'delicacy' should equally be granted to the 'poor creatures' of Africa. The flip side of this logic is to imagine white 'wives and daughters' subjected to the same treatment. This is a punitive fantasy which, as will be seen later in this chapter, some writers were not averse to deploying, but which finds its most terrible expression in the nemesis of slave rebellion.

Though he claims to be an eyewitness of the events he describes, Newton still issues a concluding disclaimer: 'the warmth of imagination might have insensibly seduced me, to aggravate and overcharge some of the horrid features' (*SAE*, 2: 116). Newton may simply want to have his rhetorical cake and eat it, but his words are a reminder of that central tension within hyperbolic realism between authenticity and incredulity. When Olaudah Equiano published his *Interesting Narrative* in 1789, he countered allegations that the book might be a white-authored fake by appealing to its authentic portrayal of slave suffering, 'the enormous cruelties practised on my sable brethren'.[22] Although such 'cruelties' occupy only a small portion of a substantial text, an early review of the book by Mary Wollstonecraft singled out for special attention the 'many anecdotes' showing the 'treatment of male and female slaves' which 'make the blood turn its course'. By comparison, she found the sections on religious conversion 'rather tiresome'.[23] If Wollstonecraft is a reliable monitor of the public mood, there was still a considerable appetite for those bloody 'anecdotes' of 'enormous cruelties' which emblazoned the evils of slavery. In his account of the middle passage, Equiano famously pushes to an extreme the cultural and moral inversions used by Newton. From the faux-naïve perspective of the newly captured narrator, European slavers are presented as cannibals, magicians and brutes. However, the most violent scenes occur later in the text when Equiano has been converted to Christianity and regards himself as 'almost an Englishman' (77). After a period of freedom, he is re-enslaved and from his ironically enlightened and elevated point of view he now witnesses the routine rape of women and children on a slave ship.[24] He contrasts this crime with the punishment of castration meted out to a male slave accused of having a sexual liaison with a white prostitute:

> as if it were no crime in the whites to rob an innocent African girl of her virtue; but most heinous in a black man only to gratify a passion of nature, where the temptation was offered by one of a different colour, though the most abandoned woman of her species. (104)

From a feminist perspective, this exposure of a sexual double standard reads like special pleading: in order to vindicate the male slave's 'passion of nature' and expose the grossly disproportionate severity of the punishment, Equiano debunks the offence of miscegenation by stressing the morally 'abandoned' status of the archetypal fallen woman, the prostitute. But the underlying message is the annihilation of the slave's sexuality and individuality: rape and castration ('cutting') are technologies of European control and power over the female and male slave body respectively. The overseers are 'human butchers, who cut and mangle the slaves in a shocking manner on the most trifling occasions' (105). Another mechanism of terror is the forcing of male slaves to beat their own wives (107). Enforced collaboration, like enforced spectatorship, was a form of humiliation and impotence which often resulted in despair and suicide.

Equiano's judgement on the 'bloody west India code' is that it would 'shock the morality and common sense of a Samaide or Hottentot' (109). This allusion to a stereotypically primitive Africa reveals another tension in Equiano's hybrid identity as a partially Europeanized or westernized African (I am sidestepping the controversy about his possible American origins, as this does not essentially change his inherited identity, a slave of African descent). Indeed, at one point in his 'interesting' story he becomes a slave trader himself, apparently without embarrassment. But it is through the appropriation of radical political discourse that he can most effectively sum up the systemic evils of slavery, and appeal to a wide spectrum of abolitionist readers. To begin with, slavery 'violates the first natural right of mankind, equality and independency'. As Hegel was to show, the tyranny of slavery also corrupts the master, who is transformed for Equiano into a figure of 'fraud, rapine, and cruelty'. Finally, slavery is an unstable institution which produces a constant 'dread of insurrection'. The parallels between this analysis and the radical critique of Old Corruption are clear. Equiano's programme of reforms conforms to liberal thinking: abolition, free education, better management of plantations and the opening up of Africa to enlightened free trade. This package of measures (aided by religious conversion) will break the cycle of fear, terror and resentment, and convert slaves into 'faithful, honest, intelligent and vigorous' subjects (111–12). The alternative is the perpetuation of fear and loathing. This dire warning is given a suitably epic gravitas by citing a passage from *Paradise Lost*. The lines are taken from Beelzebub's contribution to the debate of the fallen angels (2: 332–40). The debate, it is important to remember, is about whether or not to mount another rebellion. The lines (which are slightly modified) are worth quoting in full as they have a profound resonance, being poised on the brink of the French revolution, and providing an appropriate epic register for the scale of global imperial violence:

> . . . No peace is given
> To us enslav'd, but custody severe;
> And stripes and arbitrary punishment
> Inflicted – What peace can we return?
> But to our power, hostility and hate;
> Untam'd reluctance, and revenge, tho' slow,
> Yet ever plotting how the conqueror least
> May reap his conquest, and may least rejoice
> In doing what we most in suffering feel. (112)

After striking this warning note, the incidence of violence in the narrative dwindles. The explanation given is an aversion to repetition: 'it cannot any longer afford novelty' to relate further horrors which are 'too shocking to yield delight either to the writer or the reader' (113). The silence is broken briefly when Equiano returns to Jamaica and witnesses hangings and burnings. He decides to 'pass over numerous instances' of cruelty 'to relieve the reader by a milder scene of roguery' (172). His anecdote about a swindling 'gentleman' merchant (a mild satire on commerce) may seem like an avoidance strategy but, as is made clear, 'numerous instances' of atrocious violence are never far away.

'To sing of tortured negroes': Poetry and protest

The redaction of the slave experience into a series of metonymic, violent tableaux is even more apparent in the more confined textual space of the poem. A detailed account of a slave atrocity occupied more sheer space in a poem than in a longer prose narrative. But the reader's expectation of a poem would also be, presumably, that the poem would deliver an affective premium. The major advantage of the poem over the longer prose polemic would be its ability to make the reader feel, to compress the horrors of slavery into even more memorable tropes, images and expressions. To look at one of the most famous instances first, Thomas Cowper was initially reluctant to write his famous 'The Negro's Complaint' (1788), as he did not want to 'sing of tortured negroes'.[25] Nevertheless, at the centre of the poem is a familiar debunking of a sham Christianity which apparently condones the European use of 'knotted scourges', 'Matches' and 'blood-extorting screws' against slaves (ll. 29–30; *SAE*, 4: 74). This 'complaint' is answered by an apocalyptic fantasy of divine retribution rather than slave rebellion:

> Hark! He answers! – Wild tornadoes
> Strewing yonder sea with wrecks,
> Wasting towns, plantations, meadows,
> Are the voice with which he speaks. (ll. 33–6; *SAE*, 4: 74)

Thomas Clarkson credited Cowper's poem with spreading the abolitionist gospel as effectively as prose tracts. Set to music and printed in its thousands 'on the finest hot-pressed paper', the poem 'gave a plain account of the subject, with an appropriate feeling, to those who heard it'.[26] The 'appropriate feeling' of the poem is more sensational than Clarkson's prosaic epithet 'plain' might suggest.

But many other poets were less squeamish than Cowper in associating 'appropriate feeling' with images of 'tortured negroes'. Benjamin Rushton's *West Indian Eclogues* (1787), for example, tells the story of a failed slave revolt. Two slaves Jumba and Adoma lead an uprising in Jamaica after one of them has been whipped for defending his wife and baby against the lash. The plantation regime is presented as a spectacle of sadistic violence:

> How oft our Tyrants, at each dex'trous lash,
> With joyous looks have viewed each bleeding gash.
> How oft to these, with tortures still uncloy'd,
> Have they the *Eben's* prickly branch applied! (*SAE*, 4: 34–5)

A footnote gives additional information about this 'dex'trous' barbarism: 'The last step of this process of cruelty, is to wash the mangled wretch with a kind of pickle; or throw him headlong into the sea . . .' (*SAE*, 4: 56). Jumba's vision of vengeance is a reflection of the original offence:

> Soon shall they fall, cut down like lofty Canes,
> And (oh! the bliss) from us receive their pains.
> Oh! twill be pleasant when we see them mourn . . .
> View with delight each agonizing grin,
> When melted wax is dropp'd upon *their* skin. (*SAE*, 4: 35,
> original emphasis)

Another footnote explains that the 'leisurely' application of hot wax to gaping wounds was a common form of torture in the plantations (*SAE*, 4: 56). But Adoma's imagination looks ahead to the third stage of the cycle of violence, the terrible punishment of the gibbet. A footnote points out that some 'miserable sufferers' of the gibbet can survive for as long as a week. The reader is referred to James Ramsay's *Essay on the Conversion and Treatment of African Slaves* (1784) for authenticating evidence, but Adoma has been an eyewitness of the event:

> Oh! think on PEDRO, gibbetted alive!
> Think on his fate – six long days to survive! –
> His frantic looks, – his agonizing pain, —
> His tongue outstretch'd to catch the dropping rain;
> His vain attempts to turn his head aside,
> And gnaw the flesh which his own limbs supplied;
> Think on his suff'rings, when th'inhuman crew,
> T'increase his pangs, plac'd Plantains in his view,
> And bade him eat, – (*SAE*, 4: 38)

In the hyperbolic realism of this Dantesque scene of torture there is a concentration of 'dext'rous' violent effects and carnivalesque allusions: the comparison with Biblical crucifixion ('six long days'); the reader/viewer's identification with the slave's own 'frantic' gaze; the antithesis of the sadism of the 'inhuman crew' (the latter word also evokes the slave ship); the resort to self-cannibalism which is travestied by the mock-feeding routine; the tantalizing glimpse of pastoral balm ('dropping rain'). Such powerful and resonant literary qualities may explain why the gibbeted slave was a particularly powerful vignette of spectacular violence. Voltaire included the figure in *Candide* (1759) to point out the difference between the attractions of the Utopian El Dorado and the horrors of colonial Surinam. In the American context, Crevecoeur's famous *Letters from an American Farmer* (1782) used the scene to denounce southern slavery. Crevecoeur recalls stumbling across this 'shocking spectacle' while on the way to visit a planter friend. The slave has been partly consumed by birds:

> No sooner were the birds flown than swarms of insects covered the whole body of this unfortunate wretch, eager to feed on his mangled flesh and to drink his blood. I stood motionless, involuntary, contemplating the fate of this Negro in all its dismal latitude.[27]

In Rushton's Eclogue, the only antidote to such 'dismal latitude' is the belief that Pedro could spiritually transcend the mangled body. Jumba is certain that Pedro 'possess'd a soul, / Which nobly burst the shackles of controul' (*SAE*, 4: 39). In the fourth eclogue, however, we are presented with a rather different bursting of the shackles of control as a slave murders his wife who has been raped, a deed reminiscent of Oroonoko's honour-killing of his wife in Aphra Behn's *Oroonoko* (1688). In Rushton's poem, however, the scene's didactic and political charge is clearly aimed at a thriving abolitionist movement. In a footnote, Rushton reminds the reader that 'forcing the wives of the Negroes to a compliance' not only is morally wrong but has provoked many slave uprisings (*SAE*, 4: 60).

Rushton could draw on a number of earlier poems written from the point of view of the rebellious slave or native. The historical inspiration for these poems was probably the Coramantee revolt of Tacky in Jamaica in 1760, an event which received considerable media attention.[28] Bryan Edwards's poem 'The Negro's Dying Speech on His being Executed for Rebellion in the Island of Jamaica' (1777) presents a Tacky-like figure who is an emblem of defiance and endurance:

> Now, Christian, glut thy ravish'd eyes –
> I reach the joyful hour;
> Now bid the scorching flames arise,
> And these poor limbs devour. (*SAE*, 4: 26)

Other poems which could be cited in this context are Thomas Chatterton's, 'Heccar and Gaira: An African Eclogue' (1770), in which the hero vows to 'strew the beaches with the mighty dead / And tinge the lily of their features red' (*SAE*, 4: 7), and Thomas Day's *The Dying Negro*, which has already been discussed. The most subversive aspect of these poems is perhaps the vocalization of slave defiance. As Foucault noted, the spectacle of public execution temporarily transformed the condemned victim into a figure of power, the 'inverted body of the king'.[29] Such poems show that the idea of the slave rebellion was powerfully implanted in the literary imagination well before the San Domingo revolution of the 1790s. However, until this revolt fused Jacobinism and slavery together, slave violence was usually constructed in literature as a heroic act of individual vengeance and self-sacrifice rather than collective and ideologically motivated political resistance. On the other hand, the strong Miltonic allusions and resonances in such scenes could contain traces of the tradition of seventeenth-century 'antinomian democracy', which, according to Linebaugh and Rediker, migrated across the transatlantic plebeian community after the English civil war.[30]

In their focus on the punishment and execution of slaves, slavery poems of the late 1780s fused the grammatical and legal meanings of the 'example'. The classical rhetorical device of the *exemplum* was reduced to its starkest subject matter, the judicial 'example' or deterrent, the public spectacle of the 'mangled' body of the victim of Terror. As Marcus Wood has demonstrated, the graphic depiction of plantation 'justice' evoked the religious iconography of martyrology,[31] but the slave execution scene must equally have invited comparisons with the administration of capital punishment in mainland Europe. The slave execution was a spectacular refutation of any notion that Britain was moving away, *pace* Foucault, from the spectacle of violent public punishment. Representations of slavery brought the body of the suffering slave into the heart of British culture and made it the responsibility of that culture. A slave atrocity in the Caribbean was a slave atrocity on British territory – literally, culturally, emotionally and psychically. One of the aims of the anti-slavery campaign was to terrorize the reader and to make abolition the only form of respite for both the slave and the reader. Without reform, slavery would continue to torture both parties.

The inhumanity of the slave trade: Bristol and anti-slavery

This point can be illustrated by looking at a number of texts which emanated from Bristol writers. Bristol's status as a major slaving port made it a highly-charged, literal and imagined community in which to conduct the debate about slavery. Ann Yearsley's 'The Inhumanity of the Slave Trade' (1788), for example, asked her local Bristol reader to 'make a fellow-creature's woe / His own by heart-felt sympathy'. In order to produce this 'sympathy', Yearsley describes the execution of a rebel slave named Luco. Two forms of spectatorship are integral components of this scene. As he slowly burns to death to prolong his agonies, other slaves are forced to watch: 'his fellow slaves are ranged / To share the horrid fright'. This is a deliberate ploy by the 'planters' who, though 'to fear alone / They owe their cruel pow'r', must constantly add 'New torment with the pangs of death'. All Luco's pleas for water or a swift end are denied:

> ... The planters heed him not,
> But still prolonging Luco's torture, threat
> Their trembling slaves around.

There is an obvious correspondence between these 'trembling' spectators and the readers of the poem. If Yearsley, like the 'planters', is 'prolonging' the agony of the scene, it is to ram home the contrast between this enforced grotesque viewing and the voyeuristic ogling of the 'Christians':

> E'en Christians throng each other, to behold
> The different alterations of his face,
> As the hot death approaches. (*SAE*, 4: 146–7)

The poem's achievement is to dramatize the distinction between the two types of spectatorship: the excited gaze of the curious and the terrorized gaze of the afflicted. The challenge for the reader is to realize that violent spectacle is both an instrument of terror in reality and a mode of literary representation which offers a means of redress by exposing inhumanity. Only at this point can the terrorized reader move beyond sympathy, separate from the 'fellow-creature's woe', and attempt to turn literary into political representation. But this does not preclude the use of shock tactics and sensationalism as the first stage in the reader's edification. This process is described vividly by Anna Barbauld in a poem which attacked the rejection of the abolition bill by the House of Lords in April 1792:

> The preacher, poet, senator, in vain
> Has rattled in [Britain's] sight the Negro's chain,
> With his deep groans assailed her startled ear
> And rent the veil that hid his constant tear,
> Forced her averted eyes his stripes to scan,
> Beneath the bloody scourge laid bare the man (ll. 3–8)[32]

Lines of poetry, like the 'stripes' on the slave's body, will only 'scan' if 'bloody' reality is 'forced' upon the reader.

Ann Yearsley's former mentor Hannah More used the confessional, Evangelical mode of self-admonishment to expose the violent gaze. In her poem 'Slavery' (1788), also written in the first flush of the abolitionist campaign, she reveals:

> Whene'er to Afric's shores I turn my eyes,
> Horrors of deepest, deadliest guilt arise;
> I see, by more than Fancy's mirror shown,
> The burning village, and the blazing town:
> See the dire victim torn from social life,
> See the scared infant, hear the shrieking wife! (ll. 111–16)[33]

The poetic diction and the rather awkward nod towards verisimilitude ('more than Fancy's mirror shown') suggest that More was rather less inclined than her former prodigy to use the full force of hyperbolic realism. However, the pressure to include sensational violent detail becomes strikingly evident later in the poem when More writes her version of Yearsley's tortured slave scene:

> When the fierce Sun darts vertical his beams,
> And thirst and hunger mix their wild extremes;
> When the sharp iron wounds his inmost soul,
> And his strained eyes in burning anguish roll. (ll. 207–10)

A footnote for the third of these lines explains that 'This is not said figuratively', and informs the reader that More herself has seen 'instruments for wrenching open the jaws, contrived with such ingenious cruelty as would gratify the tender mercies of an inquisitor'.[34] This is a revealing paratextual intervention: the stereotypical reference to the Inquisition brings the histor- ical nightmare of religious persecution to bear on the 'figurative' problem of the passage, the word 'soul'. For More, the most important framework for the slavery debate is not politics or economics, though she debunks imperialism as the 'lust of gold' by the 'White Savage' (l. 249). The most heinous aspect of the inhumanity of slavery is its spiritual destructiveness: the murdering, Inquisitor-like perpetrators of slavery who 'are *not* Christians' (l. 224) deny slaves an inner life on racial grounds – 'They stand convicted – of a darker skin!' (l. 162). However, the solution to this lapse of true Christian values is Christian renewal and regeneration for all parties. The poem specific- ally denies that the unredeemed slave can be dignified with the status of a martyr. Though the violent means of death is an emotive parallel, 'No martyr's blissful visions soothe his pains' (l. 228). The real question mark hangs over the precarious spiritual integrity of the European. The poem resorts to strenuous 'Fancy' as More imagines the descent of the Evangelical cherub Mercy, whose 'generous influence steals/Till every breast the soft contagion feels' (ll. 313–14). It is Mercy, not political reform, which 'Breathes manumission o'er the rescued land' of Africa (l. 336). This 'soft contagion' is the Christian antidote to the 'mad Liberty' (l. 25) of radical politics: the latter, 'to reform a part, destroys the whole' (l. 42). This attack may have been a coded allusion to the Gordon riots of 1780 (looked at in Chapter 5),[35] but the image of the 'unlicensed monster of the crowd' (l. 25) also anticipates the anti-Jacobin crusade of the 1790s, for which More was to make such a substantial contribution with her counter-revolutionary *Cheap Repository Tracts* series. As the politics of slavery became entangled with the 'revolu- tion debate' of this decade, one of these tracts reiterated the point that only a reform of Christianity could assuage slavery's 'Horrors of deepest, dead- liest guilt'. In 'The Sorrows of Yamba, or the Negro Woman's Lamentation' (*c*.1795)[36] the 'horrors' of the middle passage are given an added dramatic edge by the first-person narration:

> Naked on the platform lying,
> Now we cross the tumbling wave!
> Shrieking, sickening, fainting, dying,
> Dead of shame for Britons brave!
>
> At the savage Captain's beck
> Now like brutes they make us prance;
> Smack the cat about the deck,
> And in scorn they bid us dance. (*SAE*, 4: 225–6)

Despite this display of another of those 'instruments' of terror (the 'cat') which More had personally seen, Yamba's salvation lies in embracing conversion. She prays for 'your massas' sins' and for the 'British sons of murder!' to be forgiven. If the stakes are high, the rewards are sublime.

The Bristol radicals Southey and Coleridge took the pursuit of the reader's guilty 'soul' in an even more sensational direction. They both made full use of the cannibalism metaphors which had become rhetorical centrepieces of the mass campaign for a sugar boycott. As the bristling propaganda made clear, few readers or listeners could escape the horrifying logic of guilt by association: to consume sugar was to consume the slave. William Fox, for example, made a grisly calculation in an extremely widely circulated 1791 pamphlet: one pound of sugar 'may be considered as consuming two ounces of human flesh'.[37] In response to this, a Cambridge bookshop advertised East Indian sweets 'uncontaminated with human gore'.[38] A newspaper poem from 1792 went so far as to transform 'white' sugar into a hallucinogenic drug:

> Go, guilty, sweet seducing food
> Tainted by streams of human blood!
> Emblem of woe, and fruitless moans,
> Of mangled limbs, and dying groans!
> To me, thy tempting white appears
> Steep'd in a thousand Negroes' tears!
> I see the lash uplifted high;
> I see the vainly-streaming eye;
> The shrunk clasp'd hands that but provoke
> Their tyrants to a harder stroke.[39]

In addition to associating 'white' sugar with the racist exploitation of black flesh (and with a history which sugar's 'whitening' would prefer to forget), the poem also points a stereotypical finger at 'white' women as the main culprits. Despite the fact that women were prominent in the sugar boycott, luxury and consumption were still troped as feminine forms of behaviour. As the Miltonic cadences indicate, to resist the 'sweet seducing' allure of the 'tempting white' substance required a manly fortitude and resolve. In one of his sonnets on slavery composed in 1794, Southey gave an exemplary demonstration of the correct response to the sight of a 'brother' slave being flogged:

> ... The scorching sun
> As pitiless as proud Prosperity,
> Darts on him his full beams, gasping he lies
> Arraigning with his looks the patient skies,
> While that inhuman driver lifts on high
> The mangling scourge. Oh ye who at your ease
> Sip the blood-sweeten'd beverage, thoughts like these

> Haply ye scorn: I thank thee, gracious God,
> That I do feel upon my cheek the glow
> Of indignation, when beneath the rod
> A sable brother writhes in silent woe. (*SAE*, 4: 244)

The 'glow / Of indignation' is a masculine blush which serves two purposes: to express what Timothy Morton calls the 'truth of colonial power and the truth of sympathetic passion', and to distinguish this 'passion' from its corrupted (or more readily corruptible) female equivalent, the 'glow' of erotic arousal or complacent, consumerist pleasure.[40]

Clearly, the cannibalistic blood–sugar trope provided a powerful new opportunity to harass the reader or listener. With breathtaking audacity, one of England's most genteel social rituals, the taking of tea, was transformed into a barbaric feeding frenzy. Probably the most sensational twist given to the trope was to compare sugar consumption to the Christian communion. This blasphemous image (or rather, image of blasphemy), a carnivalesque 'Gothic Eucharist',[41] formed the highlight of Coleridge's lecture on the slave trade, delivered in Bristol in 1795 and published in his periodical *The Watchman* in 1796 (I am of course using the published version, so readers can be taken as the equivalent of the listeners in the original delivery). With all the zeal of a missionary preacher, Coleridge subjected his audience to a highly theatricalized rhetorical battering. The lecture begins with a false promise:

> I will not mangle the feelings of my readers by detailing enormities, which the gloomy Imagination of Dante would scarcely have dared attribute the Inhabitants of Hell. For the honour of our common nature, I would fain hope that these accounts have been exaggerated . . . (*SAE*, 2: 213)

He adds that such details have been 'pressed on the Public even to satiety' (ibid.). However, as the lecture progresses, Coleridge decides that the 'enormities, at which a Caligula might have turned pale' cannot be ignored or over-exaggerated. He is also furious that the government has '*mangled* and *mutilated*' the abolition bill – this violent political behaviour ironically echoes the violence which the bill is designed to stop (*SAE*, 2: 216). Faced with such 'enormities', Coleridge asks the men in his audience to imagine how they would feel if

> a slave merchant should incite an intoxicated Chieftain to make war on your country, and murder your Wife and Children before your face, or drag them with yourself to the Market? Would you choose to be sold, to have the hot iron hiss upon your breasts, after having been crammed into the hold of a Ship, with so many fellow-victims, that the heat and stench arising from your diseased bodies, should rot the very planks? (*SAE*, 2: 218)

Gender stereotyping becomes increasingly significant as Coleridge unleashes the full force of the 'Gothic Eucharist'. Having threatened his male audience with the imaginary horrors of emasculation, he next targets the pieties of genteel women:

> Gracious Heaven! At your meals you rise up, and pressing your hands to your bosoms, you lift up your eyes to God, and say, 'O Lord! bless the food which thou hast given us!' A part of that food among most of you, is sweetened with Brother's Blood. 'Lord! bless the food which thou hast given us!' O Blasphemy! Did God give food mingled with the Blood of the murdered? Will God bless the food which is polluted with the Blood of his own innocent children? (ibid.)[42]

The climax of the lecture is a denunciation of the 'false and bastard sensibility,' which Coleridge associates with women's consumption of both sugared luxuries and sentimental literature:

> She sips a beverage sweetened with human blood, even while she is weeping over the refined sorrows of Werter or of Clementina. Sensibility is not Benevolence. Nay, by making us tremblingly alive to trifling misfortunes, it frequently prevents it, and induces effeminate and cowardly selfishness... There is one criterion by which we may always distinguish benevolence from mere sensibility – Benevolence impels to action, and is accompanied by self-denial. (*SAE*, 2: 218–19)

Women are the worst offenders in the Sadeian psychodrama of the Gothic Eucharist, just as they are often the principal victims in narratives of slave justice. Looked at in this way, anti-slavery writing would seem to be highly conservative in its construction of femininity. However, the issue of how to interpret women's consumption of images of violence at this time remains a vexed one. Jacqueline Pearson has noted how women's actual reading habits in the Romantic period did not conform to 'moralists' categories'.[43] It would be a mistake, therefore, to assume that all the Bristol women listening to Coleridge would necessarily accept his stereotypes, even if they recognized the force of his critique of sensibility.[44]

If Southey and Coleridge terrorized genteel Bristol with the Gothic Eucharist, Southey's most famous anti-slavery poem 'The Sailor who had served in the Slave Trade' (1799) turned to a more plebeian subject in order to attack Bristol's reputation as a major slaving port. According to a prefatory note, the poem was based on a local incident. After a minister discovered a sailor praying for forgiveness in a cowshed, the sailor revealed that he was trying to atone for having being forced to whip hunger-striking slaves during the middle passage. Southey's decision to turn the story into a poem attests to the penetration of print culture: 'By presenting it as a Poem the story is made more public, and such stories ought to be made as public as possible'.[45] The poem was obviously a companion piece to *The Rime of the Ancient Mariner*, as both poems showed mariners afflicted by an intolerable and self-destructive burden of guilt. But unlike Coleridge, Southey did not choose to conceal or allegorize the slavery theme. Southey's innovation was to make the humble and haunted sailor the personification of public guilt:

> So therefore we were forced by threats
> And blows to make them eat (ll. 67–8; *SAE*, 2: 429)

It is the punishment of a female slave which most wounds the sailor's sensibility:

> She twisted from the blows – her blood,
> Her mangled flesh I see;
> And still the Captain would not spare –
> Oh, he was worse than me. (ll. 81–5; ibid.)

It is worth noting that in a revised version of the poem these details were toned down:

> What woman's child a sight like that
> Could bear to look upon!
> And still the Captain would not spare
> But bade me still flog on. (*SAE*, 4: 253)

The significant deletion is the word 'twisted', which recurs in a later line: 'I see her twisting everywhere' (l. 103). Like the twisted cords of the ropes and the 'cat', the twists of the lines of poetry, or the twisting grimaces of the spectators, it is the 'twisting' slave body which energizes and terrorizes Romantic period representations of slavery. Each text, each 'twist' of the problem, awakened the same phantoms.

'Dyed over with blood': Slave rebellion and revolution

The examples of anti-slavery writing looked at so far have shown the extreme rhetorical measures which liberals and radicals were prepared to take in order to awaken the reader's conscience. Yet, we have still not looked at the most extraordinary representations of spectacular slave violence from this period. By the time Coleridge delivered his lecture in Bristol, transatlantic slavery had produced its own catastrophic revolution in San Domingo. The images of atrocity which this convulsion generated are comparable to the worst excesses of the French Terror.

Slave rebellions were a regular occurrence throughout the eighteenth century. They were usually punished with extreme cruelty. New York, for example, passed a law justifying any mode of execution which was deemed an appropriate spectacle of deterrence: this could include burnings, breaking on the wheel and hanging women in front of men.[46] As Michael Craton observes, 'decapitation was almost a rule; the severed heads were displayed on poles on the rebels' home plantations'.[47] Despite this use of Terror, rebellions continued throughout the Romantic period. For W. E. B. Du Bois, slave uprisings signified the indomitable spirit of Africa which refused to submit to the European yoke,[48] though historians are still divided about the extent to which fear of rebellion (rather than humanitarian or economic motivations) influenced the British government's decision in 1807 to abolish the slave trade.[49] Some reformers took Du Bois's view, and argued that abolition would cut off the supply of recalcitrant Africans into the slave colonies, but the persistence of post-abolition rebellions was stark evidence that slavery remained a volatile and unstable institution.

The mulattos and slaves of San Domingo began their rebellion in 1791. The rebellion was inspired by the democratic ideals of the French revolution, and was further boosted by the Jacobin abolition of slavery in 1794. Under the leadership of Toussaint L'Ouverture, the rebels successively defeated the armies of Britain, Spain and France. This was an astonishing victory, as the European powers feared the loss of trade and influence in the Caribbean and were determined to crush the slave army. San Domingo was the jewel in the crown of transatlantic slavery: by the 1790s it produced annual profits for France of £11,000,000 and sucked in 40,000 slaves each year.[50] In 1796 Britain despatched to the island an unprecedented force of 30,000 troops, the 'largest expedition ever to sail from Great Britain', according to David Geggus.[51] Very few of these troops returned home. At least 20,000 died in combat or from disease. The impact and scale of these losses cannot be overestimated. Geggus reckons that every person in Britain may have lost a family member or acquaintance to this and other conflicts in the Caribbean.[52] Britain's withdrawal in 1798 signalled the first major success for Toussaint's forces. When Napoleon revoked Jacobin reforms and attempted to restore slavery, his armies met a similar fate. In 1804, the island achieved independence and became the republic of Haiti.

In dominant ideology, however, the San Domingo rebellion figured as the worst case scenario of retaliatory slave violence. Despite the enlightened leadership of Toussaint – Thomas Clarkson described Toussaint's period of rule as a 'beautiful state of things', which was destroyed by the 'hellish expedition' of Napoleon[53] – the combination of Jacobinism and slave revolt struck fear into the European imagination. For many, the rebellion in San Domingo was stark evidence of the destructive consequences of introducing radical political ideas to 'primitive' minds. Cobbett believed that the rise of this 'Black Empire' was 'one of the most interesting and important events that ever took place, in any part of the world'.[54] Other republican uprisings, such as the one led by Julius Fedon in Grenada, seemed to confirm these fears that the whole slave system could be under threat.[55] As Robin Blackburn notes, the British press 'reported Republican atrocities against non-combatants in lurid detail'.[56] The resulting backlash undermined the progress of both abolitionism and radical democratic reform in Britain: demonologically, San Domingo was a 'black' version of French Terror.

This anti-Jacobin mood informs two texts which together comprise the most sensational representations of slavery to appear in the 1790s: Bryan Edwards's *An Historical Survey of the French Colony in the Island of St. Domingo* and John Gabriel Stedman's *Narrative of a Five Years' Expedition against the Revolted Negroes of Surinam*. Stedman's book on Surinam has received considerable critical attention, mainly because it carried illustrations by William Blake, but I want to begin with Edwards, as he wrote an account of the San Domingo rebellion as it was still unfolding.

Bryan Edwards, *An Historical Survey of the French Colony in the Island of St. Domingo* (1797)

Bryan Edwards's *An Historical Survey of the French Colony in the Island of St. Domingo* appeared in 1797, while British forces were still engaged in trying to suppress the rebellion.[57] Edwards presents the geo-political consequences of a British defeat in stark terms: 'the future fate and profitable existence of the British territories in this part of the world is at stake' (176). He presents the rebel slaves as stooges or dupes of Jacobin ideology, 'excited' into 'excesses' by the promised introduction of 'schemes of perfection, faster than nature allows'. The rebellion is a Frankenstein's monster, an 'assemblage of horrors' conjured up by 'reformers of the present day' (xxix–xxx). This Burkean demonization of revolutionary ideology figures the rebellion as an Oedipal monster which devours its parent. To emphasize the monstrosity and anarchy of the rebellion, Edwards cites Milton's description of Chaos: 'All monstrous, all prodigious things / Abominable, unutterable, and worse / Than fables yet have feigned, or fear conceiv'd'. The contradiction between this invocation of the 'unutterable' sublime and Stedman's 'duty, as a faithful historian' to 'assemble' atrocities (81) is a hallmark of hyperbolic realism: the antithetical discourses of incredulity and authenticity are in a constant state of tension.

Edwards's 'assemblage of horrors' is a series of desecrations of the white body. The intensity of the violence directed at the body of the planter may be explained in part by the planter's role in the conflict. According to Thomas Clarkson, it was not the French forces but the planters who were the primary perpetrators of cruelty against slaves: 'authors of tearing to pieces the Negroes alive by bloodhounds, or of suffocating them by hundred at a time in the holds of ships, or of drowning them (whole cargoes) by sinking and scuttling the vessels'.[58] But the slave violence can also be seen as the apocalyptic answer to the abjection and denial of the slave body during the middle passage. If the rituals of humiliation suffered by the slaves signified the negation of the slave body and the transfer of its ownership to an external agency, the outrages of slave violence described by Edwards answer the original offence by expressing an absolute refutation of the white body as a signifier of civilization. This disempowerment is more like a regime of symbolic extinction than reverse colonization. Unlike Caliban, who saw his attempted rape of Miranda as a political act – 'I would have peopled this isle with Calibans' (*The Tempest*, 1. 2. 351–2) – the Sadeian aggressors in San Domingo seem intent on obliterating, not appropriating, all vestiges of polite culture. Like Miranda, the most salient symbol of this culture is the genteel woman, but the trope of feminine vulnerability can be widened to include the family, the community and even the whole island. For Edwards, it is Jacobinism, not slavery, which has turned 'the most beautiful colony in the world into a field of desolation and carnage' (57). This spoliation is a warped mirror-image of the conventional masculinist and imperialist trope used by explorers and colonizers, in which the feminized 'interior' of an exotic land awaits penetration and conquest by the European.[59] In Burkean terms, the feminine Beauty of the island is under attack from a doubly threatening masculine sublime: the slaves embody the political savagery of Jacobinism and the natural savagery of Africa.

Stedman's rebellious slaves are a 'savage people, habituated to the barbarities of Africa'. They are associated with darkness and wildness (again, there may be a literary trace here of Caliban, the 'thing of darkness'). The slaves assemble during the night, and launch their attack upon 'the peaceful and unsuspicious planters, like so many famished tygers thirsting for human blood'. Their victims share the same virtues of powerlessness, innocence or vulnerability: 'the old and young, the matron, the virgin, and the helpless infant' (63). The focus then narrows from the community to the genteel, plantocratic family. The purpose of the atrocities seems to be to demolish the structures of patriarchy and paternalism which govern the polite family and its extended 'family' of slaves. The 'unfortunate women' of one plantation family are forced to watch their husband and father 'murdered before their faces' before being taken captive and suffering 'a more horrid fate . . . many of them suffered violation on the dead bodies of their husbands and fathers' (69). The reverse situation applies to a 'venerable planter, the father of two beautiful young ladies' who is forced to watch his daughters being 'ravished' (74). The destruction of the genteel family may function as a revenge for the lost African homeland which, as shown earlier, was often romanticized in slavery writing as an idealized organic community. But it is also an act of filial ingratitude on the part of the disloyal slave. There are strong Oedipal overtones in a scene involving a father of two 'natural sons' who tries to dissuade them from joining the rebellion. Edwards notes that the father has reared the sons with 'great tenderness' (conveniently overlooking the manner of their conception) but the father's 'soothing language' and 'pecuniary offers' are despised: the sons 'took his money, and then stabbed him to the heart' (75).

But the most remarkable desecration of the planter body is a revisiting of the atrocity of 'denatalization', a term coined by Moira Ferguson to express the violent removal of reproductive rights from the slave woman's body. A mulatto attack on a French planter and his wife produces a macabre theatricalization of sterilization:

> This unfortunate woman (my hand trembles as I write!) was far advanced in her pregnancy. The monsters, whose prisoner she was, having first murdered her husband in her presence, ripped her up alive, and threw the infant to the hogs – They then (how shall I relate it!) sewed up the head of the murdered husband in - - !!! Such are thy triumphs, philanthropy! (92)

The mock-Jacobin motto condemns but hardly explains this extraordinary exchange of body parts. The substitution of the severed head of the husband for the discarded foetus is a barely credible enactment of reverse heredity, as if the gestational and historical clock is being turned back one generation. The vignette is a grotesque travesty of a nativity scene or Caesarian section, an anti-birth which is the nemesis of a foundational moment. Like possessed surgeons, the rebels turn the 'unfortunate' female body into a site of de-creation and termination, signifying the end of white rule. In another book on the West Indies, Edwards described a similar atrocity committed during the Maroon War of 1795. A British Colonel is killed in an ambush, mutilated, decapitated, and his head 'entombed *in the ill-fated officer's own bowels*'.[60] The masculine 'head' of British military power is, quite literally, infantilized.

The few instances of planter violence in Edwards's text provide another opportunity to berate the French predisposition to cruelty. He recalls witnessing two slaves being 'broken' at the insistence of a lower-class French mob who behaved 'with the ferociousness of cannibals' (77n.). Even worse, genteel French spectators 'looked on with the most perfect composure and *sang froid*', and when some 'English seaman' mercifully strangled the slaves, their intervention was 'ridiculed, with a great deal of unseemly mirth, by the ladies' (78n.).[61] As is shown below, 'unseemly' female planter cruelty has a much more pronounced role to play in Stedman's narrative. But this scene is a reminder that Edwards, like many writers on slavery, viewed slave violence as a consequence of colonial mismanagement and abuse. In his earlier book *The History, Civil and Commercial, of the British Colonies in the West Indies*, Edwards summarized the 'Black Legend' of the Spanish conquest of the Americas:

> the whole history of mankind affords no scene of barbarity equal to the cruelties exercised on these innocent and inoffensive people. All the

murders and desolations of the most pitiless tyrants that ever diverted themselves with the pangs and convulsions of their fellow creatures, fall infinitely short of the bloody enormities committed by the Spanish nation in the conquest of the New World; – a conquest, on a low estimate, effected by the murder of ten millions of the species![62]

This is a theme looked at more closely in Chapter 3, but it is worth noting here that slave rebellion is a mirror-image of the original offence: 'cruelties exercised' on 'innocent and inoffensive people'. Faced with this burden of historical guilt, and even accepting the anti-Catholic bias of the 'Black Legend', it would be surprising if the polite reader did not, at a deep level, perceive slave violence as a form of retribution.

John Gabriel Stedman, *Narrative of a Five Years' Expedition against the Revolted Negroes of Surinam* (1796)

Newton's work has received less critical attention than John Gabriel Stedman's *Narrative of a Five Years' Expedition against the Revolted Negroes of Surinam in Guinea on the Wild Coast of South America; from the Year 1772 to 1777* (1796).[63] The book's fame has derived from the illustrations by William Blake, but recent scholarly work has focussed on other aspects of the text's sensational portrayal of plantation culture. A comparison between the published text and the original manuscript has revealed an increased emphasis on violence, a clear indicator of the popularity of spectacular violence in Romantic print culture.[64] Stedman's transgressive love affair with the slave Joanna has also attracted critical attention.[65] But the most relevant and challenging work on Stedman, for the purposes of this book, has come from Marcus Wood.[66] Wood invents the term 'plantation pornography' to explain the allegedly voyeuristic appeal of Stedman's (and Blake's) scenes of violence and nudity. For Wood, the book is not about slavery but 'white fantasies' of slavery. White authors and artists can never give the slave an authentic existence, which means that the slave body is 'little more than an open playground' of representation.[67] But rather than attack the text for its irredeemable exploitation of the slave body, I want to look at some of the ways in which Stedman constructs a compelling picture of warped planter power, defiant slave speech, and forbidden love. In particular, I want to look at a character ignored by Wood: the violent planter wife, who is a monster of envy, resentment and mischief. This figure is a flagrant anti-type of the polite woman, and a visceral illustration of the abolitionist argument that slavery dehumanized the slave-owner as much as the slave.

Despite the book's title, Stedman deals almost exclusively with planter violence. He could utilize the fact that the Dutch colony of Surinam, the setting for *Oroonoko*, had a reputation for cruelty. Stedman's determination to show the warping effects of colonial power on the planter class may be one explanation for the book's perplexing generic blend of memoir, travelogue, natural history and chronicle. One of the stylistic hallmarks of the book is the manner in which descriptions and discussions of exotic flora and fauna are succeeded seamlessly by long and detailed accounts of atrocities. It is possible that Stedman was trying to give the book an air of respectability by inserting passages of scientific interest between the bouts of sensational violence. But it may also be the case that the disconcertingly abrupt transitions from topography to Terror were designed to reflect the inhumanity and immorality of the colonial frame of mind.

When Stedman first arrives in Surinam, he is soon inducted into the colony's violent ways. After witnessing two slaves being executed for petty crimes, he is engaged in conversation by a 'decent looking man' (1: 109). This figure of respectability regales Stedman with anecdotes of two 'entertaining' slave executions. In the first story, a slave was hanged from an iron hook which skewered his ribs. After surviving for three days, he 'upbraided' a less stoical slave who was being flogged nearby with the words 'You man? – *Da say sasy?*' (1: 109). The second anecdote concerns a slave who suffered the punishment of Damiens, being torn apart by four 'strong' horses. When he was offered some water, he asked his executioner to check that it was not poisoned. According to Stedman's polite interlocutor, this witty intervention 'afforded us the greatest entertainment' (ibid.). Stedman finds this response monstrous, but his 'decent' companion is not finished: 'As for old men being broken upon the rack, and young women roasted alive chained to stakes, there can be nothing more common in this country' (1: 109–10). Those critics who are deeply suspicious of Stedman's motives might read this conversation as a device whose purpose is to preview the sensational violence which lies ahead. But the structure of the embedded anecdotes suggests that the point of this interaction is to recover the voice of the vanquished slave and to juxtapose this speech act with the nonchalant depravity of 'decent' discourse. As Foucault noted, the condemned criminal has a brief moment of cultural power during which the body on the gallows becomes 'the inverted body of the king'. Verbal interjection is a means by which the slave can impose his own meaning on his spectacular death: in the first anecdote, heroic defiance; in the second anecdote, mischievous and sacrilegious humour. The exhortation 'You man?' gives the first scene a particularly powerful emblematic quality. The words crystallize the central ethical dilemma of the slavery debate, recalling Wedgewood's famous anti-slavery slogan 'Am I not a man and a brother?' and fundamentally challenging the humanist credentials of the 'decent' spectator. In the second anecdote, the joshing and irreverent humour is actually a Freudian trap, as it does not lead to the cathartic exchange of anxieties but only to a deeper and more 'poisoned' contract of guilt for the 'entertained' audience.[68]

This complex configuration of spectacular suffering and minstrelsy anticipates the execution of the slave Neptune, probably the most famous (or infamous) scene in the book, and the source of one of Blake's most powerful engravings (Figure 1). According to Debbie Lee, Blake's illustrations

Figure 1 William Blake, 'The Execution of Breaking on the Rock', from John Gabriel Stedman, *Narrative of a Five Years' Expedition against the Revolted Negroes of Surinam* (1796)

of slave executions were 'some of the most terrifying images that would ever come before the eyes of the British public'.[69] Stedman seems to have been aware of this, as he went so far as to apologize for the 'shocking exhibition' of the 'annexed drawing' (2: 297–8). But an obvious yet overlooked point about the illustrations needs to be made. Blake's images remain non-verbal (he would never have resorted to the populist technique of inserting speech bubbles), and though this absence of language may intensify the visual mood of abjection and even stoical suffering, it does not accurately represent the text, in which there are interjections of slave speech. The attention given to Blake's illustration may also explain why the intriguing narrative coda to the Neptune execution scene has eluded critical attention.[70]

Neptune is executed for having shot his overseer in a dispute over a slave woman. The punishment for this crime of passion is to be '*broken alive upon the rack*' with no mercy stroke (2: 295). The execution is described with the lavish detail of martyrology – the fact that Neptune is a carpenter underscores the associations with crucifixion. Neptune's hand is chopped off by his black executioner, who then takes up a 'heavy iron bar, by which, with repeated blows, he broke his bones to shivers, till the marrow, blood, and splinters flew about the field; but the prisoner never uttered a sigh' (ibid.). The visceral details of the text are well in excess of Blake's illustration, and make Neptune's decision not to 'utter' a word even more remarkable. It is after the beating (and therefore in a narrative zone uncontrolled by Blake's image) that the scene takes a surprising and subversive turn. Neptune breaks his silence and begins a remarkable routine of carnivalesque comic exchanges based around the theme of the crucifixion. His first retort is to damn the departing magistrates as a 'set of barbarous rascals' (2: 296), an inversion of Christ's forgiveness of these enemies. When he is refused a mercy stroke, he jibes at Christian mercy: 'you Christians have missed your aim at last' (ibid.). The pun on the word 'aim' is quite intentional, as it combines several meanings: the merciful thrust of a weapon, the piercing of Christ on the cross, and the 'aim' or 'point' of this ritual killing, which is to make Neptune an example. Having scored these points in the manner of Foucault's condemned criminal, Neptune resorts to a more audacious mode of 'entertaining' iconoclastic humour. He sings several songs welcoming the African after-life. He discusses his trial with some onlookers but reminds them not to miss their breakfast. He asks a Jew to pay him back some money so he can purchase food and drink and be kept alive, 'which speech, on seeing the Jew stare like a fool, this mangled wretch accompanied with a loud, hearty laugh' (2: 296–7). Perhaps the joke here is a self-ironizing recognition of the power of racist humour and a skit on the stereotypical demonization of Jews as Christian-killers. The crescendo effect of this series of blasphemous gags reaches its climax with an elaborate joke on the Eucharist. Neptune begins by asking a 'sentinel' why he has no meat to eat. When the soldier replies that he is poor, Neptune offers him a 'present' of his body:

> first, pick my hand that was chopped off clean to the bones, next begin to devour my body, till you are glutted; when you will have both bread and meat, as best becomes you. (2: 297)

This mockery debunks both the Christian and voyeuristic semiotics of his execution. The cannibalistic metaphor recalls an earlier scene in which Stedman was powerless to prevent a young slave woman being brutally whipped by a 'detestable monster' who was left, 'like a beast of prey, to enjoy his bloody feast, till he was glutted' (1: 326). Neptune restyles or self-fashions the spectacle of his death into a cannibalistic ritual. Any pleasure which the reader may feel surely derives from the risqué satirical wit rather than voyeurism.[71] The sequel to the execution takes the sacrilegious humour one step further. When Stedman returns a few hours later to the savannah where Neptune was killed,

> the first object I saw was his head at some distance, placed on a stake, nodding to me backwards and forwards, as if he had really been alive. (2: 298)

This uncanny encounter is like a sequel to the earlier comic routine. Neptune's 'nodding' is a skit on the reanimated corpse of the Biblical resurrection, 'as if he had really been alive', but the nodding is also like a sign of approval aimed at Stedman. It transpires that Neptune did finally receive a mercy killing from the sentinel, 'the marks of whose musket were clearly visible by a large open fracture in the skull' (2: 299). Neptune's skilful humour had 'met its aim', as had the sentinel's musket. On closer inspection, Stedman realizes that the 'nodding' is caused by a vulture which has been feeding on the head – perhaps a 'natural' antidote to the preceding cannibalistic satire on the human variety of vulture. As if he has now exorcized Neptune's ghost, Stedman switches to a disquisition on birds of prey.

Unlike the haunted wanderers of Romantic literary texts, Stedman is not stricken by sights which 'inspire the most unfeeling reader with horror and resentment' (1: 135). This robustness may derive from his redemptive love affair with Joanna, a topic which I want to approach by placing it in the context of the book's portrayal of violence against women, female sexuality and forbidden love.

While visiting a neighbouring estate, Stedman sees a 'most affecting spectacle' of a slave girl being given 200 lashes (Figure 2). The victim is

> a beautiful Samboe girl of about eighteen, tied up by both arms to a tree, as naked as she came into the world, and lacerated in such a shocking manner by the whips of two negro drivers, that she was from her neck to her ankles literally dyed over with blood. (1: 135)

Figure 2 William Blake, 'Flagellation of a Female Samboe Slave', from John Gabriel Stedman, *Narrative of a Five Years' Expedition against the Revolted Negroes of Surinam* (1796)

This whipping of a slave woman seems a classic example of what Wood calls 'plantation pornography'.[72] But this is to privilege sexual voyeurism above other meanings. While this may be appropriate for Blake's image, it is less certain that the text responds to such an interpretation. Again, it is important to recover the narrative context for the scene, as we are told that the woman was punished for refusing the overseer's sexual advances. In other word, the rapacious sexuality of the planter class casts a shadow over the torture, and this is not a subject position which the reader would wish to associate with. This narrative detail also links the scene to the fate of Neptune, who was executed for killing an overseer in a dispute over a slave woman. In the warped culture of slavery, romantic disputes, sexual rivalries and paranoid possessiveness produce horrifically violent outcomes. One of the most 'shocking' aspects of this environment is its corruption of the planter wife. In a series of devastating encounters between white and black femininity, Stedman produces one of his most innovative violent spectacles: the Sadeian planter woman.[73]

Stedman's Sadeian woman is 'a certain Mrs S-lk-r', who is returning to her plantation on a tent-barge. One of other passengers is a slave woman who is suckling her baby. The 'innocent little creature . . . could not be hushed' so 'Mrs S.' (the abbreviation suggests 'sadist') asks for the baby to be 'delivered' into her arms. She then proceeds, 'in the presence of the distracted parent', to drown the baby. The mother leaps overboard to attempt to drown herself, but is rescued and punished for this 'daring temerity' with 300–400 lashes (1: 329–30). This scene is like a feminized version of the horrors of the middle passage: the vicious sea-captain becomes the sexually jealous plantation wife who is determined to mangle the female slave body and destroy its fertility. Mrs S. repudiates all the conventional signifiers of female virtue: sensibility, nurturing, motherhood. The motivation behind her impulsive, irrational and infanticidal rage is almost certainly the fear that her husband will be attracted to the symbolically bared breast of the slave woman. The hyperbolic violence is a form of pre-emptive self-defence and a diversion from the real threat: miscegenation. The text could be accused of allowing the patriarchal planter husband to remain textually hidden (explicit accounts of sex between planter men and slave women featured in Stedman's diary but were cut from the published version), but the depraved behaviour of the book's one genuine villainess is a startling invention. The next example of her evil handiwork occurs in a chapter entitled 'New Instances of Unprecedented Barbarity'. While he is walking on the quayside, Stedman sees another of Mrs S.'s victims:

the dreadful spectacle of a beautiful young mulatto girl, floating on her back, with her hands tied behind, her throat most shockingly cut, and stabbed in the breast with a knife in more than eight or ten different places. (2: 25)

But Mrs S. is capable of 'still greater barbarity'. When the 'infernal fiend' catches sight of a newly arrived 15-year-old slave girl who has a 'remarkably fine figure, and with a sweet engaging countenance', Mrs S.'s 'diabolical jealousy' causes her to

> burn the girl's cheeks, mouth, and forehead with a red-hot iron; she also cut the tendon-Achilles of one of her legs, thus rendering her a monster of deformity. (2: 26)

In a macabre inversion of the classical Pygmalion-Galatea myth, Mrs S. attempts to displace her own moral deformity onto the body of the slave girl, quite literally remoulding the girl in her own repressed image. In another incident, Mrs S. 'knocked out the brains of a quadroon child' (a symbol of miscegenation) and had the child's relatives decapitated (2: 27). It also seems that Mrs S. may have spawned imitators and admirers, as we are given a brief glimpse of a 'Miss Sp–n' who 'seemed to enjoy peculiar satisfaction' at ordering a young female slave 'flogged principally across the breasts' (2: 293).

The textual antidote for this murderous and vindictive psychodrama of female sexual jealousy is Stedman's liaison with Joanna. She is the embodiment of everything that Mrs S. hates: she is a quadroon who is exactly the same age as Mrs S.'s second victim when Stedman purchases her, and she is even pictured with a bared breast. The relationship produces a child named Johnnie, and Stedman describes his role as the 'reverse part of Inkle and Yarico' (2: 372), a benevolent inversion of the famous story of colonial love and abandonment which had become one of the popular paradigms of colonial experience.[74] Critical opinion is divided about Stedman's integrity: Marcus Wood is wholly unconvinced by Stedman's chivalric pretensions, calling him an 'abuser and protector', but Helen Thomas reads the romance as both daring and redemptive.[75] Stedman's claim to be the 'reverse part of Inkle' is not in fact reliable, as he leaves Joanna behind and later finds out that she has been poisoned by one of his rivals. Moreover, his son Johnnie also suffers a violent end, though ironically this takes place while serving in the British navy in the Caribbean. Stedman's forbidden love affair comes to a tragic or convenient end, depending on how much credence is given to the authenticity of his confessional narrative.

The book's other textual strategy for recuperating desecrated femininity produced another famous illustration: Blake's image of America, Europe and Asia embracing each other in the form of three naked women. Stedman states that this image of international peace and harmony is the 'emblematical' answer to the 'horrors and cruelties with which I must have hurt both the eye and the heart of the feeling reader' (2: 394).[76] Underpinned by Blake's revolutionary politics, there is no reason to doubt that the image provided a Utopian balm for the 'eye and the heart of the feeling reader'. The 'horrors and cruelties' of slavery, however, were not to be so easily erased from the public mind.

Towards emancipation

The period between the British abolition of the slave trade in 1807 and the emancipation of the slave colonies in the mid-1830s has received only modest attention from critics.[77] One reason for this neglect could be that the period seems to be less text-rich than the late eighteenth century. With the exception of the fugitive and maverick works of the Spencean radical Robert Wedderburn and the appearance of Mary Prince's ghosted autobiography in 1831, these years seem far less prolific in the production of both black writing and memorable texts by (white) Romantic writers. An obvious historical explanation for this relative scarcity is the political and agitational lull which followed abolition. Even anti-slavery stalwarts such as Thomas Clarkson argued that the ameliorative effects of abolition needed a generation to work: by cutting off the supply of fresh slaves, planters would be forced to take a more lenient and nurturing approach, which in due course would transform their slaves into a 'free and industrious peasantry' fit for emancipation.[78] This was an optimistic gloss on the situation. Planters resisted even modest further reforms such as the registration of slaves and moves to ban particularly flagrant forms of cruelty such as 'driving' and the flogging of female slaves. One consequence of this intransigence was a continuation of slave revolts and rebellions. If not on the scale of San Domingo, these uprisings were sufficient to give a fillip to the emancipationist cause. The rebellions which attracted most media attention took place in Demerara in 1823 and Jamaica in 1831. The former coincided with the founding of the Anti-Slavery Society and the publication of several major pamphlets; the latter coincided with both a major revolt in Virginia and the Reform Bill crisis in Britain.

Before these events are looked at in more detail, some account can be taken of the persistence of the idea of slave rebellion in the popular imagination in the early nineteenth century. In Maria Edgeworth's short story 'The Grateful Negro' (1802), published in her collection *Popular Tales* (1804), a slave revolt is fortuitously betrayed by a loyal slave named Caesar. Not only does this prevent bloodshed, it also vindicates the gradualist and paternalist reforms of the modernizing plantation owner Edwards, who presides over the introduction of the principles of political economy and industrial progress.[79] This liberal denial of the political agency of slave violence can be contrasted with the lively portrayal of slave resistance in a more genuinely 'popular tale' which circulated widely in different versions: *Obi; or the History of Three-Fingered Jack*.[80] The hero of the tale is the son of African parents Amri and Makro. His sole purpose in life is to be revenged upon Captain Harrop, the man who sold his parents into slavery after they had rescued him from a shipwreck – in this respect, the tale is a radical 'sequel' to the Inkle and Yarico story. Jack comes to prominence in the second Maroon war in Jamaica (1795–96), becoming 'as great a man as ever graced the annals of history' (*SAE*, 6: 292). He finally catches up with Harrop and imprisons him in a cave in Jamaica, but despite his Herculean, larger-than-life prowess and legendary fame, Jack is tracked down and killed by Squashee, a slave-cum-bounty-hunter who has been baptized to protect him against the Obi spell. Jack is beheaded, but Harrop starves to death in the cave.

The sympathies of the tale are clearly with the rebel slaves. The modern editor of the tale goes so far as to claim that the story 'unequivocally' and 'unashamedly' celebrates black rebellion, though this subversion is limited by the cultural marginality and dispensability of 'pulp-fiction' (*SAE*, 6: xxii–xxiii). In fact it could be argued, as Gramsci did, that the radicalizing of popular culture is an important revolutionary tool. There is no doubt that *Obi* exudes a strong whiff of popular, even ultra-radical Jacobinism. The Maroon rebellion is couched in the republican language of rights and 'Liberty'. Christian conversion is rejected as cant and hypocrisy, and the African religious practice of Obi (which is caricatured in Edgeworth's tale) becomes a mode of heroic resistance: Jack's grandfather, an 'Obi-man', is burned to death for not revealing Jack's hiding place (*SAE*, 6: 283). The enslavement of Jack's parents contrasts African sensibility with European barbarism. Just before their capture, Amri and Makro see a young slave woman 'mercilessly dragged along by two guides, who every now and then spirited her with a lash'. The woman dies, but her 'insensible body' is kicked by a disgruntled Christian merchant. During the middle passage, Amri faints at the sight of Makro being beaten to death as punishment for going on hunger strike: 'Oh, in what a mangled situation was his body' (*SAE*, 6: 281). Jack's crusade combines the grandeur of a revenge-tragedy with the popular exploits of the folk-hero. His ability to escape from prison recalls the feats of his namesake Jack Sheppard, but the fate awaiting Jack is far worse than mere hanging:

> he was to be slung up by his waist, forty feet from the ground, to a gallows, exposed to the sun's burning heat for three days, receiving no sustenance; on the fourth he was to be taken down, and the soles of his feet seared, and under the arm-pits; then to receive five-hundred lashes, have his heart and entrails burned before him, to be quartered, and his quarters to be hung in four several parts of the island, to strike terror to the slaves. (*SAE*, 6: 286)

This unequivocal image of 'terror' is a stark reminder that European governments during this period did not abandon the public 'mangling' of the victim as a form of punishment. This may have been a tendency on the European mainland, as Foucault argues, but it was not the case in the colonies. Slave rebellions, like other outbreaks of popular violence, exposed the brutality of State power. Such controversial images of judicial violence must surely have made a powerful impression on public opinion. In the next section of this chapter, I will suggest that the slave rebellions in Demerara, Jamaica and Virginia contributed not only to the emancipation campaign but also to the growing demand for reform of the British political system. I will also suggest that the emancipationist focus on the flogging of slave women influenced the representation of violence in Mary Prince's autobiography.

Slavery's martyrs: The Demerara rebellion (1823)

The 1823 rebellion in the former Dutch colony of Demerara was sparked by frustration at the ruling council's failure to introduce a set of 'amelioration' measures which had been recommended by parliament.[81] These included the abolition of 'driving' and the flogging of female slaves, the greater availability of religious instruction and the promotion of Christian marriage. As the Demerara administration dithered and delayed, the island's slaves, led by a black Methodist deacon named Quamina, demanded full emancipation. Though only three whites were killed, this provoked fierce reprisals. In a six-day campaign of slaughter and terror, scores of slaves were shot, gibbeted and decapitated. Many slaves were later tried and executed, including the use of ritual beheadings. Even though he tried to moderate the violence, Quamina was shot, his body gibbeted and left to hang between two cabbage trees on the plantation in which he worked.[82]

However, the main reason that the rebellion attracted media attention in England was the involvement of the British missionary John Smith. Smith had been posted to Demerara by the London Missionary Society, a movement which many planters regarded with suspicion. When it was revealed that Smith was acquainted with Quamina, the planter lobby seized on this opportunity to punish missionary do-gooders. Smith was charged with fomenting the rebellion. He was arrested but died in jail in 1824 before his case could be tried. His death became a *cause célèbre* and, in Kate Teltscher's words, a 'trigger for renewed agitation'.[83] The Demerara rebellion coincided with the launch of the Anti-Slavery Society, an organization pledged to achieving emancipation. Smith's story was a propaganda coup. His tragedy could be mobilised as an object-lesson in moral and spiritual purity which shamed slavery's supporters. In a hard-hitting pamphlet of 1824, Elizabeth Heyrick declaimed,

> Before we can have any rational hope of prevailing on our guilty neighbours to abandon this atrocious commerce – to relinquish the gain of oppression – the wealth obtained by rapine and violence, – by the deep groans, the bitter anguish of our unoffending fellow-creatures, we must purge ourselves from these pollutions.[84]

This is a familiar inversion: black innocence, humanity and suffering are the antithesis of European decadence, corruption and violence.

But despite such harangues, the public debate about the rebellion revealed the intransigence of those with vested interests. One intriguing footnote of the Demerara story concerns the famous Gladstone family. The rebel Quamina worked on the Gladstone's plantation (ironically named 'Success'), and was to this extent the Gladstone's creation. But John Gladstone, father of the future Prime Minister W. E. Gladstone, robustly resisted any moves towards reform. He argued that the 'unfortunate slaves' had been 'deluded' in their rebellion. He also warned that 'manumitted negroes' were 'idle, indolent, and slothful'. He proved this point by using the delay in the introduction of emancipation to increase the profits of Success to £10,000 per year.[85] But the most famous anti-emancipationist intervention came from George Canning, the former foreign secretary and abolitionist who also supported Catholic emancipation. In the parliamentary debate about the rebellion, which took place in June 1824, Canning opposed calls for 'immediate abolition' by drawing an analogy between the figure of the emancipated slave and Frankenstein's monster:

In dealing with the Negro, Sir, we must remember that we are dealing with a being possessing the form and strength of a man, but the intellect only of a child. To turn him loose in the manhood of his physical strength, in the maturity of his physical passions, but in the infancy of his uninstructed reason, would be to raise up a creature resembling the splendid fiction of a recent romance; the hero of which constructs a human form, with all the corporeal capabilities of man, and with the thews and sinews of a giant; but being unable to impart to the work of his hands a perception of right and wrong, he finds too late that he has only created a more than mortal power of doing mischief, and himself recoils from the monster he has made.[86]

As Chris Baldick has shown, the Frankenstein 'myth' was a cultural vehicle for expressing bourgeois fears about external threats: the French revolution, working-class radicalism, the Irish, or – as in this case – emancipated slaves.[87] The racialized 'monster' in Canning's sketch bristles with ominous sexual and violent attributes: the overdeveloped 'physical passions' are in inverse proportion to the lack of intelligence and super-ego. Given that he asked for the political debate to 'refrain from exaggerated statements, and from highly coloured pictures of individual suffering', Canning found a clever way to sensationalize his key point, that immediate emancipation would be a 'sudden and violent measure' (*SAE*, 3: 248–9). But his Frankenstein image is deeply problematic, precisely because it omits to mention the violence which has shaped the slave's existence in the first place, and which would explain why the 'infant' slave might instinctively turn towards violence (there is an obvious parallel here with the Gladstones, who refused to accept that their own 'Success' was the cradle of the rebellion). Where Canning displaces violence into the future as the outcome of emancipation, Heyrick insists that it is a systemic pretext for emancipation. Canning attributes violence to the slave; Heyrick to the European. Canning alarms his audience with the spectre of imagined European victims; Heyrick adduces the sentimental and morally righteous slave body in order to expose European guilt and spiritual contamination.

The 'cart-whip': Emancipation and the flogging debate

The trading of white and black victims in this renewed propaganda war reached a fever pitch around the issue of the flogging and sexual exploitation of slave women. These were not new causes, but the proposed reforms of 1823 gave them new prominence. A ban on flogging and the consolidation of monogamous (and ideally, Christian) marriage were two of the 'amelioration measures' which had been resisted by the Demerara council. In a pamphlet published that year, the veteran Evangelical campaigner William Wilberforce focussed his polemical energies on the physical and sexual humiliation of the female slave. In his view, the hyperbolic power given to those white and black males in positions of authority within the slavery system encouraged abuse. Slave women are forced to satisfy the black driver's 'licentious desires' even though they are 'attached' to another slave. The public flogging of slave women is 'highly indecent'.[88] White overseers are also contaminated as they become 'corrupters' not 'protectors of the purity of the young females' (*SAE*, 3: 23). In order to reform these white male 'adventurers', the restraining influence of (white) 'modest female company' and Christian marriage is required (*SAE*, 3: 55). Christianity and marriage are, for Wilberforce, more important than emancipation. Although the latter might prevent further 'transatlantic convulsions', slaves are 'not yet fit for the enjoyment of British freedom' (*SAE*, 3: 75). Christian marriage is 'the great expedient for maintaining the moral order and social happiness of mankind'. (*SAE*, 3: 26). This is the only institution which has the moral and social strength to regulate the lapsed morality of the plantation.

In order to drive this point home, Wilberforce homes in on the theme of flogging. The abolition of the flogging of slave women was seen by many reformers as a highly symbolic step forward: it not only represented the end of a cruel practice but also signified the chivalrous respect for the 'weaker sex' which underpinned civilized society. In Canning's words, 'To raise the weaker sex in self-respect, as well as in the esteem of the stronger, is the first step from barbarism to civilization' (*SAE*, 3: 229). Wilberforce takes a more sensational approach to this issue. He terrorizes his male reader into submission by imagining the substitution of white for black victims:

> is there, in the whole of the three kingdoms, a parent or a husband so sordid and insensible that any sum, which the richest West Indian proprietor could offer him, would be deemed a compensation for his suffering

his wife or daughter to be subjected to the brutal outrage of the cart-whip – to the savage lust of the driver – to the indecent, and degrading, and merciless punishment of a West Indian whipping? (*SAE*, 3: 49)

In a pamphlet published in the same year, Thomas Clarkson challenged his paternalist, patriarchal reader in exactly the same way:

to see the tender skins of those lacerated by the whip! to see them torn from him, with a knowledge, that they are going to be compelled to submit to the lust of an overseer! *and no redress!*[89]

Some critics might regard such scenes as examples of 'plantation porno-graphy'. But the point of this drastic inversion was to expose the heinous fact that, in Clarkson's words, 'the West Indian master can do what they will with their slaves' (*SAE*, 3: 126). Such power was a consequence of the legal impermissibility of the slave gaze. A master could commit 'atrocity in the sight of a thousand black spectators, and no harm will happen to him from it' (*SAE*, 3: 89). Clarkson and Wilberforce wanted to make the flogging of slave women a visual offence, even if this required some drastic imaginative distortions such as the substitution of white for black victims. The 'white slavery' flogging vignette exploded plantocratic fictions of slave insensibility by recomposing the conventional atrocity scene into a spectacular image of white self-punishment and atonement.[90]

The cracked jar: Mary Prince and the aesthetics of flogging

The emancipationist movement's investment in the trope of female flogging reached its zenith with the publication of *The History of Mary Prince, a West Indian Slave* in 1831.[91] It had been some years since the last British slave autobiography had appeared, so this work represented a triumph for the Anti-Slavery Society. The Society was responsible for rescuing this Bermudan ex-slave from obscurity and destitution, and its secretary Thomas Pringle collaborated with Prince in producing the book (his role was supposedly limited to editing the text and providing footnotes). The timing of the publication was also important, as it coincided with the political turmoil of the Reform Bill crisis. It was not difficult to see the parallels between the issues of political enfranchisement and emancipation. Mary Prince's story was an exotic and extreme extrapolation of the sufferings and aspirations of all Britain's slaves.

Prince's story is a miracle of survival, which presents spiritual redemption in punishing physical terms. From the outset, the narrative focus is on her body as a site of commodification, violent humiliation and abundant, often overpowering, sensibility. The sale of Prince and her siblings to a cruel owner is like taking 'little chickens to market' (*SAE*, 1: 347). Mary feels her 'heart would burst' at the loss of her previous mistress:

> My heart throbbed with grief and terror so violently, that I crossed my hands quite tightly across my breast, but I could not keep it still, and it continued to leap as though it would burst out of my body. But who cared for that? (*SAE*, 1: 348)

The 'violence' of her emotions (itself a political riposte against the notion of slave insensibility) counterbalances the impending violence of her new owners. The trope of the bursting body is fraught with tension: it suggests not only sublime sensibility and Evangelical religious passion, but also the malleability and vulnerability of her physical and economic condition. It is precisely this contradiction which the reader should 'care' about. A depiction of a slave auction makes clear that this is no time for 'careless' looks or 'light' responses:

> Did one of the many by-standers, who were looking at us so carelessly, think of the pain that wrung the hearts of the negro woman and her young ones? No, no! They were not all bad, I dare say, but slavery hardens white people's hearts towards the blacks; and many of them were not slow to make their remarks upon us aloud, without regard to our grief – though their light words fell like cayenne on the fresh wounds of our hearts. (Ibid.)

The aim is to shock the 'not all bad' spectator out of his or her casual indifference or 'careless' concern. Pouring cayenne pepper on fresh wounds is an apt reflexive metaphor: Mary's textual body is a visceral compound of consumable Caribbean flesh.[92] She is displayed in the street to 'strange men' who handled her like a 'butcher would a calf or lamb' (ibid.). Pringle adds some paratextual commentary on this scene by including a description of another slave auction in a footnote. In this vignette, a mother and children are 'exhibited' to farmers like a 'head of cattle', but Pringle's point is that the scene is an opportunity for sentimental intervention:

> There could not have been a finer subject for an able painter than this unhappy group. The tears, the anxiety, the anguish of the mother, while she met the gaze of the multitude, eyed the different countenances of the bidders, or cast a heart-rending look upon the children; and the simplicity and touching sorrow of the young ones, while they clung to their distracted parent, wiping their eyes, and half concealing their faces... contrasted with the marked insensibility and jocular countenances of the spectators and purchasers, furnished a striking commentary on the miseries of slavery, and its debasing effects upon the hearts of its abettors. (*SAE*, 1: 349, n.)

The viewer of this scene forms a triangular scopic relationship with the victim's 'heart-rending look' and the 'marked insensibility' of the 'abettors'. The scene is a highly self-reflexive commentary on the dangers and virtues of aestheticization: the dialectical resolution of the tension between sentimental recuperation and voyeuristic display is political intervention outside the text. Unlike the doomed slave family, the reader has the ability to turn sentiment into agency. The contrast could not be starker: the family is 'literally torn from each other', and the mother's new owner announces that he will 'teach [her] with a sjamboc (a whip made of the rhinoceros hide)' – it is almost as if he is punishing her for her pose of sentimental transcendence.

The fate of this paratextual family anticipates the sadistic regime which awaits Mary in her new position. She is beaten incessantly by her master and a 'savage mistress' (the latter figure recalls Stedman's female monsters): 'To strip me naked – to hang me up by the wrists and lay my flesh open with the cow-skin, was an ordinary punishment for even a slight offence' (*SAE*, 1: 351). One of the primary textual strategies of the narrative is to lay Mary's flesh open to physical abuse and political signification. The more she suffers, the more depraved her tormentors, and the more spectacular her redemption. Her providential status can be contrasted with the fate of her colleague Hetty, who is discovered to be pregnant. Hetty's master is unable to cope with the natural swelling of Hetty's body (there is a clear hint about paternity), so she is 'stripped quite naked, notwithstanding her pregnancy', tied to a tree and beaten until she aborts. As a consequence of this and subsequent floggings, 'her body and limbs swelled to a great size; and she lay on a mat in the kitchen, till the water burst out of her body and she died' (ibid.). Through the monstrous, abortive agency of the master, Hetty is transformed into an unnatural, Rabelaisian caricature of natural childbirth, lying on a kitchen mat like a domestic animal.

With Hetty gone, the full force of proprietorial venom falls on Mary. In a brilliant moment of textual irony, her condition is symbolized by a frail vessel, an earthenware jar which she accidentally breaks. Although 'the jar was already cracked with an old deep crack that divided it in the middle' (*SAE*, 1: 352), it becomes a touchstone for her mistress: 'I never heard the last of that jar; my mistress was always throwing it in my face'. The patent sexual and racial connotations of this cracked jar point inescapably to a repressed narrative subtext. The master has transferred his affections from Hetty to Mary, but the dominant expression of this desire is violence: 'When he had licked me for some time he [was] . . . quite wearied, and so hot . . . he sank back in his chair, almost like to faint' (ibid.). This scene could easily be regarded as plantation pornography, but the ironic effect of the erotic jargon ('licks') is actually detumescent, as the master's dubious prowess ('almost like to a faint') cannot conquer Prince's saint-like resilience of spirit. When another master beats her for her refusal to accede to his 'indecent' order to wash him in the bathtub, she remarks that to see him 'quite naked' is 'worse to me than all the licks' (*SAE*, 1: 354). Despite all the 'licks', Prince retains some control of her sexuality: another mistress is 'more vexed' than her husband about Mary's marriage to a free black, and orders her to be flogged (*SAE*, 1: 358).

But Mary Prince never completely cracks. Instead, the story of her decimated body exposes the cracks in civilization: 'There is no modesty or decency shown by the owner to his slaves; men, women and children are exposed alike.' The planters 'forget God and all feeling of shame, since they can see and do such things' (*SAE*, 1: 364). The exposed slave body exposes the owner's sinfulness. Slavery transforms Europeans into monsters, destabilizing European identity, and exposing a Jekyll and Hyde division, a 'deep crack that divided it in the middle'. As Prince remarks, 'I have often wondered how English people can go out into the West Indies and act in such a beastly manner' (ibid.). In Mary Prince's story, the exporting of European beasts is counterbalanced by the importing of her bursting heart.

The death struggles of slavery: Slave rebellion and reform 1831–1833

The Reform Bill crisis in Britain coincided with two major slave rebellions in Virginia and Jamaica. The political impact of these rebellions has received little critical attention, but the renewed focus on spectacular plantation violence undoubtedly applied pressure to the slavery debate at a crucial juncture. The scale of emancipationist activity at this time can be measured by the fact that the Anti-Slavery Society alone issued half a million tracts in 1831 and in 1832 gathered over 1.5 million signatures to petition parliament.[93] As Chapter 5 will show, the British political scene from 1830 to 1832 was in a volatile and possibly pre-revolutionary state. With the French and Belgian revolutions of 1830 as a backdrop, the Swing and Bristol riots represented a major resurgence of popular political violence. To many, the political message seemed clear: resistance to reform could lead to full-scale revolution. This logic could also be extended to the slavery debate.[94]

The insurrection in Virginia in August 1831 is probably best remembered for having produced a sensational piece of slave life writing, *The Confessions of Nat Turner* (1831).[95] Turner was the religiously inspired leader of an outbreak of violence which resulted in 50-60 whites being killed (their names were catalogued at the end of the text) and about 20 slaves being executed.[96] While awaiting trial, Turner told his story to Thomas Gray, who packaged the narrative as the slave equivalent of a 'Newgate' confession. It was published just over a week after Turner's execution in November 1831 and quickly sold 50,000 copies.[97] Contemporary interest in Turner was reignited by William Styron's 1967 novel which had exactly the same title as the original text. Styron, a white author, has been accused of appropriating and embellishing

Turner's slender narrative, but the same charge of textual dishonesty and interference has also been levelled at Gray.[98] Gray's scene-setting, prefatory comments are full of highly charged Gothic and melodramatic language. The 'bandit' Turner is a 'gloomy fanatic', plotting 'schemes of indiscriminate massacre to the whites', assisted by a 'fiendish band' with 'flinty bosoms' (130). The text is a dire warning: 'many a mother as she presses her infant darling to her bosom, will shudder at the recollection of Nat Turner, and his band of ferocious miscreants' (131).

There is certainly evidence in Turner's confession to support this view of him as a deranged, bloodthirsty religious fanatic. The text is dripping in blood. He is called to his 'work of death' (138) when, 'while labouring in the field, I discovered drops of blood on the corn as though it were dew from heaven'. He also sees 'hieroglyphic characters' representing divine figures 'portrayed in blood' on leaves of trees (137). But this discourse can also be located within a tradition of transatlantic Protestant ultra-radicalism, which Linebaugh and Rediker have called 'antinomian democracy'.[99] In Turner's vision of freedom, America represents the anti-Christ. The rebellion was originally planned for 4 July, a conscious defiance of American nationalist mythology. Turner's bloody precipitations could be interpreted as an attempt to repaint the American landscape in its 'true' colour, and to restart the symbolic clock.

The text's description of premeditated killings has the chilling brevity, clarity of purpose and ruthless detachment of the self-righteous: 'I took my station in the rear, as it was my object to carry terror and devastation wherever we went' (142); 'I sometimes got in sight in time to see bodies as they lay, in silent satisfaction' (ibid.). But the most lurid and sensational language has a strong whiff of Gray about it. One woman is ordered to lie down beside the 'mangled body of her lifeless husband' before being shot, after which Turner confesses that 'we found no more victims to gratify our thirst for blood' (144). Gray admits that 'my blood curdled in my veins' (148) as he listened to Turner's story. Given this tendency to sensationalize, it may seem odd that Gray omitted from the text a gruesome incident which he had already included in a long account of the rebellion published in a local newspaper. In this atrocity, a sleeping baby is decapitated by one of Turner's subordinates; the body is then left in a conspicuous location to act as a warning to the white community. But in the context of the *Confession*, in which the incident would fall under the agency of Turner, the vignette was probably too threatening to Gray's implied readership.[100]

But the most threatening aspect of the rebellion was its political significance. According to Herbert Aptheker, the pioneering Marxist historian of slave rebellions, the Nat Turner insurrection resonated with revolutionary significance.[101] As evidence of this, Aptheker cites a poem by Thomas Campbell which appeared in a Richmond newspaper just days before the rebellion began. The poem celebrates the Polish independence struggle and ends with this defiant couplet:

> The call of each sword upon Liberty's aid
> Shall be written in gore on the steel of its blade.[102]

In the same way that the San Domingo rebellion was inspired by the French revolution, Nat Turner's uprising could have been a response to the 'call of each sword upon Liberty's aid'. But despite the obvious parallels with other struggles for freedom, the American emancipation movement distanced itself from Turner. Abolitionists denied that their propaganda incited the Virginia uprising. Racist double standards became glaringly obvious in the debate about the rebellion in the Virginia legislature. One speaker argued that if the slaves 'were white men in oppression and bondage, I would rejoice in a revolution here'.[103] Such breathtaking hypocrisy and racism ensured the continuation of slavery in America for another generation.

But in Britain the situation was becoming critical. Turner's uprising dovetailed with a major slave revolt in Jamaica. This began at Christmas 1831 and lasted eight days. At its height it involved about 60,000 slaves (almost a fifth of the total number on the island), but despite the huge scale of the revolt there were only 14 white casualties, compared to the hundreds of slaves who were killed by militias or later executed.[104] Its leader was Sam Sharpe, a prolific Baptist preacher who had kept abreast of the emancipation debate in England. His insurrection also showed an awareness of the industrial militancy of the British working class, as the first stage of the rebellion was a general strike or 'National Holiday'. But in the expectation that the Jamaican authorities would not grant any measures of amelioration, Sharpe organized an armed resistance. Once the rebellion was crushed, there was a free-for-all of planter reprisals followed by a special assizes in which 344 slaves were given death sentences. Sharpe was executed in May 1832, the same month in which the Reform Bill finally passed through parliament, and just over a year before slavery was abolished in August 1833.

The most vivid eyewitness narrative of the rebellion was written by the Baptist missionary Henry Bleby. His openly partisan account, published some years later under the provocative title *Death Struggles of Slavery*, represents the uprising as an unequal struggle between noble-minded freedom fighters and bloodthirsty, proto-fascist planters.[105] In showing slave violence to be a justified consequence of an implacable and intransigent regime, Bleby made a clear comparison with the Reform Bill crisis in the mother country. Without reform, the slaves would 'bring their bondage to a violent and bloody termination' (2), though this was precisely the kind of language which the planters appropriated to justify their opposition to reform and their retaliatory ruthlessness. In one scene in the book, a militia leader makes a speech in the Jamaican Assembly in which he compares the insurrection to the Bristol riots: 'That the ringleaders were Baptists, is undoubted; so the ringleaders at Bristol were reformers' (25). In another, highly contrived scene, a slave is executed by firing squad and his body left on view. A white man then asks some black 'bystanders' to put their fingers in the bullet hole in the man's skull, declaiming 'You want freedom, do you? This is the sort of freedom we'll give you, every devil of you' (28). But Bleby is determined to give slave bodies the respect that they are denied by the furious planters. The first 'horrible spectacle' he witnesses is a pile of corpses,

> sixteen bodies, dragged into the road, were putrefying in the sun when we passed by, presenting a horrible spectacle . . . There lay one body, the head of which was completely stripped of flesh by the crows; and the bare scull, still attached to the partly clothed body, seemed to grin at us as we passed over it.

The macabre 'grin' recalls the grisly comic routine of Neptune in Stedman's *Narrative of a Five Years' Expedition against the Revolted Negroes of Surinam*. In an extraordinary coda to this scene, Bleby returns five years later and finds some bones, 'one or two fragments of which I carried away' (18–19). The callous planter disregard for the slave remains is converted into a moment of hagiography.

The difference between the noble slaves and the savage planters is exemplified in the titles of the two key chapters, 'Blood' and 'Negro Forbearance'. The former describes how, under martial law, the summary executions of slaves lasted for weeks. It could take as little as 90 minutes to try, condemn and execute a victim. Slaves were often hanged in twos and threes. Though 'these revolting exhibitions' (26) took place in the 'public market-place' in Montego Bay, white 'bystanders' continued 'buying and selling' – surely a withering reference to the commercial basis of slavery. But, *pace* Foucault, executions could also become spectacles of virtuous, magnanimous and defiant suffering. Many insurgents show 'undaunted bravery and fortitude', particularly the rebel leader Captain Dehaney, who as he is led out to be hanged with several others proclaims that he would not falsely incriminate missionaries: 'I won't go before my God with a lie in my mouth' (30). His godly resolve is sorely tested when his rope breaks and he has to be hanged again, but he reacts 'without a shudder' at 'the convulsive movements of his dying companions'. Despite this fortitude, Bleby does not conceal the 'sickening' violence of the execution, and the 'bloody termination' of the scene is the sight of Dehaney's 'convulsive struggles' as his body 'elbowed and pushed' the other bodies on the gallows (31). The symbolism of the language is clear: Dehaney's body is a metonym of the 'convulsive struggle' for freedom.

Once martial law is suspended, 'another system of carnage' replaces it in the form of mixed civilian and military 'slave courts', which are compared to the 'Bloody Assize' of the infamous Judge Jeffreys (35). Slaves are executed in plantations to 'strike terror into the minds of the negroes'. The trials are conducted in an insidious tone of 'levity and brutality'. Bleby gives the example of a father and son who are condemned in a mere ten minutes; their sentence ends with the insulting, humiliating remark, 'You sabbie dat?' (36). It is unsurprising that the planters, who are creatures of 'implacable cruelty' (36) seeking only 'blood, plunder, or revenge' (43), refused to co-operate with an official inquiry into the white Terror. Despite 'the licence of unlimited carnage', no whites were investigated or punished for the 'catalogue of horrors' (55).

By contrast, slave violence was a model of 'forbearance': considering 'the outrages against modesty and humanity, perpetrated upon their mothers, sisters, wives and daughters, which they had been compelled to witness', Bleby is astonished 'not that their atrocities were so many, but that they were so few' (39). He claims that planter propaganda exaggerated 'murders, rapes, and other outrages' to undermine the overwhelming case for emancipation. To prove this point, he refutes the planter version of the murder of Pearce, a militia sergeant. Pearce and his wife were allegedly tied to trees opposite each other. Pearce was forced to watch as 'a set of brutes perpetrated horrors upon her at which the heart must revolt'. The same fate met his daughters before 'the father was cut in pieces, and a portion of his bowels absolutely thrust into the mouths of his daughters' (41). This vignette utilizes the trope of anti-patriarchal disembowelling which appears in Stedman and Edwards, but Bleby gives a very different version of Pearce's death. Pearce 'very imprudently' and provocatively enters a rebel area wearing military garb. Moreover, his killers are caught and executed 'with the bloody clothes of their victim tied about their necks'. The chief assassin is decapitated and his head set on a pole on his plantation 'as an object of terror' (41). This is one of few occasions when justice might, just, have been done. The other is the execution of Sharpe, which Bleby regards as a justified punishment for plotting insurrection, but which is nevertheless a tragedy, a sacrifice to 'the polluted shrine of slavery' (118). In a concluding 'catalogue of horrors' (302), Bleby illustrates that slavery still flourishes in America, Brazil and Cuba.

Though Bleby's account did not appear until the 1850s, his indictment of planter savagery was typical of the way in which the emancipation movement used spectacular violence to discredit the plantocracy. In the aftermath of the Jamaica rebellion, reformers continued to expose the routine violence of plantation life in order to undermine planter myths of benevolent paternalism. One publication which portrayed vividly the persistence of plantation cruelty in Jamaica was Henry Whitely's innocuously titled *Three Months in Jamaica, in 1832*, a source used by Bleby.[106] Whitely was a Yorkshire Methodist lay preacher who went to Jamaica looking for work. An interesting feature of his narrative is its engagement with the 'white slavery' debate. Factory reformers in Britain often claimed that working conditions in factories were as bad as if not worse than that of plantation labour. Richard Oastler, who coined the term 'Yorkshire slavery', testified to a parliamentary inquiry in 1831 that the 'cruelties' inflicted on child-workers 'would disgrace a West Indian plantation'.[107] Bleby takes this fanciful analogy with him to Jamaica, but within 'an hour' of his arrival he is given his 'first full view of West Indian slavery' (6). He sees female slaves carrying manure for the cane fields: 'It appeared to me disgustingly dirty work; for the moisture from the manure was dripping through the baskets, and running down the bodies of the negroes' (3). The picturesque beauty of 'the enchanting scenery and beautiful humming birds' of Jamaica is immediately soiled.

Even if it could be argued that British agricultural workers suffered similar 'disgusting' conditions, by no stretch of the imagination could it be claimed that they were routinely and publicly flogged. The next 'view of west Indian slavery' is the sight of six slaves of both sexes being flogged by an overseer for minor offences. While Whitely is 'perfectly unmanned by mingled horror and pity' of the scene, the overseer reacts with 'as much seeming indifference as if he had been paying them their wages', and assures Whitely that he 'would soon get used, as others did, to such spectacles' (5–6). What follows is a catalogue of punishments which, depressingly but importantly, prove this point. The resort to flogging is so common that 'my sensibility to the sight of physical suffering was so abated, that a common flogging no longer affected me to the very painful degree that I at first experienced' (8). His desensitization is a conscious narrative strategy; his 'abated' sensibility is the first ominous step to becoming an abettor and a lost soul. But there are a sufficient number of 'uncommon' floggings which can still shock him. Predictably, most of these involve women: a mother is given 50 lashes, though she is more concerned about her 'indecent exposure than the cruel laceration of her body' (9); another mother is flogged for taking a few minutes from her work to attend to her child; and 'a very handsome brown girl' is given 10 lashes while 'the overseer and one of the bookkeepers were standing by me, but neither took the least notice' (15). Whitely is appalled by the sexual exploitation of the female slaves. The 'open and avowed licentiousness of the plantation whites' (16) is 'winked at', as is the beating of former mistresses (17).

For refusing to avail himself of the opportunities for 'licentiousness', Whitely is viewed with 'mingled contempt and suspicion' (17). His Methodism also attracts hostility, as slaves were banned from praying after the Jamaica rebellion. He is forced to flee the island after he receives death threats. His conclusion is that child labour in factories is 'very bad' and needs regulation, but slavery is 'infinitely worse' (22).

Just over a year later, British slavery came to an end with the emancipation act of August 1833. The sufferings of slaves had been 'infinitely worse' than most British readers could have imagined was possible. Hyperbolic realism was a representational tool to make the incredible credible, and to bring the astonishing and 'infinite' violence of slavery into the heart of British culture. Slavery was not the only source of spectacular violence in the Romantic period, as the rest of this study will show, but its sheer scale made it the most sustained, powerful, and haunting controversy of the age. The first wave of the anti-slavery movement anticipated the French Terror by several years, and as the next chapter will show, there are significant overlaps between both the themes and, more importantly, the forms of spectacular violence in both spheres of conflict. By the mid-1790s, spectacular violence has constructed a Sadeian universe of hyperbolic violence within the mainstream of Romantic print culture.

The claim of this chapter is that spectacular violence played an important role in representing the horrors of slavery to the British public, a process which aided both abolition and emancipation. However, my main interest in the violent gaze of slavery has been in the ways in which it constructed a new repertoire of suffering. The aesthetics of this new violent gaze gave an unprecedented cultural weight and authority to the bloody vignette. This trope generated a whole set of evil character types, and this ghastly masquerade of villainy directly challenged the moral and religious codes of European civilization. From the examples studied in this chapter (and this is only a tiny fraction of the extraordinary mass of writing which the slavery controversy produced), it is clear that the monsters of slavery were not the familiar racial or class demons of the bourgeois imagination but rather the depraved alter-egos of the enlightened, humane citizen who was the ideal implied reader or audience of anti-slavery propaganda. Even when the focus shifted to slave violence against the white body, it was clear that this was a case of the 'boomerang' effect, a terrible rebounding of imperial violence against itself. The full impact of this theatre of cruelty on Romantic literature has not yet been fully registered and explored by scholars of Romanticism. It is possible, for example, that the mangled slave body functioned as a basic archetype for all situations of extreme cruelty, and in this sense slavery could be an important source for the Gothic novel, though such a connection is beyond the scope of this study. In this chapter I have tried to show that the spectacular violence of slavery was both a political and aesthetic discourse which was grounded in eighteenth-century notions of a triangular violent gaze: most bloody vignettes utilized a visual and moral interplay between victim, perpetrator and spectator. The reader or viewer could move between these subject positions but this movement could function as a self-conscious reflection on the efficacy and pleasures of the violent gaze itself. This anxious process of violent looking was not easily resolved: Coleridge insisted that this could only be achieved by 'benevolent' intervention in the political public sphere. Spectacular violence existed uneasily but powerfully on the borders between reality and fantasy, reportage and representation, aesthetic gratification and political mobilization. It is my contention that self-awareness about the complexities of looking at real or imagined violent acts is explicitly or implicitly built into the bloody vignette, and it is this aspect of the trope which prevents the violent spectacle becoming a simple or reductive case of voyeurism.

The function of this first chapter has been to explain the 'mechanics' of spectacular violence by investigating one of its most potent sources, the representation of Romantic period slavery. The focus of subsequent chapters will be on the ways in which spectacular violence played an important role in representing other major violent events of the Romantic period, and on the ways in which this role opened up new imaginative possibilities for the Romantic imagination.

2
'Disturbed Imagination': The French Revolution

> If the mainspring of popular government in peacetime is virtue, its resource during a revolution is at one and the same time virtue and terror; virtue without which terror is merely terrible; terror, without which virtue is simply powerless. (Robespierre)[1]

> Thou heaven of earth! What spells could pall thee then
> In ominous eclipse? A thousand years
> Bred from the slime of deep Oppression's den,
> Dyed all thy liquid light with blood and tears...
>
> (P. B. Shelley, 'Ode to Liberty')[2]

The master plot of the times

Just how central is the French Terror to the development of British literary Romanticism? Put crudely, was the guillotined head the inspiration for *The Prelude*? Here is one familiar thesis: If the excessive violence of the French revolution had not taken place there would be no British Romanticism. A profound disillusionment with the Jacobin regime of Terror led the first generation of Romantic poets to abandon radical politics and to seek salvation in nature, the literary imagination and the exploration of subjectivity. Romanticism, therefore, was a sublimation, displacement or exorcism of the unbearable violence of history. The personal replaced the public; poetic idealism replaced political idealism.

This is, of course, a deliberate caricature of literary history, but its point is to underline the traditional centrality of the French revolution within any historicist construction of Romanticism. A more rigorous historical analysis would have to add that the repressive measures of the British government in the 1790s also provided an incentive for toning down radical political views. Restrictions on freedom of expression, counter-revolutionary propaganda, treason trials and invasion scares – it was these forces which produced a powerful, mythic image of Britannia endangered by violent republicanism.

This threat was deliberately exaggerated, but its intensity and cultural penetration left an indelible mark on British culture and the literary imagination. Given the undeniable fact that massacres were taking place in France, the problem of how to represent excessive violence was a marked feature in the 'revolution debate' of the 1790s. Edmund Burke's famous *Reflections on the Revolution in France* (1790) quickly established a conservative demonology of the French revolution as essentially and grotesquely violent: violence expressed graphically the unprecedented, 'unnatural' political condition of France. Radicals and liberals argued that the violence was the product of generations of tyranny and that the situation would improve as the revolution matured. But as the details of the September massacres and the Jacobin Terror became clearer, and as anti-Jacobin propaganda intensified, it proved more difficult to retain this view. The 22-year-long war with France was another site of contested bloody vignettes. The radical anti-war sentiment of the 1790s gave way to waves of patriotic, anti-Napoleonic propaganda, which relied heavily on the perpetration of French atrocities, though war poems of varying degrees of loyalty and dissent were published throughout the period.

Set against this more nuanced historical narrative, the 'repressive hypothesis' of the relationship between Romantic period literature and the violent events of revolutionary history seems a clear distortion. But the idea that Romanticism was essentially a displacement of violent historical reality has continued to command substantial critical support. The New Critical emphasis on Romanticism's quasi-Freudian sublimation of history has found an unlikely ally in the ingenious reconstructive and investigative exegeses of the New Historicists. Despite its self-conscious rejection of 'Romantic ideology', New Historicist literary criticism has not always challenged the High Romantic distaste for print culture, preferring to excavate the repressed content of canonical texts. Canon-widening has only inconsistently included the press, periodicals or popular visual culture, the places where violent history most conspicuously featured in the form of reportage and propaganda. Such sources may be drawn on to service major texts, but have no independent cultural existence as vital repositories of tropes, images and narratives. But to neglect this 'primary' level of reading can lead to serious literary-historical inaccuracies. This can be seen strikingly in Alan Liu's seminal New Historicist study *Wordsworth: The Sense of History* (1989). Liu includes press reports of French revolutionary violence in his analysis, but the point of this is to show the extent to which Wordsworth concealed and internalized his engagement with these events. The exclusive focus on Wordsworth's Romantic captaincy produces some dubious generalizations about the literary scene in the 1790s. To begin with, Liu focuses on *The Prelude*, which was unknown beyond Wordsworth's small coterie. Despite this, Liu regards Wordsworth's rejection of the French Terror, the 'master plot of the times', as representative of the zeitgeist.[3] After the

Wordsworthian renunciation, 'violence was unspeakable', and the Romantic retreat to the consolations of nature 'returned the facts of historical violence to the status of ghostly, unnatural fictions' (148, 166). Although Liu's discussion of *The Prelude* is illuminating, this conclusion is misleading and does not even accurately describe Wordsworth's poetic production in the 1790s.[4] A number of his contributions to *Lyrical Ballads*, for example, deal explicitly with 'the facts of historical violence', most notably in 'The Female Vagrant' (see Chapter 4). As we shall see, spectacular violence figured in poems and polemics by Coleridge and, more substantially, in Southey's work. His two major verse dramas of the 1790s, *Wat Tyler* and *Joan of Arc*, both imagined the destruction of the British State.[5] In addition to these well-known Romantic authors, it has already been noted that both popular and 'higher' journalism portrayed the violence in France in extraordinary detail. To show the importance of this circulation of spectacular violence in the popular print culture of the time, this chapter focuses on two such sensational works, Helen Maria Williams's *Letters from France* (1790–96), and William Cobbett's anti-Jacobin tract *The Bloody Buoy* (1797). Far from treating violence as 'unspeakable' or 'ghostly', these works construct atrocity as the defining problem of the revolution.

Another weakness of the 'Wordsworthian' reading of the trajectory of the Romantic imagination is the absence of other contexts for 'historical violence'. Even had it been the case that the French revolution proved too awful to contemplate after 1794, this would not have prevented the British reading public being exposed to the spectacular violence of the slave rebellion in San Domingo (as shown in Chapter 1), or the Irish rebellion of 1798 (see Chapter 3). The onward march of 'the facts of historical violence' renewed, reconfigured and recycled the tropes of hyperbolic realism. It is within this wider cultural matrix of representations of violence that Romantic literary texts need to be considered.

Burke's 'harrassed' sovereigns

Any consideration of the impact of the French revolution on the British literary scene has to begin with the 'revolution debate' sparked by Burke's *Reflections*. Burke had a long-standing fascination with political violence which could have derived from his Irish background. According to Luke Gibbons, Burke's theories of 'violence, pain and sympathy', first put forward in the essay on the sublime, provided a 'set of diagnostic tools to probe the dark side of enlightenment, particularly as it was used to justify colonial expansion, religious bigotry, or political repression'.[6] Before the French revolution erupted, Burke had objected publicly to the British State's excessive use of violence both in colonial settings (Ireland, India, North America) and closer to home in the harsh punishments meted out to the

Gordon rioters. In February 1788, Burke launched the impeachment proceedings against Warren Hastings by making a famous parliamentary speech in which he described Indian atrocities in graphic detail:

The innocent children were brought out and scourged before the faces of their parents; young persons were cruelly scourged, both male and female, in the presence of their parents. This was not all. They bound the father and son face to face, arm to arm, body to body; and in that situation they scourged and whipped them, in order with a refinement of cruelty that every blow that escaped the father should fall upon the son, that every stroke that escaped the son should fall upon the parent; so that where they did not lacerate and tear the sense, they should wound the sensibilities and sympathies of nature . . . it did not end there. In order that nature might be violated in all those circumstances where the sympathies of nature are awakened, where the remembrances of our infancy and all our tender remembrances are combined, they put the nipples of the women into the sharp edges of split bamboos and tore them from their bodies. Grown from ferocity to ferocity, from cruelty to cruelty, they applied burning torches and cruel slow fires (My Lords, I am ashamed to go further); those infernal fiends, in defiance of everything divine and human, planted death in the source of life.[7]

As Michael J. Franklin notes, 'India is characterized as an abused woman; the sources of her fecundity cruelly mutilated or cauterized, simultaneously spoiled and despoiled'.[8] The speech was a stage-managed set piece of sensational spectacular violence. As Burke confessed in a letter:

Oh! what an affair – I am clear that I must dilate upon that; for it has stuff in it, that will, if anything, work upon the popular Sense. But how to do this without making a monstrous and disproportioned member, I know not.[9]

Ironically, a Gillray cartoon of the same year placed Burke, along with Fox and other liberals, as one of the 'Butchers of Freedom' (Figure 3). Burke is shown as poised to strike a defenceless woman and her baby – an iconic moment of atrocity which he used to full effect in his speech on India. Gillray's appropriation of this set-piece feature of spectacular violence could not, with hindsight, have been more wounding, as Burke made the account of the mob's attack on the French queen at Versailles the rhetorical highlight of the *Reflections*.

Despite his pre-revolutionary sympathy for the abused body of the colonial or plebeian subject, it was the deposed and disposable royal body which transfixed Burke's response to the French revolution. The mistreatment and humiliation of the French king and queen was for Burke the literal

Figure 3   James Gillray, 'The Butchers of Freedom' (July 1788) © Trustees of the British Museum

and symbolic violation of tradition, authority and the customary values of church and State. It is well known that Burke was incensed by the triumphal conclusion of Richard Price's *A Discourse on the Love of our Country*, a sermon delivered in November 1789, but the significant details of that textual flashpoint have tended to be overlooked by scholars. In one key sentence, Price paints a vignette of the triumph of the people over the old regime:

> I have lived to see THIRTY MILLIONS of people, indignant and resolute, spurning at slavery, and demanding liberty with an irresistible voice; their king led in triumph, and an arbitrary monarch surrendering himself to his subjects.[10]

It is tempting to claim that the second half of this sentence, a mere fourteen words, sparked the 'revolution debate' in Britain.[11] The first half of the sentence is the sonorous, generalized rhetoric of the republican sublime, but the subsequent clause grounds this triumphal image in the specific 'glorious spectacle' (in Price's words) of the people's march on Versailles in October 1789. The image crystallizes the drama of revolutionary change into a metonymy of popular sovereignty; moreover, the deposition of monarchy takes place in the fully exposed glare of the public arena, acting as a radical antitype to the conventional pageantry of the royal procession. The captive king is a carnivalesque icon of political and social inversion, though the transfer of power takes place without violence: the king is 'led' but also 'surrenders' to the 'irresistible' popular will. The scene encapsulates the fall of absolutism, as 'arbitrary' power succumbs to the general will of the masses. The original event is transformed into political mythology; the 'glorious spectacle' is an apotheosis of both popular politics and print culture, in which the role of the 'people' at Versailles can be vicariously experienced by Price's readership. Price constructs the triumph of popular sovereignty as a vignette in which the 'light' of reason fuses with the general will.

For Burke, however, Price had summoned up a demon. The clearest indication of the efficacy of Price's rhetorical strategy is the fact that one of the central aims of the *Reflections* was to substitute a royalist narrative for Price's cameo of deposition and popular sovereignty. Burke's primary task was to restore political order and authority by reasserting the 'correct' social relations between monarch and people. This entailed the restoration of conventional aesthetic hierarchies of representation: tragic grandeur and sentiment for the monarch, grotesqueness for the people. Like many of the texts in the revolution debate, the *Reflections* was an intensely intertextual performance of hegemonic display. Burke's conquest of the public sphere would replace republican sensationalism with the traditional canons of moral respectability and polite political discourse. It would make Price the example for all budding radical orators and print radicals. Yet Burke found it impossible not to be afflicted, if not infected, by the very popular excitement he sought to banish from political debate. His own brand of sensationalist narrative effects ensured the *Reflections'* notoriety and longevity.[12]

Burke's anti-republican counter-narrative of royal 'distress' is the most famous section of the *Reflections*, a fact which underscores the degree of creative energy Burke invested in the scene. James T. Boulton calls this section of the *Reflections* the 'rhetorical and philosophical centrepoint' of the text.[13] Burke presents the procession at Versailles as a grotesque, carnivalesque parade of unnatural savagery, criminal inhumanity and, above all, female violence. He debunks the spectatorial pleasure of the event, seizing on the fact that 'several English were the stupified and indignant spectators of that triumph'.[14] Burke converts the scene into a 'triumph' of loyalist sensationalism: 'the most horrid, atrocious, and afflicting spectacle, that perhaps was ever exhibited to the pity and indignation of mankind' (117). In Burke's demonology, popular sovereignty, popular culture and popular opinion are all reviled in their own carnivalesque terms. The 'captive king' has to answer to 'the polluted nonsense of [the Assembly's] most licentious and giddy coffee-houses'; the French state is a place where 'public measures are deformed into monsters' and political reform is debased into 'assassination, massacre, and confiscation' (118–19). The leaders of the revolution are 'like the comedians of a fair before a riotous audience; they act amidst the tumultuous cries of a mixed mob of ferocious men, and of women lost to shame', truly an 'inverted order' (119). In essence, the revolution is a regicidal seizing of power, though in 1790 Burke could only make this case metaphorically and proleptically.

The counterbalance to the ferocious *poissards* is the idealized portrait of the French queen. The attack on her bedchamber is a collision of the elevated and debased extremes of femininity and social class. The 'women lost to shame' and their male cronies are placed in the balance with transcendent royal poise and beauty. Seen through the grid of Burke's aesthetic theories, the scene shows the masculine sublime terrorizing feminine beauty: 'the age of chivalry is dead'. As critics have pointed out, Burke's overheated writing may suggest a degree of complicity in what could be construed as a rape fantasy. Tom Furniss, for example, calls the tableau an 'obscene joke'.[15] But to focus discussion on the royal body is to fall into Burke's trap (in Paine's words, to 'pity the plumage' and 'neglect the dying bird')[16] as Burke's rhetorical target is the rampaging mob which represents the murderous, illicit power of popular sovereignty. Burke's ochlocracy[17] is a depoliticized, pathologized band of bloodthirsty monsters: they are 'reeking with blood'; the royal palace is 'swimming in blood' and 'strewed with scattered limbs and mutilated carcasses' (this hyperbole shows Burke's determination to turn the scene into a bloody vignette of atrocity); the triumphal march to Paris on October 6 is a violent Dionysiac or Saturnalian orgy, comprising

> the horrid yells, and shrilling screams, and frantic dances, and infamous contumelies, and all the unutterable abominations of the furies of hell, in the abused shape of the vilest of women. (122)

This is Burke's answer to Richard Price's 'people, indignant and resolute, spurning at slavery, and demanding liberty with an irresistible voice'. Here there is no articulation of revolutionary change, only the hellish charivari of pre-social anarchy. Burke's image of the furious crowd was certainly not new, but the subsequent course of the revolution made his fantasy of sublime violence and royal distress seem like a historical prophecy. As Chapter 5 will show, the demonic image of the spectacular mob became a potent feature of counter-revolutionary propaganda in the 1790s, and it was to haunt the literary and visual imagination well into the nineteenth century.[18]

Initially, however, Burke did not have it all his own way. *Reflections* provoked a flurry of counter-attacks, the most famous of which was Thomas Paine's *The Rights of Man* (1791–92). All these ripostes debunked Burke's Versailles fantasy. Paine accused Burke of writing 'Quixotic' nonsense and producing 'tragic paintings' and 'flagrant misrepresentations' instead of history.[19] Paine rewrites the Versailles incident in neutral language, simply calling the crowd 'a very numerous body of women, and men in the disguise of women' (62). Paine countered Burke's fawning monarchism with a lofty republicanism, denying that the royal couple's private space was invaded. In

Paine's rewriting of the event, the disturbance is not mindless violence but a politically motivated act, the result of genuine fears that the king was about to escape and betray the revolution. In the finale to Part One of *The Rights of Man*, Paine announced famously that the present day was an 'age of revolutions', but he added that he was referring to peaceful revolution 'by reason and accommodation', not 'convulsions' (146). The examples of America and France had shown that 'convulsions' were the result of the failure of an *ancien régime* to introduce enlightened political reforms. In the conservative imagination, however, popular violence and popular justice was instinctual, mindless and purely destructive, the antitype of civilization.

All the replies to Burke were intertextual reworkings of the original text.[20] Burke's sentimental worship of the queen was an easy target.[21] As the eponymous hero of Charlotte Smith's republican novel *Desmond* (1792) puts it, mocking Burke's famous declamation on the decline of chivalry, '*a thousand pens will leap from their standishes*... to answer such a book'.[22] Mary Wollstonecraft in *A Vindication of the Rights of Men* (1790) debunked Burke's account of the 'outrages of a day' at Versailles by placing it within a larger canvas of the poverty and suffering of the common people:

> Did the pangs you felt for insulted nobility, the anguish that rent your heart when the gorgeous robes were torn off the idol human weakness had set up, deserve to be compared with the long-drawn sigh of melancholy reflection, when misery and vice are thus seen to haunt our steps?[23]

For Wollstonecraft, Burke's monarchist narrative is an index of his exclusive politics and his irrational worship of power. She refutes his claim that royal suffering is the epitome of tragic pathos by identifying two types of 'sympathetic emotion' which are activated at the sight of 'distress', or an 'affecting' narrative:

> We ought to beware of confounding mechanical instinctive sensations with emotions that reason deepens, and justly terms the feelings of *humanity*. This word discriminates the active exertions of virtue from the vague declamation of sensibility. (1: 52)

As was shown in Chapter 1, this critique of passive or 'vague' sensibility was also deployed by Coleridge in the anti-slavery campaign. Like Coleridge, Wollstonecraft cannot separate 'the feelings of *humanity*' from their political context. The civic humanist 'active exertions of virtue' can only flourish, she adds sharply, 'amongst equals' (1: 55). In *Vindication of the Rights of Women* (1792) she explained revolutionary violence as the outcome of political repression, not social predisposition: 'The bent bow recoils with violence, when the hand is suddenly relaxed that forcibly held it'.[24] In her more definitive study of the revolution, *An Historical and Moral View of the Origin and Progress of the French Revolution; and the Effect it has Produced in Europe* (1794), she put the same point more pithily: 'the French became suddenly all sovereigns'.[25] She also gave a more Burkean, sympathetic account of the 'harassed' sovereigns at Versailles:

> The sanctuary of repose, the asylum of care and fatigue, the chaste temple of a woman, I consider the queen only as one, the apartment where she consigns her senses to the bosom of sleep, folded in its arms forgetful of the world, was violated with murderous fury. (6: 204, 209)

Even here there is a republican, deflationary qualifying clause which refuses to give the queen a transcendental humanity, 'a woman, I consider the queen only as one'. Wollstonecraft also demystifies the 'female mob' by explaining its composition as a mix of half-starved Parisians and loyalist male *agents provocateurs* in female disguise; it is the latter 'monsters' (acting for the Duke of Orleans) who are primarily responsible for instigating the 'brutal violation' of the queen's apartment, and who ensured that the incident would become one of the most 'mysterious' and 'blackest' of the revolution (6: 205–6).[26] Though she does not deny the aesthetic and political power of the 'violation' – she even goes so far as to assign to it 'the commencement of the reign of anarchy' (6: 212) – Wollstonecraft refigures the incident as an example of duplicitous monarchist spectacle: an apposite critique of Burke and the ideology of legitimacy he expounded.

Wollstonecraft could have been influenced by the republican historian Catherine Macaulay, who argued that Burke's stricken queen was a sentimental trap for the reader. For Macaulay, Burke's cloying depiction of 'regal distress' is meant to '*enslave* our affections' and 'captivate the imagination', but it merely duplicates Burke's royalist 'delusions of fancy'.[27] Macaulay cleverly conflates representation and affect – the real victim of the scene is the reader. Again, the republican counter to the royalist and loyalist aesthetics is to democratize sensibility. The collective heroism of the people, Macaulay adds, is a truer and nobler subject for sublime art. In similar vein, Joseph Towers contrasted Burke's 'pathetic representations of the supposed suffering' of the royal couple with the 'freedom and happiness of more than twenty-five millions of people'.[28] Like other radicals, Towers explains the violence at Versailles as the understandable response of a newly liberated people afflicted by food shortages and a serious threat of counter-revolution.[29] Towers also inverts the chivalric exhortation of Burke's 'historical romance', preferring that 'the nation' should draw swords 'in defence of the liberties of their country' (1: 108, 98). In the republican scale of historical justice, 'an imprisoned monarch is an inconsiderable evil compared with that of an enslaved nation' (1: 97). Unfortunately for this radical critique, the execution of the king in January 1793 was a propaganda gift to loyalists.

Burke's demonization of the people was the target of some intriguing and striking irony in James Mackintosh's *Vindicæ Gallicæ* (1791). Mackintosh displaces the Burkean imagery of the people's violent licentiousness onto Burke's style: 'he can advance a group of magnificent horrors to make a breach in our hearts, through which the most undisciplined rabble of arguments can enter in triumph'.[30] Mackintosh does not deny that popular violence occurred, but he disputes its barbarity. To begin with, some excesses were inevitable in the circumstances: 'the passions of a *nation* cannot be kindled to the degree which renders it capable of great achievements, without endangering the commission of violence and crimes' (1: 332). Moreover, popular violence is open and direct: 'the wild justice of the people has a naked and undisguised horror . . . while murder and rapine, if arrayed in the gorgeous disguise of acts of state, may with impunity stalk abroad' (1: 323). The phrase 'gorgeous disguise' is a powerful encapsulation of the radical critique of the conservative political mythology of mob rule. Burke's hagiographic portrait of royalty gave radicals an opportunity to debunk the cult of monarchy. A 'calm survey' of the Versailles imbroglio, says Mackintosh, shows simply 'the shock of one day's excesses committed by a delirious populace' who feared the king's betrayal (1: 329). As for the demise of chivalry, Mackintosh explains this as a byproduct of modernity, 'the diffusion of knowledge and extension of commerce' (1: 330). Burke's royalist fantasy is converted into an Enlightenment narrative of popular progress.

Despite this enterprising republican counter-mythology of popular violence, the course of the revolution from the summer of 1792 to the end of the Terror in 1794 provided a massive amount of ammunition to the reactionary opposition, and destabilized the liberal and radical analysis of popular violence as a mirror or 'boomerang effect' of tyranny. The representation of spectacular violence remained a contested discursive site, though the balance of power swung towards demonization.

'The hour of carnage is arrived': The revolutionary massacre

The summer of 1792 was a turning point in the French revolution. In the wake of the Brunswick manifesto and the threat of invasion, the revolution entered a more radical phase. The storming of the Tuileries on 10 August marked the final demise of the monarchy and heralded the establishment of the French republic. In early September, hundreds of prisoners were massacred in response to rumours that priests and captured Swiss guards were engaged in counter-revolutionary conspiracies. A new mode of death appeared in the form of guillotine, a 'democratic' and highly portable technology which became the symbol of the Jacobin Terror of 1793–94. The British reading public, already bombarded by the horrors of slavery, were subjected to a new torrent of violent reportage, sensational propaganda and bloody vignettes. In the Introduction to its volume for 1792, the *Annual*

Register remarked that the 'atrocities of democracy' in France provoked 'mingled astonishment and terror' (viii). The Burkean vision of Dystopian Terror seemed to be unfolding.

One of the first reports of the 10 August massacre appeared in *The Times* on 16 August. The report is by a 'regular correspondent' who describes himself (I assume it is a he) as an 'unwilling spectator' whose 'blood freezes at the very recollection of the massacre'. The slaughter of Swiss guards by sans-culottes is presented as one-sided, an act of 'cool, deliberate, and premeditated revenge' which 'makes humanity shudder'. Many of the Swiss guards 'underwent a sort of mock trial' before being beheaded, while the 'mob' watched 'coolly'. As was shown in Chapter 1, the 'cool' gaze was a standard signifier of the inhumanity of those who ordered, perpetrated or abetted atrocities. Note also the emphasis on carnivalesque justice, the ritual of the 'mock trial', the inversion of order and authority. The *Annual Register* reported that at the end of the day, 'nought but bloody banners grace the turrets and spires of this once admired city of Paris' (*Annual Register* (1792), 759). The revolutionary flags are conspicuous by their absence of inscription; they are reduced to being mere signifiers of primitive violence, power and non-meaning, the anarchic antithesis of order and tradition. Another English eyewitness, John Moore, similarly presented the 'massacre' as a rout of the codes of civilized warfare (and by implication, civilization itself).[31] Visiting the scene on 11 August, he is shocked to see that the 'stripped' corpses of the Swiss guards had been left 'exposed' (1: 58). For Moore, there had been no 'finer battalion of infantry in Europe', and he recalled having seen them recently 'in all the pride of health and military pomp' (1: 59). The degrading disposal of their bodies is an intentional rejection of military etiquette: 'Many of the bodies were thrown into the flames – I saw some half consumed' (1: 61). This is too much for Moore, and 'sick at the sight, I hurried from this scene of horror', but not before he contrasts his manly sentiment with the unnaturally 'curious' gaze of sans-culotte women: 'The garden and adjacent courts were crowded with spectators, among whom there was a considerable proportion of women, whose curiosity it was evident was at least equal to their modesty' (1: 58). There is only one Burkean conclusion to be drawn from such behaviour: 'such furies do not deserve the name of citizens' (1: 60).

For those who were opposed to the French revolution, its republican transformation in 1792 represented the final collapse of any legitimacy. The crescendo of violence, beginning with the events of 10 August and reaching a climax in the execution of the king in January 1793, was interpreted as the bloody death of the ideals of the revolution, rather than its apocalyptic rebirth. In conservative mythology, the revolution had executed itself. As *The Times* announced on 8 September, the rule of 'mobocracy' signified that 'the Revolution in France is at an end'. In order to drive this point home, the newspaper's reports of the September massacres were extremely graphic and elaborate (it is also worth noting that the newspaper later described the Terror (24 March 1794) as 'a new Septemberizing'). The paper makes clear that every account is based on 'eye-witness' testimony and is 'not in need of exaggeration' (10 September), a good example of the central features of hyperbolic realism. The motives of the mobocracy range from recidivist instinct, a 'base, cruel and degenerate nature', to the despicable politics of envy and class vengeance. This latter point is exemplified by the fact that the most prominent of the mob's sacrificial victims is a prime example of the socially elevated female, the Princess de Lamballe – following the principles of sensibility, it was a *de rigeur* feature of spectacular violence that a distressed genteel woman was a more sentimental and affective figure than a distressed lower-class woman. Although *The Times* states that 'decency forbids us to repeat' the 'circumstances' of her death, the report goes on to describe how, for refusing to take a republican oath, 'Her thighs were cut across, and her bowels and heart torn from her, and for two days her mangled body was dragged through the streets'. In a 'private letter' from a 'reluctant spectator', which was printed in the 11 September issue, the Princess's 'fidelity to her Royal and hapless Mistress' the Queen is given as the motive for the mob's fury – in other words, killing the Princess is a substitute for killing the Queen. The *Annual Register* reported that the Princess's head was stuck on a pike and exposed to the King and Queen as a clear warning that they should 'expect the same fate' (58). According to John Moore, the Queen 'instantly fainted' at the sight of this 'most cruel of spectacles' (1: 317, 318). However, the *Annual Register*'s report ends with a reassuring sentimental touch: 'The head, though bleeding, was not disfigured, and her fine light hair still curling around the pike' (58). In this respect her death anticipated the cult of the martyr which was to surround the execution of the royal couple in 1793.

The grisly death of the Princess Lamballe became an iconic moment in reports of the September massacres. It is almost certain that she is the model for one of the most sensational acts of violence in Romantic fiction, the mob's murder of the Prioress in Matthew Lewis's Gothic novel *The Monk* (1796):

They tore her one from another, and each new tormentor was more savage than the former. They stifled with howls and execrations her shrill cries for mercy; and dragged her through the streets, spurning her, trampling her, and treating her with every species of cruelty which hate or vindictive fury could invent. At length a flint, aimed by some well-directed hand, struck her full upon the temple. She sank upon the ground bathed in blood, and in a few minutes terminated her miserable existence. Yet though she no longer felt their insults, the rioters still exercised their impotent rage upon her lifeless body. They beat it, trod it, and ill-used it, till it became no more than a mass of flesh, unsightly, shapeless, and disgusting.[32]

But in this instance the mob also meets a violent end, as the nunnery which they have set alight collapses on top of them, producing 'mingled shrieks of the Nuns and the Rioters' (358). As shown in Chapter 5, this trope of the rioting mob's auto-destruction was firmly ingrained in the popular imagination by this time.

The Princess Lamballe was a high-profile casualty of French revolutionary violence, but she was not of course the only female victim. As discussed in Chapter 1, the grisly logic of revolutionary and subaltern violence led to the sacrificial slaughter of entire genteel families. Such moments gave the parent and child one last chance to bond:

> The Countess de Chevre, with her five children, the oldest not eleven years of age, were massacred at her house, *Rue de Bacq*, on the 3rd, and their bodies exposed before the door. The children were first assassinated before the eyes of the parent. She bore this infernal sight with a fortitude almost supernatural; she embraced the bleeding head of the youngest, and met her fate with heroic contempt. The wretches first cut off the arms that sustained her last sad comfort, and then severed her head from her body. (*Gentleman's Magazine* (1792), 855)

Once the Terror formalized and institutionalized the mass execution of such victims, the redemptive 'final moment' became an increasingly familiar scene, as will be shown shortly. But a final embrace with a loved one (an action which was travestied in the infamous mass drownings of the Vendée) did not prevent further desecration of the bodies of the ruling class. When a marchioness and her daughter are found to have committed suicide, 'the mob, thus disappointed, cut the lifeless bodies into pieces' (ibid., 856). On the other hand, when two priests are told to eat human flesh before being burned alive, they manage to cheat their captors by 'embracing each other' and leaping into the fire voluntarily (*The Times*, 11 September). A similar scene takes this scenario of cheating death to almost surreal regions of representation. The hyperbolic realism evokes Freud's 'uncanny' blurring of the line between life and death:

> an old Swiss gentleman... who before the revolution had some place under government, was thrown alive into a fire kindled of furniture belonging to the different Hotels of the Emigrants. Thrice he ran from the flames, and as often was driven back; at last, with their pikes, the sanguinary monsters pinned him there, and insultingly demanding him to sing *ca ira*, danced around the fire, singing themselves, in the true spirit of North American savages. (*Gentleman's Magazine* (1792), 855)

The allusion to 'North American savages' is not whimsical – as will be shown in Chapter 4, the American revolutionary war produced a vigorous public controversy about the British policy of hiring 'savage' American Indians. The prolonged death and ritualistic burning of prisoners also evokes obvious comparisons with the fate of many slaves, as shown in Chapter 1. But the 'savage' violence of the French revolution was occurring in the streets of a European capital city, not in the remoter regions of the empire, and this proximity of geography must have heightened the impact, the drama and the terror of the reportage. According to *The Times*, class vengeance was being meted out on the flimsiest of excuses, for example against any person 'who had the appearance of a gentleman' (11 September). Paris was being transformed rapidly into a necropolis: 'the streets of Paris, strewed with the carcases of the mangled victims, are become so familiar to the sight, that they are passed by and trod on without any particular notice' (ibid.). The *Gentleman's Magazine* reported that 'the streets have this morning exhibited a spectacle of the mangled bodies and heads of the priests who were yesterday massacred; and the multitude who follow this cannibal feast are singing choruses expressive of their joy' (855). There is an abundance of macabre inventiveness on display. A Swiss officer is ordered to dress the hair of a fellow officer before removing the scalp, 'and to be cautious not to spoil his head-dress, saying it was too fine a head to put upon a pike'. When the officer refuses, he is killed and his head is sawn off by two women (*The Times*, 12 September). Another example of the 'dressing' of victims involves a family who are roasted alive after being stripped and 'washed with oil' while 'the mob were singing and dancing round the fire' (ibid.). A pastry cook makes pies 'de la viande des Suisses', and a citizen brings the heads of his parents to the local Jacobin club in order to inspire vengeance against 'aristocrats' (ibid.). Alan Liu interprets these anecdotes as examples of the 'jokework of death', 'sublime slapstick', the grim humour of 'brigand violence'.[33] It is difficult to know to what extent the reading public tuned in to this 'slapstick', though Gillray's extraordinary cartoons would suggest that there was an appetite for 'the jokework of death'. Gillray's response to the September massacres was 'Un petit Souper a la Parisienne – or – A Family of Sans-Culotts refreshing after the fatigues of the day' (Figure 4), a print which shows a sans-culotte family feasting on the bodies of their victims. Like the 'Gothic Eucharist' of anti-slavery writing, this was yet another sensational mobilization of the trope of cannibalism.

There was far less difficulty understanding the political lesson to be drawn from the carnage in Paris: 'Read this ye ENGLISHMEN, with attention, and ardently pray that your happy Constitution may never be outraged by the despotic tyranny of Equalization' (*The Times*, 12 September). This warning recycles the trope of an 'outraged' Britannia in distress, a satirical picto-graphic tradition which began in the period of 'Wilkes and Liberty' (see Chapter 4). If chivalry had expired in France (the 'outrage' at Versailles is an implied allusion), Englishmen could reassert their patriotic masculinity and prevent the beautiful yet vulnerable English constitution being mangled by the savage, republican sublime.

Figure 4   James Gillray, 'Un petit Souper a la Parisienne – or – A Family of Sans-Culotts refreshing after the fatigues of the day' (September 1792) © Trustees of the British Museum

'Violators of freedom': Helen Maria Williams, *Letters From France* (1790–95)

In the event, it was a radical Englishwoman who produced some of the most popular reportage on the French Terror.[34] In *Letters Written in France* (1790), *Letters from France* (1792–94) and *Letters Containing a Sketch of the Politics of France* (1795), Helen Maria Williams's response to the French revolution's increasingly violent character captured vividly the 'Romantic' curve of sublime enthusiasm followed by anxious disenchantment. Williams the writer was no stranger to spectacular violence. Before she took up residence in France in 1790, she had already attacked imperial violence in her poem *Peru* (1784), and had contributed to the anti-slavery campaign with *A Poem on the Bill Lately Passed for Regulating the Slave Trade* (1788). The latter poem praised a new law which imposed limits on the numbers of slaves which ships could transport. It was hoped that this measure would mitigate some of the horrors of the middle passage: '*one* dire scene for ever clos'd' (l. 34).[35] However, in order to keep up the pressure for abolition, the poem dwells on this 'dire scene' several times, attacks the 'dull sense' (l. 283) of those who can 'view unmov'd' (l. 221) slave suffering, and questions whether the 'Eloquence' of poetic 'Fancy' can 'add one horror more' to the 'tale of woe' (ll. 321, 350, 337). In her valedictory poem 'A Farewell, for Two Years, to England' (1791), Williams expresses an exasperation that progress towards abolition has stalled.[36] She considers the irony that revolutionary France may 'snatch this deathless wreath' (l. 198) from Britain, as it was 'Albion' which 'taught' France, 'long in slav'ry sunk', to break 'her fetters' (ll. 128–30). Though anti-slavery writers 'with fruitless zeal the tale of horror trace' (l. 157), Williams's 'zeal' for the political efficacy of 'the tale of horror' is undiminished. Addressing the enslaved 'Captive race' (l. 167), she reiterates the power of spectacular violence. If 'all the force display'd / By glowing Genius' is applied to the abolitionist cause,

> When, with that energy she boasts alone,
> She made your wrongs, your ling'ring tortures known;
> Bade full in view the bloody visions roll,
> Shook the firm nerves, and froze the shudd'ring soul! –
> As when the sun, in piercing radiance bright,
> Dispelling the low mists of doubtful light,
> Its lustre on some hideous object throws,
> And all its hateful horror clearly shows...
> How swift had Britons torn your galling chain. (ll. 169–79)

The continuing 'bloody visions' of transatlantic slavery are contrasted with the fledgling revolutionary violence of the manumitted French: 'That purifying tempest now has past' (l. 129). This 'purifying' violence is the sublime antidote to the horrors of slavery. In the poem on the slave trade, as noted above, Williams shows a typical self-consciousness about hyperbolic realism. The 'heighten'd tint' (l. 338) of Fancy is no match for the sublime power of 'the Truth' (l. 339), but the difference is expressed, ironically, through the poetic conceit of two stormscapes: fancy is 'The storm that hangs along the glade' (l. 342), but this is no match for the sublime power of Truth, 'where the wintry tempests sweep / In madness, o'er the darkened deep' (l. 345). In 'A Farewell, for Two Years, to England', the 'purifying tempest' of revolutionary violence is 'a transient storm / Flung o'er the darkened wave' of the Seine (ll. 117–18). The Biblical and Miltonic cadences suggest a profound if terrible creativity, and the final, ostensibly reassuring line of this vignette – 'No more the trembling waters feel the blast' (l. 119) – is actually profoundly disturbing: the gestatory trope adds to the scene a Blakean, 'heighten'd tint' of Orcan sexual energy or, more conventionally, distressed femininity. As Williams moved from old England to new France, it was uncertain whether the 'trembling waters' of the new French constitution would produce Sin and Death, or Glad Day. The future direction of Williams's emotional and political commitment to both countries, and the degree of stress on her 'filial heart' (l. 197), would depend on this outcome.

In addition to being a Romantic author who experienced the French revolution at first hand, her unique contribution was to fashion her position as a female foreign correspondent into a personification of sensibility. As she witnessed the Fête de la Fédération in 1790 she enthused: 'it is very difficult, with common sensibility, to avoid sympathizing in general happiness. My love of the French revolution, is the natural result of this sympathy; and therefore my political creed is entirely an affair of the heart' (*LWF*, 91). The tone of this is mildly playful – in another description of the same event, she notes that the 'sublime' Fête 'addressed itself at once to the imagination, the understanding, and the heart', and added 'it required but the common feelings of humanity to become in that moment a citizen of the world' (*LFF*, 1: 9). But Williams challenges her readers not to fall in love with the spectacle of a jubilant new nation: 'the enthusiastic spirit of liberty displays itself, not merely on the days of solemn ceremonies . . . but is mingled with the gaiety of social enjoyment' (*LWF*, 93). The revolution is an 'enthusiastic' display of beauty: 'liberty appears in France adorned with the freshness of youth, and is loved with the ardour of passion' (93). The counter-spectacle to this revolutionary romance is the Gothic sublime of the ancien régime, the 'old gloomy Gothic fabric which they have laid in ruins' (*LWF*, 92). This allusion is both literal and metaphorical – it evokes the discarded political system and its most potent material symbol, the Bastille. Williams also reveals that this binary opposition between emancipatory romantic present and cloistered Gothic past has a deeply personal significance:

the old constitution is connected in my mind with the image of a friend confined in the gloomy recesses of a dungeon, and pining in hopeless captivity; while, with the new constitution, I unite the soothing idea of his return to prosperity, honours, and happiness. (*LWF*, 93)

Although Williams's friend was a real person who was imprisoned on the whim of an aristocrat, Williams is also drawing on the proliferation of apocryphal prison stories generated by the fall of the Bastille. Central to this mythology was the idea of the forgotten prisoner who had languished in a cell for years until liberated by the revolution. Sometimes known as Count Lorges, this figure was celebrated in waxwork exhibitions and was still sufficiently in vogue to influence Dickens's characterization of Dr Manette in *A Tale of Two Cities*. The fable predates the French revolution, as it occurs in an episode called 'The Captive' in Sterne's *A Sentimental Journey* (1768), but as David Bindman notes, the legendary prisoner was 'a conflation of many of the stories which gathered around the Bastille in the eighteenth century'.[37] Williams alludes directly to the myth earlier in the text (*LWF*, 770).[38] But the Gothic mode was not to maintain this significance for Williams. As we shall see, her disenchantment with the revolution can be gauged by the shift in her use of Gothic discourse. As Fred Botting has argued, radicals in the early 1790s used the Gothic to signify 'everything that was old-fashioned, barbaric, feudal and irrationally ungrounded'. This was an attempt by Paine, Woll-stonecraft and other radical writers like Williams to debunk Burke's 'Gothic nostalgia'. But Botting also notes that 'these invocations of the word Gothic in defences of revolution were written before the Terror in France gave new weight' to conservative writers.[39] As Williams witnessed the revolution's fall from grace, she increasingly turned to the aesthetic and narrative resources of Gothic to convey the revolutionary resurrection of sublime tyranny and spectacular violence.

But in the honeymoon period before 1792, Williams treated examples of revolutionary violence as lover's tiffs. She admits that she is chilled by sight of the 'lanterne', but explains that some 'irregularities' are inevitable. She even resorts to chilling utilitarian logic and argues that the revolution was achieved at a 'far cheaper rate' of casualties than might have been predicted (*LFF*, 1: 47). Her account of the 'memorable night' at Versailles sides with the queen against the 'savage ferocity' of the poissards (*LFF*, 1: 48), but this distaste for militant plebeian women is balanced by Williams's praise for their part in the storming of the Bastille (*LWF*, 75; *LFF*, 1: 22–3), and her spirited defence of French female patriotism (*LWF*, 78–9). During a visit to England, she is shocked by the distortions of the British media:

> I hear of nothing but crimes, assassinations, torture, and death. I am told that every day witnesses a conspiracy; that every town is the scene of a massacre; that every street is blackened with a gallows, and every highway deluged with blood . . . to me, this land of desolation appeared drest in additional beauty beneath the genial smile of liberty. (*LFF*, 1: 123)

This confident reassertion of the ascendancy of the beautiful over the Gothic sublime was not to last, but Williams's reputation as a revolution-lover was sufficient to make her the butt of some unsisterly, Burkean ridicule by another female poet, Anne Grant:

> Equality's new-fangled doctrines she taught;
> And murder and sacrilege calmly surveyed;
> In the new pandemonium those demons had made;
> Seine's blood-crimsoned waters with apathy eyed,
> While the glories of old father Thames she decried.
> (Anne Grant, 'A Familiar Epistle to a Friend' (1795), ll. 181–5)[40]

The allusion to the parliament of the fallen angels in *Paradise Lost* is not simply poetic affectation: in the anti-Jacobin lexicon, Milton represented the regicidal reality of political revolution. As shown below, nothing reveals Williams's fugitive sympathies more clearly than her anti-revolutionary use of Miltonic allusion to convey the Gothic horror of anarchy and Terror.

Like most paradises, the Utopia of the French revolution did not survive for long. In Williams's narrative, it is on the night of 2 September 1792 that the 'violators of freedom' take control and Paris is transformed into a 'theatre' of 'inhuman violence'. She laments the sights which Parisians have witnessed:

> They have beheld, in the room of the pure and sublime worship of liberty, the grim idol of anarchy set up, and have seen the altar smeared with sanguinary rites. They have beheld the inhuman judges of that night wearing the municipal scarf which their polluting touch profaned, surrounded by men armed with pikes and sabers dropping with blood – while a number of blazing torches threw their glaring light on the ferocious visages of those execrable judges, who, mixing their voices with the shrieks of the dying, passed sentence with a savage mockery of justice, on victims devoted to their rage. They have beheld infernal executioners of that night, with their arms bared for the purposes of murder, dragging forth those victims to modes of death at which nature shudders – (*LFF*, 2: 2–4)

The sensational 'heighten'd tints' in this vivid description would not be out of place in *A Tale of Two Cities*. The scene combines the tropes of brutal masculinity, sacrilege and mock-justice into a powerful literary cocktail of inconceivable violence and violation: indeed, as was seen in anti-slavery writing, the limit point of representation is marked by the typographical device of the dash. In Williams's emerging demonology, the 'grim idol of anarchy' is the monstrous prodigy of a dysfunctional revolutionary leadership whose 'pure and sublime worship of liberty' has deteriorated into 'inhuman' authority. The Jacobin leaders Robespierre, Danton and Marat are a diabolical Miltonic trinity: Danton's position in the hierarchy, relative to Robespierre, is the equivalent of Beelzebub to Satan in *Paradise Lost*, 'next to him in power, and next in crime' (ibid.; see *Paradise Lost*, 1: 79–80). Robespierre, like the Gothic, is 'gloomy and saturnine' (ibid.). This malign intelligence has unleashed plebeian fury onto the streets of Paris. Williams makes clear that there is a class distinction between instigators and perpetrators. She attacks 'bourgeois' liberals for being 'pusillanimous witnesses' to the carnage (as will be seen throughout this study, the genteel spectator of violence is a particular focus of anxiety for writers). Like Satan's paternity of Sin and Death, this derogation of duty is a travesty of political succession, the triumph of the 'fanatics of liberty, fierce as the fanatics of superstition', who have summoned up a second 'St. Bartholemew'. The regressive enthusiasm of fanaticism has replaced the sublime enthusiasm of sensibility, humanity and enlightenment:

> Ah! what is become of the delightful visions which elevated the enthusiastic heart? . . . This was indeed the golden age of the revolution. – But it

is past! – the enchanting spell is broken, and the fair scenes of beauty and order, through which imagination wandered, are transformed into the desolation of the wilderness, and clouded by the darkness of the tempest. (*LFF*, 2: 3–4)

The sublime 'darkness of the tempest' has succeeded the 'purifying tempest' and 'trembling waters' of expiatory violence depicted a few years earlier in 'A Farewell, for Two Years, to England'. The Miltonic echoes in this elegy give the passage both poignancy and tension. The language evokes, for example, Satan's lament for the loss of the 'happy fields' of heaven:

> Farewell, happy fields,
> Where joy forever dwells! Hail, horrors! hail,
> Infernal World! and thou, profoundest Hell,
> Receive thy new possessor—one who brings
> A mind not to be changed by place or time. (*Paradise Lost*, 1: 249–53)

The Satanic point of view neatly combines both the 'fallen' revolutionary perspective and the twisted new regime of diabolical power. Williams may also be alluding to a speech by Belial in the pandemonium debate:

> To be no more. Sad cure! for who would lose,
> Though full of pain, this intellectual being,
> Those thoughts that wander through eternity,
> To perish rather, swallowed up and lost
> In the wide womb of uncreated Night. (*Paradise Lost*, 2: 146–50)

The Miltonic subtexts brilliantly dramatize the loss of 'the golden age of the revolution' – the decline from pastoral to Gothic, from enlightenment to barbarism, from intellectual ideals to anarchic reality – while preserving some of the Romantic glamour and complex, antinomian morality of Satanic defiance. But the complexity of Williams's feelings can be gauged by the fact that the tapestry of literary allusion may also incorporate a reference to the famous apocalyptic dénouement of Pope's 1743 *Dunciad*:

> Lo! Thy dread empire, CHAOS! is restor'd;
> Light dies before thy uncreating word;
> Thy hand, great Anarch! lets the curtain fall,
> And universal darkness buries all. (IV: 653–6)[41]

Pope's poem casts a devastating mock-heroic shadow over the imagining of the demise of the French revolution.

In a final attempt to define the difference between the old evils of despotism and the new evils of anarchy, Williams reworks the river metaphors which she first used to convey the hyperbolic violence of slavery. In these changed circumstances, despotism is like a stream which drains water from the surrounding countryside but offers the occasional 'spot of scanty verdure' (another image of lost pastoral innocence which parallels the more famous, Wordsworthian 'spots of time'). By comparison, anarchy is like a tidal wave, 'the impetuous torrent that sweeps over the land with irresistible violence, and involves every object in one wide mass of ruin'. Despotism is venerable and naturalized; its violence is mostly hidden (like its Gothic 'gloomy towers' and 'solitary dungeons'), whereas the violence of anarchy (like Satan's incestuous offspring Death) is unsophisticated, impulsive, public, and indiscriminate (*LFF*, 2: 11). This is an exact inversion of the radical defence of popular violence which was premised on its directness and 'openness': as James Mackintosh asserted, 'the wild justice of the people has a naked and undisguised horror... while murder and rapine, if arrayed in the gorgeous disguise of acts of state, may with impunity stalk abroad'.[42] But Williams could at least find some consolation in the logic of her sublime metaphors and argue that natural disasters are temporary convulsions: 'the French revolution is still in its progress, and who can decide how its last page will finish?' (ibid.). Williams could not have seen the irony in the reflexive literary language of her phrase 'last page', as her arrest during the Terror (she was imprisoned from October to November 1793) could have ensured that her own production of 'pages' would come to an abrupt end.

But it was the arrest and execution of the French king which represented the next fatal error in the revolution's page-turning 'progress'. Williams may have been anticipating the king's fate when she called the September massacres a 'savage spectacle' (*LFF*, 2: 11). In Shakespeare's *Julius Caesar*, Brutus insists that the assassination of Caesar must be motivated by sound republican principles, 'else this were a savage spectacle' (*Julius Caesar*, III.i.223). The Shakespearean allusion to regicide is echoed in Williams's description of her feelings when she saw the 'captive' king:

> The long page of human history rushed upon the mind – age after age arose to memory, in sad succession, like the line of Banquo; and each seemed disfigured by crimes or darkened by calamity. (*LFF*, 2: 128)

The 'last page' of the Utopian revolution has been absorbed into the 'long page' of violent, monarchical European history. The allusion to the king-killing, guilt-ridden *Macbeth*, which must have influenced Wordsworth's use of the same allusion in his troubled account of the Terror in *The Prelude*, seems designed to give the French king some tragic grandeur, though the parallel does not resolve the ideological tensions of the scene. The comparison between the king and Banquo is only partially successful, as Banquo was the victim, not the agent, of monarchical in-fighting. If the French king is a victim, he is a victim of the discredited system of 'crime' and 'calamity' which Williams believed the revolution was now imitating, another ironic 'boomerang' effect. As the Terror of 1793–94 unfolded, Williams looked for other relevant 'figures' with which to render the spectacular disfiguring of the revolution.

Perhaps unsurprisingly, given the fact that Williams was imprisoned under the Law of Suspects, it is the 'figure' of distressed femininity which is foregrounded in her reports of the 'violators of freedom'. Indeed, Gary Kelly sees a Burkean gendering of politics as one of Williams's central rhetorical strategies. Kelly states that Williams' historical schema is premised on a distinction between Girondin and Jacobin republicanism: the former is feminine, charming, alluring and beautiful; the latter is masculine, brutal and sublime.[43] In terms of strict historical fact, the Girondins were not quite the 'illustrious martyrs' (*LCS*, 2: 78) of Williams's vision, as many Girondin leaders voted to execute the king. But rhetorically, romance had regressed to folk tale: the Holy Grail elbowed out by Bluebeard. The dramatic core of Williams's narrative is a series of captivity stories. Once again, she is the personification of revolutionary sensibility. Ironically, it is those 'gloomy' dungeons, which had previously signified the discarded Gothic tyranny of the ancien régime, which become the dominant and domineering setting. The captivity vignettes pour new wine into an old bottle. The dungeons are full of genteel prisoners, not festering relics like the Count Lorges. A significant proportion of these well-dressed victims are women, the classic sentimental victims of sublime cruelty. Finally, the Jacobin appropriation of the Gothic machinery of incarceration is the prelude to a modernized 'last page' of extinction, a meeting with the 'daily spectacle' (*LCS*, 2: 7) of the republican guillotine.

Williams's narrative of the Terror reads like a real-life Gothic melodrama, an exhibition of 'images of horror' (*LCS*, 1: 4), a 'dark drama of which France has been the desolated scene, and Europe the affrighted spectator' (*LCS*, 1: 28). The first rumours of the Terror are like 'hollow noises that roll in the dark gulph of the volcano' (*LCS*, 1: 5). The revolutionary tribunal is 'a shrine consecrated to infernal deities' which is 'reeking with the sacrifice of human victims' and is run by 'monsters' (*LCS*, 1: 247). Most of these 'monsters' are sadistic, megalomaniacal men: 'Brutality, as well as terror, was the order of the day' (*LCS*, 1: 30). The first individualized portrait of such a monster appears during Williams's incarceration in the Luxembourg. This is the 'wretch' Henriot, veteran of the September massacres and newly appointed commander of Paris National Guard:

his fierceness seemed to be of that kind which belongs to a cannibal of New Zealand; and he looked not merely as if he longed to plunge his sabre into our bosoms, but to drink a libation of our blood. He poured forth a volley of oaths and imprecations, called out how many guillotines must be erected for the English, and did not leave our chamber until one person who was present had fainted with terror. (*LCS*, 1: 29–30)

In order to give a 'heighten'd tint' to this confrontation, Williams adds an allusion to stereotypical 'native' savagery, but the trope of cannibalism and sacrifice also evokes the reportage of the September massacres (which first brought this beast to power) and equivalent scenes of sadistic cruelty in anti-slavery writing. Note also that one of the women faints, a dramatic enactment of the impact of the discourse of Terror on feminine sensibility and an extreme subject-position for the female reader. But as Williams's pages unfurl, it becomes clear that female victims are not restricted to the roles of abject and passive suffering.

To begin with, Williams praises those women who demanded to see their husbands. Such women are evidence that 'the force of sensibility' can overcome 'female weakness' (*LCS*, 1: 41). Ironically, the 'force of sensibility' which epitomized the birth of the revolution has become the heroic means to resist its excesses. But the most spectacular demonstration of this strength is the 'admirable firmness' (*LCS*, 1: 213) of Girondin, monarchist and Jacobin women in the face of death. In a series of heightened last moments, Williams reasserts the superior moral and physical beauty of femininity. Most famously, we see Madame Roland (*LCS*, 1: 195–202), Marie-Antoinette, and Charlotte Corday. The latter's death is given a sentimental, even sensual 'heighten'd tint': as she goes to the guillotine, she 'blushed deeply', and her exposed head 'exhibited this last impression of offended modesty' (*LCS*, 1: 135). Similarly, Madame Desmoulins dies 'with the serenity of an angel' (*LCS*, 2: 36). This feminine stoicism further enrages the male captors. The consequence is that 'the fury of these implacable monsters seemed directed with peculiar virulence' against women prisoners (*LCS*, 1: 214). A group of young women from Verdun go to the scaffold 'like nymphs adorned for a festival' (*LCS*, 1: 216). A peasant's baby is torn away from her bosom on the scaffold, and not even the 'piercing throes of maternal tenderness' could prevent her execution (*LCS*, 1: 215). When a public accuser notices the 'firmness' of a large group of women, he remarks: 'I must go and see if they show the same effrontery on the scaffold, even if I should lose my dinner' (*LCS*, 2: 72). In the Vendée, Collot d'Herbois, whom Williams compares to Gengis Khan, Caligula and Salmoneus, 'ordered three ladies, who had thrown themselves at his feet to implore his mercy, to be tied for six hours to the scaffold where their husbands were to be executed' (*LCS*, 2: 161).[44] Despite this exemplary display of female anti-Jacobin 'firmness', the mere fact of Williams being a practitioner of spectacular violence was condemned by the loyalist press. The *Gentleman's Magazine*, for example, concluded that she had 'debased her sex, her heart, her feelings, her talents, in recording such a tissue of horror and villainy' (LXV (1795), 1030). It was as if Williams's Girondin sensibility still harboured a tainted Jacobinism. Boswell was so outraged by her candour that he removed the adjective 'amiable' from his description of her in the *Life of Johnson*.[45]

The apotheosis of the disfigurement of femininity is Liberty itself. She has been 'transformed into a Fury, who, brandishing her snaky whips and torches, has enlarged the limits of wickedness' (*LCS*, 2: 212). This is the monstrous caricature of anti-Jacobin satire, the inversion of the idealized figure of Marianne (see, for example, Rowlandson's dyptich 'The Contrast').[46] As Vivien Jones notes, Williams seems to be colluding with counter-revolutionary propaganda: 'Though Liberty is the victim of monsters, tyrannic monstrosity is nevertheless displaced onto a woman'.[47] But for Williams this is a price worth paying in order to debunk the Terror's Robespierrian semiotics. She presents the Festival of the Supreme Being as the antitype of the Fête de la Fédération. In the mock-epic, 'polluted' Jacobin festival, the symbols of redemptive, pantheistic nature are contaminated by the violent gaze: 'the scent of carnage seemed mingled with these lavish sweets; the glowing festoons appeared tinged with blood; and in the background of this festive scenery the guillotine arose before the disturbed imagination' (*LCS*, 2: 89). Robespierre is 'the high priest of Molock', a 'foul fiend' who presides over a 'daily sacrifice of human beings' (*LCS*, 2: 90). The gory visions summoned up by Williams's 'disturbed imagination' recall the 'blood–sugar' phantoms of anti-slavery literature. In another recycling of the trope of violated femininity, pastoral beauty is now 'tinged with blood'. The countryside surrounding Paris is 'haunted' by 'vulgar despots' who cast their 'polluting glance on nature' and 'tread with profane steps her hallowed recesses' (*LCS*, 2: 2–3). Bloody ghosts are everywhere. The revolutionary jury cannot function 'without being haunted by the mangled spectres of those whom they had murdered the preceding day' (ibid.). One of the most 'heighten'd' Gothic scenes imagines the fate of imprisoned Jacobin leaders:

> along those subterraneous galleries where all the light which entered was 'darkness visible', terrific phantoms covered with blood seemed to pursue their steps, and with menacing looks prepared to drag them to abysses of deeper horror; they fancied they saw the headless trunks of murdered victims encumbering the ground . . . while the knife of the guillotine, like Macbeth's aerial dagger, hung suspended before their affrighted imagination. (*LCS*, 2: 18)

This melodramatic fantasy of retributive justice reworks the Miltonic and Shakespearean allusions which were first used in the account of the king's execution. The ironic parallel is intentional, as the Jacobin Pretenders are now confronting the same haunted fate as those more illustrious deposed princes (Satan, Macbeth, Richard III) summoned up by the literary roll-call. But it is women who are most susceptible to being visited by the dead. This sensitivity to spectral spectacle is one measure of the 'force of sensibility', but the gift of a sentimental sixth sense is also a curse. For example, an 'unfortunate young lady' is driven mad in her cell by apparitions of the 'mangled spectres of her murdered parents' (*LCS*, 2: 104). More significantly, Williams herself comes to personify the 'disturbed imagination'. Even after the Terror has subsided, Paris to her still resembles a necropolis:

> I saw in the vehicles of death the spectres of my murdered friends. The magnificent square of the revolution, with all its gay buildings, appeared to me clotted with blood, and incumbered with the dead. (*LCS*, 1: 177)

The red flags on confiscated buildings remind her of Defoe's plague-ridden London, where every infected house 'was marked with a bloody sign of the cross' (*LCS*, 1: 178).[48] For Williams, there was only one way to escape from the spell of this disturbing and disturbed imagination: to flee to the Rousseauistic, restorative pastoral and political beauties of Switzerland.

Despite her denunciations of the revolution's excesses, Williams did not abandon her faith in republicanism, and argued that 'the cause of liberty is not the less sacred, because sanguinary monsters and sordid savages have defiled her temple'.[49] Wollstonecraft also expressed a sanguine, long-term view, though her biological metaphor anxiously conflates ideas of purgation, putrefaction, farting and decomposition. She states that the body politic will eventually cleanse itself, though in the short term, the 'excrementitious humours exuming from the contaminated body will excite a general dislike and contempt'.[50] In *The Prelude*, Wordsworth utilized a similar 'disturbed' medical metaphor to explain his misguided, youthful attachment to revolutionary thinking:

> I took the knife in hand
> And stopping not at parts less sensitive,
> Endeavoured with my best of skills to probe
> The living body of society
> Even to the heart; I pushed without remorse
> My speculations forward; yea, set foot
> On Nature's holiest places. (X (1805), ll. 873–9)

This extraordinary passage has connotations of rape, defilement and forbidden scientific and intellectual experimentation (there is a clear line of descent to *Frankenstein*). It is as if the heartless Wordsworth, extracting the heart out of the body politic, personifies the ruthless and perverted ideals of the French revolution. It is another reworking of the trope of sublime masculine power trampling on the sanctity of feminized virtue and beauty: 'Nature's holiest places'.[51] The image echoes two earlier scenes in this section of *The Prelude*. The first scene describes a singular act of disloyalty in which Wordsworth attends a literal 'holy place', a patriotic church service. Instead of offering prayers 'for our country's victories', he 'Exulted in the triumph of my soul, / When Englishmen by thousands were o'erthrown' (X (1805),

l. 295, ll. 285–6).[52] The second scene recounts his response to 'those atrocities', the September massacres. Owing a clear debt to Williams, he describes being haunted by 'ghastly visions' of 'tyranny, and implements of death', but he also imagines being put on trial 'Before unjust tribunals'. His attempts to plead his innocence are hampered by 'a sense / Of treachery and desertion in the place / The holiest that I knew of, my own soul' (X (1805), ll. 400–15). Wordsworth's guilt about polluting holy places is so overdetermined that it is difficult to know exactly what the 'unjust tribunal' represents. It is obviously a nightmare of Jacobin persecution – 'all perished, all' (X (1805), l. 360), but it could also be the British treason trials of 1794 – 'a tool of murder' (X (1805), l. 65), or even a reprimand for the unmentionable abandonment of Annette Vallon. Ultimately, it is Wordsworth's 'o'erthrown' soul which requires restitution.

As these anxious metaphors demonstrate, the spectacular violence in France had indelibly 'disturbed' the literary and political imagination. The bloody vignette had become one of the central, defining problems of the revolution debate, and one of its key rhetorical moments. Romantic writers had to come to terms with the long shadow which spectacular violence cast over the literary imagination. This did not necessarily mean resorting to silence or evasion – indeed, as we shall see, atrocity figured as a key component in anti-war polemic. But, as the next text to be discussed will show, spectacular violence was a formidable counter-revolutionary weapon, and the challenge for Romantic authors was to try to avoid being tainted by guilty association with France's 'democratic' crimes.

'The dark catalogue': William Cobbett, *The Bloody Buoy* (1797)

In 1797, a book appeared in Britain which carried one of the most extraordinary 'Table of Contents' to be published in the Romantic period (Figure 5). The book was *The Bloody Buoy* by 'Peter Porcupine', the American pen-name for William Cobbett.[53] The complete title of the work is worth quoting in full to convey its dramatic effect: *The Bloody Buoy, Thrown out as a Warning to all the Political Pilots of all Nations. Or a Faithful Relation of a Multitude of Acts of Horrid Barbarity, Such as the Eye never witnessed, the Tongue never expressed, or the Imagination conceived, until the commencement of the French Revolution. To which is Added, An Instructive Essay, Tracing these Dreadful Effects to their Real Causes.* At this stage in his journalistic career, Cobbett was an ardent anti-Jacobin, and his 'partisan account of the horrors of the French revolution' was a contribution to the continuing suppression of radicalism in Britain.[54] Cobbett threw his full weight behind the demonization of Jacobinism as an essentially murderous political regime. He prepared the ground for *The Bloody Buoy* in two earlier pamphlets, *On the Emigration of Dr Priestley* (1794) and *A Bone to Gnaw the Democrats* (1795).[55] Both these

T A B L E

OF SOME OF THE

MOST STRIKING FACTS.

Figure 5   William Cobbett, Table of Contents of *The Bloody Buoy* (1797)

works use accounts of atrocities in order to debunk and discredit radical support for French republicanism. As Raymond Williams puts it, 'Cobbett is an effective narrator, but also a master of guilt by association'.[56] The effect of Jacobinism, according to Cobbett's evidence, is to bring about 'a system of anarchy, that has changed the airy amiable French into a set of the most ferocious inhuman bloodhounds', and he warns the reader: 'fix your eyes on this theatre of carnage' (1: 29, 1: 136). *On the Emigration of Dr Priestley* recycles the iconic martyrdom of the 'much lamented unfortunate' Princess de Lamballe (30), while *A Bone to Gnaw the Democrats* focuses on the 'carnage' in the Vendée. The sentimental emphasis is placed on the violation of genteel women: 'the first ladies of the city were led to the tree of *Liberty* (of *Liberty!*) and there made to take the hands of chimney-sweepers and common felons!' (138). Cobbett concludes with the claim that the revolution is responsible for about two million murders, including 250,000 women and 24,000 'Christian priests' (139).

Yet, despite adducing hyperbolic statistics, the 'theatre of carnage' takes up no more than ten pages of these pamphlets. In *The Bloody Buoy*, Cobbett expanded his canvass to a massive 260 pages, a magnitude which allowed him to include scores of 'unedited' vignettes of spectacular violence (and even then, he insisted that he could have filled many more volumes). The public in America and Britain clearly responded to this profusion of images of atrocity, as the tract sold well.[57] *The Bloody Buoy* takes the logic of hyperbolic realism to its logical conclusion: in Cobbett's own words, it is a 'dark catalogue' (a2) of atrocities, all of which can be authenticated by reference to already published sources.[58] This stress on authenticity is the counterweight to the extreme sensationalism of the 'Table of Contents'. None of these 'crimes' would have been necessarily unfamiliar to the general reader (as this chapter has shown), but their concentration into a catalogue creates a spectacular effect of rapid and relentless violence. For example, the 'Instructive Essay' mentioned at page 126 is listed as just another item. In fact this essay is a lengthy exposition of the 'real causes' of these 'dreadful effects' and occupies almost half the book. But this level of detail is omitted, as it would detract from the visceral, mimetic impact of the 'dark catalogue' of Contents: the raw, unmediated reportage of Jacobin excesses.

These journalistic and commercial flourishes make *The Bloody Buoy* a more aggressively populist and didactic work than Williams's anxious, autobiographical correspondence. The whole point of Cobbett's propaganda is its unoriginality and impersonality: in quasi-forensic fashion, Cobbett is selecting, assembling and condensing a body of historical evidence against the revolution. These atrocious micro-narratives should, like the horrors of slavery, speak for themselves. In order to bolster the veracity of his sources, Cobbett claims, disingenuously, that the British media have been far too lenient towards the revolution – his aim is to 'tear aside the veil' of silence and euphemism (xv). He also 'has taken particular care to mention the work, and even the page, from which each fact is extracted' (ibid.). Strangely, Helen Maria Williams is not one of these sources – if Cobbett discarded her as a Jacobin sympathiser or 'unsex'd female', he overlooked the extent to which her portrayal of the Terror was antagonistic and sensational. Cobbett's forensic display of his sources does not prove that their version of events is true, but it does allow him to claim that he is not inventing incidents.[59] His 'impartiality and undaunted adherence to truth' (xiii) implies a primitivist appeal to direct reportage shorn of metaphorical embroidery and personal reflection, the antithesis of Williams's use of literary conventions. In this respect *The Bloody Buoy* is a deeply un-Romantic and unliterary document, but its flagrant exploitation of the resources of popular print culture makes it one of the period's starkest verbal constructions of spectacular violence.[60]

It is not possible to examine all the bloody vignettes which are contained in Cobbett's 'dark catalogue'. Some vignettes are tiny, and none occupy more than a couple of pages. They are organized around two stages in the revolution's progress: the killing of priests who refused to take the oath of allegiance to the new revolutionary government, climaxing in the September massacres; and (the bulk of the cases) the annihilation of the counter-revolution in the Vendée, where the focus is on the killing of women and the desecration of the family. Cobbett's main source for priest-martyrs was Abbé Barruel's *The History of the Clergy during the French Revolution*, a work which appeared in an English translation in 1794. Barruel justified his focus on martyrdom by stating that 'it is a pleasure to deliver to posterity the fortitude of martyrs, not the cruelty of assassins', though the claim is hollow, as 'cruelty' is depicted in lavish detail.[61] Cobbett's borrowings from Barruel form a dramatic restatement of a familiar theme: the overthrowing and perversion of the social and moral order. The first few vignettes are displaced Oedipal dramas. A young priest is killed in front of his father: the killers ignore 'the cries and lamentations of the father' and 'extend the son before him a bleeding corpse' (6). Conversely, a father is killed in front of his son, 'whom they besmeared with his blood' (ibid.). An even more spectacular variant on this theme is an incident which occurred during the September massacres (and was reported in *The Times*), which tells of a son who takes the heads of his non-juror parents to a Jacobin Club as a pledge of his loyalty. He is called a 'parricide' (15) to convey the sense of the overturning of the natural, patriarchal hierarchy. This scene is followed immediately by the example of a father who condemns his son – 'nor would the barbarous father quit his child till he saw his head severed from his body' (16). The father's actions are 'applauded' by the Convention 'as an imitator of the republican Brutus' (17). This is a sharp allusion: through this atrocity Cobbett is debunking the revolution's self-mythologizing as the reincarna-tion of classical republican virtue. Brutus had famously condemned his own sons to death as enemies of republican Rome, an event captured vividly in

Jacques Louis David's revolutionary painting 'Brutus Receiving the Bodies of His Sons from the Lictors' (1789).

The transitional scene between the September massacres and the Vendée is the arrival of the revolutionary tribunal in Lyon (there is of course no mention of loyalist atrocities). The tribunal hosts a mock religious procession followed by 'undistinguished butchery' which makes blood run 'in the gutters' (21–2). Apart from the anticipation of *A Tale of Two Cities* in this scenario, it is also worth noting the *double entendre* of the word 'undistinguished', which conveys the ideas of 'indiscriminate' and 'vulgar' slaughter. The latter meaning is a comment on the social origins and evil banality of the revolutionary committee's leaders, who act in the name of the government (Cobbett insists that his source, *Trials of Members of the Revolutionary Committee*, makes clear where the true blame lies, and that these are not maverick actions). The chief villains are the ex-actor Collot D'Herbois, who turns his fiefdom into a theatre of carnage, and Carrier the 'assassin-general', 'the bloodiest of the bloody', (36), a megalomaniac who 'ordered a woman to be shot at her window, merely because she looked at him' (40). These men and their low-bred associates transform the urban landscape into a necropolis of violated bodies, unbridled desire and disrespect for the dead. The polite family is subjected to multifarious forms of destruction. For example, two women are tied to a guillotine while their husbands are executed, 'and their blood sprinkled over them', like a mock religious baptism (23). This blasphemous imagery also occurs in one of the most extreme examples of 'diabolical cruelty' which Cobbett claims he can muster, the tying of four children to the posts of a guillotine while their parents are executed and the blood 'dropped on their heads' (114). Female beauty is a curse which attracts the masculine violent sublime: the 'prettiest of the women' are saved from the infamous 'republican marriage' (the tying together and drowning of naked men and women) only to 'endure the more than infernal embraces of these monsters' (69). Carrier has a particular hatred of women – he selects women prisoners for sex and then 'being satiated with their charms, sent them to the guillotine' so that no one else can have them (40).

But the most sensational account of mass rape is a flagrantly racist reworking of the Burkean trope of the extinction of chivalry. This encounter describes the kidnapping in Nantz of a group of 'pretty women' by a group of ex-slaves (49–52). The incident is clearly an opportunity for Cobbett to attack both Jacobinism and anti-slavery by showing the heinous consequences of emancipation (the fact that the book was published while the British army was being decimated in San Domingo is perhaps no coincidence). In Cobbett's demonological universe, the rampaging manumitted slave is the shadowy accomplice of the upstart sans-culotte, a worst-case scenario of the political folly of democratic extremism. The incident is a virulently aggressive attempt to debunk the idea of the entry of blacks into civil society.

As soon as 'these people claimed their rights as citizens' they show their grat-itude to their Jacobin liberators by claiming their own rights of black sexual conquest and vengeance over white women. Cobbett relishes the oppor-tunity to show the contradiction between this recidivist behaviour and the slaves' new existence as '*Americans*' – the racist joke is that the Jacobin ban on the word 'negro' confers only a veneer of respectability. In this respect, the black rapists are a metonymy of the false ideals, self-interest and patholo-gical violence of the revolution. Cobbett's political target is the revolutionary ideology which has given rise to the situation in the first place. This explains the way he constructs the vignette as an abortive attempt by the Jacobin authorities to keep control over the situation. A group of officers are sent to the house where the women are being kept captive: 'The poor creatures were crying and groaning; their shrieks were to be heard at half a mile distance'. The captors will not relinquish their '*prey*', even when it is pointed out that 'the French empire contained *no slaves*'. There is of course a double irony here, as the (white) Jacobins are equally guilty of taking women captive, but this offence can be effaced behind the unspoken racism of the accusa-tion. Perhaps this embarrassing parallel is the real reason that the officers withdraw and leave the women to their fate. The '*prudence*' of the officers is vilified by Cobbett as the absolute death of chivalry, the failure to rescue 'five of their lovely country-women exposed to the nauseous embraces of a set of filthy merciless monsters'. The point of this racist abuse is to excoriate the last vestiges of honour from the 'pusillanimous, rascally Frenchman' who have failed the ultimate test of racial loyalty and compassion 'which rouses all the feelings of manhood'. Cobbett's tirade is a demonstration of such arousal, a textual punishment of the debased 'manhood' of both the effete Jacobin officers and the 'monstrous' black captors. Cobbett is sending an alarming message to the supporters of anti-slavery: beware the lethal combination of phoney republican idealism and black vengeance. As shown in Chapter 1, the slave rebellion in San Domingo was a spectacular factor in the slowing of the pace of anti-slavery in Britain in the 1790s. To its detractors, the rebellion seemed like a colossal extrapolation of Cobbett's ominous scene.

As Cobbett's account of the Vendée massacres builds towards a crescendo, his vignettes paint a picture of a depraved killing culture which disregards, transgresses and inverts the normative relations between life and death. A hospital becomes a 'slaughter-house', a maternity ward a site of infanticide and human waste: one witness 'saw several infants, some yet palpitating, and other drowned in tubs of human excrement' (54). Like a macabre travesty of Foucauldianism, hospitals and prisons become interchangeable. There is a grisly pun on women's 'confinement' in a scene in which a woman gives birth in prison in a standing position: 'Such an object I never saw; she was crawling with vermin; her lips were blue; death had already seized her' (73). Monstrous birth is a reality: women 'delivered in the very lighters, among water and mud . . . They with the fruit of their conjugal love, went to the bottom together' (115–16). There is an implicit symbolism here: the love of life and liberty, like the ideals of the revolution, has sunk into a debased miasma of monstrous procreation. 'We are, you see, up to our eyes among the dead bodies and pretty girls' says one Jacobin commander (86). Babies and children are simply obstacles between Jacobin desire and the mother's body: one Jacobin leader 'murdered several infants at the breast, and afterwards tried to lie with the mothers' (115); another is seen to 'jump and dance on the dead body of a child' (86).

It seems that in this psychopathic culture of death, there is an intention to ridicule, debase, appropriate or discard the reproductive potential of the old order. This drama is played out on the womans's body. The climax of this subset of atrocity is the 'denatalization' of drowning women, the victims of the infamous *noyades* (mass drownings) and 'republican marriages' (the tying together of naked men and women before their boat is sunk). In the anti-Jacobin imagination, as Adriana Craciun has noted, the latter 'parodied liberalized sexual relations' and comprised a travesty of the Robespierrean union of Virtue and Terror.[62] In a variation on earlier scenes of infanticide, two women have their babies confiscated: in the first example, 'the horrid villains tore the child from her body, stuck it on the point of a bayonet, and thus carried it to the river' (116); in the second instance, there is an even worse calamity, which is signalled by Cobbett's interjection 'great God! my heart dies within me'. This time the villains 'ripped open the wombs of the mother [and] tore out the palpitating embryo, to deck the point of a pike of liberty and equality' (ibid.). Note the parallel between Cobbett's sympathetic but metaphorical arrest ('my heart dies within me') and the extracted, 'palpitating', heart-like foetus which becomes another Jacobin emblem of heartlessness. The parturient imagery gives Cobbett's comment that he has 'led the reader through rivers of blood' a peculiarly literal application. The river Loire, poisoned and polluted by corpses, is also a breeding ground for the monstrous progeny of the revolution. Cobbett's river Loire is connected imaginatively, if not geographically, to Maria Williams's image of the 'trembling waters' of the Seine.

In Cobbett's hell, Jacobin power can literally be measured by the numbers of exposed corpses and body parts. By 'exposed' I mean both highly conspicuous and naked. Nakedness signifies dehumanization, abjection and abuse, but the absence of clothes is also the result of the trade in death. The legion of 'old-clothes dealers' who thrive on massacres complain that 'clothes being shot through sunk their value' (85). The remedy is 'to strip the prisoners naked before execution'. Though such comparisons are anachronistic, there are other chilling anticipations of the imagery of the Nazi holocaust: the allegation that leading Jacobins 'wore *boots made of human skin*. Robespierre did not flay his people figuratively' (240); and a Jacobin governor watching executions, 'attended by a band of music, which played while this inhuman butchery lasted' (251). In the Nantz necropolis, the Loire disgorges its human offal:

> I have seen heaps of human bodies gnawed, and partly devoured by the dogs and the birds of prey; which latter were continually hovering over the city, and particularly near the water side. (75)

A similar sight, 'a heap formed of the bodies of women who had been shot', produces a macabre political joke: 'the soldiers, laughing, called this horrible spectacle the *mountain*, alluding to the mountain of the National Convention' (70). But this reduction of the revolution to piles of bodies could also describe Cobbett's methodology: heaping corpses in front of the reader. His book is a mimesis of the 'mountain' of body parts, a body-count in which bodies count.[63] After he has piled up bodies for over a hundred pages, Cobbett produces an apocalyptic statistical comparison with which to conclude his devastating account. He claims that the Jacobins have destroyed, 'in one city in France, a population equal to that of the capital of the United States' (118). If the Americans are not vigilant in repelling French ideas of democracy, Cobbett does not discount 'even the head of our admired and beloved President rolling on a scaffold' (225). As in France, republicanism could turn on its head. But the message was also directed at British loyalism and its fears of regicidal Jacobin plotting. Despite the fact that only a decade earlier the 'admired and beloved' Americans had accused the British of committing atrocities in the revolutionary war, it was now important to unite in the face of the common enemy.

Napoleon and the miseries of war

The gruelling war with France and Napoleon's rise to power in the late 1790s impelled a fresh wave of atrocity stories into the British public sphere. The widespread fear of a French invasion inspired a resurgence of apocalyptic, Francophobic and anti-radical propaganda. As H. T. Dickinson notes, 'popular conservatism and militant loyalism kept domestic radicalism at bay so long as it could be convincingly linked with the anarchy of the French revolution and the military aggression of Napoleon'.[64] Gillray's cartoon 'Promis'd Horrors of the French Invasion. – or – Forcible Reasons for negociating a Regicide Peace' (1796) imagined revolutionary atrocities on the streets of London, including the birching of Pitt and the hanging of his ministers (Figure 6). Gillray's fascination with political violence has led some critics to suspect that he covertly relished the spectacle of the overthrow of the British government, but there is no doubting that he bolstered the stereotype of the anarchic, bloodthirsty, depraved, even cannibalistic Jacobin.[65]

Cobbett threw his full journalistic weight behind this vilification. Announcing the launch of his *Political Register* in September 1800, Cobbett warned

Figure 6   James Gillray, 'Promis'd Horrors of the French Invasion. – or – Forcible Reasons for negociating a Regicide Peace' (October 1796) © Trustees of the British Museum

his readers about the French threat: 'Had they the means, they would exterminate us to the last man'.[66] Three years later, at the height of the invasion fears of 1803, Cobbett produced a powerful piece of anti-Napoleonic propaganda, 'Important Considerations for the People of this Kingdom'. The tract was distributed 'to every parish in England and Wales' in order to drum up national support for renewing the war and ending the Treaty of Amiens (2: 81).[67] In line with other popular denunciations of Napoleonic power published at this time, Cobbett stresses the duplicity and cruelty of French rule in conquered territories. This approach has been dismissed by Leonora Nattrass as 'the tried and tested formula of crude atrocity stories', but the text repays serious critical attention.[68] The contrast between fake republican promises of freedom and prosperity and the atrocious reality of occupation is treated as 'indisputable evidence' (2: 89) of the French designs upon England. To borrow a phrase from Coleridge, the didactic aim of the pamphlet is to 'repel an impious foe', but instead of Coleridge's highly Romantic, agonized self-doubts and subjective anxieties, Cobbett opts for reportage. He gives a brief survey of the 'evidence' of French Terror in Egypt, Holland, Switzerland and Germany (this list would later include Spain). This 'long and black catalogue of French cruelties towards the people of other countries' (2: 85) echoes the 'dark catalogue' of *The Bloody Buoy*, and the appalling picture of conquest and atrocity recalls the horrors of the Vendée. However, in order to maximize the impact of the hyperbolic realism of his narrative, Cobbett does not make this comparison evident, even though most of the examples of 'brutality never heard of before' (2: 90) can be found in *The Bloody Buoy*. Cobbett wants his readers to be shocked, outraged and patriotically stirred, so he presents Napoleonic brutality as novel and unprecedented in its scale, ferocity and ruthlessness. Wherever possible, Napoleon is made an accomplice of the slaughter. The French army in Egypt massacres over 3000 Turks at Jaffa 'with musquetry and grape shot, stabbing and cutting to death the few who escaped the fire, while he himself looked on, and rejoiced at the horrid scene' (2: 86). The latter detail is a classic 'heighten'd tint' of spectacular violence.

Such literary license was designed to assist loyalist propaganda in transforming Napoleon, 'this rapacious, this bloody minded tyrant', into the personification of evil, and the malign intelligence behind all the actions of the French military. In Cobbett's narrative, Napoleon's standard ploy is to promise liberation and impose Terror – as Coleridge puts it in 'France: An Ode' (1798), 'to tempt and to betray!' (l. 84).[69] This pattern of disillusionment and treachery recalls the lost hopes of the French revolution. The tragic pathos is nowhere better illustrated than in the betrayed pastoral virtue of the Swiss: 'the earth was strewed with their dead bodies, and while the flames ascended from the once happy dwellings of this valiant and innocent people, the hard-earned and long-preserved liberties of Switzerland expired' (2: 88). Again, there is an echo of Coleridge's poem here: 'From bleak Helvetia's icy caverns sent – / I hear [Liberty's] groans upon her bloodstained streams!' (ll. 66–7). As this apocalyptic extinction of liberty moves inexorably towards Britain, the Germans suffer three months of scorched earth: 'from one end of the country to the other, we trace the merciless ruffians through a scene of conflagration and blood' (2: 91). The key effect here is the sublime sense of national catastrophe, the fate awaiting Britain if Napoleon is not defeated. The closing section of the pamphlet is a Dystopian prophecy of conquest and enslavement which goes beyond anything imagined by Gillray or Coleridge:

> They would introduce their own bloody laws, with additional severities; they would divide us into separate classes; hem us up in districts, cut off all communication between friends and relations, parents and children, which latter they would breed up in their own blasphemous principles; they would put badges upon us, mark us on the cheek, on our heads, split our ears, or clothe us in the habit of slaves. (Ibid.)

There is a final, Orwellian touch to this chilling but ironic scenario of imperial subjection being imposed on imperial Britain: French 'extortions and atrocities' would be 'universal' (ibid.).

The emblazoning of French military atrocities was a hallmark of popular anti-Napoleonic propaganda during this period.[70] One broadside took the form of a Proclamation announcing that a French invasion will *'violate the Wives and Daughters of our People'*.[71] Another broadside revived the popular genre of an imaginary dialogue in which John Bull faces up to his opponent. In *Plain Answers to Plain Questions, in a Dialogue between John Bull and Bonaparte*, the following exchange takes place:

> *John Bull*: Why have you suffered your soldiers to burn so many towns, shed so much innocent blood, destroy cottages as well as palaces so indiscriminately, murder in cold blood thousands of poor men, and ravish thousands of poor women, in Italy, in Egypt, in Syria, and lately in Hanover?
>
> *Bonaparte*: . . . I did not merely suffer it – I encouraged it. – My object has always been to strike terror.

When John Bull asks about plans to invade Britain, the reply is: 'I won't tell you. It would make your hair stand on end' (102–3). The sensational use of faux-reticence was also a feature of pamphlet called *A Peep into Hanover; Or, A Faint Description of the Atrocities Committed by the French in that City*. Despite the euphemistic title, the 'faint description' includes the following scene, printed in capital letters:

> Even in the public street, women of the highest rank have been violated by the lowest of that brutal soldiery, in the presence of their husbands and fathers, and subjected at the same time to such additional and indescribable outrages as the brutal fury of the violators, enflamed by drunkenness, could contrive. (148)

An even more sensational broadside had the Gothic title *Horrors Upon Horrors; or, what are the Hellish deeds that can surprise us, when committed by the Blood-Hounds of that Arch-Fiend of Wickedness, the Corsican Bonaparte?* It purports to be the 'true and faithful narrative' of a refugee German blacksmith who has witnessed many atrocities, beginning with the gang-rape of a mother. Though the woman is breastfeeding, her baby is 'dashed against the floor'. When her young son fights back like a 'little tiger' (an ironic echo of the soldiers who behave 'like so many tigers'), all her children are bayoneted 'and thrown out of the door upon a dung-hill'. The blacksmith hopes to reach England, 'the only free and happy country that is left in all Europe' (201–3).

However, the tide of anti-Jacobin propaganda did not prevent many Romantic-period poets emphasizing the brutality, futility and human wastefulness of war.[72] Taking his lead from Godwin's denunciation of war in

Political Justice (discussed in Chapter 5), Shelley summed up anti-war sentiment in his 'Declaration of Rights' of 1812: 'Man has no right to kill his
brother, it is no excuse that he does so in uniform. He only adds the infamy
of servitude to the crime of murder'.[73] Southey and Coleridge were particularly active in producing anti-war texts in the 1790s. Both of Southey's two
major works of the decade, the unpublished *Wat Tyler* (1794) and *Joan of Arc*
(1796), imagine the violent destruction of the English State, and Southey
trawled history for examples of republican martyrs and victims of tyranny.[74]
Southey's 'Ode to Terror' (1791) presents a whole 'wreck'd army' as a casualty
of war, but the key sentimental figures are a mother and a child:

> The mother to her breast,
> On the heap'd snows reclining, clasps her child,
> Not to be pitied now, for both are now at rest.

This vignette was recycled in some of Coleridge's hard-hitting anti-war
journalism. In his periodical *The Watchman* (1796), Coleridge published two
excerpts from a British soldier's first-hand account of the disastrous Flanders
campaigns.[75] In the first excerpt, the soldier sees a 'beautiful young woman'
who has frozen to death while feeding her baby. The most telling sentimental
detail is the 'instantly congealed' stream of excess milk on the 'exposed'
breast: a literally frozen image of 'denatalization', the violated ideal of maternity. As Philip Shaw has noted, 'the representation of familial decimation
proved to be a powerful tool against the state',[76] so it is unsurprising that
Coleridge was attracted to the emotional power of this vignette, recycling
it in the unpublished *The Vision of the Maid of Orleans*, written in the same
year.[77] In this new context, the scene is displaced historically to form a
key moment in Joan of Arc's transformation into a national hero. Having
ascended a mountain for religious inspiration, she witnesses an atrocity. In
this version of the vignette, the husband of the dead mother is still alive,
and he is able to recount how their village was 'seized and fired' (l. 234) by
English soldiers. Joan's response is a righteous echo of this villainy: indignation 'fires' her eye (l. 257) and sets her on her mission of nationalist
vengeance. Her transcendent violence is the answer to war's desecration of
the female body. Women are also the principal victims of Coleridge's second
excerpt from the soldier's memoirs, which describes the British shelling of
a nunnery. The 'piercing' shells of the British 'instantaneously destroyed, or
miserably mangled the whole Sisterhood'. The phallic language intentionally
conflates sexual, military and religious violence.

Coleridge made an even more sweeping denunciation of British and
European imperial violence in 'Ode on the Departing Year', a poem
published in the *Cambridge Intelligencer* in December 1796. After noting the
anniversary of the death of Catherine the Great, an 'exterminating Fiend'
(l. 56), a footnote points out that the same date is also the anniversary

of the Russian siege of Ismail, a battle fought in 1790 in which 'THIRTY THOUSAND HUMAN BEINGS, MEN, WOMEN AND CHILDREN' died 'in cold blood'.[78] Coleridge goes on to accuse British imperial policy of being responsible for global atrocities: the decision to invade revolutionary France led to 'the smoking villages of Flanders and the putrefied fields of La Vendée'; the detestable Slave-Trade' in Africa has produced 'unnumbered victims'; in India there are 'the millions whom a rice-contracting governor caused to perish'; and in America, there has been 'the recent enormities of the Scalp-merchants' (1: 165–6).

Despite the prevalence of this violence, Coleridge prefaces the excerpts in *The Watchman* with an attack on the reader's complacency: 'The horrors of war must be re-commenced – Let those who sit by the fire-side, and hear of them at a safe distance attentively peruse the following' (238). This is reminiscent of his more ferocious lampooning of female sensibility in his 'Lecture on the Slave Trade', also published in *The Watchman*. The finger-wagging admonishment shows the constant need to reiterate the radical impact of spectacular violence as a mode of discourse resistant to 'safe' consumption. Helen Maria Williams made a similar point about the 'distant' spectatorship of war:

> The soldier climbing precipices, or scaling walls, to fall with indiscrim-
> inate rage on the old, the infant, and the defenceless, and to convert
> flourishing cities into one vast cemetery, is only a being of romance to
> those who have lived at a distance from such scenes. (*LCS*, 2: 194)

Whether such a reprimand was really required is less important than the fact that writers like Williams and Coleridge thought it was necessary. The most famous example of this shaming of the *hypocrite lecteur* occurs in Coleridge's 'Fears in Solitude' (1798), a key text in the 'Romantic' disenchantment with the French revolution. Coleridge targets the patriotic glamorization of war:

> We, this whole people, have been clamorous
> For war and bloodshed, animating sports,
> The which we pay for, as a thing to talk of,
> Spectators and not combatants... (ll. 90–3)[79]

Coleridge focuses his animus on those groups in society who are defined by their exclusion from combat:

> ... Boys and girls,
> And women that would groan to see a child
> Pull off an insect's leg – all read of war,
> The best amusement for our morning meal! (ll. 101–4)

These are rather cheap points to score, as Coleridge is surely not suggesting that women and children should prove their mettle in actual combat. As in the slavery debate, it is genteel women who are singled out as the most susceptible and impressionable consumers of images of violence. But the lower-class male also merits Coleridge's derision. This attraction of war for this 'poor wretch' – a tag which suggests unfitness for combat as well as vulgarity – is an immersion in gung-ho fantasies and armchair strategy. He becomes a 'fluent phraseman' of 'dainty terms' and 'abstractions', a set of 'empty sounds' which sanitize violence:

> ... as if the wretch,
> Who fell in battle doing bloody deeds,
> Passed off to heaven, *translated* and not killed. (ll. 116–18)

Both these 'wretches' are victims of a commercial society which packages war as a form of entertainment and thrilling spectacle. War has become a product of a society addicted to luxury. If this tendency is not halted, the nation will become 'A selfish, lewd, effeminated race' (l. 57). In order to resist feminization, a manly and principled representation of war is needed. Explicit violence is not precluded, but it should not be glorified. Coleridge must have been alert to the fact that he is snared in his own logic: poets are also 'spectators and not combatants'. But as Mark Rawlinson has commented, Coleridge was responding to the 'the strategic necessity of disseminating fearful images of war to generate patriotism'.[80] Simon Bainbridge also believes that Coleridge saw his poetic role as sensitizing the reader to the horrors of war.[81] This may explain why the poem opens with a chilling contrast between the poet's rural retreat – a 'nook' in which the 'humble man ... dreams of better worlds' (ll. 14, 26) – and the poet's vision (or spectacle) of an invasion. He imagines,

> Ev'n now, perchance, and in his native isle,
> Carnage and screams beneath this blessed sun! (ll. 41–2)

Coleridge's 'Romantic' poetic intervention into the invasion panic is premised on three displacements: the switch from the city to the pastoral 'nook' as the emblematic heartland of England, and the symbolic and literal terrain which must be defended against violation;[82] the opening up of a moral and aesthetic gap between the poet and commercial society and print culture; and the grounding of the poem in the poet's subjective reflection on events, the guarantee of a humane and humanist aesthetics. It can be assumed that these mediations provide the necessary distance for the poet (and the reader) to 'read' war dispassionately, but this does not solve the problem of the poem's function as a patriotic call-to-arms: the reader is exhorted to 'Repel an impious foe' (l. 136). The born-again, Burkean

Coleridge – 'a son, a brother, and a friend, / A husband and a father who revere / All bonds of natural love' (ll. 174–5) – is obliged to stereotype the French as savage, 'mingling mirth / With deeds of murder' (ll. 138–9). The justified violence of the 'natural' British, on the other hand, is bloodless: they will 'repel' and 'render' the French enemy without carnage: 'may we return / Not with a drunken triumph' (l. 148). The alliteration enacts national differences: the 'r' allotted to the British forces (repel, render, return) is the assertive, manly rebuttal of the treacherously emollient 'm' of French aggression (mingling, mirth, murder). The word 'render' is also multivalent. 'Fears in Solitude' is a poem which strives to 'render' a nation in crisis: to repay a debt, to present for inspection, to strip away layers of fat (luxury), to make the body politic lean and healthy through a correct 'reading of war'. But the idea of melting down fat could also recall the traditional contrast between the over-refined and effeminate French, represented emblematically by an emaciated fop, and the corpulent John Bull's, the 'roast beef of England'. In other words, John Bull will render or cannibalize his puny opponent. This is a subtle inversion of anti-Jacobin caricatures of sans-culotte cannibalism, seen most spectacularly in Gillray's 'Un petit Souper a la Parisienne'. But the final court of appeal for the poet's 'fears' is conventional religious authority: 'the sweet words / Of Christian promise (words that even yet / Might stem destruction)' (ll. 60–2). The idea that 'sweet words' can 'stem destruction' valorizes the poem's attempt to 'repel' the spectacle of war and to rehumanize the nation: to defend heath, hearth and home from 'invasion' by French soldiers and debased textual pleasures.

One possible culmination of this phase of Romantic resistance to the allure of spectacular violence comes in the preface to the second edition of *Lyrical Ballads* (1800), where Wordsworth attacks the contemporary taste for 'outrageous stimulation' and 'extraordinary incident', and insists that 'the human mind is capable of excitement, without the application of gross and violent stimulants'.[83] In fact violence figures prominently and sensationally in several poems in *Lyrical Ballads*: *The Rime of the Ancient Mariner* is now regarded as an allegory of the slave trade;[84] 'The Thorn' and 'The Mad Mother' are about infanticide;[85] and 'The Female Vagrant' (analysed in Chapter 4) depicts atrocities in the American revolutionary war. It is also worth a reminder that 1798, when *Lyrical Ballads* first appeared, was a year not only of invasion fears but also of the Irish rebellion – indeed, this republican revolution on British soil erupted only one month after Coleridge composed 'Fears in Solitude'. As will be shown in Chapter 3, the rebellion was preceded by a brutal regime of Terror, and it is quite possible that the crisis in Ireland affected the tone and themes of these poems under discussion. The most direct reflection of this tense mood was Coleridge's sensational poem 'Fire, Famine, and Slaughter. A War Eclogue', published in *The Morning Post* in January 1798.[86] The poem is an extrapolation of the accusation made in the footnote to 'Ode on the Departing Year', that Pitt's war-mongering policy led to 'the putrefied fields of La Vendée'. But the line 'By the light of his own blazing cot / Was many a naked Rebel shot' (ll. 56–7) is strongly suggestive of Ireland. If this is the case, the most seditious sentiments in the poem have an eerily predictive quality. The figure of Famine pledges revenge against the aggressor:

> I'll gnaw the multitude,
> Till the cup of rage o'erbrim:
> They shall seize him and his brood,

and Fire adds, 'They shall tear him limb from limb' (ll. 69–72).[87] In an 'Apologetic Preface' which Coleridge added to a much later reprint of the poem, he berated his 'seething imagination' for exaggerating the horrors of war, and claimed that the 'many vivid, yet fantastic forms' in the text were not based on 'observation' or 'realities'.[88] But this was just another disingenuous attempt to disown his radical past.[89] In his poems, lectures and journalism, Coleridge used spectacular violence to attack government policy. Pulling off legs and limbs could be justified if it furthered the cause of peace and reform.

Bloody hands

The war with Napoleon finally ended in 1815, but the critique of war continued. Indeed, the battle of Waterloo, which cost around 50,000 casualties in one day's fighting, was viewed by many writers as a Pyrrhic victory.[90] The Allied Powers' restoration of the Bourbons was reviled by radicals as a treacherous step back into 'legitimacy'. This was despite the fact that Napoleon's repressive occupation of Spain had attracted fierce condemnation from Romantic authors. In the first Canto of *Childe Harold's Pilgrimage* (1812), Byron asked:

> Ah! Spain! How sad will be thy reckoning day,
> When soars Gaul's Vulture, with his wings unfurl'd,
> And thou shalt view thy sons in crowds to Hades hurl'd. (1: LII)[91]

Goya also etched a series of French atrocities called 'The Disasters of War', though these were not published at the time.[92] But these criticisms of Napoleonic policy did not let the British government off the legitimist hook. In the third Canto of *Childe Harold's Pilgrimage* (1816), the hero's visit to the Waterloo battlefield is an opportunity for Byron to rail against monarchism: 'Shall we, who struck the Lion down, shall we / Pay the wolf homage?' (III, XIX).

Byron continued his debunking of the glories of war in Cantos VII–VIII of *Don Juan* (1822). His critique of imperial violence is displaced historically onto the sacking of the Turkish city of Ismail by the Russians in 1790.[93] As noted above, Coleridge identified this battle as an example of the imperialist savagery of Catherine the Great, an 'exterminating fiend'. Byron focuses his anger on Catherine's 'exterminating' commander, General Suwarrow: 'Hero, buffoon, half-demon and half-dirt', a 'Harlequin in uniform' (VII, 55). It is not difficult to detect the ghost of Wellington behind this lampoon, but Byron like Coleridge also attacks the cultural glorification of war. The popularity of the military 'bullet-in' (VII, 21) is ridiculed: 'Think how the joys of reading a *Gazette* / Are purchased by all agonies and crimes' (VIII, 125). Hyperbolic realism is a reality check, an antidote to the facile 'joys of reading'. As the city is taken,

> ... the heat
> Of carnage, like the Nile's sun-sodden slime,
> Engendered monstrous shapes of every crime (VIII, 82)

But Byron is reluctant to textually engender too many 'monstrous' crimes: 'It is an awful topic, but 'tis not / My cue for any time to be terrific' (VIII, 89). Instead of being 'terrific', he resorts to a sentimental subplot in which Juan rescues a beautiful child from the clutches of two Cossacks. Byron does use the atrocity motif of a pile of bodies, in this case 'a yet warm group / Of murdered women' (VIII, 91) under which the child is burrowing in a desperate attempt to find maternal protection, but the narrative focus is on the child's survival. She is rescued in the nick of time, as the Cossack sabres 'glittered o'er her little head' (VIII, 93), though the 'slender streak of blood' on her face is a reminder of 'how near / Her fate had been' (VIII, 95). Unlike her numerous predecessors, the girl does not suffer defilement, though that is not the case for a group of older women:

> Some odd mistakes too happened in the dark,
> Which showed a want of lanterns or of taste ...
> ... six old damsels, each of seventy years,
> Were all deflowered by different grenardiers. (VIII, 130)

It is difficult to defend the humorous tone of this vignette. Whereas the child is sentimentally protected, the rape of 'old damsels' is regarded as a comically implausible 'crime', and a moment of zeugmatic, light relief. Simon Bainbridge has robustly defended Byron's use of sexual metaphors to expose the barbarities of warfare: 'Byron's critique of imperialism links sexual and territorial aggressiveness'.[94] But it does seem that the theme of rape in *Don Juan* is made to conform to the poem's satirical imperative, to be 'a little quietly facetious upon everything'.[95] It may be Byron who at this juncture shows a 'want of taste' and lacks enlightenment.

However, if this scene is one facetious step too far, it is counterbalanced by the way in which the poem typically reflects on its own poetic practices and ambiguities. Byron concludes the battle scene with a cunning comment on the problematic of making war a topic for amusement. He describes how Suwarrow communicates his victory to the Empress in the form of a rhyming couplet, translated into English as 'Glory to God and to the Empress. Ismail's ours' (VIII, 133). In a brilliant reflexive moment, Byron exposes the reality of the 'bloody hands' behind this inappropriately literary text. When Catherine the Great receives the letter, she is amused by Suwarrow's rhyme, which makes a 'dull' couplet out of 'The whole gazette of thousands whom he slew' (IX, 60). The 'dullness' of imperial intelligence is only half the joke: the real 'crime' is the willful disregard for the reality of war. As Bainbridge remarks, Suwarrow's 'fatuous and inappropriate' couplet is a foil for Byron's republican poetic practice, to reveal 'what *things were*'.[96] The scene is a powerful reminder of the radical value of spectacular violence, and the need to show 'the worst which pen expresses' (VIII, 123).

The violence of the French revolution, like the horrors of slavery, placed the bloody vignette firmly on the literary and cultural landscape of Romanticism. The French revolution added the new crime of 'democratic' atrocity to the lexicon of spectacular violence, and as we have already seen in Chapter 1, the San Domingo slave rebellion was portrayed as a direct descendent of this modern evil. The older form of British imperial violence also persisted in anti-war rhetoric, but this was rebutted by loyalist propaganda which concentrated on invasion fears and Jacobin and Napoleonic atrocities. The Romantic author faced a difficult challenge: to limit Jacobin excesses while resisting the hysteria of the patriotic call to arms. Romantic literary texts were not silent on the issue of spectacular violence, but there is a distinction between the degree of candour and graphic detail in what I have called the higher journalism, and the more 'composed' texts of mainstream Romantic authors, though this distinction should not be exaggerated. But it is certainly the case that Romantic popular print culture continued to be the main repository of an extraordinarily rich and disturbing repertoire of violent tropes and micro-narratives. As the next chapter on the Irish rebellion of 1798 will show, the lag between reportage and literary texts continued to grow. This does not invalidate either response, but it shows that it was increasingly difficult for writers to confront the trauma of violent history without a breathing space.

3
'The Most Distressful Country': The Irish Rebellion of 1798

> Q What have you got in your hand?
> A A green bough.
> Q Where did it first grow?
> A In America.
> Q Where did it bud?
> A In France.
> Q Where are you going to plant it?
> A In the crown of Great Britain.
>
> (Catechism of the United Irishmen)

> I met with Napper Tandy,
> And he took me by the hand,
> Saying, How is poor old Ireland,
> And how does she stand?
> She's the most distressful country
> That ever yet was seen;
> They are hanging men and women,
> For the wearing of the green! (Irish ballad)

> I expect to be accused of a desire for renewing in Ireland the scenes of
> revolutionary horror, which marked the struggles of France twenty
> years ago. But it is the renewal of that unfortunate aera, which
> I strongly deprecate, and which the tendency of this address is
> calculated to obviate.
>
> (Percy Bysshe Shelley, An Address, to the Irish People, 1812)[1]

The Irish rebellion of 1798 was the closest that Britain came to imitating
the French revolution. Yet the event still barely figures on the landscape
of Romanticism. One reason for this neglect could be the apparent absence
of Romantic literary texts which represent the rebellion, a gap which this
chapter should begin to fill. A further reason could be the ameliorative
shape of the course of events: the defeat of the rebellion and the Act of

Union may have created the impression that the rebellion was relatively easily absorbed into a Whiggish historical narrative of reform. But another explanation for the scholarly neglect of the rebellion is the hyperbolic violence of the conflict. Following the example of the horrors of slavery, the French revolution and the American wars, Romantic print culture responded vigorously to the Irish rebellion and established it immediately as a potent source of spectacular violence. But at the same time as Romantic readers consumed the bloody vignettes of the conflict, the proximity of the event must have evoked grave fears and anxieties: if the rebellion succeeded, what next? As Ruan O'Donnell notes, the rebellion was 'the most serious armed domestic challenge faced by the British state throughout the long eighteenth century' – note the use of the word 'domestic'.[2] On the other hand, the bloody brutality of British policy in Ireland was also a glaring political and moral excrescence. Looked at either way, the rebellion was and has remained a colossal political embarrassment to British history and culture. The aim of this chapter is therefore twofold: to show how the rebellion was constructed as an event of spectacular violence, and to trace some of the literary responses to the rebellion in Romantic historical fiction. As will become clear, it took almost 30 years for the first, full-frontal fictional retelling of the rebellion to be published. This literary landmark was made possible by the generic innovation of Scott's historical novel, and the fact that Ireland was in the throes of a new mass political movement.

Atrocities on both sides

At his trial for High Treason in 1798, the United Irish leader Wolfe Tone declared,

> For open war I was prepared but if, instead of that, a system of private assassinations has taken place, I repeat, whilst I deplore it, that is not chargeable on me. Atrocities, it seems, have been committed on both sides... I detest them from my heart.[3]

As the Miltonic allusion indicates – Moloch recommends 'open war' in the fallen angels' debate in Pandemonium (*Paradise Lost*, 2: 50) – Tone believed that the high-minded and virtuous republican ideals of the Irish rebellion had degenerated into unjustified sectarian violence, 'atrocities... committed on both sides'. Like the French revolution which inspired it, the Irish rebellion was another Paradise Lost. From the outset, these 'atrocities' have dominated the cultural construction of the rebellion.[4] This response has always existed in a state of tension with that other possible interpretation of events: 1798 was the violent realization of the worst British anti-Jacobin fears, a full-scale republican revolution, an 'open war' on British soil which resulted in an astonishing 20,000–30,000 casualties, the majority of whom were Irish peasants, in little more than a few months of fighting – 'probably the most concentrated episode of violence in Irish history' according to Roy Foster.[5] On the other hand, the rebellion was a Catholic uprising, a 'religious war' which led to a series of infamous rebel massacres at Vinegar Hill, Wexford Bridge and Scullabogue.[6] By considering a range of primary sources, including newspaper accounts, eyewitness testimonies, poems and songs, the aim of this chapter is to show that the rebel massacres were constructed by a predominantly loyalist press as the 'essence' of the rebellion: a jacquerie of out-of-control sectarian fanatics, an 'enthusiastic', religiously based reincarnation of Jacobinism which could only be finally exorcised by Union with England.[7] The second part of the chapter will consider the representation of the rebellion in Romantic fiction. The obvious choice of text to begin with is Maria Edgeworth's 'national tale' *Ennui* (1809), but I will also look at two examples of what Ina Ferris has called 'novels of insurgency': Charles Maturin's *The Milesian Chief* (1812), and more substantially, Michael Banim's *The Croppy* (1828).[8] Finally, I want to suggest that Walter Scott's novel *Old Mortality* (1816), which deals with the Covenanter conflicts of late seventeenth-century Scotland, can be read as an allegory of the 1798 rebellion.

Given the paucity of critical interest in the Irish rebellion within Romantic studies, it is worth a brief recap of the basic chronology. By 1798, the proscribed, Presbyterian-led United Irishmen had joined forces with the underground, militant movement Defenderism. This was a powerful alliance: a hysterical government report painted a garish picture of guerilla violence, 'midnight murder, robbery and outrage'.[9] The final piece of the revolutionary plan was put in place when the French agreed to collaborate in a co-ordinated invasion and uprising. The Protestant-dominated Ascendancy administration in Ireland (a 'knot of low jobbers', according to Burke),[10] aided by the newly founded loyalist organization, the Orangemen, conducted a campaign of 'systematic government terror' against all those suspected of nationalist sympathies.[11] Forms of punishment included burning down houses, the notorious pitch-capping, and summary executions (Figures 7 and 8). Despite the arrest of most of the United Irish leadership in March 1798, an 'open' rebellion broke out in late May. After some early successes, particularly the setting up of the so-called 'republic' of Wexford, the rebels were defeated at New Ross and Vinegar Hill. The French invasion in August was repelled by Generals Lake and Cornwallis, and a state of 'white Terror' persisted for many months, despite mass amnesties for rebels who renounced their nationalist political allegiance. The United Irish leaders turned king's evidence and, understandably, distanced themselves from the carnage.

Almost immediately, this idea of a fatal gap between an enlightened Protestant leadership and a sectarian peasantry became a leading interpretation of the rebellion's failure. In one of the earliest histories of the rebellion, James Gordon stated that the conflict 'was made a religious war by the lower

Figure 7   'Pitch-cap' punishment

classes in the south of Ireland', whose 'ignorance and bigotry' inflamed
the 'sanguinary and cruel' excesses of all 'successful insurrections of the
populace'.[12] William Hazlitt summed up the problem with a characteristic
dogmatic flourish:

Figure 8 Summary hanging of Irish rebels

> Catholics may make good subjects, but bad rebels. They are so used to the trammels of authority, that they do not immediately know how to do without them; or, like manumitted slaves, only feel assured of their liberty in committing some Saturnalian license. A revolution, to give it stability and soundness, should first be conducted down to a Protestant ground.[13]

Notice the references to slave rebellion and the familiar liberal explanation of the violence of the early stages of the French revolution. In Hazlitt's schema, the suddenly 'manumitted' Catholics in Ireland behaved with the same violent 'license' as their enslaved and benighted equivalents in San Domingo or Paris.[14] In a highly prejudicial way, Hazlitt contrasts this recidivism with the rationality of Protestant 'stability and soundness', though he must have known that numerous United Irish leaders and commanders were actually Catholic. History was also commandeered in order to bolster the idea that the rebellion was a revival of seventeenth-century Catholic Terror. An example of this propaganda was Richard Musgrave's *A Concise Account of the Material Events and Atrocities which Occurred in the Present Rebellion with the Causes which Produced Them*, which traced a line of descent from the 1798 rebellion to the Catholic massacres of 1641. Musgrave's book was rushed into print in 1799, before he had finished his important and widely cited *Memoirs of The Different Rebellions in Ireland* (1801).[15] But nationalists could also appropriate the same conflict, placing the emphasis on Protestant Terror: 'Cromwell in Ireland – the Irish nearly exterminated', in Thomas Moore's sardonic words.[16] However, no event seemed to confirm the regressive, loyalist interpretation of the 1798 uprising more clearly than the rebel massacres at Vinegar Hill, Wexford Bridge and Scullabogue. These incidents were captured in a series of remarkably vivid images produced by George Cruikshank as illustrations for W. H. Maxwell's *History of the Irish Rebellion* (1845). In the absence of an Irish Goya, Gillray or Zoffany, Cruikshank's images (Figures 9–11) have become the most widely used and cited visual record of the massacres.[17] Cruikshank's Scullabogue scene has even been called 'the most potent propaganda image of the entire rebellion'.[18] Further reference to these images will be made below, but it is worth pointing out at this stage that the main rebel weapon, the pike, lent itself to stylized graphic representation. The sight of skewered bodies carries an immediate dramatic impact well suited to Cruikshank's aim of discrediting the rebellion. In the context of the 1840s, Cruikshank was undoubtedly scoring political hits against the resurgent Young Ireland movement, which would stage its own abortive and diminutive rebellion in 1848.

'Direct and open violence': Ascendancy terror

Before looking at the rebel massacres in more detail, it is important to remember Wolfe Tone's condemnation of 'atrocities . . . committed on both sides'. Some account must be taken of the regime of Ascendancy Terror and loyalist violence which preceded and provoked the rebellion. As stated in the secret 'Address of the United Britons to the United Irishmen' of January 1798, 'Ireland has always been the object of direct and open violence, England of fraud'.[19] Several songs in the United Irish songbook *Paddy's Resource* (1795) give voice to this mood of fear, repression and indignation.[20] A song called 'The Victim of Tyranny' (39) shows the response of a landlord when he discovers that his tenant's 'heart to Erin yearn'd':

> Even with the ground my cot did raze,
> And fir'd my substance dearly earn'd.
> Unmov'd, remorseless now he sees,
> My cottage falling as it burns,
> My wife for mercy, on her knees,
> From him, with ruthless frown he spurns.

A tactical comparison between this ruined cottage and its Wordsworthian equivalent illustrates the difference between the effects of repressive government in England ('fraud') and Ireland ('direct and open violence'). In Wordsworth's anti-war poem 'The Ruined Cottage' (composed in the year of the rebellion in 1798, though not published until 1814 as part of *The Excursion*),[21] the iconic humble building has fallen into decay after 'the plague of war' (l. 136) has caused an economic blight in the English countryside. But there is no 'direct violence', and the war is in a 'distant land' (l. 269). Note also that the 'unmov'd' landlord in the United Irish song resembles the figure of the sadistic slave-owner or slave-ship captain, though 'unmov'd' implies its nemesis, forced 'removal' by revolutionary action. Another song called 'Fly to Arms, Brave the Field' (55–6) is a nationalist rallying cry for vengeance. It takes the scorched earth narrative one step further, and appropriates the trope of violated femininity:

> When you behold your village burn,
> Or to the bleeding peasants turn;
> When Virgin screams assail your ears,
> The houseless child and mother's tears,
> Then all the softer feelings spurn,
> And for revenge and glory burn . . .
> No more to female weakness yield,
> But fly to arms, and brave the field!

For the United Irishmen (the stress here is on 'men'), the age of chivalry is about to commence. Stereotypical 'female weakness' is both an inspiration and a hindrance. The 'softer feelings' of sensibility must give way to manly, patriotic action. Nationalist masculine valour must rescue a feminized, powerless Irish people from the brutality of the 'colonial sublime'.[22] The United Irish leader Myles Byrne recalled that the state of the country, previous to the insurrection, is not to be imagined; except by those who witnessed the atrocities of every description committed by the military and the Orangemen, who were let loose on the unfortunate, defenceless and unarmed population.[23]

Byrne also called the mass shootings of prisoners at Wicklow 'one of the most bloody deeds that took place that was ever recorded in Irish history since the days of Cromwell' (ibid.). From this perspective, therefore, subaltern excesses could be seen as a justified, proportionate or simply inevitable 'boomerang' response to what Marianne Elliott calls the 'great Orange fear'.[24] In Thomas Moore's *Memoirs of Captain Rock* (1824), the Captain refers to 'the atrocities committed by some members of my own Family, during the paroxysm of that re-action which the measures of the Government had provoked', an emphasis overlooked by those who attacked Moore for allegedly underplaying endemic peasant violence.[25] The counter-productive policy of repression was even admitted at the highest level in the British state. When General Abercrombie took command of government forces in Ireland in early 1798, he was shocked to find the army 'in a state of licentiousness which must render it formidable to everyone but the enemy'.[26] So the situation conformed to the familiar cycle of repression and revolt: the 'licentiousness' of State power provokes (in Hazlitt's words) the 'Saturnalian license' of 'manumitted slaves'. But it was the 'paroxysm' of 're-action', in Moore's words, which attracted most attention, even though this violence killed far fewer people.[27]

'Saturnalian license': Rebel massacres

According to the revisionist Irish historian Tom Dunne, the date of 5 June 1798 is etched at the centre of the Irish rebellion and its meaning. On that one day occurred both the battle for New Ross – a military 'turning point' (151) in which about 1500 rebels were killed – and the rebel massacre at Scullabogue barn, in which over a hundred men, women and children were burned to death.[28] For Dunne, 'every reading of 1798 is lit by the lurid flames of Scullabogue' (108).[29] Moreover, when news of the New Ross defeat reached Wexford, scores of prisoners were executed on Wexford Bridge – the Irish rebellion's equivalent of the September massacres. As one of the leading Irish historians of the rebellion, Dunne is fully aware that there is a loyalist bias in many primary sources. But his concern is to correct the 'distortion' (141) of nationalist historiography which – in order to counter the myth of the sectarian, Catholic jacquerie – has gone too far in the other direction, and marginalized the rebel massacres as a maverick aberration or blip, a temporary loss of United Irish control over the Wexford 'republic'.[30] In Dunne's eyes, the United Irish 'unthinking idealism', a habit of mind he associates with 'bourgeois revolutionaries' (274), must bear more responsibility for the violence.[31] But more significantly, he argues that nationalist 'distortion' (or is it a counter-distortion?) makes the rebellion 'a matter of ideology rather than of killing' (139).[32] Dunne takes the idea of a 'Saturnalian license' seriously, as he reckons that the rebels constructed their massacres with a 'sense of theatre' (252–3). Far from being an instinctual chaos of mob carnage, rebel atrocity was a conscious performance, a ritualization of killing power. Though Dunne does not make the comparison with the French revolution or other examples of spectacular violence from the period, many of his primary sources did exactly that, and envisaged a reincarnation or emulation of Jacobin violence. James Gordon, for example, in his *History of the Rebellion in Ireland in the Year 1798* (1801), compared the rebel captain Thomas Davis to Robespierre and 'other unfeeling monsters in the French revolution'. Gordon also claims that the fate of the prisoners at Wexford was decided by 'a kind of judicial body, not improperly denominated the Bloody Committee'.[33] Taking these responses into account, it may be the case that anti-Jacobin tropes were an accurate reflection of the symbolic, semiotic and narrative organization of the massacres. Roy Foster can also be cited in this context, as he has called the rebellion 'sansculottism, Irish style'.[34]

It would of course be a 'distortion' to see this 'theatre' of violence as narrowly premeditated and scripted, and indeed the local United Irish leadership in Wexford did try to exert control over the situation. The clearest example of this concerns the massacres at Vinegar Hill, when possibly hundreds of prisoners being held in a windmill were executed (Figure 9).[35] In order to exert

Figure 9   George Cruikshank, 'Rebel Executions of Prisoners on Vinegar Hill', from W. H. Maxwell, *History of the Irish Rebellion* (1845)

some control over the situation, Bagenal Harvey and Edward Roche (the new rebel commander-in-chief) issued a Proclamation on 7 June 1798. Addressed 'To the People of Ireland, Countrymen and Fellow Soldiers', it declared:

> thanks to the Almighty Ruler of the Universe, that a total stop has been put to those sanguinary measures which of late were but too often resorted to by the creatures of government, to keep the people in slavery . . . In the moment of triumph, my countrymen, let not your victories be tarnished with any wanton act of cruelty.[36]

This was too optimistic. Once the unbridled 'cruelty' began, it soon acquired (at least, in most of the reportage) a predictable set of carnivalesque, 'Saturnalian' features: lords of misrule, Amazonian women, cannibalistic rituals, the desecration of the family and drunkenness. There was also a conspicuous role for the 'fanatical' figure of the priest-warrior. The *Annual Register's* report of the Vinegar Hill killings described a mock religious ceremony:

> More than 500 victims were thus sacrificed to the spirit of fanatical rancour, and the last moments of the unhappy sufferers were embittered by the most refined cruelties. Murphy [a rebel priest], on horseback, and raising a large crucifix in his arms, frequently adjudged sentence, after the mockery of a trial, and denounced the terrors of eternal punishment upon the expiring heretic. (*Annual* Register (1798), 113)

The *Annual Register* also reported that rebels took an 'oath of extermination' in which they promised 'by the blessed Virgin Mary, that I will burn, destroy and murder all heretics, up to my knees in blood. So help me God' (ibid., 124). This figure must have evoked the memory of seventeenth-century 'enthusiasm', but there was also a closer and more ironic parallel with the royalist, counter-revolutionary priest-soldiers of the Vendée uprising. For Helen Maria Williams, the Vendée was a 'feudal' region which harboured 'fanatical clergy' determined to retain their privileges:

> what gave the rebellion its fiercest rage was the fanaticism of which the priest inspired, who marching at the head of their columns, bearing the crucifix in his hand, pointed out to his followers the road to victory or heaven. (*LCS*, 1: 119–20, 124)[37]

In the tradition of spectacular violence, even this figure could be appropriated and change political allegiance. Musgrave lampooned the blessing of rebel soldiers as little more than 'an expiation for the horrid crimes that they had been committing'. This offering of 'immolated human victims to the Deity' is for Musgrave a continuation of the barbarous practices of 'Mahomet', the ancient Celts, and the Inquisition.[38]

The 'Saturnalian' religious iconography of the rebellion was not restricted to the violent, fanatical priest. As already noted, the Scullabogue massacre (Figure 10) brought into the 'theatre' of Irish violence one of the most shocking acts of atrocity, the cannibalistic 'Gothic Eucharist'. According to Musgrave, the rebels at Scullabogue 'took pleasure in licking their spears'; one rebel 'said he would try the taste of Orange blood; and that he dipped a tooth-pick in a wound of one of the protestants who was shot, and then put it into his mouth'.[39] The *Annual Register* reported that a rebel 'satisfied his ferocious thirst' by 'dipping his fingers in the wounds of some scarce-dead corpse, or passing his tongue over the red point of his pike' (124). In his account of being a rebel prisoner-of-war at Wexford, Charles Jackson recalled being forced to shoot another prisoner and almost being made to 'wash my hands in his blood'.[40] These are sensational details, but not necessarily unexpected. The Romantic reader was already familiar with this trope, particularly from the anti-sugar campaign, where sweetened drinks were likened to drinking slave blood (see Chapter 1), but also from the reportage of the French revolution (see Chapter 2) and accounts of American Indian 'savagery' (see Chapter 4). Significantly, Dunne does not dispute that

Figure 10 George Cruikshank, 'Rebel Massacre at Scullabogue', from W. H. Maxwell, *History of the Irish Rebellion* (1845)

acts of cannibalistic behaviour took place but interprets the behaviour as a conscious display of 'rebel bravado', not innate savagery.[41]

Like other 'theatres' of Terror and counter-Terror, the Irish rebellion's spectacle of violence shows a breaking down of taboos concerning the sanctity of the body and the distinction between life and death. In Charles Jackson's eye-witness account of the killings on Wexford Bridge, one man refuses to die:

> Mr Robinson was the next: he was piked to death. The manner of piking was, by two of the rebels pushing their pikes into the front of the victim, while two others pushed pikes into his back, and in this state (writhing with torture) he was suspended aloft on the pikes till dead. He was then thrown over the bridge into the water. They ripped open the belly of poor Mr Atkins; and, in that condition, he ran several yards... [42]

This 'uncanny' animated corpse was possibly too disturbing a figure to find its way into Cruikshank's illustration (Figure 11). In the reports of the Scullabogue massacre, there are other victims who run the gauntlet of life and death. In a detail which Cruikshank does feature (Figure 10), Musgrave notes that a child who managed to crawl out of the Scullabogue barn was piked and thrown back into flames (1: 528). In the bloody Romantic vignette, such

Figure 11 George Cruikshank, 'Rebel Massacre on Wexford Bridge', W. H. Maxwell, *History of the Irish Rebellion* (1845)

an atrocity is often closely associated with the violation of women, although there was some variance in the early sources here. Musgrave claims that 'The rebels made a constant practice of violating women who came into their hands' (1: 454), whereas Gordon insists that 'Amid all their atrocities the character of the fair sex was respected', unlike the 'opposite behaviour' of royal troops (213–14).[43]

But it was not only as victims that women figured in the 'Saturnalian' cast of the rebellion. As in the French revolution, rebel women were portrayed as Furies and Amazons – the Burkean, demonic antitype of the 'fair sex'. This stereotype conveniently diverted attention away from those radical Irish women (like Mary Joy McCracken) who were active organizers and thinkers, and whose role has been largely hidden from history (to the extent that this book is a study of cultural mythologies rather than a work of history, it is also guilty of this effacement).[44] On Wexford Bridge, the rebel Dixon's wife is described by Charles Jackson as literally stage-managing the 'entertaining spectacle' of the massacres, transforming the bridge into 'a magnificent wooden fabric, ill adapted, from the beauty and gaiety of its appearance, for such hideous exhibitions'. Even this brief cameo captures the carnivalesque sense of an inverted culture, the debasement of 'beauty and gaiety' into 'hideous' violent display. The 'gaiety' of healthy communal social life is replaced by a drunken orgy of violence and the transgression of traditional gender roles. Dixon himself resorts to type, and 'prepared his immediate followers for their bloody work by whiskey' (151). In Musgrave's narrative, 'the mob, consisting more of women than men, expressed their savage joy on the immolation of each of the victims, by loud huzzas' (17). The *Annual Register* reported that

> these barbarities were heightened by the frantic exultation of the women who followed in troops. They kissed and congratulated their fathers, brothers, and husbands; and stimulated them to fresh deeds of blood. (108)

These women are the Maenadic cheerleaders of the Irish rebellion. The detail was not lost on Cruikshank. In his version of the execution of a prisoner on Wexford Bridge (Figure 11), women are shown on either side of the bridge in a state of drunken, abandoned voyeurism.

However, once the rebels were defeated, the bridge did not immediately return to its former glory of 'beauty and gaiety'. Its function as an arena of 'hideous exhibition' was appropriated by government troops. As Jackson notes, this 'melancholy occasion' was the 'reverse' of the earlier spectacle:

> The bridge was the general scene of execution, as it had been of massacre. The head, after death by hanging, separated from the body, which was commonly thrown in the river, as had been the bodies of the massacred protestants, was fixed aloft on the courthouse.[45]

Some victims received a more 'theatrical' treatment. The head of John Kelly, a high-ranking United Irish officer, was used as a football and kicked into the street where his sister lived. She 'had the misfortune to come to the window at one point and was confronted with the spectacle'.[46] The cycle of violence continued, and the bloody vignettes multiplied on both sides.

'The ferocity of civil war': Reprisals

The historian Thomas Bartlett notes that 'in certain areas of the country nothing short of a 'White Terror' had been unleashed in the aftermath of the rebellion'.[47] British commanders in the field would not have disputed this interpretation of the situation. General Sir John Moore noted that 'My wish was to excite terror, and by that means to obtain our end speedily', and General Lake expressed his regret at 'being obliged to order so many men out of the world'.[48] A serving officer reported to *The Times* that in Carlow 'Executions still go on here – both shooting and hanging' (2 June 1798). The report goes on to describe the storming of the town of Ballytore, near Carlow: 'It having appeared that the greater part of the inhabitants had assisted the rebels, the military burnt the town, with the exception of a few houses belonging to well-disposed people'. That final detail 'well-disposed' is a nice conflation of political and class affiliation, and another example of the plebeianizing of the rebellion. In another attack on Carlow, according to an eyewitness named William Farrell, loyal troops burned down 'cabins' full of 'men, women and children, innocent and guilty, even all burned together in one common mass'. Farrell cites this massacre as a counterweight to Scullabogue:

> here were forty Scullabogues in Carlow and very little said about it from that day to this. Perhaps those people who justly complain of Scullabogue ought to recollect that it was themselves or their party who first set the example.[49]

James Gordon felt obliged to describe some examples of loyalist atrocities, even though his 'natural bias' was towards Protestantism. Gordon relates how soldiers of the Ancient British regiment mutilated the body of Father Michael Murphy after the battle of Arklow: they 'took out his heart, roasted the body, and oiled their boots with the grease which dripped from it!'[50] The loyalist Jonah Barrington was forced to admit that 'during these most sanguinary scenes, the brutal conduct of certain frantic Royalists was at least on a parallel with that of the frantic rebels'.[51] The aftermath of the battle for New Ross was described vividly by a serving loyalist soldier named James Alexander. He recalled seeing 'terrible and disgusting spectacles', including many carcasses reduced to a cinder, some of which were partly reduced to ashes... What infatuated desperadoes! Scarcely any of them, but piously wore scapulars. Mr Wheatly, of the Ross infantry, took off hundreds of them, and shewed them with as much glee as an Israelite in King David's time might be supposed to exhibit as many foreskins of Philistines![52]

Another soldier witnessed a less metaphorical version of this circumcision ritual:

One thing I would particularly notice here, is the *ferocity* of civil war. It has barbarities, not now practised in the national wars of Europe. Among those whom I saw lying dead, numbers had their foreskins cut off. In one spot, where seven had fled to a house, in which they were killed, their bodies had been brought out to the roadside, where they lay, shamefully uncovered, and some of them greatly mangled.[53]

This account was published in 1819, the year of the Peterloo massacre. It may not have taken too huge a leap of the imagination to see a parallel between the two events, though the 'barbarities' in Ireland were much more extreme. One of the worst atrocities which the soldier recalled was the hanging of a rebel in the town of Gorey:

The man was scarcely suspended, when the officer of the party fired the contents of two pistols into the body, and then drew his sword and ran into it. I then turned from the sight with disgust; but those of my comrades who staid told me, that the body was lowered down from the tree, upon the road; that the soldiers of the party perforated it with their bayonets, cut off the head, cut it in pieces, and threw them about, tossing them in the air, calling out, "Who will have this?" They then dug a hole on the opposite side of the road, and buried the body and the mangled pieces of the head, in the presence of a few of the unhappy man's friends. (18)[54]

The crucial rhetorical factor here is not the gruesome detail but the fact that the soldier-narrator 'turned from the sight with disgust'. In order to register the full horror of spectacular violence, the narrator is pushed to the limit of what can be personally witnessed. With this guarantee of basic humanity in place, the scene can be continued at second hand, though there is still a question mark concerning the role of the soldiers who chose to carry on looking – their testimony is invaluable, though the reader may be left wondering why they did not also turn away in disgust. The available points of view for the reader are distributed between the three spectator positions in the scene: the 'disgusted' narrator, the curious (or compelled) soldiers, and the 'unhappy friends' of the victim.

'Croppies lie down': From reportage to poetry

An example of the speed with which the sectarian interpretation of the rebellion passed into literature is a little-known poem with a revealing title: *Ierne: An Elegy; Lamenting the Horrors of the Rebellion in Ireland, As Particularly Exemplified by the Massacre of the Amiable Miss Clifford, Residing in the House of the Rev. Mr Haydon, in the County of Wexford, Together with Himself and His Whole Family, In Consequence of Her Singing 'Croppies, Lie Down'*, published in 1798.[55] I have cited the full title as it seems to express its political and moral outrage in the fact that the 'amiable' heroine has been killed for the seemingly insignificant offence of singing a song. As cited in a footnote, the poem was based on an incident which appeared in 'several News-Papers of the day' (5). In *The Times*, 2 June 1798, a letter from a British officer serving in Carlow describes the murder of a clergyman and his daughter. Her 'beauty' and 'virtue' make her 'the admiration of the country', but her fate is sealed when, one evening after dinner, she sings the loyalist song 'Croppies Lie Down'. Her song is overheard by one of the servants, and the next day the family is massacred. The servant plunges a pike into the 'beautiful bosom' of Miss Clifford, exclaiming: 'There you d-d wh-e, take that for your Croppy lie down'. To cap the atrocity, 'four infants were not spared, but tossed in hellish sport on the point of spikes'. What *The Times* did not report was the fact that 'Croppies Lie Down' was a loyalist soldier's song which stereotyped the Irish rebels ('croppies') as cowardly and barbaric. The song's refrain is a thinly veiled euphemism for the killing of rebels. Whether wittingly or not, the clergyman's daughter was participating in the rebellion's propaganda wars, and for her servant, we can surmise, this made her exactly the kind of target imagined in the song:

> The rebels so bold, when they've none to oppose,
> To houses and haystacks are terrible foes;
> They murder poor parsons and likewise their wives,
> At the sight of a soldier they run for their lives;
> Whenever we march over country and town
> In ditches and cellars the croppies lie down.
> Down, down, croppies lie down.

> While thus in this war so unmanly they wage
> On women, dear women, they turn their damn'd rage;
> We'll fly to protect the dear creatures from harm,
> They'll be sure to find safety when clasped in our arms;
> On love in a soldier no maiden will frown,
> But bless the brave troops that made croppies lie down.
> Down, down, croppies lie down.[56]

In the erotics of this encounter, in which the woman's body is the prize, loyalist chivalry is the redemptive answer to the 'unmanly' rebel violence which substitutes pikes for vigorous sexuality ('On love in a soldier no maiden will frown'). In the poem, the political significance of the real-life heroine's body is augmented by two further factors: her close association with Anglicanism, the loyal religion of the State (contrast the Dissenting Presbyterianism and the Catholicism of the United Irishmen); and the implicit comparison to Marie-Antoinette facing an 'infernal Robespierrian sect' (4). There is even a suggestion of Jacobin vampirism: "Tis monstrous lips alone could savage suck / The virgin blood . . . virtuous, fair.' (7). A footnote to these lines stresses their realism:

Lest this picture should seem exaggerated, instance only the Deposition stating the rebel spearmen licking their bloody spears! And one aged man literally torn limb from limb, and his scattered remains not only refused internment, but, horrid! actually thrown to the Pigs!!! (Ibid.)

The footnote is clear evidence that literary texts struggled to reflect the sensational 'deposition' of violence in the print culture. In the wake of this awkward attempt to bridge the gap between catastrophic historical reality and the decorum of poetry, the text proffers a sentimental resolution in the figure of General Cornwallis. As the hero of both America and India, he personifies patriotic and patriarchal virtues. He is 'the state chirurgeon' with a godlike power 'to conciliate or coerce' (15–16). The epitome of 'manly' English authority and responsible power, he resolves the political and sexual tensions in the poem and heals the body politic after it has been 'torn limb from limb'.

Two other aspects of this poem are worth pursuing. The first concerns the significance of the epithet 'amiable' (the 'amiable Miss Clifford') in eighteenth-century theories of the pleasures of sublime violence. In a 1775 essay entitled 'An Enquiry into those kinds of Distress which excite Disagreeable Sensations', John and Anna Laetitia Aikin (later Anna Barbauld) argued that 'no scenes of misery ought to be exhibited which are not connected with the display of some moral excellence or agreeable quality', otherwise 'the mind is rather stunned than softened by great calamities'.[57] In order to illustrate this point, a comparison is made between the suffering of an American Indian and a polite woman:

We are less moved at the description of an Indian tortured with all the dreadful ingenuity of that savage people, than with the fatal mistake of a lover in the Spectator, who pierced an artery in the arm of his mistress as he was letting her blood. (199)

The racial stereotyping lying behind this juxtaposition becomes clear in the next point: 'nothing, therefore, must be admitted which destroys the grace and dignity of suffering; the imagination must have an amiable figure to dwell upon' (200–1). In Bakhtinian terms, it is 'classical' beauty which guarantees the moral success of a scene of 'distress'. The Irish peasant, like the savage Indian, is excluded from this 'amiable' aesthetic.

One further aspect of the poem's construction of 'amiable' female distress is worth attention: the relationship between the genteel woman and the servant. In a comment on the character of Thady in Maria Edgeworth's novel *Castle Rackrent*, Terry Eagleton notes,

> In the revolutionary 1790s, previously trusted family retainers suddenly revealed their hostility to their masters, and this was particularly unnerving for genteel women, dependent as they were on socializing with their servants.[58]

Like the rebellious slave, the murderous servant was the epitome of ingratitude, disloyalty and recalcitrance. The triangular relationship between master, daughter and servant was a model of European imperial rule, an echo of the Prospero–Miranda–Ariel configuration in *The Tempest*. The servant was also crucial for the success of the social aspirations of the middle class and the creation of women's 'special sphere' of domestic virtue and elevated leisure. Taking these additional factors into account, it is possible that the most 'amiable' figure in the poem is not the heroine but the magisterial Cornwallis, who puts the pieces of this aesthetic and political structure back together.

The national tale and the 'novel of insurgency'

According to Ina Ferris, it was not until the 1820s that the Irish novel engaged directly and substantially with the theme of the Irish rebellion. Before the appearance of the 'novel of insurgency' in that decade, there was a huge disparity between literature and the wider print culture. In the latter domain, the rebellion was 'by no means discursively invisible', but the 'flurry of memoirs, ballads, analyses, and other texts' made little direct impact on fiction, where the theme remained a 'troubling undercurrent' (135). The emergence of the 'national tale' – a hybrid genre existing on the borders of romance, the sentimental novel, the Gothic novel and the historical novel – gave novelists such as Sydney Owenson (Lady Morgan) and Maria Edgeworth the opportunity to explore the vexed issues of Irish national identity and culture. But it was in Edgeworth's *Ennui* that the 'troubling undercurrent' of the Irish rebellion was first heard and felt. The marginalization of the Irish rebellion within Romantic studies has tended to give the impression that Edgeworth's novel was unique in taking up the theme of the rebellion. One of the aims of this section of the chapter is to correct that bias and, following on from Ferris's work, to give a more prominent place to the 'novel of insurgency'.

'Sans culottes of Ireland': Maria Edgeworth, *Ennui* (1809)

Maria Edgeworth was well qualified to write a novel about the Irish rebellion. She and her father were caught up in the second phase of the insurrection and only narrowly escaped with their lives. Richard Lovell Edgeworth was in no doubt about the catastrophic scale of the events unfolding around him:

> the sans culottes of Ireland are immured to blood and murder . . . an insurrection of such people who have been much oppressed must be infinitely more horrid than any thing that has happened in France.[59]

In the summer of 1798, the Edgeworths were forced to evacuate their home in Edgeworthstown and flee to Longford to avoid the advancing French and Irish forces. Ironically, on arrival in the town, Maria's father was suspected of rebel sympathies, and he was almost lynched by a loyalist mob.[60] 'Because my father was not an Orangeman, they concluded he must be a rebel . . . No French mob was ever more sanguinary in their dispositions' wrote Maria to a friend.[61]

Maria drew on this traumatic encounter with rough justice in her novel *Ennui*, written in 1804 (just one year after Robert Emmett's failed uprising in Dublin) and published by Joseph Johnson in 1809. The action of the novel, which follows the fortunes of a devitalized English owner of an Irish estate, is set during the period of the rebellion. For defending a Catholic tenant against loyalist violence, the hero Glenthorn is suspected of being a 'trimmer *or* a traitor' (247). Like Edgeworth's father during the 'horrors of Longford',[62] Glenthorn is almost lynched by a mob, but later the same tenant (the blacksmith Christy, who is actually Glenthorn's step-brother and the true heir) shows his gratitude by informing Glenthorn about a rebel plot, led by the servant Kelly, to capture or kill him. In Wolfe Tone's terms, the rebellion figures in the novel more as 'private assassination' than 'open war'. Glenthorn's easy victory over this conspiracy means that the novel can avoid bloody conflict: in the narrator Glenthorn's words, 'I am sorry I have no bloody battle for the entertainment of such of my readers as like horrors' (268). As Marilyn Butler has noted, this squeamish representation of the rebellion is historically 'fantastical', but was probably intended to appeal to a post-Union, cosmopolitan readership. By constructing the rebellion, in Butler's words, 'thinly', the novel provides an appropriate distance from Ireland's 'bloody' recent past.[63] However, when placed in the tradition of spectacular violence, and in the light of the reportage examined in the first part of this chapter, it is possible to do some further probing of the novel's historical and political reticence.

The first point to note is that in order to rescue his reputation with his gentry peers, Glenthorn enlists as a soldier. Though we are told only of his 'indefatigable exertions in the field' (247), the reference is a window onto a whole historical panorama of violent 'exertion'. The novel does not enlighten us further, but the reference is a tantalizing invitation to speculate about Glenthorn's 'indefatigable' role in the rebellion's 'bloody battles'. Glenthorn presents his silence about the rebellion as a principled resistance to sensationalism, but the other motivating factor may be embarrassment or guilt about his precise participation in unspeakable 'horrors'.

A second revealing lacuna emerges from Glenthorn's role as a magistrate. Shortly before he is disinherited, Glenthorn's last public act is to examine the conspirators. The issue of their guilt is, however, a source of considerable textual ambivalence. Although all the men are clearly legally guilty, the consequence of this is too terrible or embarrassing for the narrative to acknowledge. Glenthorn claims that he has only a 'confused recollection' of their fate:

> The men were, I believe, all committed to gaol, and Joe Kelly turned king's evidence... as to any further particulars, I know no more than if I had been in a dream. (273)

The men's fate dissolves into the narrator's barely credible amnesia, and again leaves open the question of precisely what he (and by extension, the novel) is 'committed' to. There are major unresolved literary and ideological tensions in those two crucial qualifiers 'I believe... in a dream'. As Freud showed, a dream is a mode of revelation, 'one of the *detours by which repression can be evaded*'.[64] The novel's attempt to repress history is only partially successful. Tom Dunne argues that the 'confusions and narrative breakdowns' in the novel result from the inability of Irish culture to come to terms with 'the reverberating nightmare and horror of 1798'. Similarly, Brian Hollingworth observes that the 'narrative inconsistencies' in the text betray 'Edgeworth's discomfort with the contrived answers which she is providing to her own uncertainties' about the 'the years immediately following the rebellion'.[65] Narrative 'breakdowns' are highly symptomatic, and can reveal as much as they conceal. The evasiveness of *Ennui* collapses historical trauma into romanticized, allegorical personal crisis. The truth about Glenthorn's birth emerges when his true mother, the nurse Ellinor, pleads for the life of her son Ody, who is one of the prisoners. Momentarily, it is possible that Glenthorn will have to 'commit' his own brother, but the situation is redeemed when Ellinor realizes that she has made a mistake, and Ody is not a prisoner after all. The shock of her revelation, which 'engrossed all my powers of attention' (273), is given as the reason why Glenthorn cannot remember what happened to the prisoners, but this is unconvincing – indeed, the device functions like a self-conscious goad to the reader to also lose their 'powers of attention'. Nor is the plot device of the changeling a persuasive nationalist allegory for removing British 'powers' in Ireland. Glenthorn's disinheritance is a poor substitute for the 'dream' of an Irish republic; the 'magical realism' of the dénouement is a comic burlesque of nationalism, as the new, rightful owners are feckless, extravagant, inept and vulgar.[66] Glenthorn Castle burns down, and Christy offers Glenthorn his old job back. The 'dream' of a nationalist Ireland lies, literally, in ruins.

'Like Emmet's insurrection': Charles Maturin, *The Milesian Chief* (1812)

Ruins are also a significant presence in Charles Maturin's heavily Gothicized version of the rebellion, *The Milesian Chief* (1812).[67] This novel has few pretensions to historical verisimilitude. It is an unabashed anti-nationalist fable which tells the story of a fictionalized rebellion led by the disinherited Connal, a Byronic figure who lives in the ruins of his family's ancestral castle. The novel's overblown Gothic flourishes have prompted Terry Eagleton to dismiss the text as a 'lurid parody' of the national tale, but this is too harsh, and the novel is worth serious if brief consideration.[68]

Connal is a reluctant rebel leader. He inherited from his grandfather 'the frantic idea of wresting Ireland from the English hand' (3: 49), but once his 'brain cooled' he realized that 'it was impossible for Ireland to subsist as an independent country' (3: 52). The novel is historically vague: the rebellion which Connal leads 'seemed like Emmet's insurrection, the isolated and hopeless attempt of a single enthusiast' (2: 143).[69] Connal is given some Satanic grandeur but the tone waivers on the brink of mock-epic derision: he is described at one point as 'proudly eminent' over 'the fallen host of inferior spirits, awed by his strength, dazzled by his brightness, lost by his example' (2: 202). However, there is no vagueness or ambiguity concerning the horrors of the violence which the civil war unleashes. After a hard-won victory, Connal manages to prevent his troops committing atrocities (3: 14), but later his men deteriorate into 'a rabble mad for rapine' (4: 48). One young captured officer (who turns out to be Connal's brother Desmond) is pursued by

> thirteen or fourteen rebels, like wolves after their prey, pursuing him with pikes and scythes, not so much to kill as to mangle and tear. (4: 51)

On the eve of the final battle, Connal reflects grimly on the carnage he has witnessed, and admits that the price of rebellion is too high. He has seen soldiers 'so gashed and mangled, that of humanity not even the form remained' (4: 79). Connal's musings reinforce the idea that the conflict in Ireland is pre-modern, regressive and recidivist, 'so totally unlike to modern war' that it 'seemed like the contest of two savage nations' in which the poorly armed rebels rely on their 'wildness' to inflict significant losses on the more disciplined army of the government (4: 86). Ina Ferris has argued that this depiction of war as 'brutal inhuman effects' has the effect of 'puncturing the idealizing moves of nationalist myth-making'.[70] This is a fair point, though this 'puncturing' of violent rebellion was not restricted to Maturin. It was also in 1812 that Shelley went to Dublin and proselytized for Catholic emancipation and repeal of the Union, stressing in almost every paragraph that violence would be futile: 'out of the frying-pan into the fire . . . it is the heart that glows and not the cheek'.[71] It is also worth adding that Maturin's 'brutal' construction of an Irish revolution adds nothing to the dominant anti-nationalist 'myth-making' which constructed the 1798 rebellion as a sectarian, 'Saturnalian' throwback.

A more original comment on the rebellion emerges from the novel's conclusion. All the main characters meet 'brutal' ends: Connal and his brother are shot, and Connal's lover Armida poisons herself while grasping his corpse (another 'uncanny' tableau). Moreover, there is no reassuring, concluding imagery of post-Union progress; this contrasts with the ending of *Ennui,* in which Glenthorn Castle is being rebuilt for its reinstated owner. According to Katie Trumpener, *The Milesian Chief's* pessimistic portrayal of 'the violence of history' differs from the dialectical narrative method of the historical novel (typified by Scott's *Waverley*), in which history has 'a retro-active meaning, purpose, and alibi'.[72] These are suggestive comments: the national tale's failure to engage fully and realistically with the processes of history can be seen as a weakness which is corrected by its successor genre, the historical novel; on the other hand, the refusal to subscribe to a notion of Whiggish historical progress can be interpreted as a form of subversion or resistance, an aesthetics of absence. As Terry Eagleton argues, the trauma of the Irish rebellion left nineteenth-century Irish writers in a dilemma. Irish history was 'larger than life' and demanded attention, but it was also an 'imminently overwhelming history' which had fractured Irish consciousness and culture so profoundly that novelistic realism – the literary ideology of a confident bourgeois class – struggled to establish itself. In particular, notes Eagleton, any realistic representation of Ireland which suggested that Irish culture was degenerate or backward could be viewed as 'unpatriotic'. Hence, Irish writing of the Romantic period is more renowned for the emergence of a non-realist sub-genre, the 'Protestant Gothic' (the best example of which is Maturin's *Melmoth the Wanderer*), than it is for literary realism.[73]

Appropriately, the next two texts to be considered are from the next stage of literary development which followed the national tale. Both are historical novels: Banim's *The Croppy* and Scott's *Old Mortality*. In the light of the comments by Eagleton and Trumpener, the focus of the discussion will be on the ways in which these novels negotiate 'violent history' in order to find 'meaning' and 'purpose'.

'National carnage': Michael Banim, *The Croppy* (1828)[74]

Michael Banim's *The Croppy: A Tale of 1798* is an innovative novel: the 'first attempt at a fullscale historical novel on the Wexford rebellion' by the 'first Irish national-popular novelist'.[75] It was published just one year before Catholic Emancipation, and the climate of mass political agitation generated by Daniel O'Connell's Catholic Association may have prompted Banim to revive the spectacular violence of the rebellion as a reminder of the dangers of blocking reform.[76] He could also draw on the recent memory of the 'Rockite' disturbances of the early 1820s. Seen in this way, the novel's violent means justified its pacific ends. Banim himself declared that his aim was to promote 'a good and affectionate feeling between England and Ireland'.[77] In W. J. McCormack's words, this required Banim to 'to trim the material' of his novel 'so as to smooth the excited temper of the times'.[78] But it remains to be seen whether the novel's construction of the rebellion conforms so neatly to this agenda of 'affectionate', reconciliatory and pragmatic political sentiments.

From the outset, it is clear that the rebellion is defined by its excessive violence: in Wolfe Tone's words, 'atrocities committed on both sides'. Before the narrative begins, the novel's Dedication refers to the 'recent results of misrule'. Taking a lead from Scott, the first chapter is given over entirely to the rebellion's historical background. We are told that the 1798 'conspiracy' existed 'amongst Irishmen of every rank and sect' (1: 1). The origins of the 'conspiracy' are traced back to the Irish Volunteers of the 1780s, the first modern 'national band' led by 'reflecting citizens, as well as chivalrous soldiers' (1: 3). This is clearly Banim's ideal of an enlightened nationalist movement; the key word, as will become clear, is 'reflecting'. The United Irishmen are the 'last of the Volunteers', a group of 'reasoning men' who foster a 'philosophical feeling of brotherhood' (1: 11). But this elevated leadership has not been maintained. To begin with, 'their inferiors' in the rural south are busy 'cutting each other's throats' in response to the government's terror tactics (1: 18–19). The Catholic peasant's 'delusion' that all Protestants are Orangemen is blamed in part on the propaganda efforts of United Irish 'emissaries', and on the Irish peasant's sectarian desire for revenge 'without time being afforded him to reflect' (1: 23). The emphasis on lack of 'reflection' is revealing – as Jon Mee has shown, this type of irrational collective behaviour was regarded in the Romantic period as a hallmark of political extremism and 'enthusiasm'.[79] Banim also condemns the United Irish alliance with the Defenders. The United Irish 'found it convenient to make the parish Defender a national revolutionist', despite the fact that a Defender was 'but too well prepared, by the examples he had been set, to brutalize the name even of civil war' (1: 20). But the Orangemen are also culpable: they represent a 'covenant . . . to exterminate Catholics all over Ireland' (ibid.).

All the sides in the conflict are apportioned some of the blame for the resulting carnage. This critique is reminiscent of what Lukacs identified as the 'epic' balance of Scott's historical novels. It also resembles the views of the contemporary revisionist Irish historian Tom Dunne, who places spectacular violence at the centre of the rebellion, and gives the United Irishmen their share of the blame for the rebel atrocities.

Also like Scott, Banim weaves together historical events with a romantic plot. In *The Croppy*, the main characters revolve around a love triangle which features Eliza Hartley, her villainous, bigamous fiancé Sir William, and her ex-lover Talbot. Eliza's father Sir Thomas Hartley is a benevolent landowner who belonged to the United Irishmen until the organization was proscribed in 1794. Sir Thomas is determined not to take sides, but the cataclysmic forces of history make it impossible for a man of his stature, influence and background to remain on the sidelines. The year 1798 is a 'baleful year' of 'such scenes of convulsion, of carnage, and of horror, as, to this day, leave a shuddering recollection amongst the inhabitants of our country' (1: 123). Banim reinforces the stereotypes of anti-nationalist reportage in his description of rebel peasants who 'brought into the field the darkest religious prejudice', and who 'could not enlighten themselves... with an account of why they hated' (1: 156). But he also insists on the savagery of loyalist Terror, citing General Abercrombie's denunciation of a 'licentious and disorderly' militia. These troops have a 'half-bandit feeling of duty' (1: 159), and will not flinch at killing 'at the lonely road-side' (1: 165). At this stage in the novel, the only question is the extent to which Banim will follow up this preparatory exegesis with scenes of spectacular violence: the reader is not disappointed. The power of these scenes, as we shall see, derives not only from their content, but from the foregrounding and thematization of the gaze of Terror. The reason for Sir Thomas's refusal to join the rebels is that he is already haunted by imagined 'pictures' of their violence. In his eyes, the rebellion is 'stalking, even to the shrine of Freedom, through national carnage, ruin, and demoralization'; it is an 'impure fire' of patriotism (1: 274–5). He has no doubt that the 'lower orders' will commit 'the most atrocious as well as the most superfluous outrages', and he confesses that 'the frightful picture of their common barbarities is ever before my eyes, searing me from all participation in your cause' (1: 276).

In fact the first of the novel's set-piece 'barbarities' is a loyalist attack on a rebel village. In the build-up to this incident, the novel introduces Captain Whaley, a fanatical and ruthless Orangemen. He is a magistrate and yeoman cavalry commander who believes that 'croppies' should be 'bled into loyalty' (2: 97). Whaley's inhumanity is symptomatic of the deteriorating national situation and the 'results of misrule'. The novel states that the arrest of the United Irish leaders in March 1798 could have been followed by 'wise measures of conciliation' (2: 37). But the government preferred the imposition of martial law and the provocative tactics of Terror, symbolized by pitch-capping or 'scalping' (the reference to Indian violence is intentional). Banim's condemnation of this violence takes the form of a direct appeal to his English readers' consciences: he exhorts 'free and proud Englishmen!' to remember that 'bodily torture' is a throwback to 'Despotism's most darling mode of coercion' (2: 37–9).[80] Whaley's 'darling' sidekick is Saunders, a cowardly sadist who knows 'the sore spot between the shoulders' (2: 98). After a tip-off from an informer called Nale, Whaley the 'Orange blood-hound' (2: 131) leads a raid on a village. The foregrounding of the sense of spectacle has an almost cinematic quality. The villager Shawn-a-Gaw has a 'distended eye' (2: 141) as he watches his cottage razed to the ground. Saunders flogs a man 'with much ostentation' (2: 142). In graphic silhou-ette, another group of soldiers 'challenged the eye' as they strangle a boy in order to extract information (2: 142–3). At this point in the slaughter Sir Thomas Hartley arrives on the scene and the narrative adopts his point of view. Seen through Hartley's outraged sensibility, Saunders's victim has an expression 'such as humanity would weep at'. On purely humanitarian grounds Sir Thomas, whose heart is 'sickened' by the sight, instinctively tries to intervene, but he is rebuffed. He then attempts to implore Whaley to stop the killing, only to find that Whaley is conducting the torture of the boy, 'a scene of surpassing horror'. Examining 'the lad's spasmed features', Whaley remarks that 'these Croppies have the lives of cats'. Sir Thomas's plea to Whaley crystallizes the liberal objection to Terror: 'is it by such acts as these that you hope to bring back the wretched people to a sense of their duty?' (2: 145–8). Whaley's determination to kill the croppy boy, despite the entreaties of his mother and Sir Thomas, is only foiled by a false report from another prisoner that the rebel army is about to attack. After witnessing this atrocity, Sir Thomas is dragged inexorably into the conflict. The rebels try to claim him as a leader, and although he refuses the offer he is subsequently arrested and tried for treason. The narrative focus then switches to rebel violence, but again this violence is constructed through the eyes of several characters.

The most significant of these characters is Father Rourke, a rebel priest and commander who is almost certainly based on the Boolavogue 'priest and patriot' Father John Murphy.[81] As has been shown, the reportage of the rebellion usually portrayed such figures as fanatics, but Rourke is more complex and rounded than this. His nature is humane, but he is resigned to the grim, cyclical logic of the conflict. He notes that even if the Orange oath of extermination is a myth, 'Orangemen act as if it were true'. He cannot see that the peasantry has much room for manoeuvre: the alternative to resistance is to 'stay at home, to be flogged like a negro, or strung up by the blaze of his own cabin'. For Rourke, most of the fighting is a series of 'tit for tat' reprisals. Like Bagenal Harvey and other real-life United Irish leaders, Rourke tries to prevent rebel excesses, but this is difficult in a climate where loyalists are shooting 'every straggler, wearing a peasant's coat' (2: 244–5).

Rourke's 'realistic' point of view is similar to that of the novel. For example, the narrator intervenes to correct one rebel's 'greatly exaggerated' report of a victory over the 'murtherers' of 'Ould Ireland' (2: 128), but another report of the shooting of 25 peasants at Cullen is not disputed (2: 129). It is significant that the novel ends with a chilling vignette of Rourke's execution on Wexford Bridge (3: 318). The fact that 'the weight of his colossal body' breaks the rope is surely a powerful symbolic moment: his corpse represents the huge potential and lost hopes of the rebellion. The scene is followed by a brief coda which points out that the 'promises' of the Union 'have not yet been conceded', despite the rebels of 1798 being 'goaded to the field' (3: 316). The rebellion was a 'colossal' price to pay for deferred reforms.

Most of the rebel violence is viewed through the eyes of the disreputable Sir William, who spends much of his time frantically searching for his wife. Unlike Rourke, Sir William is apolitical, unprincipled and self-serving. This opens up the possibility that the depiction of rebel atrocities at Enniscorthy, Vinegar Hill and Wexford are coloured by his heightened emotions. This argument cannot be pushed too far, but it is a factor which has been ignored by critics. Ferris calls these scenes 'compelling if lurid', but 'lurid' barely does justice to the ways in which the novel interacts with the tradition of spectacular violence.[82] The 'lurid' scenes of mob rule and mob violence conform to a very familiar pattern. At Enniscorthy there is a 'general licentiousness' (2: 260) and 'unbridled rioting' (2: 261). The 'ferocious visitors' are shown 'trampling indifferently the heaped bodies of comrades and foes' as they 'plunder the abandoned houses, and pour into their parched throats whatever liquor they could seize upon'. They show no mercy as 'they dragged their trembling wretches from their places of concealment, to be piked in the streets, already too deeply stained with blood' (2: 259). As Cruikshank appreciated, the pike was the distinctive and emblematic rebel weapon (village forges were often prime sites of government raids). In the novel, the pike signifies the brutality and backwardness of the rebels' culture of violence. Pikes are 'rude weapons' designed to inflict 'cruel slaughter' (2: 21). They are 'fit instruments' of 'civil strife' where 'chivalrous feelings, as well as chivalrous display, seldom find a place' (2: 253). However, not all the mob violence is unchivalrous. At Wexford, a town full of terrified female refugees who have 'rushed, unconsciously, through flame, and shot, and shout, and groan' (2: 282), we are reassured that no 'female honour was outraged' (3: 6).

The devastating aftermath of the battle for Enniscorthy is a particularly powerful moment. The scene is a travesty of the neo-classical tradition of the topographical 'prospect'. Instead of conveying visual pleasure and social harmony to the eye, the landscape evokes a 'fearful' and 'general horror'. In cinematic terms, the panorama gives way to close-ups of individual distress and depravity. The heaps of bodies are a macabre comment on the shattered ideals of the United Irish republican brotherhood. At the centre of the carnage is the 'wild figure' of the Croppy, the reincarnation of sans-culotte recidivism:

Masses of dead or motionless bodies, choking, along with black thatch and broken furniture, the narrow streets, were fearfully indicated to the eye, a few wild figures only stalking through them; – and if the spectator, curious to analyse the general horror, but descended the hill-side, he might perceive that the intoxicated Croppy often slept out, amongst these groups of dead, his deep debauch of the previous night; that, in some instances, his unconscious head rested on the corpse of his comrade, and in others was pillowed upon the silent breast of his party opponent – perhaps upon that of the victim of his own particular vengeance; and the figures which had appeared in motion from the hill-top, would now prove to be some moaning woman, who came to turn the face of the slain peasants, searching for the remains of near and dear relatives; while others, with garments tucked round them to avoid the stain of blood, prowled amongst the dead of the other side, only in quest of plunder. (2: 287–8)

The visual effect of this open-air necropolis is like a cross between Gillray, Goya and Cruikshank. This episode also introduces the novel's only full-blown rebel villain, a man called Murtoch Kane. He is a figure of 'inherent malignity' who is 'still remembered' for the 'cold-blooded murders' on the 'rocky hill' outside the town (2: 271). This 'rocky hill', which has connotations of Golgotha, is Vinegar Hill, the site of the windmill massacres. The novel subscribes to the view that this atrocity was the work of disreputable characters like Kane, 'men, demons rather, to be found in all communities, whose natural disposition was murderous', and who wreaked havoc in the absence of United Irish leaders (3: 21). The massacres are witnessed by Sir William, who believes mistakenly that Eliza is being held in the windmill. The scene is carefully composed. The first visual detail is a flag which carries the motto 'Liberty or Death', though the effect of a faint breeze is that only the word 'Death' is visible (3: 27). Beneath this emblem, appropriately, 'the rocks and the burnt grass were reddened, and lifeless bodies, frightfully gashed, lay here and there amongst them' (3: 27). The blasted landscape and dismembered bodies merge into a 'fearful indicator' of death. The mock-trial and execution of the prisoners is reminiscent of the imagery of the September massacres. Shawn-a-Gaw is the principal interrogator, while Murtoch Kane is the main executioner. Gaw dispenses life and death casually; if someone speaks up for a victim they are spared with 'carelessness' (3: 33).

The novel is more reticent about the Scullabogue and Wexford Bridge massacres. The absence of set-piece descriptions of these two incidents challenges the idea that Banim's sole purpose was to completely discredit the rebellion. Scullabogue is only mentioned in a footnote (3: 233–4). It is a 'horrid remembrancer of the times we would illustrate', though Banim does not resolve whether 'the general body of the armed peasants' were to blame, or whether it was an act of 'maddened' vengeance. The curious reader is referred to 'historians or apologists' for further information.[83] Rather than dwell on rebel depravity, Banim is more interested in showing the heroic endeavours and tragic folly of the crucial battle for New Ross. After sustaining huge losses – 'heaps and heaps of their own slain' – the rebels are within sight of a historic victory when they revert to type, 'seized upon whatever liquor they could find' and become a 'powerless rabble', unable to withstand a counter-attack (3: 258–63). As Dunne has shown, the defeat at New Ross was the turning point in the conflict, a classic moment of 'open war'.[84] Banim reinforces anti-Jacobin stereotypes of mob fecklessness to explain poor military tactics, but his extrapolation from this recidivist behaviour is ominous: he notes that, should 'the war-cry be given' again, the Irish people would 'rush at each other's throats' and 'enact scenes' as 'terribly vivid' as any in the book (3: 58–9).

The Croppy is an ambiguously nationalist text. As Dunne has remarked, the novel is a 'vivid, courageous and illuminating' exposé of the 'results of misrule'.[85] It employs the myths and tropes of mindless mob rule, but it places atrocities within the cycle of Terror and counter-Terror. Behind this spectacular violence is the ghost of Wolfe Tone and the lost Utopia of a renewed Ireland. In the words of a United Irish song,

> When th'all glorious work is done...
> Detested wars shall ever cease,
> In kind fraternization,
> All will be harmony and peace,
> And the whole world one nation.[86]

This sentiment lies behind one of the novel's most poignant scenes. As a group of rebels take the oath of the United Irishmen, the narrator intervenes to literally highlight those 'philosophical' passages of the oath which are beyond the comprehension of the new recruits. The particular phrase which is singled out is '*a brotherhood of affection among Irishmen of every religious persuasion*' (2: 29).[87] These italicized words represent the unattainable constitution of a free Ireland: 'a vision of a non-sectarian, democratic and inclusive politics', in the more recent words of Kevin Whelan.[88] The lost 'brotherhood of affection' is the destabilizing discourse behind Banim's stated claim that the purpose of the novel was to foster 'a good and affectionate feeling between England and Ireland' – the competing meanings of national 'affection' represent an irresolvable ideological gulf between liberal and radical readings of the novel's depiction of Irish history. The narrator's textual interpolation is like a futile *deus ex machina*, an attempt to change the course of history by insisting on a correct reading of the point at which human agency commits itself to revolutionary collective action. It is the failure of this higher political and 'philosophical' ideal which explains the rebellion's fatal misreading of revolutionary history, not the innate savagery of the Irish people.

'Gory figures': Walter Scott, *Old Mortality* (1816)

The influence of Walter Scott on Banim's *The Croppy* may have been more than just generic. In the concluding part of this chapter, I want to suggest that we can read Scott's *Old Mortality* as an allegory – or indirect representation – of the Irish rebellion. Although this novel is about the Scottish Covenanter wars of late seventeenth century, it dwells extensively on atrocities committed by both the rebel 'enthusiasts', personified by Balfour Burley, and the regime of state Terror, personified by Claverhouse. As John Sutherland notes, 'At the heart of *Old Mortality*, then, is not rebellion but war crime...atrocity runs through [the novel] like a crimson thread'. The conflict in the novel, Sutherland continues, is 'entirely ideological', with no 'glamorous nationalism' or chivalry.[89] Sutherland's comments could equally apply to Romantic-period constructions of the Irish rebellion. The *Annual Register*'s characterization of the rebellion as 'illustrating the depths of crime into which religious and political fanaticism may plunge the half civilized and the misguided' (*1798*, iv) would be a fair gloss on the mood of Scott's novel. A similar assessment of the Irish rebellion is made by Musgrave: he notes that it proved 'how far fanaticism can extinguish all religious and moral principle'.[90] In relation to Scott's novel, Robert Maniquis has argued that 'the old language of Terror', the 'prophetic violence' of 'Calvinist fanatics' which is 'spoken by the Scottish rebels...would be read directly through the recent memories of 1793'.[91] But the Irish rebellion was both historically and culturally closer to Scott than the French Terror, so it surprising that neither Maniquis nor Sutherland consider the Irish 'fanatics' war as a closer parallel.[92] In *The Croppy*, for example, the Orangemen make a 'covenant to exterminate Catholics all over Ireland' (1: 20).

But the comparison also fits Scott's 'epic' methodology of showing (in Tone's words) 'atrocities...committed by both sides'. The most chilling moments in the novel are all examples of State Terror. The 'dismal spectacle' of Claverhouse's triumphal entry into Edinburgh is reluctantly witnessed by the wavering hero Morton. This 'ghastly procession' (a phrase which anticipates the 'ghastly masquerade' of Shelley's *The Mask of Anarchy*) has the macabre inventiveness, the 'brutal mockery' and grotesque semiotics of spectacular violence. Morton sees

> two heads borne upon pikes, and before each bloody head were carried the hands of the dismembered sufferers, which were, by the brutal mockery of those who bore them, often approached towards each other as in the attitude of exhortation or prayer.[93]

Even worse is to come. Behind these 'bloody trophies' are 'the heads of others who had fallen . . . some on pikes and halberds, some in sacks, bearing the names of the slaughtered persons labelled on the outside' (387). To his horror, Morton recognizes some of these names. He also witnesses first-hand the interrogation and torture of a recalcitrant Covenanter. This Gothic display of power is highly stylised:

> A dark crimson curtain, which covered a sort of niche, or Gothic recess in the wall, rose at the signal, and displayed the public executioner, a tall, grim, and hideous man, having an oaken table before him, on which lay thumb-screws, and an iron case, called the Scottish boot, used in those tyrannical days to torture accused persons. (393)

On refusing to divulge information about Burley, the rebel is then tortured by having his knee crushed with a wedge and mallet. The most chilling aspect of this ritual is the juridical coolness of the tribunal, which includes the attendance of a 'well-dressed' doctor whose role is to 'regulate the torture according to the strength of the patient' (394).[94] Like many feeling spectators of violent spectacle, Morton's 'blood boiled within him at witnessing such cruelty' (394). After eventually fainting, the prisoner is executed within half an hour, his head and hands chopped off, and his body 'disposed of according to the pleasure of the Council' (395). Scott adds a footnote at this point to authenticate the macabre 'wit' or ingenuity of this public humiliation of the rebel body:

> The pleasure of the Council respecting the relics of their victims was often as savage as the rest of their conduct. The heads of the preachers were frequently exposed on pikes between their two hands, the palms displayed in the attitude of prayer. (577–8)

Such moments in the novel seem like classic examples of Scott's Lukacsian radicalism: Scott does not idealize the rebels, but the hypocrisy of State 'savagery' brings out Scott's nationalist instincts. Morton is also shocked to see defeated rebel soldiers being given no quarter by government troops:

> the pursuing dragoons, whose wild shouts and halloo, as they did execution on the groups whom they overtook, mingled with the groans and screams of their victims, rose shrilly up the hill. (366)

Katie Trumpener points out that the perception of an anti-Covenanter bias in the novel provoked fellow Scot John Galt to write a riposte, *Ringhan Gilhaize, or The Covenanters* (1823).[95] However, the novel's main target, and the focus of much of its imaginative energy, is the abuse of State power, and the contradictions between means and ends. If the novel can be interpreted as an allegory of the Irish rebellion, it performs a scathing analysis of double standards regarding the use of 'savage' violence. The key figure here is of course Claverhouse, the flawed representative of modernity and historical progress. Scott was fascinated by Claverhouse: one sign of this is the fact that Claverhouse's portrait had a prominent place in Scott's study.[96] But the admiration was tempered by the knowledge that Claverhouse was a ruthless and zealous agent of English colonial policy. In an attempt to deal with these ambivalent feelings about Claverhouse, Scott devises a brilliantly witty means to embarrass and expose him. After ordering the summary execution of rebel soldiers, Claverhouse makes a flowery speech which argues that all deaths in war are a 'lottery' in the epic quest for fame. As this declamation of 'martial enthusiasm' ends, as if on cue, 'a gory figure, which seemed to rise out of the floor of the apartment, stood upright before him' (378). This spectral apparition is actually Mucklewrath, the most fanatical of the Covenanters, who has been fatally wounded but overlooked by Claverhouse's guards. He lambasts Claverhouse in the elevated, Biblical, 'enthusiastic' language of Protestant Terror, and calls on him to answer 'for this innocent blood' (ibid.). In this comic, theatrical encounter, it is as if Claverhouse has summoned up his diabolical alter-ego, the spectre of guilt and retribution which haunts many scenes of spectacular violence. Lockhart's observation that the novel had 're-animated' the 'stern and solemn enthusiasm' of the Covenanters seems particularly apposite here.[97] The 'gory figure' is sensational, satirical and self-referentially emblematic – the phrase can obviously refer to both a linguistic trope and a physical body. The last word, however, is with the (physically and emotionally) 'unmoved' Claverhouse:

> I must see that my blackguards grind their swords sharper; they used not to do their work so slovenly. – But we have a had a busy day; they are tired, and their blades blunted with their bloody work. (379)

The 'bloody work' of *Old Mortality* exposes, as the *Annual Register* commented in relation to the Irish rebellion, the 'depths of crime into which religious and political fanaticism' can take a nation. But in its stripping and debunking of warfare's idealism and sentimentality, it also shows that the State and its opponents reflect each other's 'gory figures'.

This chapter has tried to show that the shockwaves generated by the rebellion of 1798 were not just felt in Ireland. Despite the Act of Union, the scale and impact of the rebellion's violence produced an unstable faultline in Romantic literary sensibility. It may never be possible (or desirable) to lay Wolfe Tone's ghost to rest, but in the absence of more intensive research into the rebellion, this monumentally 'distressful' event will continue to haunt and harass Romantic studies.

4
American 'Savagery'

...on my American plains I feel the struggling afflictions...
(Urthona to Orc, in William Blake, *America*, 1793)[1]

...the Indians' misfortune has been to come into contact with the most civilized nation in the world, and also, I would add, the greediest, at a time when they are themselves half barbarians, and to find masters in their instructors, having enlightenment and oppression brought to them together.
(Alexis de Tocqueville, *Democracy in America*, 1835)[2]

Sadistic slave-owners, vengeful slaves, megalomaniacal sans-culottes, cannibalistic soldiers, fanatical sectarian peasants – the cast list of the performers of spectacular violence is already extensive but by no means complete. This chapter will look at another prominent player in the grim theatre of bloody Romanticism, the American Indian. However, as the title of the chapter indicates, Indian violence was only one component of bloody conflict in America, and it is essential to place the demonized figure of the 'savage' Indian in this wider geopolitical and cultural context.

Forsaken pantisocracy

In 1794 the young Romantic poets Samuel Taylor Coleridge and Robert Southey, who were students at Cambridge and Oxford respectively, devised a scheme to establish a small socialist community on the banks of the Susquehanna river in Pennsylvania. They named this Utopian community 'Pantisocracy', a Greek word meaning 'equal rule by all'. Coleridge hoped that Pantisocracy and 'aspheterism' (the common ownership of property) would 'make men necessarily virtuous by removing all Motives to Evil – all possible temptations'.[3] He also wrote a sonnet called 'Pantisocracy' to celebrate the scheme:

> No more my visionary soul shall dwell
> On joys that were; no more endure to weigh
> The shame and anguish of the evil day,
> Wisely forgetful! O'er the ocean swell
> Sublime of Hope, I seek the cottag'd dell
> Where Virtue calm with careless step may stray,
> And dancing to the moonlight roundelay,
> The wizard Passions weave an holy spell.
> Eyes that have ach'd with Sorrow! Ye shall weep
> Tears of doubt-mingled joy, like theirs who start
> From Precipices of distemper'd sleep,
> On which the fierce-eyed Fiends their revels keep,
> And see the rising Sun, and feel it dart
> New rays of pleasance trembling to the heart.[4]

The poem is a self-conscious fantasy, a cross between a millennial dream and an idealistic political scheme which will bring personal and collective liberation from Miltonic 'evil days'. America figures as a place of fairy-tale deliverance – 'dancing to the moonlight roundelay'. It is the virtuous antithesis of a clapped-out moral, social and political system which is internalized as 'distemper'd sleep', a mood of Terror and counter-Terror. The symbolic voyage across the Atlantic will render the traveller 'wisely forgetful' of these nightmares of history. America is rebirth, regeneration, the reawakening of sensuous life and sunny republican virtue in a Rousseauesque 'cottag'd dell'. In other words, the poem is an expression of a deeply Romantic love affair with a country steeped in the mythology of Utopianism. Like Cupid's arrow, the poem is itself a 'dart' seeking to pierce the reader's heart. And like many infatuations, the effervescent 'wizard Passions' soon fizzled out – Pantisocracy remained a potent dream.[5]

Consider now, by way of contrast, two of the poems in Coleridge and Wordsworth's landmark collection *Lyrical Ballads*, first published in the autumn of 1798, in the immediate wake of the Irish rebellion (as noted in Chapter 2, it is likely that the rebellion influenced the tone and themes of Wordsworth and Coleridge's writing at this crucial time, in particular the two poems under discussion here). Wordsworth's anti-war poem 'The Female Vagrant' presents a very different picture of America from the Utopia of 'Pantisocracy'.[6] The poem is a ballad narrated by the 'female vagrant' of the title, who tells her life story. She describes how economic hardship in the English countryside propelled her husband into joining the army. When he is sent to fight in the American revolutionary war, she accompanied him, but the experience in America is defined by disillusionment, loss, devastation and carnage. They arrive in the 'western world, a poor, devoted crew' (l. 117), but devotion is no armour against the horrors of war:

> Oh dreadful price of being to resign
> All that is dear *in* being: better far
> In Want's most lonely cave till death to pine,
> Unseen, unheard, unwatched by any star;
> Or, in the streets and walks where proud men are,
> Better our dying bodies to obtrude,
> Than dog-like, wading at the heels of war,
> Protract a cursed existence with the brood
> That lap (their very nourishment) their brother's blood.
>
> The pains and plagues that on our heads came down –
> Disease and famine, agony and fear,
> In wood or wilderness, in camp or town –
> It would thy brain unsettle even to hear.
> All perished; all, in one remorseless year,
> Husband and children! One by one, by sword
> And ravenous plague, all perished. Every tear
> Dried up, despairing, desolate, . . . (ll. 118–33)

Note the generic marker of spectacular violence, the admission that we have reached a limit point of representation: 'It would thy brain unsettle even to hear' (l. 129). Though she survives this carnage and is placed on a British naval ship, the narrator remains haunted by memories of war. The 'late terrific sleeps' (l. 145) of the passage back to Britain are an illusory respite. Like the 'distemper'd sleep' which summed up the repressive condition of British life in Coleridge's 'Pantisocracy', the effect of the trauma is that she is doomed to replay in her memory the horrific scenes which she witnessed (in contemporary parlance, this might be regarded as post-traumatic stress disorder):

> Ah! how unlike those late terrific sleeps!
> And groans, that rage of racking famine spoke,
> Where looks inhuman dwelt on festering heaps!
> The breathing pestilence that rose like smoke!
> The shriek that from the distant battle broke!
> The mine's dire earthquake, and the pallid host
> Driven by the bomb's incessant thunderstroke
> To loathsome vaults where heartsick anguish tossed,
> Hope died, and fear itself in agony was lost!
>
> Yet does that burst of woe congeal my frame,
> When the dark streets appeared to heave and gape,

While like a sea the storming army came,
And Fire from hell reared his gigantic shape,
And Murder, by the ghastly gleam, and Rape
Seized their joint prey – the mother and the child!
But from these crazing thoughts, my brain, escape!
(ll. 145–60)

However, she cannot 'escape' these 'crazing thoughts' – note that the word 'crazing' carries a hint of 'increasing', as well as its core meaning of driving crazy. Her social destiny in England is to become a beggar or 'vagrant', a Romantic outcast who personifies America's vanquished potential:

Three years a wanderer, often have I viewed,
In tears, the sun towards that country tend
Where my poor heart lost all its fortitude . . . (ll. 262–4)

This is a powerfully poignant moment, as the turn towards the west was traditionally a trope of the Utopian potential of America. Note the contrast in the solar imagery in the two poems: in Coleridge's 'Pantisocracy', 'the rising Sun' brought 'New rays of pleasance trembling to the heart'; in the later poem, the sun sets over a land of catastrophic violence and loss in which personal identity is obliterated rather than rediscovered or reinvented. Moreover, the conspicuous romance conventions of the first poem are shattered by the hyperbolic realism of the latter poem. In a footnote to 'The Female Vagrant', Wordsworth claimed that

All that relates to her sufferings as a soldier's wife in America, and her condition of mind during her journey home, were faithfully taken from the report made me by a friend who had been subjected to the same trials and affected in the same way.[7]

The unnamed vagrant joined the ranks of outcasts and wanderers who populate the British countryside in Romantic literature, and who form an alternative social and political geography to the mythic, Burkean culture of 'national contentment' which patriotic, anti-Jacobin propaganda disseminated in the 1790s and beyond.[8]

The other poem in *Lyrical Ballads* which took up a conspicuously American theme (or a displaced Irish theme) is Wordsworth's 'The Complaint of a Forsaken Indian Woman'.[9] Based on the Indian custom of abandoning those who are too sick to keep up with migratory journeys, the poem imagines the final sentiments of a mother who is close to being frozen to death. Wordsworth's introductory comments express a disinterested, anthropological curiosity about this contemporaneous practice of exposure, and there is no obvious suggestion that the poem is an attempt to either condemn or recuperate noble savagery. In a similar vein to anti-slavery texts, the 'forsaken' mother is a mouthpiece of natural sensibility and humanity. She bewails the loss of her child (who has been given to another mother) though she does not criticize her tribe. Compared to 'The Female Vagrant', this damaged and moribund female narrator is not a victim of injustice and violence. Her plight is the consequence of a customary fate which is harsh but not vindictive. The closest that Wordsworth comes to implying that the practice is cruel – and as this chapter will show, cruelty is a key word in this context, as American Indians were stereotyped as being notoriously cruel in their tactics of warfare and in particular their treatment of prisoners of war – is his comment that 'It is unnecessary to add that the females are equally, or still more, exposed to the same fate'.[10] The qualifier 'or still more' grates, as it is a hint that Indian culture is intolerant of female weakness. But if this is criticism, it remains veiled, as if Wordsworth is fully aware that he could so easily open the floodgates of anti-Indian prejudice (note that there is no mention of Indian violence in the depiction of warfare in 'The Female Vagrant'). Wordsworth deflects some of the anxieties raised by the remark by referring the reader to his 'very interesting' source, Samuel Hearne's *A Journey from Prince of Wales's Fort in Hudson's Bay to the Northern Ocean*, published in 1795. Hearne's book was one of the many examples of eighteenth-century travel and exploration writing which exerted a considerable influence over the Romantic imagination.[11] However, the conscientious or enthusiastic reader who consulted Hearne's book would have been confronted with a much more 'savage' picture of Indian customary behaviour than Wordsworth's 'very interesting' citation might suggest. Famously, the book contains a sensational description of a massacre of Innuits by Indians at the Coppermine river in 1771. This incident was regarded by contemporary readers as a centerpiece of Hearne's book, a 'synecdoche' of the whole text, according to I. S. McLaren.[12] If we apply New Historicist methods of displaced contexts to 'The Forsaken Indian Woman', it is possible to argue that the Coppermine massacre is a constitutive ('forsaken') absence in the poem. The invasion of this hyperbolic violence into the poem (a reproduction of the original 'ambush' of the Innuits) places Wordsworth's mildly hostile representation of Indian female distress under considerable interpretive pressure.

Hearne witnessed the slaughter of Innuits by American Indians when he was searching for the mythical north-west passage on behalf of the Hudson's Bay Company. Hearne presents himself as a reluctant observer, a 'neuter in the rear' of his company of explorers and Indians. The Indian attack took place at night, so the Innuit victims rush out of their tents naked and terrified. Typically, the most sensational vignettes involve the killing of women. Most spectacularly, Hearne is brought into collision with the brutal killing of a young female Innuit:

[she was] killed so near me, that when the first spear was stuck into her side she fell down at my feet, and twisted round my legs, so that it was with difficulty that I could disengage myself from her dying grasps.[13]

There could not be a stronger contrast between this death scene and the solitary 'complaint' of Wordsworth's forsaken Indian woman. Hearne's Innuit victim is verbally silent but her physical resistance forces Hearne to literally embrace her death. Her 'dying grasps' (a close correlation of dying 'gasps') claw for meaning. She is 'twisted' round his legs, paralyzing normal motion until the significance of her death is acknowledged. There is also a strong verbal echo of the use of the word 'twisting' in Southey's 'The Sailor who Served in the Slave Trade' (see Chapter 1). The Innuit woman's Indian 'murderers' take full opportunity to goad Hearne with sexual banter, asking him if he 'wanted an Esquimaux wife', even though she is 'twining round their spears like an eel!'. 'Twining' recalls 'twisting', as if again the victim uses her violated body to insinuate meaning into her death. The serpent imagery reinforces the sexual connotations of the assault (though this does not mean that the scene itself is erotic), and there may also be a suggestion of an imminent Ovidian metamorphosis. But supplicant gestures do not deter the Indians, who continue to ogle at women's corpses in a manner it would be 'indecent to describe'. Their next victim is an older woman, whose age does exempt her from sexual humiliation: '[They] aimed at torture, rather than immediate death, as they not only poked out her eyes, but stabbed her in many parts very remote from those which are vital' (*TEE*: 3: 75–6). Hearne's compassionate or sympathetic gaze is supposedly the antithesis of this savagery. A reluctant observer and an enlightened man of feeling, he states that he shed many tears recalling this massacre, though this sentimental response sits awkwardly alongside his remarkably resilient (even hardened) behaviour at the time. Within only hours of the massacre taking place, he has supper with the Indians and resumes his sublime quest, though the reader may find it less easy to abandon (or forsake) the twisted and mangled bodies left behind.

The point of the discussion so far is to introduce the idea that the image of America in the Romantic period was deeply conflicted. This is hardly a new or surprising notion, but the aim of this chapter is to identify spectacular violence as a significant faultline around which various cultural anxieties about American national life and identity were confronted and navigated. After 1783 America was a newly independent country with deep Utopian roots. For many Romantic-period writers and readers on both sides of the Atlantic, America represented ideals of freedom and democracy which were still unobtainable in Britain: 'For empire is no more, and now the lion and wolf shall cease', bellowed William Blake in *America: A Prophecy* (1793). But many of the same writers found it difficult to reconcile the image of America the pristine modern nation founded on tolerance and diversity with the violence of its history, the horrors of the war which emancipated it from Britain, the continuing existence of chattel slavery, and the parlous fate of its indigenous peoples. In Hector Crevecoeur's seminal foundational text *Letters from an American Farmer* (1782),[14] America is constructed as a republican Utopia scarred ignominiously by war and slavery. In order to expose the horrors of slavery, we are presented with the 'shocking spectacle' (178) of a caged slave which Crevecoeur once came across when on his way to visit a planter friend. The slave has been hanging for two days, and he has already been partially consumed by insects and birds. Crevecoeur has one bullet in his rifle, but instead of using it for a mercy killing, he fires it to clear away the 'hideous' birds:

> No sooner were the birds flown than swarms of insects covered the whole body of this unfortunate wretch, eager to feed on his mangled flesh and to drink his blood. I stood motionless, involuntary, contemplating the fate of this Negro in all its dismal latitude. (178)

The attempt to preserve the dignity of the slave body is futile: the birds consume his flesh and blood in a hideous travesty of the Christian Eucharist. In an 'uncouth dialect' the slave then makes an ironic request for water: 'Tanky you, white man; tanky you; puta some poison and give me' (ibid.). The slave's fate symbolizes the poisoned waters of the American dream. He is a 'living spectre', a haunting emblem of political and moral failure. As Crevecoeur 'meditates' on such contradictions in American society, he is led to a Swiftian or even Freudian conclusion:

> We certainly are not that class of beings which we vainly think ourselves to be; man, an animal of prey, seems to have rapine and the love of bloodshed implanted in his heart. (174)

This is a 'dismal' recidivist narrative, which flows in the opposite direction to the onward march of Enlightenment progress and universal benevolence. Indeed, Crevecoeur's idea of history as a primitive cycle of devastation masquerading as progress would not be out of place in the Frankfurt School:

> What little political felicity is to be met with here and there has cost oceans of blood to purchase, as if good was never to be the portion of unhappy man. Republics, kingdoms, monarchies, founded either on fraud or successful violence, increase by pursuing the steps of the same policy until they are destroyed in their turn, either by the influence of their own crimes or by more successful but equally criminal enemies. (176–7)

This is a sweeping and largely rhetorical condemnation of the 'successful violence' of political power, but it establishes a framework for the theme of this chapter. The chapter's title 'American savagery' is deliberately ambiguous, and indicates that 'savage' violence in this period does not emanate solely from its most stereotypical representative and personification, the American 'savage' or indigenous American Indian. Following the example of Burke and Paine, this chapter will interpret spectacular or sublime violence as a fundamental instrument of global terror wielded by colonial and imperial oppressors. In the long historical perspective, indigenous peoples are not the aggressors but the desperate victims of barbaric European domination. For America as a whole (north, central and south), this process of violent subjection began with the Spanish conquest (the so-called 'Black Legend'), a topic discussed in more detail shortly. This period is followed by the introduction of transatlantic chattel slavery (see Chapter 1). In the pre-Romantic era, wars between France and Britain transformed North America into what Fenimore Cooper called a 'bloody arena' of European conflict. And at the beginning of the Romantic period the American revolutionary war produced atrocity propaganda on both sides of the conflict. Within this larger framework of history, this chapter concentrates on two memorable examples of Indian violence which made a significant impact on Romantic period writing and culture. By highlighting these two events, the aim is to consider the ways in which different genres of writing and visual imagery recycled and reworked the tropes and myths of 'savage' violence.

The first incident (though it will figure towards the end of the chapter) is the Fort William Henry massacre of 1757. This took place during the early stages of the Seven Years' War between Britain and France, a conflict in which Britain eventually gained the substantial prize of Canada. After Fort William Henry was surrendered to the French, about 2000 British prisoners of war and their families were attacked by Indians who were under French command. The ambush resulted in 70–100 deaths and the taking of some 600 prisoners.[15] According to Ian K. Steele, the massacre became an instant sensation and remained 'powerful in American folk memory' as it crystallized white settler fears of Indian cruelty, providing a pretext for further measures of pacification.[16] An early report in the *New York Mercury*, for example, described the incident as an attack of 'Indian blood hounds' in which 'the throats of most, if not all the women, were cut, and their bellies ript open, their bowels torn out and thrown upon the faces of their dead and dying bodies'.[17] Over 60 years later, the importance of the massacre in 'American folk memory' can be gauged by the fact that it formed the central incident in Fenimore Cooper's *The Last of the Mohicans* (1826), a seminal early American novel.

The second incident to become a media sensation was the murder of Jane McCrea. This occurred in 1777, during the early stages of the American revolutionary war. McCrea was a young American woman who was engaged to be married to a British officer, but on her way to join him she was attacked and scalped by a band of Indians who were in the pay of the British. That, at least, was the dominant, sentimentalized version of her demise. In fact there were various versions of the murder in circulation which undermined the stereotype of irredeemable Indian depravity. Other accounts included a mix-up between the Indians, and even that she had been shot mistakenly by the Americans.[18] But the incident was a propaganda coup for the Americans, as it exposed British complicity with Indian savagery. As we shall see, the story was headline news on both sides of the Atlantic. It has even been argued by historians that the controversy changed the tide of the war, as it gave the American forces, then at low ebb, 'the strongest possible argument in favour of resistance'.[19] General Burgoyne surrendered at Saratoga on 13 October 1777, less than 3 months after the murder, and when news of the surrender reached London on 3 December, many believed that the war was effectively lost.[20] John Vanderlyn's painting of the McCrea murder (c.1804) soon established itself as the most famous single visual image of Indian cruelty from the Romantic period. As 'one of the first major artworks of the new nation, the painting fueled sexual and racial anxieties and vividly reminded Americans that Indians during the Revolution were "merciless savages"', argues Colin Galloway.[21] The image also featured as a plate for Joel Barlow's 1807 epic poem *The Columbiad* (Figure 12), a text which is discussed at the end of this chapter.

A third incident is also worth mentioning, as it achieved a degree of notoriety among British Romantic authors. In July 1778 a large force of Mohawks led by the loyalist commander Major John Butler killed hundreds of patriot militia and their dependants in the Wyoming Valley. There were immediate rumours that a massacre of civilians had taken place. American outrage led to a major counter-offensive under the command of General John Sullivan. The motto of this expeditionary force was stark: 'Civilization or death to all American savages'.[22] In the popular imagination, however, the Wyoming Valley 'massacre' became another case of Indian cruelty and British connivance. In a lecture delivered in 1795, Coleridge made a sensational allusion to the massacre in order to undermine the war against revolutionary France:

> Universal massacre ensued. The Houses were destroyed: the Corn Fields burnt: and where under the broad Maple trees innocent Children used to play at noontide, there the Drinkers of human Blood, and the Feasters on human Flesh were seen in horrid circles, counting their scalps and anticipating their gains. The English Court bought Scalps at a fixed price![23]

Some years later, Thomas Campbell used the massacre as the basis for his poem *Gertrude of Wyoming* (1809). Though the text is critical of British war policy, it shies away from scenes of spectacular violence.[24] The Wyoming Valley massacre is an important event, but for the purposes of this chapter I have found the other two incidents to be richer sources of literary allusion and generic transformation.

Figure 12 'The Murder of Lucinda', from Joel Barlow, *The Columbiad* (1807)

The aim of this chapter, therefore, is to consider Indian violence as part of a complex configuration of colonial power in which 'savages' are agents, pawns and victims of colonial conflict. As Sartre noted memorably in his Preface to Fanon's *The Wretched of the Earth*, subaltern violence is the 'boomerang' effect of colonial domination: 'it is not *their* violence, it is ours, which turns back on itself'.[25] As we shall see, Edmund Burke and other critics of British war policy in America put forward remarkably similar views.

'The unparalleled sufferings of an innocent and amiable people': Las Casas and Spanish cruelty

Before we turn to the representations of eighteenth-century conflict in America, it is useful to revisit that deep stratum of cultural memory in which America is 'created' out of European violence. As David Hume noted sceptically in his essay 'Of the Original Contract' (1752), the power of most governments has always been based on violence rather than popular consent.[26] The story of the Spanish conquest of the Americas was one of the most glaring examples of this. In De Tocqueville's words, the Spanish had committed 'unparalleled atrocities which brand them with indelible shame'.[27] According to the critic Tzvetan Todorov, the genocidal treatment of indigenous Americans by the Spanish was an unprecedented crime. The period from the end of the fifteenth century, when America was 'discovered' by Columbus, to the middle of the sixteenth century saw 'a population diminution estimated at 70 million human lives. None of the great massacres of the twentieth century can be compared to this hecatomb'. This 'hecatomb' was the consequence of massacre, enslavement and disease. Todorov adds the qualifying remark that 'the Spaniards are not worse than the other colonial powers; it just so happens that they are the people who occupied America at the time, and that no other colonising power has had the opportunity, before or since, to cause the death of so many at once', but this does not absolve the Spanish from having 'invented' the modern massacre. Todorov defines this as a form of 'atheistic murder' which can be distinguished from 'sacrificial' or legal execution. The massacre exceeds any religious, political, legal or social function; it is the exercise of Terror and mastery for its own sake, and it 'heralds the advent of modern times'.[28]

Todorov's primary source, and the figure most responsible for the textual 'invention' of the 'modern' massacre, is Bartolemé Las Casas, the key propagandist of Spanish cruelty in the New World. His *A Short Account of the Destruction of the Indies*, first published in the sixteenth century, and known in England as *Tears of the Indians*,[29] was the classic account of the excesses of the Spanish conquest.[30] Like Cobbett's *The Bloody Buoy*, Las Casas's text (Figure 13) is a quintessential work of spectacular violence, as it is essentially an anti-epic catalogue of atrocities, based allegedly on Las Casas's own eye-witness testimony. Like the standard eighteenth-century anti-slavery

Figure 13 Frontispiece of Bartolemé Las Casas, *Tears of the Indians* (1656)

narrative, Las Casas constructs the American Indians as innocent pastoral victims and noble savages, 'quiet lambs' devoured by Spanish 'Tygers, Wolves and Lions' (3). The sensational repertoire of 'savage' practices recorded by Las Casas established a benchmark for subsequent representations of atrocities. After only eight pages we are presented with a series of vignettes of atrocities committed by Spanish military forces in Hispaniola (8–10). These include ripping open the bellies of pregnant women and 'taking out the Infant to hew it in pieces', or on other occasions the soldiers would 'run both Mother and Infant, being in her belly quite through at one thrust'; laying bets on who could 'with most dexterity either cleave or cut a man in the middle, or who could at one blow soonest cut off his head'; smashing children's heads against rocks and then 'with a strange and cruel derision they would call upon them to swim'; hanging up to 13 natives at the same time before burning them alive, 'blasphemously . . . in honour of our Redeemer and his Apostles'; burning native Lords and Nobles under a 'gentle fire' to 'melt them away by degrees'; hunting runaways with hounds; and instigating a culture of reprisals in which 100 Indians are executed for every Spaniard killed. The base motive is gold, and the principle tactic of rule is Terror, but the Spaniards also become sadistic: 'being delighted with new kinds of torments, [they] daily increased their cruelty and rage' (20). As seen in previous chapters, all these types of cruelty recur in later representations of spectacular violence. So does the figure of the sadistic ruler or master, an archetypal 'tyrant' who re-emerges in the Romantic period as the captain of the slave-ship, the plantation overseer or the Jacobin commander. In Las Casas's text, one of the first appearances of this villain is the governor of Guatemala, who 'encouraged' the Spanish settlers 'in wickednesse' (52–3). For example, after discovering that Indians had dug pits with stakes to trap unwary Spanish soldiers, he ordered Indians to be thrown into one such pit, including 'women big with childe . . . till the pit was full' (48–9). Under his jurisdiction a sick mother hangs herself and her child before she can be captured, but her dead child is still fed to the dogs (63); another Spaniard feeds a live Indian child to his dogs (64). Captive Indians who are being transported by ship are thrown into the sea if provisions on ships become low (an anticipation of the *Zong*). Two-hundred Indian men are castrated and left to bleed to death (107). Communities are rounded up and crammed into buildings which are then burned. Dismemberment (cutting off hands, noses and ears) is used as a form of punishment or simply as a mechanism of Terror (126).

There is a remarkable if depressing similarity between this litany of atrocity and its eighteenth-century equivalent – it is as if Las Casas had written a training manual rather than an exposé of 'kinds of torments'. But there is another aspect of his approach which prefigures later writing: his awareness of the credibility gap and fatigue factor in hyperbolic realism. Las Casas admits that there is a difficulty in representing the scale and horror of the slaughter he has witnessed. He states that although there is 'no language, no art or humane science, that can avail to recite the abominable crimes', he is compelled to present graphic scenes, though each is only 'one of a thousand' (34). He is aware of the danger that he can 'cloy the reader' (42), but he claims that he has a duty to depict the horrors in 'their own lively colours' (131). One striking example of such a 'lively' incident uses the literary device of direct speech to dramatise a conversation between two Spanish soldiers who are hunting runaway slaves. One of the men remarks, *'Give me a quarter of your Indian for my dogs, and tomorrow when I kill one I will pay it you again'* (130). The chilling dehumanization of this casual sadism strives to rhetorically overwhelm any doubts the reader may have about the authenticity of the conversation.

But Las Casas is also, famously and ironically, associated with the introduction of the transatlantic slave trade. In order to protect the American Indians, Las Casas proposed to the Spanish government that it would be more efficient and economical to import African slave labour to the Americas. This astonishing double standard was exposed by Samuel Johnson in an essay published in his journal *The Idler* in 1759, during the Seven Years' War. The essay is a masterly display of ventriloquism, as it is purportedly a speech by an Indian chief who bemoans the spoliation of his native country:

Many years and ages are supposed to have been thus passed in plenty and security; when at last, a new race of men entered our country from the great ocean. They inclosed themselves in habitations of stone, which our ancestors could neither enter by violence, nor destroy by fire. They issued from these fastnesses, sometimes covered like the armadillo with shells, from which the lance rebounded on the striker, and sometimes carried by mighty beasts which had never been seen in our vales or forests, of such strength and swiftness, that flight and opposition were vain alike. Those invaders ranged over the continent, slaughtering in their rage those that resisted, and those that submitted, in their mirth. Of those that remained, some were buried in caverns, and condemned to dig metals for their masters; some were employed in tilling the ground, of which foreign tyrants devour the produce; and when the sword and the mines have destroyed the natives, they supply their place by human beings of another colour, brought from some distant country to perish here under toil and torture.[31]

Though he is not named, most educated readers would identify Las Casas as the strategist behind the establishment of the transatlantic slave trade. As we shall see, those Romantic authors who lionized Las Casas in order to attack colonialism simply left this aspect of his career out of the picture, but the irony of the dual role was not lost on the historian William Robertson. In his influential *The History of America* (1777), he acknowledges Las Casas as the 'avowed patron of the Indians' who succeeded in 'opening the eyes and softening the heart' of the Spanish conquerors. Conversely, Robertson notes that Las Casas revived the trade in human slaves, an 'odious commerce' long banned in Europe. In order to 'save the Americans from the yoke', argues Robertson, Las Casas substituted the new slavery of Africans.[32] In the context of the emerging anti-slavery movement, Robertson's Las Casas was a villain not a hero. He personified the striking hypocrisy and double standards of European imperial power.

However, Robertson's comments did not prevent radical authors celebrating Las Casas's heroic role as the 'avowed patron of the Indians'. In Helen Maria Williams's poem *Peru* (1784), Las Casas is the 'protector of the Indians' who lives up to his reputation not by writing but by chivalrous intervention.[33] As Alan Richardson notes, Williams was so intent on bringing the heroic Las Casas into the story that she defied historical accuracy and gave him the highly contrived function of a deus ex machina.[34] Las Casas is so offended at the sight of a human sacrifice – 'In human blood that hallowed Altar steeps, / Libation dire! while groaning Nature weeps' (ll. 501–2) – that he physically rescues a tortured Peruvian priest. Williams's literary politics are a duplication of Las Casas's radical sensibility: 'the unparalleled sufferings of an innocent and amiable People afford the finest subjects for true pathos' (vii–viii). Following in her hero's footsteps, she pledges her support for nationalist liberation struggles in Chile (94).

Las Casas's 'patronage' of the Indians also features in Richard Brinsley Sheridan's anti-war play *Pizarro; A Tragedy* (1799), though Las Casas is joined by a whole bevy of colonial radicals.[35] Based on Kotzebue's *Die Spanier in Peru* (1796), and first performed in May 1799, the text sold well, reaching sales figures of some 29,000 (a considerable achievement, as the printed text cost 5 shillings).[36] Sheridan may have been influenced not only by Kotzebue but also by the recent tribute paid to Las Casas in Bryan Edwards's *The History, Civil and Commercial, of the British Colonies in the West Indies* (1793). In order to convey the authenticity and power of Las Casas's atrocity scenes, Edwards indulges in typographic histrionics: 'my hand is trembling as I write, and my heart devoutly wishing it could be proved to be false'.[37] Sheridan's approach is less fulsome, as Las Casas is a relatively minor though important character in the play. The celebration of Las Casas is in inverse proportion to the demolition of the reputation of the eponymous Pizarro. Sheridan cleverly puts the most strident criticisms of Pizarro into the mouths of those closest to him: his proto-feminist mistress Elvira, whose determination to speak out against the abuse of power is founded on an analogy between the treatment of slaves and women – the latter are treated 'as playthings or as slaves!' (6); his ex-general Alonzo, the play's genuine hero, who has defected to the Peruvian army out of disgust that Pizarro and his legions have betrayed their original noble ideals – 'lured by the abhorred lust of gold' (41); his secretary Valverde, who calls Pizarro a 'licensed pirate – treating men as brutes, the world as booty' (2); and of course the 'aged Las Casas'. According to Elvira, Las Casas is the only uncorrupted member of Pizarro's ruling council, though Pizarro blames Las Casas's 'canting precepts of humanity' for Alonzo's decision to defect.

The play opens in epic fashion on the eve of the decisive battle for Quito. In the council of war, Las Casas makes a last-ditch, impassioned attempt to find a peaceful settlement, accusing the Spaniards of committing 'foul barbarities which your insatiate avarice has inflicted on this wretched, unoffending race'. He curses their 'homicides', but unable to change their minds, he retreats to the forest to become a hermit (7–10). His mantle is assumed by Elvira, the personification of radical sensibility. When a defiant captive Peruvian is murdered on stage, she embraces the 'martyr'd innocent' and declaims 'Would I could fly these dreadful scenes' (14–15), but unlike Las Casas her options as a kept woman are more limited. It takes a final showdown with Pizarro's ruthlessness to drive her into leaving him (a clever inversion of the conventional trope of the deserted woman). When Alonzo is captured, Elvira pleads for Pizarro to be lenient, but Pizarro's growing inhumanity is evident when he is presented with a captured Peruvian baby: 'What is the imp to me – Bid them toss it into the sea' (71). Once she is free of his control, Elvira becomes an avenging nemesis. Resembling the real-life Charlotte Corday, she even tries to become a female assassin. When she is arrested, she insists that her motive was not 'woman's anger' but political zeal, 'to have rescued millions of innocents from the blood-thirsty tyranny of one' (60). She finally succeeds in killing Pizarro by distracting him in his final combat with Alonzo (the play is not so radical as to deny the audience the satisfaction of a traditional dénouement in which the male hero kills the villain). So Pizarro is supplanted by his benevolent, model colonizer Alonzo, who has helped the Peruvians reach a state of grace: 'by gentleness from error won' (42).

In this fantasy of colonial resistance and reconciliation, the Peruvians are the outright winners: 'Content sits basking on the cheek of Toil' (42–3). The play denies that the Peruvians practised human sacrifice, and gives the noble Peruvian general Rollo the last word on the difference between Inca and Spanish violence:

THEY, by a strange frenzy driven, fight for power, for plunder, and extended rule – WE, for our country, our altars, and our homes. (22)

In the context of the continuing anti-Jacobin repression of the late 1790s, these sentiments are a flagrant radical appropriation of the patriotic language of Burke. However, as we have seen, Burke was a fierce critic of the excessive violence of British colonial policy, and, could he have known, he may have been privately impressed to see his views echoed by a Peruvian rebel.

With this longer historical perspective in mind, it is now necessary to look at the key event which made America an icon of freedom in the Romantic imagination, the revolutionary war of the 1770s and 1780s.

'That barbarous and hellish power': War, propaganda and atrocity

From the moment the first shots were fired in the American revolutionary war (1775–83), it was clear that this was to be a war of violent propaganda.[38] The first British newspaper reports of the fighting at Lexington, in May 1775, focused on atrocities. The pro-American *Public Advertiser*, a daily London newspaper, published the following description of the battle, based on an American source:

> Last Wednesday, the 19th of April, the Troops of his Britannic Majesty commenced hostilities upon the people of the Province, attended with Circumstances of Cruelty not less brutal than what our venerable ancestors received from the vilest Savages of the Wilderness... The savage barbarity exercised upon the bodies of our unfortunate brethren who fell, is almost incredible. Not content with shooting down the unarmed, aged and infirm, they disregarded the cries of the wounded, killing them without mercy, and mangling their bodies in the most horrid manner... not one instance of cruelty, that we have heard of was committed by our victorious Militia.[39]

On the other side, the pro-government paper the *London Gazette* did not publish its 'official version' of the battle until 10 June, and predictably this report reversed the agency of atrocity: 'such was the Cruelty and Barbarity of the Rebels, that they scalped and cut off the Ears of some of the wounded Men who fell into their hands'. In between these two accounts, the radical activist John Horne Tooke was prosecuted for promoting a relief fund for the families of those Americans who, in his words, were being 'inhumanly murdered by the King's troops'. Tooke's advertisement, which appeared in seven newspapers, was the only case of press censorship in Britain directly arising from the war, and earned Tooke a one-year jail sentence in 1777.[40]

Note that so far there has been no mention of Indian violence; it is the generic 'rebels' or 'King's troops' who are scalping and mutilating prisoners. Throughout the war, there were constant reports of non-Indian atrocities. These stories reflected the extremely lethal nature of the conflict. There were approximately 25,000 rebel casualties: this means that about one in eight of all rebel soldiers died – the equivalent of about two million deaths today. A similar number of slaves also perished. Ray Raphael singles out the 'escalating violence' of the war in the southern states for particular attention, 'each atrocity justifying a more brutal response'. One American officer noted that 'the people, by copying the manners of the British, have become perfectly savage'.[41] It was in this theatre of war that one of the most infamous loyalist massacres was perpetrated by Banastre Tarleton, the lover of the British feminist author Mary Robinson. In 1780, at the high point of British conquests in the south, Tarleton's troops massacred prisoners taken from Abraham Buford's regiment. This led to tit-for-tat reprisals under the banner 'remember Buford'. The rebel Moses Hall later recalled one such incident: 'I heard some of our men cry out, "Remember Buford", and the prisoners were immediately hewed to pieces with broadswords'. Although Hall was initially 'unmanned' by this experience, he quickly forgot his 'distressful feelings for the slaughter of the Tories, and I desired nothing so much as the opportunity of participating in their destruction'.[42] The American press also lost no opportunity to report British 'savagery' against American women. For example, one newspaper reported that

Besides the sixteen women who had fled to the woods to avoid their brutality and were there seized and carried off, one man had the cruel mortification to have his wife and only daughter (a child of ten years of age) ravished . . . [A]nother girl of thirteen years of age was taken from the father's house, carried to a barn about a mile, there ravished, and afterwards made use of by five more of these brutes.[43]

Even without the inclusion of specifically 'Indian' cruelty, therefore, the American war figured in the public imagination as hyperbolically violent. It was not uncommon for public figures to invoke apocalyptic language to characterize the hostilities. In a speech made in 1777, the British commander General Burgoyne threatened the rebels with 'reluctant' but righteous extermination:

I trust I shall stand acquitted in the eyes of God and men in denouncing and executing the vengeance of the state against the wilful outcasts. The messengers of justice and of wrath await them in the field: and devastation, famine, and every concomitant horror, that a reluctant, but indispensable prosecution of military duty must occasion, will bar the way to their return.[44]

Indian 'savagery' functioned within this larger rhetorical matrix of hyperbolic violence.

The powerful discursive transition from 'unnatural' colonial or rebel violence to naturalized but exploited subaltern violence was used to striking effect by the most famous of all the political writers who helped to 'create' America: Thomas Paine. In his revolutionary pamphlet *Common Sense* (1776), Paine described all forms of government as a necessary evil: 'Government, like dress, is the badge of lost innocence; the palaces of kings are built in the ruins of the bowers of paradise'.[45] Monarchy is the least enlightened political system, argues Paine, as it is inherently violent: the king is a 'crowned ruffian' (79) and 'monarchy and succession have laid (not this or that kingdom only) but the world in blood and ashes' (78). Although Paine is defending the national interests of America, he regards imperialism as a global scourge – like Burke, he sees a commonality of interest between the disenfranchised and oppressed around the world. The British rule of America is 'a long and violent abuse of power' and 'the cause of America is in great measure the cause of all mankind' (65). In order to dramatize his argument further, Paine uses those well-established Oedipal and familial metaphors which symbolized the relationship between Britain and America:

> But Britain is the parent company, some say. Then the more shame upon her conduct. Even brutes do not devour their young, nor savages make war upon their families. (81)[46]

Paine could have in mind here some lines from Thomas Day's poem *Ode for the New Year 1776*: '*Britain*, terror of the world no more, / Turns on herself, and drinks her Children's gore!'[47] In Paine's narrative, the moment of the familial rupture, when this ultra-savage Oedipal violence begins, is what he calls the 'massacre' at Lexington. This event is like a mythic Fall from grace, when the king

> with the pretended title of FATHER OF HIS PEOPLE can unfeelingly hear of their slaughter, and composedly sleep with their blood upon his soul. (87)

In Paine's propaganda, the king is more like the cannibalistic, child-killing Saturn than a caring father figure. This infanticidal slaughter is augmented by the 'stirring up' of those traditional savages, slaves and Indians:

> There are thousands and tens of thousands, who would think it glorious to expel from the continent, that barbarous and hellish power, which hath stirred up the Indians and Negroes to destroy us; the cruelty hath a double guilt, it is dealing brutally by us, and treacherously by them. (93)

This scenario was the realization of the worst fears of patriot Americans. At the outbreak of hostilities, there had been a concerted effort by the Continental Congress to persuade the Six Nations of Indian tribes to remain neutral. The Congress's Address to the Indian Council couched its appeal in the figurative language of familial discord:

> *England* we regard as the father; the island may be compared to the son . . . This is a family quarrel between us and *Old England*. You *Indians* are not concerned in it.[48]

While this racialized metaphor excludes native Americans from the white 'family' of civilization (which, ironically, was undergoing a catastrophic rift), the Address shows that separatist Americans were absolutely clear where the political blame lay for the 'cruelty' of the war. In order to rally his (male) American readers into revolutionary action, Paine unleashes the full force of the imagery of Terror:

> But if you say, you can still pass the violations over, then I ask, Hath your house been burnt? Hath your property been destroyed before your face? Are your wife and children destitute of a bed to lie on, or bread to live on? Have you lost a parent or child by their hands, and yourself the ruined and wretched survivor?... If you have, and can still shake hands with the murderers, then are you unworthy the name of husband, father, friend, or lover... This is not inflaming or exaggerating matters, but trying them by those feelings and affections which nature justifies... I mean not to exhibit horror for the purpose of provoking revenge, but to awaken us from fatal and unmanly slumbers. (85)

Paine is not of course immune from using the well-honed convention of distressed femininity, though as we shall see, he was able to draw on a rich tradition of political rather than exclusively sexual iconography:

> Ye that tell us of harmony and reconciliation, can ye restore us to the time that is past? Can ye give to prostitution its former innocence... There are injuries which nature cannot forgive; she would cease to be nature if she did. As well can the lover forgive the ravisher of his mistress, as the continent forgive the murders of Britain. (93)

It is worth noting here that Paine also used the familial metaphor to attack slavery. In his pamphlet *African Slavery in America* (1775), Paine drew a sharp analogy between the hereditary principle in monarchy and slavery: in the latter, 'if the parents were justly slaves, yet the children are born free', and 'one may, with as much reason and decency, plead for murder, robbery, lewdness and barbarity, as for this practice' (54). Inheriting the condition of slavery, Paine insists, is the Gothic antitype of monarchical 'succession'. The same trope of derogation of paternal duty is used in Paine's bristling attack on British rule in India. In his pamphlet *Reflections on the Death of Lord Clive*, also published in 1775, Paine anticipates Burke's revelations about colonial atrocities. Paine's India is a 'loud proclaimer of European cruelties', a 'bloody monument of unnecessary deaths' (57). Paine imagines accompanying Clive to India, where instead of deference there is desolation:

> The wailing widow, the crying orphan, and the childless parent remember and lament... Fear and terror march like pioneers before his camp,

murder and rapine accompany it, famine and wretchedness follow in the rear. (58)

He also imagines the ageing, ruined Clive as a proto-Romantic figure, a guilt-ridden wanderer. When Clive is served dinner,

> the crimson coloured port resembles blood . . . the joyous toast is like the sound of murder, and the loud laughs are groans of dying men. (61)

This spectral trope is very similar to the 'blood–sugar' trope of the anti-slavery campaign. But like many examples of spectacular violence, Paine's sensationalism is underpinned by an appeal to factual accuracy. In a foot-note, Paine cites a parliamentary investigation of 1773 which looked into the conduct of various governors of Bengal. Paine quotes the chairman of the committee – ironically, General Burgoyne, not yet posted to America – who warns that 'the reports contained shocking accounts to human nature, that the most infamous designs had been carried into execution by perfidy and murder' (58n.).

The 'stirring up' of American Indians, therefore, was just one move in a global chess game of domination, exploitation and abuse.

'As if done by ourselves': Indian cruelty and British war policy

Thomas Paine was not the only vitriolic critic of Britain's hiring of American Indians in the revolutionary war, as the policy was attacked on both sides of the Atlantic. Famously, the American Declaration of July 1776 (echoing Paine's *Common Sense*) claimed that George III had

> endeavoured to bring on the inhabitants of our frontiers, the merci-less Indian savages, whose known rule of warfare, is an undistinguished destruction of all ages, sexes and conditions.[49]

Reflecting this mood, Thomas Day's anti-war poem *The Desolation of America* (1777)[50] imagines the scenario of an American man and wife who are fleeing from the advancing British forces. They are trapped between the battlefield and a dark forest which contains a second enemy, the Indian. The father hears terrible sounds that would normally 'mollify a British heart'. Presum-ably the British reader, like the embattled father, is a creature of sensibility, unlike the British soldiers who are on the rampage and unmoved by

> The virgin's shriek, who trembling in the dust,
> Weeps the pollution of a ruffian's lust;
> The mangled infant's wail, that as he dies,
> Looks up in vain for pity from the skies. (19)

The mother has also witnessed the sadism of the 'horrid soldier':

> His unrelenting hand the wound prepares
> For those, whom ev'n the fiery deluge spares;
> Inspires new fury to the sinking flame;
> Or stabs the suppliant babe, and calls it fame. (8)

But the most sinister threat lurks in the 'dark forest'. The 'fell Indian, Britain's ready aid' (9) is waiting to pounce:

> Torture and death alone his thoughts employ;
> Blood his delight, and havoc all his joy. (25)

The British and the Indians are the Scylla and Charybdis of this anti-war vignette.

In the British press, concerns were expressed that Indians were unstable, unreliable and unassimilated allies, whose violence, once aroused, could not be contained. The *Annual Register* for 1777 declared the 'object and design' of Indian warfare was 'not to fight, but to murder; not to conquer, but to destroy' (144). The *Annual Register* was also sceptical about the wisdom of General Burgoyne's widely reported Address to the Indian Congress in June 1777. The journal pointed out the contradiction of a policy designed to 'excite [the Indians'] ardour in the common cause, and at the same time to repress their barbarity' with a set of constraints which 'were not of force wholly to restrain their ferocity' (146). This criticism refers to Burgoyne's simultaneous attempt to both incite and restrain Indian violence. Burgoyne told the Indians that they could 'strike at the common enemies of Great Britain and America – disturbers of public order, peace, and happiness – destroyers of commerce, parricides of the state' (note the Oedipal image again), but also insisted that civilians and prisoners 'must be held sacred from the knife or hatchet', except for those of the enemy who had committed 'acts of barbarity' themselves. Burgoyne added that Indians would be paid for scalps (a policy which drew some of the most hostile condemnation), though they were only 'allowed to take the scalps of the dead, when killed by your fire and in fair opposition'.[51] An American poem lampooned Burgoyne's speech as rabblerousing and bloodthirsty:

> Thousands of *Indians* I've supplied with knives,
> To scalp your dearest children and your wives;
> If I but nod the savage army flies,
> And naught is heard but shrieks and female cries.[52]

Even the *Annual Register* declared that Burgoyne's manifesto was 'calculated to spread terror' as it threatened the rebellious Americans with 'all the calamities and outrages of war, arrayed in their most terrific forms' (146–7, 155). Moreover, argued the periodical, the policy of inciting the 'indiscriminate rage' (156) of the Indians was counterproductive, as it alienated public opinion and galvanized the rebels. The example chosen by the *Annual Register* to illustrate this point was the murder of Jane McCrea, which 'struck every breast with horror'. Hence, 'the advantages expected from the terror excited by these savage auxiliaries . . . produced a directly contrary effect' (ibid.).

Edmund Burke lent his inimitable oratorical and rhetorical weight to this clamour of disapproval. In a draft petition written in late 1775, Burke derided the 'degenerate' hiring of Indians and slaves. Britain had abandoned 'making War' in that 'generous, open and humane procedure' which had formerly 'distinguished this gallant nation'. Instead, Britain was unleashing

> every Class of savages and Cannibals the most cruel and ferocious (known) to lay Waste with fire hatchet [and] with Murders, and Sanguinary Tortures of the Inhabitants, the most beautiful Work of Skill and Labour by which the creation and name of God was ever glorified.[53]

In terms of Burke's own aesthetic theory, the masculine, sublime violence of pro-British Indians is violating the pristine feminine beauty of America. In 'Address to the Colonists' (January 1777), Burke berates the fact that slaves, who had been 'sold to you on public faith' (a rather feeble vindication of the slave trade), were now 'employed to cut the throats of their masters'. This refers to the British policy, instigated by Lord Dunmore, the governor of Virginia, of promising manumission for slaves who joined British regiments. In reality, the volunteer slaves were treated shabbily, and at the end of the war most fled the country.[54] But for Burke, the strategy was a prime example of the British government's betrayal of the principles of 'just' colonization: 'They are the real rebels to the fair constitution and just supremacy of England'. To ally with 'these fierce tribes of Savages and Cannibals, in whom the traces of human nature are effaced by ignorance and barbarity' is for Burke the moral equivalent of miscegenation, 'fleshing them in the slaughter of you [the colonists]'. The cruel Indian is a violent prodigy of British malevolence:

> cruelties too horrible and full of turpitude for Christian mouths to utter or ears to hear, if done at our instigation (by those who, we know, will make war thus if they make it at all) to be, to all intents and purposes, as if done by ourselves. (281–2)

Burke reiterated this point pithily in another speech: 'to employ them was merely to be cruel ourselves in their persons' (357). Burke's spectral trope is damning: behind every act of Indian cruelty lurks the 'horrible' hand of the British.

Burke ended the Address with a warning: though he has a 'thorough detestation of the whole War; and particularly the mercenary and savage War, carried on or attempted against you', he pleads with the Americans not to be swayed by the 'seductions' of separatists. No doubt he had Paine in mind, as Burke was fully aware that the incidence of 'cruelties too horrible and full of turpitude for Christian mouths to utter or ears to hear, if done at our instigation' was a propaganda coup for the rebels.

The climax of Burke's assault on the British alliance with Indians was his three-hour 'Speech on the Use of Indians'. The speech was delivered in parliament on 6 February 1778 in support of a failed motion demanding an inquiry into the policy (the motion was defeated by 223 votes to 137). According to the *Parliamentary Register*, it was 'the very best speech' he had 'ever delivered' (361).[55] Burke does not attack the Indians on essentialist, racist grounds – he specifically dismisses the importance of their 'being of one colour or another' – but highlights their culture of savage warfare, a

> way of making war; which was so horrible, that it shocked not only the manners of all civilized people, but far exceeded the ferocity of all barbarians mentioned in history.[56]

This uncivilized, regressive cruelty includes 'gratifications arising from torturing, mangling, scalping, and sometimes eating their captives in war' (ibid.). The speech then moved into the register of hyperbolic realism: 'He then repeated several instances of this diabolical mode of war, scarcely credible, and, if true, improper to be repeated' (ibid.). These 'several instances' of 'scarcely credible' violence have been lost, but that is not the case with the rest of the speech. Burke castigates the British recruitment of slaves as an incitement to rebellion:

> what murders, rapes, and enormities of all kinds, were in the contemplation of all negroes who meditated an insurrection? He lastly asked what means were proposed for governing these negroes, who were 100,000 at least; when they had reduced the province to their obedience, and made themselves masters of the houses, goods, wives and daughters of their murdered lords? (359)

In order to debunk Burgoyne's 'perfectly unintelligible' insistence on Indian restraint, Burke 'painted in very strong colours the horrid story of Miss Mac Ray, murdered by savages on the day of her marriage with an officer of the King's troops' (358). Some indication of the 'strong colours' of this vignette can be gleaned from Burke's draft notes for the speech:

> that hair dressed for other purposes that morning torn from her head to decorate the infernal habitation of cruelty and barbarism . . . her body

a mangled ghastly spectacle of blood and horror, crying through an hundred mouths to that whose image was defaced for Vengeance'. (363–4)

The sensational power of this cameo has led Luke Gibbons to speculate that Jane McCrea is the prototype for Burke's famous description of the beleaguered Marie-Antoinette at Versailles.[57] The *Public Advertiser* expressed reservations about the heightened 'colourings' of this potent mix of sentimentalism and sensationalism:

[the] shocking cruelties generally exercised by Savages on their Foes... were described with a Pathos which melted the Auditory almost to tears and filled them with the utmost Horror... But his colourings, we hope, for the Honour of Human Nature, were too High. (361)

This prim response may have underestimated the political connotations of the vignette. The displaced sexual connotations of McCrea's murder – she was allegedly on route to meet her British fiancé, hence 'that hair dressed for other purposes that morning' – were surely meant to reflect badly on General Burgoyne, and rape, as we have seen, was a familiar metaphor of colonial domination. Indeed, it is not pushing symbolic logic too far to see the violation of McCrea as a displacement of the 'unnatural' alliance of the British and the Indians. In the words of the 1778 *Annual Register*, Burke's performance successfully denounced 'those shameful, savage and servile, alliances and their barbarous consequences' (113). The death of Jane McCrea was a high-profile 'barbarous consequence' of this 'shameful' military mating. These interlinked erotic and political themes were explored and developed at a cultural level in the literary response to the McCrea sensation.

Jane McCrea and distressed femininity

Burke's model of proxy violence is employed in what may be the first American novel: Michel René Hilliard d'Auberteuil's *Miss McCrea: A Novel of the American Revolution* (1784).[58] Lewis Leary calls this text 'the first book-length prose narrative to deal wholly with a national American incident and with America as the entire scene of action' (5). Hilliard had a reputation as a liberal: his previous book on the horrors of slavery in San Domingo had been proscribed in France, and this was one reason why he transferred his residence to America when the war broke out. By the time his novel appeared, the war was over and the McCrea story was heavily sentimentalized in American propaganda.[59] A popular version of her tragedy exaggerated her vulnerability by making her both younger and jilted. In fact, as Leary points out, her lover Lieutenant David Jones was not faithless, and on hearing the news of her death he either resigned or deserted (14). Other versions of her murder did not so easily fit the sentimental conventions of distressed femininity.

These included wrangling between squads of Indians, and even the possibility that she had been shot mistakenly by Americans. Hilliard followed Burke's example by framing a sensational and sexualized account of her death within a hard-hitting political critique of Britain's exploitation of the Indians. The imaginative license afforded by the fictional format allowed Hilliard to develop this critique in some particularly effective ways.

The novel opens with a vivid, spectacular description of a brutal British attack on New York:

> After swarms of ferocious and well-disciplined German soldiers were debarked on Long Island, brutal and bloody crimes were committed there by them... The blood of the [American] soldiers, mingling with the flowing brooks, had reddened the edges of the seas... The bloodthirsty Germans were on every street, and with an excess of wine to add to their barbarism they killed anyone who obstructed their way. (23–4)

At this point in the narrative it is the mercenary Germans who represent the British policy of proxy violence. The 'flowing' American blood which reddens the Atlantic captures the sense of catastrophic sacrifice; it also conveys the idea of the contamination of the 'natural', familial relationship between the two warring countries. The assault on New York sets the scene for the introduction of the 16-year-old heroine (in fact she was in her mid-20s) who is in a highly vulnerable predicament, 'alone in her father's house' (24). When British soldiers burst into her house, she is prepared for the worst, and it seems to the reader as if the novel is bringing her fate forward. The British officer Captain Belton has a melodramatically ferocious appearance: 'his fiery eyes seemed only to foretell death; blood covered his face'. But his reaction to the sight of the heroine is the novel's first peripeteia, as he is transformed instantly (though precariously, as is soon apparent) from proto-Gothic villain into Burkean, chivalric gentleman. In his 'sweet and tender voice' he tells Jane,

> You are the most beautiful girl in this land. We have not come to fight enemies such as you. We put our weapons down. If I dare to enter your house, it is only to give you protection; my companions and I are entirely at your command. (25)

In time-honoured romance tradition, this homily is enough to make Jane fall in love with the enemy. As she is tending his wounds, her father, a wealthy trader who is preparing to evacuate to Albany, finds the couple in a suggestive pose. Outraged, he demands that he be allowed to leave with his daughter, but Belton persuades him not to 'hazard being detained in the countryside by raging soldiers who had been rendered uncontrollable by arrogance in victory' (28), and leaves a guard posted on the door. An interesting scene then takes place. The incarcerated father and daughter have two contrasting visions of the war. Nathaniel, a republican upholder of 'liberty' and 'natural rights', is obsessed by the 'odious events' that have already marred the war, and 'saw nothing but young girls cornered and trembling at the licentious conduct of an unrestrained grenadier, Indians armed with hatchets, and villages on fire' (29). For Jane's father, the war is defined by spectacular violence, and his obsession with 'young girls cornered and trembling' is an ominous foreshadowing of his daughter's demise. Jane, on the other hand, has an equally active and disturbed imagination. Her mind is full of 'licentious' fantasies of Belton's military prowess:

> She imagined she saw him triumph over an American regiment single-handed; she imagined she saw an enemy saber strike his forehead, and his arm plunge a sword into the ribs of the audacious rebel who had dared to wound him. (29)

Psychoanalytically, this 'audacious' fantasy is clearly about freeing herself from her father's influence and transferring her affections to Belton, a hero with 'the dignity of Mars and the beauty of Apollo' (32). Likewise, her father's violation fantasies could be a displacement of his resentment about his daughter's disloyal affections (we are told that she is being led 'astray' (31) by her naiveté), and his desire to punish her. The disturbing psychoanalytic dynamics are symptomatic of the function of the characters as allegorical personifications of the wider national and political context. It seems that the narrative is moving against the grain of sentimentality by presenting Jane as indulging in fantasies of escape from American rather than British patriarchal authority. If it is the case that Jane associates personal and sexual liberty with the romanticized violence of British military power, her nemesis at the hands of brutal Indians has the disturbing force of poetic justice. The gender politics of this narrative resolution are deeply conservative, warning the reader about the dangers of female independence and romantic autonomy (Jane is killed in the 'wild', anti-social space of a dark wood, a place traditionally associated with sexual transgression and danger). The message would seem to be that Jane's fatal error is a unique consequence of the disruption of familial relations caused by the war. With this upheaval safely in the past, the normative, dutiful and domesticated feminine virtues of the new republic will be restored.[60] In this interpretation of the narrative, the principle motivation for the allegorizing of British-Indian perfidy is sexual politics, as if the novel has to work extra hard to prevent the spectre of an emancipated Jane emerging from the clutches of her captors.

In the wake of the father and daughter's violent day-dreams, the novel depicts another example of British atrocities. In an attempt to disrupt the British advance, retreating New Yorkers implement a scorched earth policy, including 'several women' who 'stabbed themselves at the moment of capture' (34), thereby denying all forms of booty to the enemy. The reprisals are swift, as the British 'killed anyone they caught trying to revive the fire. Several arsonists were thrown into the fire they themselves had kindled' (35). From this low ebb, which captures the mood of the American retreat to Valley Forge, Jane begins to 'revive the fire' of her feelings for Belton. When word gets out that she is Tory (or loyalist) sympathizer, the local community ostracizes her, though her 'ardour' eventually triumphs over public opinion. The same passion is then put into a correspondence with Belton. This is conducted via a scheming Irish servant Betsy, who arranges a tryst in a remote woodland cottage. However, Belton's sensibility has become hardened by the war, and instead of the 'sweet and tender' words of their first meeting, he tries to rape her. Jane's protestations bring him back from the brink, and she is able to 'triumph over a seducer' (49), but she still loves him. He returns to England leaving her desolate, but after several months he pledges to return with Burgoyne 'to conquer your country and you in order to possess you forever' (50). Jane is now 'thrilled with pleasure' at the news of British victories (53). Belton is a signifier of the old country's treacherous codes of aristocratic chivalry and honour.

The novel's representation of the murder combines direct political statement with a new plot device. Indian violence is blamed squarely on the British:

The Ministers of England added, so to speak, a new horror to the scourge of war, paying fifteen guineas for each murdered American's scalp. The officers of Burgoyne's army kept these Indians continually intoxicated in order to increase their ferocity and to encourage them to murder and commit atrocities. These simple people did not love cruelty for its own sake but for the reward offered by the Europeans. It is not, then, upon them but that our horror for the crimes should fall but upon the nations that provoked them, nations that dared to call themselves civilized. (58)

In order to vindicate the Indians while remaining faithful to the savagery of the murder, Hillard introduces a new and wholly fictitious character, the Indian chief Kiashatu. The noblest character in the novel, he tries desperately to save Jane's life. In a flagrant departure from the dominant version of the murder, both Jane and Betsy are stripped naked and tied to a tree. After Betsy is killed, the delay in dispatching Jane is blatantly eroticized. The Indian warriors 'stared desirously at her charms' (58), and her precious hair, which is 'long enough to serve as a veil for her modesty' (59), no doubt adds to her attraction (Hilliard's notebook was even more explicit, stating that Jane's captors 'performed on her all that their fury and brutality could suggest').[61] But this lascivious gaze is disrupted by Kiashatu's chivalrous irruption into the spectacle. Though the odds are overwhelming and he cannot save Jane, he does exact justice on the warrior who kills her. Kiashatu's hatchet 'split open the warrior's chest and heart' (61), an appropriate revenge for a heartless deed. Kaishatu takes Jane's scalp to Belton and then commits suicide, insisting that Belton do the same. Belton refuses, but shortly after is fatally poisoned by an Indian arrow in an ambush. The symbolism of his death is a convincing political allegory, as it is the British who have poisoned the natural beauty of America, turned the Atlantic red with American blood and inebriated the Indians with liquor. Jane McCrea's fifteen-guinea scalp is an emblem of the 'new horror' of a displaced and commercialized warfare in which 'nations that dared to call themselves civilized' act through their 'savage' deputies.

Clearly, Jane McCrea's iconic distress functioned as a national symbol of the violation of America. But it is important to recognize that the cultural power of the imagery of female peril did not derive solely from the eighteenth-century sentimental tradition, but also from an iconographic tradition of political propaganda which was constantly recycled and appropriated. From the 1760s onwards, many political cartoons show either Britannia or America (who at this time is always represented by an Indian woman) in situations of danger or distress. Conflict with America could be represented as an attack on either or both of these figures. A striking example of this is the two-part *The Colonies Reduced. Its Companion*, a cartoon which appeared in the *Political Register* in 1768 (Figure 14). The upper design is a copy of Benjamin Franklin's 1766 cartoon *Magna Britannia: Her Colonies Reduced*. Britannia is in a forlorn, mutilated condition, having lost her limbs which represent the colonies. The allusion to the disabled Roman general Belisarius reinforces the amputation motif. The lower design shows France rescuing America from Britannia. The message is that British aggression towards America will only benefit Britain's enemies: the treacherous Earl of Bute encourages Spain to attack Britannia from behind (the assault resembles an act of anal rape), while the Dutch exploit Britain's naval weakness. In *The Able Doctor, or America Swallowing the Bitter Draft* which appeared in the *London Magazine* in May 1774, America is held down by Mansfield and Sandwich, while Lord North pours tea down her throat (Figure 15). Britannia cannot bear to look and covers her eyes, while France and Spain look on eagerly. Britannia's anguished response is a sentimental signifier of the familial basis of the relationship between the two countries. The Oedipal theme is also clear in *The Parricide. A Sketch of Modern Patriotism*, published in the *Westminster Magazine* in April 1776 (Figure 16). Britannia is restrained by so-called 'patriots' (including Fox and Wilkes) who are actually making her vulnerable to attack by America. Gillray's *Britania's Assassination, or the Republican's Amusement* (May 1782) is like a sequel to *The Parricide*: a headless, mulilated Britannia is assaulted by a fox (Fox) and other anti-war politicians, while America, France, Spain and Holland steal parts of Britannia's body (Figure 17).

As these examples make clear, the figure of the abused female body had a very wide currency in British graphic political satire, where it served both

Figure 14   The Colonies Reduced. Its Companion (1768) © Trustees of the British Museum

Figure 15   The Able Doctor, or America Swallowing the Bitter Draft (1774) © Trustees of the British Museum

Figure 16   The Parricide. A Sketch of Modern Patriotism (1776) © Trustees of the British Museum

Figure 17 James Gillray, *Britania's Assassination, or the Republican's Amusement* (May 1782) © Trustees of the British Museum

anti-radical and radical aims. As Chapter 5 will show, the abject female is also at the centre of popular visual representations of the Peterloo massacre and other government attacks on civil and political liberties in the Romantic period. The sentimental and realist modes of representation did not replace the satirical; the co-existence of these traditions provided Romantic readers and audiences with an alternative means of response to the narrowly sentimental or sympathetic identification with the victim. The same paradigm needs to be applied to the Jane McCrea controversy in order to appreciate its full cultural and political impact.

Indian victims: Captivity, cruelty and revenge

The focus so far has been on the writing and visual imagery generated by the American revolutionary war, but as noted at the beginning of this chapter, in the discussion of Wordsworth's use of Samuel Hearne, there were many other popular sources for representations of the violence of American Indians, particularly the accounts of travellers, explorers and captives. This section of the chapter looks at some of these sources in order to show that even the most negative and stereotypical portrayals of Indian cruelty are often represented within politicized frameworks of colonial conflict, cultural relativism and the inexorable cycle of violence.

The popular image of the Indian balanced bloodthirsty violence in battle with legendary fortitude under torture, symbolized by the famous 'death song'.[62] As Tim Fulford argues, scenes of Indian torture may begin as sensational 'sadomasochistic' fantasies, but they often turn into an unsettling and challenging exploration of the parallels between Indian and European cultures of excessive violence.[63] Take, for example, the very hostile depiction of Indian violence in James Adair's *The History of the American Indians* (1775). Adair describes in detail the ritualized torture of captives from rival tribes. The burning alive and mutilation of the prisoners is a spectator sport: 'Unspeakable pleasure now fills the exulting crowd of spectators, and the circle fills with the Amazon and merciless executioners'. The victim is gradually made insensible after being attacked by the 'contracted circle'. He is then scalped, dismembered and his 'exterior branches' carried away in 'shameful, and savage triumph'. True to the tradition of hyperbolic realism, we are told that this is the 'most favourable treatment', and that other 'doleful tragedies' are even worse. But a series of comparisons is then invoked: 'nothing can equal these scenes, but those of the merciful Romish inquisition'. The role of women in an auto-da-fe is also highlighted: supposedly they 'sing with religious joy, all the while they are torturing the devoted victim' (*TEE*, 1: 8–9). If there is 'sadomasochistic' pleasure in this scene, it is mediated or heightened through a series of misogynistic and anti-Catholic stereotypes which close the gap between self and Other, white and red, European and Indian. Extreme violence is shown to be a form of cultural rather than natural behaviour, and this rule applies equally to Europe.

One of the most fertile sources for descriptions of Indian torture was the increasingly popular genre of the captivity narrative.[64] In the American revolutionary war, the genre was utilized by the Americans to boost national morale, and some of the early narratives of female capture, such as the story of the escapee Hannah Dustan, who scalped her captors, were reprinted in great numbers.[65] In the earlier period of Anglo-French conflict, however (the moment of the Fort William massacre), anti-Indian representations could be implicitly or explicitly directed at the French. This may explain the popularity of Peter Williamson's famous captivity narrative *French and Indian Cruelty*, first published in 1756 and reprinted many times.[66] According to Linda Colley, 'if there was a popular British classic about Native Americans in this period, this was certainly it'.[67] This text established a benchmark for the sensational representation of spectacular, hyperbolic Indian violence, but as we shall see, this did not preclude the text making some major criticisms of British settler policy and practices.[68] In fact Williamson's misfortunes begin when he is kidnapped in Scotland as a young child and taken to America to be sold into slavery. This leads Williamson to rate white slavers as worse than Indians, as the latter do not have the benefit of Christianity (4). The title of the book refers to his second fall. Having established himself as a respectable settler, he is captured by Indians who are paid per scalp by the

French – this anticipates the proxy violence of the British in the later revolutionary war. The Indians are 'undaunted and blood thirsty monsters' (10) whose 'various and complicated' atrocities could 'fill a large volume' (17). As some of the anthropological observations make clear, there is a non-violent side to Indian culture, but French lucre and liquor have inflamed naturally violent tendencies. Even without this incentive, the Indians have many grisly customs such as the ritual of euthanasia. Williamson describes the killing of an old man who has his brains dashed out by a child who has to be lifted up so can reach the head: 'Thus are they from their youth inured to barbarity!' (23–4). Much of the book is a catalogue of these barbarities. For example, an elderly farmer is forced to watch his wife scalped and raped before he is in turn abducted and tortured. He is whipped, painted, scorched and the white hairs are plucked from his head (perhaps the motivation here is to destroy the symbolic value of the white male patriarchal body). He is told 'He was a fool for living so long, and that they should shew him kindness in putting him out of the world' (15–16). From the mouths of three newly captured prisoners, Williamson hears many other tales, including that of a family 'cut in pieces, and given to the swine', and even worse, the story of a man who is 'roasted before he was dead' and then eaten: 'his head made what they called an *Indian* pudding' (18). This macabre humour anticipates what Alan Liu has called the 'jokework' of the reportage of the September massacres (see Chapter 2). The execution of Williamson's three fellow prisoners is the most graphic moment in the book. It is worth quoting in full as it shows clearly that the discourse of spectacular violence was fully active across a range of cultural sources, and cannot be pinned down to one sphere of conflict or genre of writing:

> two of them were tied to a tree, and a great fire made round them, where they remained till they were terribly scorched and burnt; when one of the villains with his scalping knife, ript open their bellies, took out their entrails, and burnt them before their eyes, while the others were cutting, piercing and tearing the flesh from their breasts, hands, arms and legs, with red hot irons, till they were dead. The third unhappy victim was reserved for a few hours longer, to be, if possible, sacrificed in a more cruel manner; his arms were tied close to his body, and a hole being dug deep enough for him to stand upright, he was put there in, and earth ram'd and beat in all around his body up to his neck, so that his head only appeared above ground; then they scalp'd him, and there let him remain for three or four hours in the greatest agonies; after which they made a small fire near his head, causing him to suffer the most excruciating torments imaginable, while the poor creature could only cry for mercy in killing him immediately, for his brains were boiling in his head: Inexorable to all his [com]plaints they continued the fire, whilst shocking to behold! his eyes gushed out of their sockets; and such agonizing torments did

the unhappy creature suffer for near two hours, 'till he was quite dead! Then they cut off his head, and buried it with the other bodies; my task being to dig the graves, which feeble and terrified as I was, the dread of suffering the same fate, enabled me to do. (19)

But the settlers also commit atrocities:

our men were busily employed in cutting, hacking and scalping the dead Indians; and so desirous was every man to have a share in wreaking his revenge on them, that disputes happened among ourselves, who should be the instruments of further shewing it on their lifeless trunks, there not being enough for every man to have one wherewith to satisfy himself. (38)

The vague sexual connotation of the word 'satisfy' only adds to the *frisson* of this vignette. Having cast lots, one half of the men 'with half-pleased countenances' watches the other half 'treating [the Indians'] dead bodies as the most inveterate hatred and detestation could suggest' (39). The distinction between settler and Indian collapses completely when it is revealed that the settlers are 'rewarded handsomely' for the 50 Indian scalps they gather (40). As David Hume noted in *An Enquiry Concerning the Principles of Morals* (1751), so-called 'civilised Europeans' had discarded 'all restraints of justice, and even of humanity' in their dealings with Indians.[69]

Though it dwells on Indian atrocities, Williamson's book has a surprisingly liberal conclusion. Williamson supports Indian grievances against corrupt and immoral traders and recommends 'regulating the trade'. The real villain of the story is the rogue trader:

getting beyond the law, executing unheard of villainies upon the poor natives, committing crimes which modesty forbids to name, and behaving in a manner too shocking to relate. (92–3)

This economic explanation of the reasons for Indian defection to the French studiously avoids reducing the problem to racial stereotypes. In such conditions, argues Williamson, the Indians develop 'a rooted prejudice against us' (93). Logically, therefore, this 'prejudice' lies behind the atrocious treatment of settler captives, and the 'unheard of villainies' of settler violence rebound in a classic 'boomerang' effect.

Anti-French sentiment also lies behind the account of the Fort William Henry massacre in Jonathan Carver's influential *Travels through the Interior Parts of North America, in the Years 1766, 1767, and 1768* (1778), the principal source for Fenimore Cooper's *The Last of the Mohicans*. Carver served as a volunteer in the British fort which surrendered to French forces under Montcalm. When the retreating British troops and civilians were attacked by Indians, Carver was captured and witnessed the massacre at close hand.

The clarity of his memory is presented as the guarantee of both historical veracity and sensational affect:

> Every circumstance of the adventure still dwells on my remembrance, and enables me to describe with greater perspicuity the brutal fierceness of the Indians when they have surprised or overpowered an enemy. (*TEE*, 1: 29)

Though 'the power of words' struggles to convey the 'horrid scene', Carver foregrounds the most despicable act of Indian savagery, cannibalism: 'many of these savages drank the blood of their victims, as it flowed from the fatal wound'. But Carver makes clear that he is much more shocked by the indifference of the French 'body of ten thousand Christian troops' who refuse to intervene. The 'French officers walking about at some distance, discoursing with apparent unconcern' are the antithesis of Carver's (and, we assume, the reader's) 'concern' (*TEE*, 1: 35–6). The French are monsters of unfeeling inhumanity who fail to respond to the extreme suffering of others. To rub this point in, the French failure to pass the basic test of sensibility is contrasted with the noble actions of an 'English gentleman of some distinction' who helps Carver escape and is killed for his heroism (*TEE*, 1: 37–8).

With French culpability firmly in place, Carver finds three ways to textually retaliate against the Indians. His first means of revenge is a fantasy of divine providence and poetic justice, as we are told that most of the ambushers will subsequently die of smallpox, 'an equal havock to what they themselves had done'; the few that survive 'were transformed by it into hideous objects', the flesh made emblematic of the sin (*TEE*, 1: 42). The second reprisal is a striking example of white 'Amazonian intrepidity' *pace* Hannah Dustan, in which a woman named Rowe turns the tables on her captors and scalps them (*TEE*, 1: 50). The third and most prolonged act of justice is a classic scene of inter-Indian torture. Carver focuses on one Indian victim who is bound to a tree and used as target practice by children. Throughout this ordeal, the captive sings his legendary death-song, recalling 'the different barbarous methods' he has used on captives from his torturers' tribe.[70] This defiant discourse gives him 'inconceivable pleasure from the recital of the horrid tale' (*TEE*, 1: 55). Another victim recites to his tormentors the ways he 'devised for them the most excruciating torments' and reminds them that he

> had stuck their bodies full of sharp splinters of turpentine wood, to which he then set fire, and dancing round them enjoyed the agonizing pangs of the flaming victims.

At the point of maximum subjection to violent spectacle, the response of these Indian warriors is to return its force as a mode of defiance. This extraordinary 'bravado' is eventually terminated: 'one of the chiefs ran to him, and ripping out his heart, stopped with it the mouth from which had issued such provoking language' (*TEE*, 1: 57). The victim literally has his heart in his mouth, and it difficult not to perceive this punishment as a piece of 'jokework'. The grammatically ambiguous word 'provoking' (rather than 'provocative') is a reminder that spectacular violence is a textual event which provokes (produces) provoking (shocking and heartless) language.

After this textual mauling, Carver makes clear that Indians are more generous towards female captives. He refutes the standard assumption that captive women are raped: even 'women of great beauty' have been carried through 'retired forests' and have 'lain' by their captors' sides 'without receiving any insult' (*TEE*, 1: 58). The women are 'distributed to the men' and 'do not fail of meeting with a favourable reception', including marriage (*TEE*, 1: 61). Against the grain of the Jane McCrea myth, and in line with many female captivity narratives, the destiny of the genteel white woman is a trans-cultural existence as an Indian wife. In mainstream literature, however, miscegenation remained a largely taboo topic, deeply submerged beneath the stereotypes of violation and transgression. This is the case in Fenimore Cooper's seminal frontier novel *The Last of the Mohicans*, to which we now turn.

'The bloody arena': James Fenimore Cooper, *The Last of the Mohicans* (1826)

James Fenimore Cooper's *The Last of the Mohicans* was published in 1826, more than 40 years after the end of the American revolutionary war, and over 60 years after the end of the Seven Years' War.[71] The book has gained a reputation as the 'bloodiest and most troubling of Cooper's five Leatherstocking novels', to quote Terence Martin.[72] At the centre of the novel is the Fort William Henry massacre, an incident which had become deeply ingrained in American popular memory.[73] From the vantage point of post-revolutionary nationalism, Cooper makes it clear from the outset that eighteenth-century America was a theatre of colonial conflict. The 'cold and selfish policy of the distant monarchs of Europe' (15) transformed the 'wooded scenery' of north America, previously the pastoral birthright of its 'untutored possessors', into a 'bloody arena' of 'strife and bloodshed' (16–17). For the white settlers, 'the terrific character of their merciless enemies', the Indians, 'increased, immeasurably, the natural horrors of warfare', but Cooper insists that the cultural demonization of the Indian was an exaggerated response, a 'magnifying influence' which 'set at nought the calculations of reason' (18–19). These opening comments establish an historical and political framework for perceiving Indian violence as both sensational and distortedly hyperbolic. The 'terrific' nature of Indian violence can be registered, but not without forgetting the 'magnifying influence' of geopolitical conflict. The extent to which the narrative colludes with or resists the 'magnifying' of Indian violence is one of the central critical problems for any reading of the novel.

The novel places the Fort William Henry massacre at the centre of the narrative: Chapters 15–17 out of a total of 33. This positioning reinforces the historical significance of the event. As John McWilliams notes,

> the fall of Fort William Henry serves as a lens upon the past, as a central historical exemplum around which a particular view of white-red and intercolonial conflicts can be developed.[74]

In similar fashion to Hilliard d'Auberteuil's novel *Miss McCrea*, Cooper separates the Indians into two groups. The villainous Hurons, personified by Magua the 'subtle savage' (173), are allied with the French. The honourable Mohicans, represented by Uncas and Chingachgook, help the British, though they are loosely commanded by the ambiguous figure of Hawk-eye, the white frontiersmen. The 'good' Indians carry traces of noble savagery, but it is clear that they are now pawns in the colonial game of domination. Chingachgook, for example, carries 'a tomahawk and scalping knife, of English manufacture' (39), and Hawk-eye lowers his taciturn mask at one point to berate the fact that 'the evil has been mainly done by men with white skins'. The result is divide and rule, 'turning the tomahawk of brother against brother' (257). The characterization of the dastardly Hurons may seem out of step with the 'epic' balance of the historical novel, but this demonization reflects the novel's post-revolutionary consciousness. As McWilliams notes, the Hurons were remembered by the Americans as 'the most visible and feared of Iroquois tribes' (407) as they had sided with the British in the revolutionary war. This typology produces a complex historical schema in which the Indian perpetrators of the Fort William Henry massacre are destined to be punished by the later American victory over the British. At the same time, this redemptive teleology effaces any mention of American violence against the Indians, including the ongoing, post-revolutionary policy of clearances and containment.

Cooper was aware that the graphic depiction of the massacre could disturb some of his readers. In his 1826 Preface he noted that 'young ladies, whose ideas are usually limited by the four walls of a comfortable drawing room' would find the book's gory realism 'shocking' (6). This may or may not have been the case, but this condescending remark ignores the fact that women Romantic readers were familiar with spectacular violence, including, as will be seen shortly, the popular genre of the female captivity narrative. Cooper modelled his account of the massacre on Carver's, but as Steele has explained, Cooper was 'more accurate' than Carver in showing that the motivation for the attack was not 'unprovoked Indian savagery' but an enraged response to the French withdrawing a promise of booty.[75] The French under Montcalm are doubly culpable: having provoked the violence, they fail to intervene to prevent its escalation. Like Carver, Cooper regards the 'cruel apathy' (204) of the Christian French as less forgivable than the customary, 'terrific' violence of the Indians: 'the armed columns of the Christian king stood fast, in an apathy which has never been explained' (202). As McWilliams notes,

> By the careful pacing and central placement of this scene, the worst atrocity in Cooper's bloody work is revealed to be the moment when the forces of Christian civilization tacitly acquiesce in 'savage' practices. (409)

Montcalm's indifferent spectatorship is the obverse of a civilized, sympathetic response to human (in this case, specifically white) suffering.

After pointing the finger of blame clearly at French negligence and collusion, the narrative unleashes the full force of 'terrific' Indian violence. The attack commences with the iconic murder of a mother and her baby. A 'savage' who covets a 'gaudy shawl' dashes out the brains of a baby and then 'mercifully' tomahawks the mother. This is a shocking detail in a mainstream realist novel, though in fact, as Steele notes (198), such incidents were a set-piece of captivity narratives. Indeed, in Mary Jemison's bestselling *A Narrative of the Life of Mrs. Mary Jemison*, an atrocity-laden captivity narrative published just two years earlier in 1824, there is an account of an incident in which her husband Hiokatoo captured 'several infants, whom Hiokatoo butchered or dashed upon the stones with his own hands'.[76] Cooper's novel appears less sensational when placed alongside Jemison, though his refusal to describe 'the revolting horrors that succeeded' the killing of the mother and child is a typical moment of hyperbolic dramatization. His pose of squeamishness does not prevent him including Carver's most sensational detail, the frenzied drinking of the 'crimson tide' of blood (199). Moreover, in the aftermath of the massacre, it is the sight of a 'confused mass of dead' (207), a heap of festering women's bodies, which leads the novel's hero Hawk-eye to vow vengeance. This 'sad spectacle' is positioned, significantly, in 'the centre of the plain'. The 'revolting horror of the exhibition' provokes Hawk-eye to harangue his Mohican friends Uncas and Chingachgook: 'shall the Hurons boast of this to their women when the deep snows come?' (208). Behind this comment lies the driving force behind the novel's plot: the chivalric quest to protect and retrieve the novel's two heroines Cora and Alice. From the outset, their captivity is a dramatic device for enforcing the lurking, predatorial and sexualized violence of Magua and his tribe, and for valourizing the countervailing endeavours of Hawk-eye and the Mohicans.[77] The echoes of Jane McCrea are legion, and it is quite possible that Cooper may have seen John Vanderlyn's painting of McCrea on display in New York in either 1816 or 1826. When the women are captured by Magua, the symbolic function of the genteel female victim is made explicit. Alice is tied to a tree, 'looking like some beautiful emblem of the wounded delicacy of her sex' (125). Similarly, Cora's ordeal is a melodramatic re-enactment of the McCrea legend:

the breast of the Huron was a stranger to any sympathy. Seizing Cora by the rich tresses which fell in confusion about her form, he tore her from her frantic hold, and bowed her down with brutal violence to her knees. The savage drew the flowing curls through his hand, and raising them on high with an outstretched arm, he passed the knife around the exquisitely moulded head of the victim, with a taunting and exulting laugh. (129)

Cora is more fortunate than her predecessor, as on this occasion she is rescued in the nick of time. But the 'brutal violence' of Hawk-eye and his Indian colleagues narrows the gap between the victor and the vanquished:

the honest, but implacable scout, made the circuit of the dead, into whose senseless bosoms he thrust his long knife, with as much coolness, as though they had been so many brute carcasses. He had, however, been anticipated by the elder Mohican, who had already torn the emblems of victory from the unresisting heads of the slain. (131)

The 'beautiful emblem' of the violated female body has been replaced by the male body's 'emblem of victory'. The 'brutality' of the heroes' violence is presumably mitigated by the fact that the bodies of their enemies are 'brute carcasses' and 'senseless bosoms'. That key detail – 'the breast of the Huron was a stranger to any sympathy' – makes the 'bad' Indian the 'emblem' of inhumanity (absence of sensibility is far more important in this context than absence of Christianity), and the antithesis of the 'exquisitely moulded' figure (essentially hair and breasts) of the female captive. The sacrosanct female body marks the limit of acceptable violence and civilized values. But this still leaves considerable latitude for 'implacable' violence against the male body. It is a moot point whether Hawk-eye's 'cool' piercing of Indian corpses is more or less shocking than the highly melodramatic, 'exulting' sadism of the Huron Magua.

The dual depiction of Indians as savage and honorable may have expressed Cooper's liberal guilt and anxiety about the inevitability of war-fuelled progress. As Cooper wrote the novel, American political debate was full of proselytizing for President Jackson's removal policy of 1830, aided and abetted by a spate of popular stories which depicted the Indians as stereotypical savages.[78] Just a few years later, De Toqueville announced gloomily that 'I have met the last of the Iroquois; they were begging.'[79] But the novel's historical setting and narrative structure imply that the 'end' of authentic Indian culture was the result of the pre-revolutionary exploitation of the Indians by the Dutch, British and French. The epic lament for the 'last' of the Mohicans is a deeply racialized, consoling historical fiction. Indeed, Cooper's positive portrayal of Uncas the Mohican warrior king was attacked by some early reviewers for its idealization of the Indians.[80] But Chingachgook's concluding words still carry a chill: 'The pale-faces are masters of the earth, and the time of the red-men has not yet come again' (394). The extinction of the Indians was an object-lesson in the dangers which could befall the 'superior' white races if they did not guard against the lethal effects of war, exploitation and mongrelization.[81]

The narrative solution to this ideological problem was to transfer primitive Indian virtues to the new breed of white American hero: the frontiersman, a hybrid figure who polices the border between the civilized and the 'savage', and whose *raison d'être* is the continuing conquest of the mythic American wilderness. As Cooper declared in the 1831 Introduction to the novel, Hawk-eye (also known as Natty Bumppo, Leatherstocking and the Long Rifle) is one of those 'half wild beings who hang between society and the wilderness' (9).[82] The model for Hawk-eye was the legendary Daniel Boone, a hero of the revolutionary war and the 'most emotionally compelling myth-hero of the early republic'.[83] In his memoir entitled *Adventures of Colonel Daniel Boon* (1784), Boone represented the Indians as irredeemably savage, and he celebrates their pacification as the arrival of the new millennium:

> Providence... has turned a cruel war into peace, brought order out of confusion, made the fierce savages placid, and turned away their hostile weapons from our country! May the same Almighty Goodness banish the accursed monster, war, from all lands, with her hated associates, rapine and insatiable ambition. Let peace, descending from her native heaven, bid her olives spring amidst the joyful nations; and plenty, in league with commerce, scatter blessings from her copious hand. (*TEE*, 1: 138–9)

This is reminiscent of Pantisocracy – the recovery of America's Utopian birthright. In reality, of course, the repression of Indians and slaves was to continue for decades.

The goddess of cruelty: Joel Barlow's *The Columbiad* (1807)

The final literary text to be looked at in this chapter is the generic antithesis of Cooper's realist exploration of the passing away of America's indigenous epic culture. Joel Barlow's *The Columbiad* (1807) was the first full-blown American epic poem.[84] Dedicated to 'the love of rational liberty' (x), the poem was an attempt to take stock of America's cultural identity as a newly independent democratic nation.[85] Barlow first explored this theme in an earlier version of the poem entitled *The Vision of Columbus* (1787). As the title implies, the epic conceit of the poem is that Columbus is given visions of America's future by a deity – in this case Hesper, the genius of the west. In the revised text, the historical perspective is expanded to include the war with Britain. Though Hesper tries to give Columbus the Whiggish reassurance that the story unfolding before him has a happy ending, he is repelled by the scenes of

Spanish atrocities. The conventions of epic are used to transform Columbus into an outraged viewer of the spectacular violence of American history. His reaction to seeing the 'gold and carnage' of Cortez's career in Mexico is fierce:

> On these fair fields the blood of realms to pour,
> Tread sceptres down, and print thy steps in gore,
> With gold and carnage swell thy sateless mind,
> And live and die the blackest of mankind. (ll: 325–8)

The sense of violation is emphasized by the allusion to Milton's Paradise:

> Not that fair field
> Of Enna, where Proserpin gath'ring flours
> Her self a fairer Flour by gloomy Dis
> Was gather'd, which cost Ceres all that pain
> To seek her through the world. (*Paradise Lost*, IV: 268–72)

Though Milton's comparison is negative (the 'real' Paradise is superior to its imaginary, classical antecedents), the reference to the abduction of Proserpine clearly foreshadows the fall of Eve. In Barlow's poem, the loss of those 'fair fields' is also a symbolic Fall from grace, but it is caused by a literal act of dispossession. The onset of the European making of America is to 'print thy steps in gore' – history is written in blood. The function of the Romantic epic is to bear 'all that pain', and to recover the lost beauty of the 'fairer flower'. Cortez is a grotesque travesty of republican virtue: he 'treads scepters down' for the basest of motives (gold), which is the polar opposite (we can assume) of the high-minded motives of the rebels who had defeated the armies of George III.

In the poem's account of the revolutionary war, the 'blackest' deeds are now perpetrated by the British. Significantly, that key word 'sateless' is transferred from the Spanish conquerors to the violence of the new oppressors:

> Crowds of wild fugitives, with frantic tread,
> Flit thro' the flames that pierce the midnight shade,
> Back on the burning domes revert their eyes,
> Where some lost friend, some perished infant lies.
> Their maim'd, their sick, their age-enfeebled sires
> Have sunk sad victims to the sateless fires. (V: 527–32)

As this vignette shows, Barlow recycles the tropes and themes of wartime anti-British propaganda. Though the poem mentions numerous examples of 'sateless' British and Indian cruelty, the text focuses on two atrocities. One of these, perhaps unsurprisingly, is the fabled Jane McCrea, who is thinly disguised as a character called Lucinda. In Barlow's version of the murder, her lover arrives at the scene too late to save her, but he gets his revenge by killing the two Indians as they are 'disputing' her 'gory scalp, the horrid prize of blood' (VI: 681–2). Within the context of spectacular violence, this 'horrid prize of blood' could be a synecdoche for America itself. The murder is yet another example of the 'sateless' lust for 'gold and carnage' imprinting its bloody marks on the feminized 'fair field' of American virtue. Like Proserpine, Lucinda / McCrea is about to be 'gathered' by the forces of darkness. In order to heighten her desirability and value, her appearance is sexualized: 'her kerchief torn betrays the globes of snow / That heave responsive to her weight of woe' (VI: 677–8). The conquest of Lucinda is simultaneously erotic and mercenary: 'the scalps by British gold are paid' (VI: 671). But commodification is also dehumanization – 'No marks distinguish, and no man can know' the destiny of Lucinda's 'sacred spoil' (VI: 623–4). The job of remembering the victim is left to the distinguishing and distinguished 'marks' of epic poetry. Its role is to bear the 'weight of woe', to act as the conscience of bloodily imprinted history, and to sentimentally elevate the victims of conflict: 'the tale, ye nations, hear; / Eternal ages, trace it with a tear' (VI: 617–18).

Unlike the reworking of the McCrea legend, the second atrocity which the poem focuses on produces a much more memorable and original contribution to the discourse of spectacular violence. Barlow turns his attention to the appalling fate of those American prisoners of war who were incarcerated on British ships in New York harbour. In modern parlance this crime would be called prisoner abuse, but at the time it overlapped with both slavery and captivity narratives. Barlow's source was almost certainly Ethan Allen's *A Narrative of Colonel Ethan Allen's Captivity* (1779).[86] According to Linda Colley, this was 'the most famous captivity narrative published during the war'.[87] The book recounted Allen's gruelling two years on board a prison ship, an experience he likened to the middle passage (78–80), and which led him to conclude that the British were 'a murdering and cruel enemy' (57). In order to amplify the horrors of the prison-ship scene, Barlow made a striking aesthetic decision. He utilized that most conspicuous of non-realist epic conventions, the 'machinery' or participation of the gods, and invented a new deity: the Goddess Cruelty. Given the fact that such inventiveness was more normally the métier of the eighteenth-century mock-epic, this was a high-risk poetical strategy. But the new goddess's role is to act as the apotheosis of Terror, and her insertion into the poem is a striking recognition of the cultural authority of spectacular violence in Romantic period literature. The scene is a classic vignette of 'sateless' cruelty, and is worth quoting at some length:

> She comes, the Fiend! Her grinning jaws expand,
> Her brazen eyes cast lightning o'er the strand,
> Her wings like thunder-clouds the welkin sweep,
> Brush the tall spires and shade the shuddering deep;

She gains the deck, displays her wonted store,
Her cords and scourges wet with prisoners' gore;
Gripes, pincers, thumb-screws spread beneath her feet,
Slow poisonous drugs and loads of putrid meat;
Disease hangs drizzling from her slimy locks,
And hot contagion issues from her box.
O'er the closed hatches ere she takes her place,
She moves massy planks a little space,
Opes a small passage to the cries below,
That feast her soul on messages of woe;
There sits with gaping ear and changeless eye,
Drinks every groan and treasures every sigh.
Sustains the faint, their miseries to prolong,
Revives the dying and unnerves the strong.
But as the infected mass resign their breath,
She keeps with joy the register of death.
As tost thro' portholes from the encumber'd cave,
Corpse after corpse fall dashing in the wave;
Corpse after corpse, for days and months and years.
The tide bears off, and still its current clears;
At last, o'erloaded with the putrid gore,
The slime-clad waters thicken round the shore. (VI, 45–70)

The reason for the goddess's existence is the unprecedented nature of the offence. She descends to oversee 'New modes of cruelty' (VI: 3) introduced by the British. Unlike some of their antecedents – cannibalism, the Inquisition, Barbary piracy – these 'new' forms of cruelty cannot hide behind the relativist 'cloak' of primitive zeal or custom. The goddess represents the catastrophic regression of those who 'change the British for the brutal heart' (VI: 20). As an emblem of American nationalist propaganda, Cruelty is the nemesis or de-creation of America, a counterblast to the sublime revolutionary energy of Blake's Orc or Albion. It is as if she is transforming America into a floating necropolis, a stationery version of the slave-ship *Zong*: 'Corpse after corpse fall dashing in the wave; / Corpse after corpse, for days and months and years' (in an authenticating footnote (423–4), Barlow claims that 11,000 Americans died over a period of 18 months on just one prison ship called the *Jersey*). Eventually, the Atlantic ocean, 'That laves, that purifies the earth and sky' (VI: 3) will itself expire. The monstrous goddess is a creative amalgam of Milton's Sin, Pope's Dullness, and Pandora – 'hot contagion issues from her box'. She is the ultimate, sublime female Fury, a Maenad to end all Maenads, the most violent, vindictive and 'unnatural' female in Romantic literature. Her sadism is 'sateless': she 'Sustains the faint, their miseries to prolong, / Revives the dying and unnerves the strong'. As the accompanying illustration to the text shows, female power is stereotypically associated with masculinity (Figure 18). That

Figure 18 'The Goddess Cruelty', from Joel Barlow, *The Columbiad* (1807)

key visual signifier of female gender, the breast, is concealed by shadow, while the brooding and sadistic face is very masculine, and the arms are muscular.

But there are two further ways to read the 'register of death' in this image. The first way is to consider the aesthetic composition of the illustration. If a diagonal line is drawn from bottom right to middle left, the picture divides neatly into two halves. The dividing line follows the angle of the barrel of the cannon under which there is a corpse – clearly a symbol of the war which has summoned this demon into existence. In the bottom left corner is the realistic depiction of the prisoners, their supplicating faces, hands and arms poking through the grill of the hold in a classic attitude of abjection. In the upper right corner is the 'presiding' genius of Cruelty reading her book of death. On the one side, there is history and realism (supported by authenticating footnotes and statistics); on the other side, the mythologizing conventions of the literary epic. The formal separation of the two modes of representation could imply that Barlow wanted the goddess to be perceived as a self-conscious device of literary artifice, a kind of artistic and moral special measure. Put the other way round, the splicing together of the two modes of representation is barely credible. The goddess hovers precariously on the edge of Miltonic kitsch, the creation of the 'machinery' of theatrical stage and lighting effects.

Another way to interpret the image is to consider its political iconography. Clearly, as a presiding emissary of specifically British cruelty, the goddess represents a version of Britannia. But there are no visual indications of this, just as there are no signifiers of femaleness. Indeed, if the image is taken out of context, it would be difficult to identify any national characteristics in the composition. Again, this adds to the sense that the goddess is a temporary interloper, a visitation summoned up by the dire circumstances of revolutionary war. This interpretation is reinforced by a footnote in which Barlow notes that the atrocity of the prison ships was a crime which ran 'contrary' to the 'freeborn' spirit of English national character which Barlow revered (424). English savagery is not excused, but it is at least an historical aberration. The goddess is a spectacular textual event, but she belongs in the epic past, when the fate of nations was decided by catastrophic warfare.

Barlow's use of historical hindsight may appear to have resolved the tensions in the image, but there is a lingering problem. The shock value of the realist part of the composition comes from seeing white prisoners where there would normally be slaves. By coincidence, the poem was published in the same year in which Britain abolished the slave trade. But the pictorial allusion to the middle passage is so strong that if the viewer dwells on the picture for any length of time, it is difficult not to see the helpless white faces and arms changing colour. The end of the war and the creation of America as an independent nation – the ostensible vanishing point or teleology of the tableau – did not bring about the emancipation of the American slaves who are the constitutive absence in the image. De Toqueville commented that emancipation was a 'question of life and death' for southern whites, and he prophesied with uncanny accuracy that emancipation would bring about an increase in 'race prejudice'.[88] In *The Columbiad*, Hesper commands the new American nation to be consistent and eradicate slavery: 'purge all privations from your liberal code' (VIII: 392). This harangue is an uncomfortable reminder that Cruelty may simply have changed sides at the end of the war. Seen from this perspective, Barlow's goddess is a displacement of the Other within America, the externalization of a deeply ingrained internal flaw.

5
Unruly People: The Spectacular Riot

> ... impressing the mind of the spectator with an idea, as if not only the whole metropolis was burning, but all nations yielding to the final consummation of all things.
>
> (Report on the Gordon riots, *The Political Magazine*, June 1780)[1]

> ... the rioters were masters of the city; the government of the mob had begun
>
> (Report on the Bristol riots, *Annual Register*, 1831)[2]

The theme of this chapter is slightly different from previous chapters. Although the chapter studies acts of spectacular violence on the British mainland, this violence has a significantly different character to the atrocities studied so far in this book. First, it is collective violence; second, the target of the violence is property not people. In one sense, therefore, we are dealing with 'bloodless' rather than bloody vignettes, but the aim of this chapter is to show that Romantic popular violence was constructed out of many of the same tropes as the more atrocious violence which has been the theme of this book so far. In particular, crowd violence was nearly always represented as 'savage': recidivist, mindless, instinctual, depraved. Yet this resort to quasi-anthropological tropes of primitive behaviour co-existed with an underlying fear that the mob also represented revolutionary popular politics. It is this tension between pathologization and politicization which generated what I am calling the 'spectacular' mob, the spectre of popular insurrection which haunted bourgeois culture until well into the nineteenth century. This is another topic which needs to be more integrated into Romantic studies: like Frankenstein, Romanticism created a monster which it was also desperate to disown.

'A short-lived mischief'

This chapter will argue that it was the Gordon riots of 1780 and not the French revolution which established the paradigmatic British riot of the

Romantic period and beyond – what I am calling the 'spectacular' mob. As previous chapters have demonstrated, the imagery of popular violence took on a new and indelible 'Jacobin' intensity in the 1790s, but the essential traits and narrative features of this violence were already in place: licentious-ness, anarchy, recidivism, infantilism, self-destruction, Amazonian women, deficient, corrupt or negligent leadership, and brutal state retribution. It is this mythic, carnivalesque crowd which haunted the bourgeois imagination until well into the nineteenth century, and which so heavily influenced the cultural construction of actual Romantic period 'disturbances' – the Priestley or 'Church and King' riots, the Luddites, Peterloo, Cato Street, Swing and the Bristol Reform Bill riots. The significance of these events did not only derive from their 'real' historical agency but from the way they were moulded by a mythologized and demonized discourse of popular violence. Seen from this cultural perspective, it is possible to challenge the widely held view that the Romantic period saw a clear transition from the Georgian 'age of the mob' to the more disciplined and heavily policed 'claim-making' crowd.[3] In the Romantic imagination, there is only a single, spectacular riot.

There are several reasons why it is important to recognize the emergence of the spectacular riot. First, it shows that eighteenth-century revolutionary or proto-revolutionary popular violence was not, at least initially, regarded as a 'foreign', and therefore innately un-British form of behaviour, though anti-Jacobinism worked hard to fix this notion in the public mind. Second, it shows that yet another important source of spectacular violence was firmly in place at the beginning of the Romantic period, and that subsequent represent-ations show a familiar pattern of appropriation and reconfiguration. Third, it locates the sublime 'Otherness' of spectacular violence firmly on British soil: unlike slavery, the French revolution, the Irish rebellion and the American war of Independence, the riotous mob of the Gordon or Bristol riots belonged in a very literal sense to the British social and political system. Paradoxic-ally, this explains the cultural imperative to relocate the mob outside of the public sphere, and to 'explain' popular violence as a reversion to irrational, lower-class, instinctual behaviour. At one level, this was simply an evasion of political responsibility, but it was also a response to a deep-seated fear of popular justice. This anxiety was not restricted to counter-revolutionaries; it was also a serious cause for concern for radicals and liberals.

An apposite illustration of this problem can be found in the way in which Godwin contrasted the horrors of war and popular violence. In *Political Justice* (1793), Godwin castigates warfare as a barbarous tool of State policy, but this does not mean that he condones insurrectionary violence. He argues that the only justified wars are those fought to liberate others from tyranny. Otherwise, war is tool of oppression and a waste of human life. To press this point home, Godwin invokes the aid of 'imagination' to envisage a 'visit' to a battlefield:

> Here men deliberately destroy each other by thousands without any resentment against or even knowledge of each other. The plain is strewed

with death in its various forms. Anguish and wounds display the diver-
sified modes in which they can torment the human frame. Towns are
burned, ships are blown up in the air while the mangled limbs descend
on every side, the fields are laid desolate, the wives of the inhabitants
exposed to brutal insult, and their children driven forth to hunger and
nakedness... these scenes of horror [are] the total subversion of all ideas
of moral justice... in the auditors and spectators.[4]

The timing of this tirade is important, as it coincided with the beginning of the war against revolutionary France. Godwin paints a spectacle of
wanton violence, a Swiftian or Voltairean debunking of the 'causes' of war.
In Godwin's radical 'imagination', there is no real enemy, only a politically
constructed enemy. His vignette is also an *exposé* of the way in which war
spills over into Terror: note the atrocities against civilians ('wives... exposed
to brutal insult'), and the resulting social devastation. Echoing the republican sentiments of Thomas Paine, who likened war to a game of Faro played
by monarchical governments, Godwin's aim in presenting 'scenes of horror'
is to jolt the reader into rethinking the 'moral justice' of war.

But this attack on legitimacy and patriotism does not mean that Godwin is
uncritical of revolutionary violence. The violent course of the French revolution in 1792–93 posed a dilemma for many radicals. As Saree Makdisi notes,
'It was, then, simply the *possibility* of an urban insurrection – armed or otherwise – that terrified the government, the propertied classes, and the polite
reformers, as well as the liberal-radicals themselves'.[5] In the early stages
of the French revolution, 'liberal-radicals' like Godwin explained excessive
popular violence as the natural consequence of a sudden release from years
of oppression, but they also believed or hoped that this phase would pass
away relatively quickly. When this failed to happen, the radical theory
of short-lived hyperbolic violence came under pressure. Godwin tried to
refine the radical analysis by drawing a quantitative and qualitative distinction between 'anarchy' and 'despotism'. If 'anarchy has slain its hundreds,
despotism has sacrificed millions upon millions'. Anarchy is 'a short-lived
mischief', admittedly a 'dreadful remedy', but a 'sure one' born of 'men
rendered mad with oppression, and drunk with the acquisition of new born
power'; despotism, on the other hand, is 'all but immortal' (3: 296). But
this explanation was insufficient to exorcise the demons of popular violence
from the text, and at the end of *Political Justice* Godwin returned to the
theme. He assures his middle-class readers that his 'levelling principles' will
not – as anti-Jacobin propaganda trumpeted – excite the 'barbarian' lower
orders into a 'massacre'. But he does more than simply issue this denial.
Once again he invokes the 'imagination' to visualize a scene of carnage, in
this case an urban massacre rather than a battlefield:

the instruments of massacre are actuated with all the sentiments of fiends.
Their eyes emit flashes of cruelty and rage. They pursue their victims

from street to street and from house to house. They tear them from the arms of their fathers and their wives. They glut themselves with barbarity and insult, and utter shouts of horrid joy at the spectacle of their tortures. (3: 467)

This 'spectacle' is the nemesis of popular politics. Yet, Godwin still tries to convince the reader (or himself) that a 'moment of horror and distress' will lead to 'ages of felicity', and that 'the first opening and illumination of mind will be attended with disorder'. Godwin's massacre is simultaneously excessive and explicable: 'massacre is perhaps the most hateful scene, allowing for its momentary duration, that any imagination can suggest' (3: 467–8).

Godwin's simultaneous fascination and revulsion reflects the climate of counter-revolutionary fear and intimidation which existed in Britain during the 1790s. To 'imagine' popular violence was to imagine the overthrow of the government, a potentially treasonous act. But the idea of extreme, even apocalyptic violence taking place in the streets of British cities was not new. As Ronald Paulson has argued, it was the Gordon riots which provided 'the context in which many English people naturally saw the events of 14 July 1789'.[6] Out of the Gordon riots emerged a new force in British cultural history – the spectacular mob.

The 'June days' of 1780: The Gordon riots

The Gordon riots erupted in London in June 1780. The political background to the riots goes back to 1778, when the government passed a Catholic Relief Bill. The Bill granted modest new civil rights for Catholics, primarily concerning education and property ownership, but this was enough to rouse fierce opposition from militant Protestants. Under the leadership of Lord George Gordon, the newly formed Protestant Association successfully blocked the introduction of the new law in Scotland, and flushed by this success turned its attention to getting the Bill repealed in England. On 2 June 1780, as MPs were voting on this issue, a crowd of around 50,000–60,000 protestors assembled in St George's Fields in order to present a petition to parliament. Gordon claimed that the petition contained 120,000 signatures, though a more accurate figure is in the region of 44,000. The violence began on a small scale with the jostling and intimidation of MPs. But when the repeal vote was overwhelmingly defeated (6 in favour of repeal, 192 against), the violence quickly escalated. The first targets were Catholic chapels and properties and the homes of politicians who had supported the Bill. The latter included Sir George Saville, Lord Sandwich and Lord Mansfield. But the destruction soon widened beyond sectarianism to include symbols of State power, most famously Newgate prison, which was attacked on 6 June. When the gatekeeper refused to hand over the keys, the prison was burned down, and over 300 prisoners were released, 4 of whom were on death row. On the same day, the Bank of England was assaulted. It seemed to many observers that the violence had assumed an insurrectionary and apocalyptic character. The *Annual Register* called the night of 7 June a time of 'infernal humanity . . . one of the most dreadful spectacles this country ever beheld . . . every thing served to impress the mind with ideas of universal anarchy and approaching desolation'.[7] Dr Johnson spoke of a 'time of terror', and William Cowper described a 'Metropolis in flames, and a nation in ruins'.[8] Nathaniel Wraxall saw a resemblance between the Gordon riots and the Peasants' Revolt, comparing Gordon to 'Wat Tyler and Jack Cade, the incendiaries of the Plantagenet era'.[9] The mob's contempt for genteel property implied a degree of class-consciousness. For example, Lord Mansfield's house in Bloomsbury was vandalized 'with the utmost relenting fury': his 'superb' furniture and library of around 1000 books, his 'rich wardrobe' and 'some very capital pictures' were all burned in the street, and the wine from his cellars 'plentifully bestowed it on the populace' (*Annual Register* (1780), 261). The City of London authorities were initially slow to intervene, but a force of 10,000 troops was eventually brought into the capital to restore order. Their impact was lethal: 210 rioters were killed outright, and 75 fatally injured; there were 450 arrests; 62 rioters were sentenced to death, of whom 25 were hanged, and 39 transported.[10] The destructiveness of the riots was unprecedented. According to John Stevenson, the Gordon riots were 'the largest civil commotion in England since the Monmouth Rebellion', and Robert Shoemaker notes that this was the only occasion when the Georgian mob 'threatened to take over the city'.[11]

Although the riots may have seemed like an outbreak of Protestant Terror, a 'paroxysm of religious phrenzy', in Burke's words,[12] no Catholics were killed by the rioters, and this led to speculation (which has continued to the present day) that the riots may have had covert political motives to unseat Lord North's unpopular pro-American war government. Indeed, historians are still excavating new meanings for the riots: Peter Linebaugh, for example, finds evidence of infiltration by the culture of transatlantic plebeian republicanism.[13] The issue of 'direction' or leadership is an important factor in the discursive construction of the spectacular riot: conspiratorial theories concerning the motivation of the rioters provided a degree of mystique which aided the transition from fact to myth. As we turn, therefore, to the transformation of the Gordon riots from history into cultural legend, it is the carnivalesque or Saturnalian features of the narrative which demand attention: inverted power, transgression, taboo, and the grotesque body. Symbols of authority are destroyed and desecrated in a process can be linked to what Bakhtin calls decoronation (though strictly, as we shall see in relation to the Bristol riots, decoronation involves the crowd taking over such sites). There are potentially two striking symbols of decoronation in the Gordon riots. The first is the destruction of Newgate, the English precursor of the Bastille (Figure 19). When Dickens recreated the riots in his novel *Barnaby*

Figure 19   'The Burning and Plundering of Newgate and Setting the Felons at Liberty by the Mob' (July 1780)

Rudge (1841), he made the burning of Newgate and the release of the prisoners a centrepiece of the narrative. His letters to his publisher Forster show that Dickens was infected by the 'anarchic' power of the mob: 'I have just burnt into Newgate, and am going out in the next number to tear the prisoners out by the hair of their heads'; 'I have let all the prisoners out of Newgate, burnt down Lord Mansfield's, and played the very devil... I feel quite smoky when I am at work'.[14] A second, conspicuous moment of demotic power is the attack on the Bank of England. As the *Annual Register* observed, 'any rational mind' could understand the disastrous 'consequences' of the storming of this building (*Annual Register* (1780), 262). But I want to propose a different climax to the carnivalesque, mythic version of the riots: the attack on Langdale's distillery. This is the point at which the recidivist, infantilist 'mob' auto-destructs in a drunken orgy. Self-destruction is the most spectacular signifier of the sociopathic tendencies of mob-rule; it is the logical outcome of an absence of super-ego, discipline and elevated leadership. The imagery of an imploding anarchy represents the anagnorisis of what Freud called the 'herd instinct'. The spectacular power of this mock-triumphal moment was captured vividly by Thomas Holcroft, a source used by Dickens:

> But powder and ball do not seem to have been so fatal to them as their own inordinate appetites. Numbers, it is said, and at various places, died with inebriation, especially at the distilleries of the unfortunate Mr. Langdale, from whose vessels the licquors ran down the middle of the street, was taken up by pailfuls, and held to the mouths of the besotted multitude; many of whom killed themselves with drinking non-rectified spirits, and were burnt or buried in the ruins... at Newgate likewise many of them had made so free with the liquor that they could not get away, and were burnt in the cells. In the streets men were lying upon bulks and stalls, and at the doors of empty houses, drunk to a state of insensibility, and to a contempt of danger: boys and women were in the same condition, and so many of the latter with infants in their arms.[15]

The political subtext is clear: the mob are 'non-rectified spirits' reverting to a pre-social, 'savage' behaviour. A similar description can be found in another, later source which Dickens probably knew, George Lillie Craik's *Sketches of Popular Tumults; Illustrative of the Evils of Social Ignorance* (1837). This book, along with Carlyle's *The French Revolution*, which was published in the same year, re-presented the imagery of popular violence for the Victorian literary imagination. In Craik's account of the attack on Langdale's, 'Many indeed drank themselves literally dead, and many more, who had rendered themselves unable to move, perished in the midst of flames'.[16] In *Barnaby Rudge*, the rioters are immolated in a Miltonic 'hideous lake' of burning alcohol (Figure 20).[17] Such scenes can encode bourgeois society's worst fears about the plebeian underclass without straying too far from the historical facts. The ideological function of the quasi-anthropological discourse of recidivism is to both register and contain the primitive violence of the crowd by turning it against itself. Additionally, this scene is confirmation of the irrationality of the mob, the abnegation of any higher purpose behind the violence. As Dickens puts it,

> the great mass never reasoned or thought at all, but were stimulated by their own headlong passions, by poverty, by ignorance, by the love of mischief, and the hope of plunder. (483)

In actual fact, even this epicentre of the riots showed some evidence of 'discipline', as fire engines were allowed to put out fires in nearby buildings.[18]

Figure 20   Hablot K. Browne, 'Rioters', from Charles Dickens, *Barnaby Rudge* (1841)

But the narrative conventions of the mythic riot are predominantly mock-epic. Leaders are mock-leaders: riff-raff, criminals, impostors, women, or even 'well-dressed' genteel defectors or agitators. Riots, like the aristeia of the mock-epic, propel social outcasts into the historical limelight. In Holcroft, the mob is infiltrated by 'those miscreants, who always mingle with the mob, whose trade is plunder' (23). For Craik, the difference between genteel and plebeian leadership distinguishes a true rebellion from a riot. The former is a 'mixed association of men from every rank in the community'; the latter is a mob of the 'very lowest orders' with a poor 'mental culture', led by urban 'desperadoes and renegades' (104–6). Craik must have known that the trials of the rioters revealed precisely such a 'mixed association' of social ranks, but this fact is ignored.[19] The infantile, spectacular mob is a much more useful ideological tool. It can be easily manipulated by unscrupulous and sinister demagogues like Gordon – 'just now the reigning hero' as the poet George Crabbe observed[20] – and it reveals its true cowardice when faced with the phallic intervention of the law. In Craik, the 'feeble' rabble are 'scattered like chaff before the wind' when the 'natural strength of established society' is 'aroused and directed' (84). In *Barnaby Rudge* the rioters are also easily dispersed: 'a single company of soldiers could have scattered them like dust' (482). This trope of abject surrender glosses over the lethality of troops using rifles and grapeshot against clubs and firebrands.

But once the 'natural strength of established society' has been restored, the tone changes from condemnation to regret or pathos. This is another reason for the spectacular riot's cultural durability and accessibility. With the threat of violence extinguished, the focus changes to its terrible consequences: in Craik's words, 'the miserable end of so many of the unhappy wretches' (23). The perpetrators of popular violence are transformed into pathetic victims of delusion, appetite and folly. Britain's bloody penal code is exposed as a harsh and brutal punishment (it is worth a reminder that in all the cases of rioting looked at in this chapter, all the offences were against property). Public execution is at best a horrific deterrent, at worst a counter-spectacle of retaliatory violence.[21] The chastened, even tragic tone of the final phase of the spectacular riot was an attempt to turn the affective spotlight on the abuses of State power. The desire to punish the offenders conflicted with deep-seated liberal beliefs in the constitutional safeguards against tyranny. As Charles James Fox declared inimitably in relation to the riots, it was better to be 'governed by a mob than a standing army'.[22] Burke regarded the use of the army in the Gordon riots as 'establishing a military on the ruins of the civil government'. Even though he was threatened personally as a Catholic sympathizer, and had to defend himself with his sword, Burke feared that martial law would turn London into 'Paris, Berlin or Petersburg', and that 'scenes would ensue, at which he was chilled with horror only to think of' (603). Burke also advised that only six ringleaders should be executed; the remaining 'thoughtless' plunderers should be treated leniently. Otherwise, the 'carnage', which 'resembles a Massacre than a sober execution', would backfire, and penal laws 'lose their Terror'.[23] For Burke, these 'ringleaders' were justified targets, not only because of their actions but because they were socially qualified to be *bona fide* leaders. As George Rudé discovered, the trials and special assizes revealed the composition of the rioters to be predominantly 'sober workmen'.[24] Burke's advice was ignored and 25 people were executed 'near the spot where the felonies they were guilty of had been committed'.[25] The victims included women and teenagers. As Burke might have predicted, this ensured that the spectacular riot would preserve a space to criticize the 'Terror' of the State. Dickens's account of the executions captures the Burkean mood of solemnity, pathos and indignation:

> there had been many such sights since the riots were over – some so moving in their nature, and so repulsive too, that they were far more calculated to awaken pity for the sufferers, than respect for that law whose strong arm seemed in more than one case to be as wantonly stretched forth now that all was safe, as it had been basely paralysed in time of danger... [A] boy was hanged in Bow Street; other young lads in various

quarters of the town. Four wretched women, too, were put to death. In a word, those who suffered as rioters were, for the most part, the weakest, meanest, and most miserable among them . . . (698)

E. P. Thompson has described the Gordon rioters as 'a half-way house in the emergence of popular political consciousness . . . a mixture of manipulated mob and revolutionary crowd'.[26] The function of the spectacular riot was to contain the threat of 'popular political consciousness' by foregrounding the 'manipulation' and irrational destructiveness of popular violence. The spectacular riot is the antithesis of Thompson's customary 'moral economy', in which 'behind every form of popular direct action some legitimizing notion of right is to be found' (73). After 1780, as Shoemaker notes, 'Attitudes towards the mob would never be the same again',[27] but it is important to recognize the role of cultural fantasy in this reaction. It was the Gordon riots, not the French revolution, which put the image of the 'revolutionary crowd' firmly in the public eye and 'formed part of the consciousness which people carried into the revolutionary era'.[28] Gillray's 1788 caricature 'The Butchers of Freedom' (Figure 3) provides striking evidence that a visual language of urban massacre existed in British culture prior to the French revolution. As noted in Chapter 2, the placing of Burke at the centre of this scene is a breathtaking irony, as if Gillray sensed that Burke was about to become the major exponent of the idea of the Jacobin mob. But Gillray is also caught in this irony, as his later anti-Jacobin cartoons tried to efface the similarity between English and French popular violence. In David Bindman's words: 'though the sans-culottes are presented in British caricature as uniquely and essentially French, the typological origins of their representation, with a few refinements, are to be found in contemporary perceptions of the London rather than the Paris mob'.[29] In this complex interplay of cultural innovation and amnesia, the revolutionary crowd emerges as imminent and Other, familiar and remote, historical and spectral, real and fantastical.

The 'fierce rushing crowd' in the 1790s

Godwin's anxious attempt to find a way to promote the virtues of 'anarchy' was symptomatic of the unstable and threatening place which popular violence held in the public political sphere. As the propaganda wars of the 1790s heated up, the invoking of the spectacular mob became one of the most reliable weapons of counter-revolutionary loyalism.[30] The aim was to make revolutionary ideas synonymous with violence and dangerous delusion, and to secure popular assent for repressive measures against radicals. This campaign was a huge distortion of the actual intentions of the overwhelming majority of mainland British radical groups in the 1790s. Excluding the situation in Ireland, and accepting the possibility of revolutionary plotting by O'Coigley and the United British in 1798, there is no substantial evidence that British radicalism was prepared to use any form of violence other than the constitutional 'right of having and using arms for self-preservation and defence',[31] and even this last resort was never tested.[32] The collapse of the Treason Trials in 1794 testified to this fact, but this defeat did not prevent the government continuing to restrict the rights of free speech and assembly. As E. P. Thompson notes, Charles James Fox's habeas corpus Bill of 1792 may have prevented the onset of an English White Terror.[33]

Given this climate of fear and intimidation, it is understandable that many radicals and liberals were wary of the whole idea of popular violence. As Jon Mee argues, an anxiety about violence afflicted the inspirational discourse of quasi-religious 'enthusiasm' which was a major tributary of radical ideology: 'amiable sympathies that seemed to be the basis of civic society teetered on the edge of the unruliness of the crowd.'[34] Every radical writer faced the problem of being tarred as an incendiary demagogue. Godwin was so concerned about this that he went so far as to lampoon 'Political Associations' in language that would not have been out of place in the loyalist Association for the Preservation of Liberty and Property against Republicans and Levellers: 'all is delusion or tumult' (4: 146).[35] The tumultuous mob was the spectre haunting the radical movement. By 1803, a year of heightened invasion fears, Coleridge struggled to exorcize the demon of popular violence from his imagination. In a poem called 'The Pains of Sleep', he berates his unconscious for 'entempesting anew' and plunging him into guilty association with the mob:

> But yester-night I prayed aloud
> In anguish and in agony,
> Up-starting from the fiendish crowd
> Of shapes and thoughts that tortured me :
> A lurid light, a trampling throng,
> Sense of intolerable wrong,
> And whom I scorned, those only strong !
> Thirst of revenge, the powerless will
> Still baffled, and yet burning still !
> Desire with loathing strangely mixed
> On wild or hateful objects fixed.
> Fantastic passions ! maddening brawl !
> And shame and terror over all ![36]

As Wordsworth put it in *The Prelude*, the 'froward multitude' were a lurking force who 'Murmur (for truth is hated, where not loved)' (*Prelude* (1850 text), 7: 531–6). In Robert Bage's 'Jacobin' novel *Hermsprong* (1796), the eponymous hero displays his political mettle by quelling a riot of Cornish tin miners, and cuffing a 'turbulent' heckler.[37] This paternalist solution to popular violence shows a close affinity between radicals and conservative

Evangelicals. In Hannah More's 'The Riot', one of her Cheap Repository tracts series, Tom Hod is persuaded by the loyal Jack Anvil to desist from participating in a bread riot. Tom sees the error of his ways:

> So I'll e'en wait a little till cheaper the bread,
> For a mittimus hangs o'er each rioter's head.
> And when of two evils I'm asked which is best,
> I'd rather be hungry than hang'd, I protest.[38]

Fear is the corollary of obedience.

So if the sympathies of all radical writers, in Mee's words, 'teetered on the edge of the unruliness of the crowd', it required considerable courage to present popular violence in a positive light. One solution to this problem was to relocate such violence in an 'allegorical' setting that was displaced historically, geographically, or politically. For example, Blake's depiction of the 'fierce rushing' crowd in his 'prophetic' poem *America* (1791–93) may carry a more radical charge than has been previously recognized by critics. As David Erdman first postulated, Blake was probably recalling the Gordon riots (which Blake may have participated in), but Saree Makdisi has argued that the image has deeper and more radical roots in seventeenth-century antinomianism and republicanism.[39] For Makdisi, this places Blake outside the 'liberal-radical' consensus, though Makdisi accepts that the text had a very limited circulation. Blake's liminality can be compared to the more populist aesthetics of Robert Southey, who re-created the Peasant's Revolt in his historical verse-drama *Wat Tyler* (1794). It is still unclear why Southey decided not to publish *Wat Tyler*, as his equally subversive *Joan of Arc* appeared in 1796 with impunity. One explanation could be that it is only in *Wat Tyler* that we see the revolutionary power of popular violence. This may have accounted for Southey's caution, despite the fact that the poem explicitly condemns undisciplined mob rule. It is surely no accident that radical publishers issued unauthorized editions of *Wat Tyler* during the post-war revival of mass agitation and the 'monster meeting'.

Unlike the anxious 'liberal-radicals', some plebeian radicals were more audacious in their response to loyalist smears and intimidation. In one sense this was, quite literally, a 'token' response. A shortage of coins in the mid-1790s led to a craze for collecting privately produced tokens. The radical author and activist Thomas Spence set up business as a coin dealer and began to issue his own currency of tokens with radical engravings. These included 'End of Pitt', which shows a hanged man who is easily identifiable as the Prime Minister, and another coin called 'Tree of Liberty', which shows four men dancing round a maypole topped by Pitt's head.[40] It is not known how many of these coins were produced, but the number of extant tokens attests to their popularity, and the device was also used by loyalists – indeed, one reply to 'End of Pitt' uses exactly the same image (though it is worth noting that the viewing public was familiar with the motif of the hanged politician from Gillray's cartoons). In the paper medium, radicals flirted with regicidal representations, including 'Citizen' Lee's broadside 'King-Killing' and John Thelwall's allegory 'King Chaunticleer'.[41] Another radical response was to produce examples of loyalist or royalist atrocities. This was the motivation behind the fable of Count Memmay's feast, an anecdote which circulated in radical culture in the 1790s. According to Thelwall, who recounted the incident in his lectures, Memmay was an 'infernal' French aristocrat. He invited some guests to a 'civic feast' to celebrate the French revolution, and then proceeded to blow them up:

> the whole assembled multitude (men, women and children) were scattered through the air, and their mangled carcasses were found by their patriotic friends weltering in blood, – a spectacle of horror which no tongue can describe, nor heart can scarcely conceive.[42]

In Godwinian terms, this is the treacherous, time-honoured violence of 'despotism'. It was a standard radical argument that the principal source of public violence was the State and its ancillaries. The historical evidence supports the radical case. As John Stevenson notes, 'the most widespread manifestations of popular feeling' in England in the 1790s were anti-radical, not Jacobin.[43] Despite all the propaganda to the contrary, it was loyalist mobs which burned effigies of Thomas Paine and broke up Thelwall's lectures. Even more spectacular was the attack on Joseph Priestley and other Birmingham Dissenters in July 1791. This incident has become known as the 'Church and King' riots, though the label is misleading. As we shall see, the counter-revolutionary character of the violence did not prevent the government punishing the ringleaders. This severe response was not simply about upholding the law: the State feared the anarchic energies of the spectacular mob more than it welcomed the triumph of the loyal mob.

'Electrical patriotism': The Priestley riots of 1791

The Priestley riots began when loyalists attacked a Birmingham hotel on 14 July 1791.[44] Inside the hotel was a group of liberals and Dissenters who were having an annual dinner to celebrate the French revolution. The atmosphere in the weeks and months preceding the meeting had been increasingly tense. The most famous member of the Birmingham 'friends of freedom', Joseph Priestley, had been accused of harbouring revolutionary and subversive views. The *Gentleman's Magazine*, for example, dubbed him the 'arch-priest of Pandaemonium liberty'.[45] Fearing that his presence at the meeting might be used as an excuse for further intimidation, Priestley stayed at home, but this did not prevent the loyalist mob setting fire to the hotel and attacking the meeting-houses and homes of Dissenters. As was the case in the Gordon riots, the reluctance or refusal of the local authorities to intervene led to accusations of pre-meditation and collusion. Priestley avoided personal injury but could not prevent the destruction of his library and laboratory. Had the riots stopped at this point, they would have been sectarian and narrowly 'patriotic' in character, but as in the Gordon riots, the scale of the violence fanned out to include symbols of authority such as prisons and the homes of magistrates. It was the nascent class-consciousness of the violence which alarmed the government, overrode considerations of 'loyalty', and which led to the punishment of the ringleaders. In April 1792, 17 rioters were tried, 4 were convicted, and 2 hanged.[46] Despite these prosecutions and compensation payments, the riots had the effect of diminishing the power of the Dissenting intellectuals in the region. Priestley fled to London and then emigrated to America. As anti-Paineite hysteria gripped England, the Association for the Protection of Property and Liberty against Republicans and Levellers set up a local branch in Birmingham.

Clearly, the Priestley 'disturbance' warranted the 'Church and King' label in the contribution which the riots made to the suppression of radicalism in the 1790s. But, in Macherayan terms, the cultural 'work' of the riots helped to consolidate the idea of the spectacular mob. The flagrant distortions of loyalist propaganda testify to an underlying anxiety that the spectacular genie may have been once more released from the bottle. Gillray's cartoon *The Birmingham Toast*, for example, which was published on the first day of the riots, shows Fox, Horne Tooke, Priestley and Sheridan at the celebratory dinner, though none were actually present. Another cartoon called *The Hopes of the Party* shows the same group preparing to cut off the king's head. These efforts to deflect the focus of attention away from the mob can be contrasted with contemporary reportage in which the violence shows conspicuous features of anarchic excess, manipulation, recidivism and self-destruction. In the anonymously authored *An Authentic Account of the Dreadful Riots in Birmingham* (1791), the sense of violent spectacle is immediately heightened in the way in which the loyalist mob is presented as prodigious (numbering about 10,000) and extremely menacing. Before they embark on their orgy of destruction, the rioters burn an effigy of Priestley in front of his house.[47] Lurking behind the mob is the sinister hand of the agitator: according to an unnamed eyewitness, the crowd has 'a degree of system which it is almost incredible to suppose' (4). But the clinching detail is the climactic self-immolation. The location for this debacle is Baskerville House, home of the Dissenting merchant John Ryland. After setting fire to the house and ransacking the wine-cellar, the rioters are consumed in their own flames, 'one so much burnt, that he was recognised only by the buckle in one of his shoes. What could be collected of his remains have just been taken away in a basket'. Another rioter 'was found with his legs burnt off, and a bottle of spirits or wine in each pocket'. The final tableau could easily be transposed almost word for word into *Barnaby Rudge*: 'A great number of the mob were lying in a state of the most insensible drunkenness on the green' (6). The *Annual Register* reported that 'many of the rioters who were drunk, perished in the cellars, either by the flames, or suffocation by the falling of the roof'.[48]

Priestley's own narrative of events also stressed the spectacular violence of the riots. In his pamphlet *An Appeal to the Public on the Subject of the Riots in Birmingham*, Priestley cites one of his own sermons in which he condemned anti-radical bigotry:

> If even burning alive was a sight that the country would now bear, there exists a spirit which would inflict that horrid punishment, and with as much cool indifference, or savage exultation, as in any preceding age of the world.[49]

The destruction of his house and laboratory is composed as a set-piece act of spectatorship. After fleeing his house, Priestley and a friend return later that night to witness the violence (as one local historian has noted, Priestley was 'presumably unrecognized'):[50]

> It being remarkably calm, and clear moon-light, we could see to a considerable distance, and being upon a rising ground, we distinctly heard all that passed at the house, every shout of the mob, and almost every stroke of the instruments they had provided for breaking the doors and the furniture. (30)

What follows next is an intriguing twist on the trope of arson and self-immolation. When they find themselves without any source of fire, the rioters try to 'get fire from my large electrical machine' (30). This attempt to steal Priestley's scientific fire is a bizarre Promethean allusion which highlights the mob's anti-intellectualism. *The Times'* report of the riots (one of the Appendices in Priestley's pamphlet) added a further colourful dimension to this figuration. The newspaper explained the ferocity of the mob's actions as a justified response to hearing the radical diners allegedly toasting 'Destruction to the present government. The king's head upon a charger' (133). The effect of this toast on the loyalists was that 'a kind of electrical patriotism animated them to instant vengeance' against 'these modern reformers' (133–4). In this vignette, 'electrical' energy is transferred from dangerous modernity to the righteous Terror of 'patriotic' normality. Priestley saw things rather differently, of course, and lamented that his private papers were left to the mercy of the 'illiterate mob' (41–2). As Uglow notes, 'book-burning' is an 'abiding image' of the riots (448), but she fails to add that the scene was already part of the repertoire of the spectacular riot: the same fate befell Lord Mansfield's library during the Gordon riots, and, as we shall see, the scene recurs in the Bristol riots of 1831.

The spectacular Priestley mob resembles Burke's philistine Jacobins, the supposed nemesis of high culture. This idea comes across strongly in a pamphlet called *Views of the Ruins of the Principal Houses destroyed during the Riots at Birmingham* (1791), a series of engravings showing some of the most prominent buildings before and after the riots. The images are set out as a set of tragic tableaux, and the visual message of the 'before and after' format is that the riots are an offence against genteel property, not simply an attack on Dissenting or radical ideas. As R. B. Rose has noted, 'It was not always clear whether rich dissenters were attacked because they were dissenters, or because they were rich'.[51] But the mere possibility of the re-emergence of the spectacular mob with its 'fickle' allegiances was enough to rattle the government.[52] As the Home Secretary Lord Dundas put it, the government feared 'the sudden rising of the lower classes of people who may be instigated by the same levelling principle which has been the causes of the disturbances in Birmingham'.[53] The Priestley rioters may have been, in E. P. Thompson's assessment, a 'late backward eddy of the transitional mob, before the Paineite propaganda had started in earnest the formation of a new democratic consciousness', but they were also a confirmation of the cultural power of the 'anarchic', carnivalesque mob of spectacular violence.[54]

'Savages are much alike all over the world': George Walker, *The Vagabond* (1799)

George Walker's popular anti-Jacobin novel *The Vagabond: A Novel* (1799) provides compelling textual evidence of the existence of the spectacular riot in the Romantic imagination. In order to tar radicals with the brush of popular violence, Walker's satirical story anachronistically merges the Gordon riots with the contemporary political scene. In his Dedication to the Bishop of Landaff, Walker claims that he chose the format of the novel as 'an attempt to parry the Enemy with their own weapons', and to deflate the '*political romance*' of radicalism.[55] As noted above, there is in fact very little indication that radicals used literature to promote incendiary violence, but Walker is contributing to a loyalist demonology which made radicalism synonymous with, among other things, a propensity to incite massacre. Walker's decision to conflate the Gordon riots and 'Jacobin' violence shows that the earlier disturbance still exerted a powerful hold on popular memory. Walker also utilizes the global reach of spectacular violence, as the novel's anti-Pantisocratic dénouement takes place in the 'savage' territory of the American Indians.

In Chapters 5–7 of the novel the Gulliverian narrator-hero is unwittingly swept up into a prominent role in the Gordon riots. The anachronism is glaring, as he has just attended a lecture by John Thelwall, rechristened in the novel as 'Citizen Ego'. In an overheard private conversation, 'Citizen Ego' illuminates his orator friends on how to manipulate and swindle the audience by whipping up radical aggression: 'If I mention a Government spy, I always set the room in roar' (92). His comrade responds enthusiastically: 'Talk about revolutions, taxes, ropes, and axes, till you set his brains a-whirling, and then you may pick his pocket with all the ease in nature' (93). Shortly after this scene, the hero, who is a naïve convert to radicalism, finds himself in the middle of the Gordon riots. His chaise is accosted by 'a parcel of ragged fellows' who demand his money. His chivalric response is to challenge one of them to personal combat. After defeating a 'great-boned Irishman' (108) in a bare-knuckle fight (a coded allusion to the political menace of the Irish), the hero is fêted by the mob. He is immediately approached by a 'man, dressed like a chimney-sweeper' (a sartorial signifier of plebeian politics) who 'engages' him as a leader:

> The ignorant believe they are fighting for religion, but we guide them and direct them where the storm shall fall. The passions of men must be raised, their rational senses must be confounded with terrific reports, before the mass can be roused; but there are always a sufficient number of profligates and vagabonds to join in with any thing. (108)

The description of the Gordon riots which follows is based on a close knowledge of Holcroft and other newspaper sources. Despite the fact that it is written from the mock-celebratory point of view of the hero, this remains the most detailed Romantic literary account of the riots. Walker debunks the radical discourse of liberty by presenting the violence as sheer plunder and destruction: 'the energies of the people are unresistable when determined on emancipation, and *unopposed*'; 'Pickpockets, cut-purses, shop-lifters, and felons of every denomination, hailed the dawn of returning freedom' (110–11). The hero's remark 'To say truth, my figure was not a little hideous' (111) may be a wry self-referential joke, as his hideous appearance is clearly a metaphor for the 'hideous' bloodlust of popular violence:

> To see the enemies of liberty perishing in heaps before the burning sword of retributive justice; to see the rage of lust despoiling those disdainful beauties . . . how dear must such a scene be to the friends of liberty and universal man; nor should the paltry consideration of two or three thousand being massacred, to satiate private revenge, be taken into account of so great, so immortal a consideration. (116)

Walker's satirical version of the Gordon riots allows him to settle scores with contemporary radicals. In the attack on the Bank of England the hero's mentor Stupeo is shot and is believed to have been killed. Given that Stupeo is meant to be Godwin, this is a sensational way to dispose of one of the principal authors of 'political romance'. When he resurfaces later in the story, Stupeo is given the opportunity to express a view on the Priestley riots: 'that must have been a mob hired by the government . . . had it been a republican mob, it would have been a different thing; we should then have had a fine display of rational principles' (183). The self-deflating hypocrisy of the remark is apparent, but from a factual and radical perspective the joke falls doubly flat – as we have seen, Godwin went out of his way to denounce popular justice in language that has much in common with Walker's satirical histrionics.

Walker reserves an even more 'savage' fate for Stupeo / Godwin than being gunned down at the Bank of England. When his plan to establish a Pantiso-cratic community in the America wilderness fails, he is captured and burnt at the stake by American Indians. This demise is presented as a form of violent poetic justice: Stupeo 'perished in the heat of his own ideas' (241). Walker further enhances the satirical clout of the scene by alluding to other sources of spectacular violence. There is an implied comparison between Indian and slave violence in the racialized description of the Indians as 'black children' and 'sons of nature' (240). Taking a lead from Burke, Walker also makes a connection between Indian and Jacobin violence. In a footnote he cites a passage from William Playfair's *History of Jacobinism* (1798) which describes a Jacobin atrocity, and adds the comment that 'savages are much alike, all over the world' (241n.). In this fantastical loyalist vision, the new savage is consumed by 'his own' shadow.

Frame-breaking: Byron and the Luddites

In 1816, a year of mass meetings and political turbulence in post-Waterloo Britain, Lord Byron penned the 'Song for the Luddites':

> As the Liberty lads over the sea
> Brought their freedom, and cheaply, with blood,
> So we, boys, we
> Will die fighting, or live free,
> And down with all kings but King Ludd!
>
> When the web that we weave is complete,
> And the shuttle exchanged for the sword,
> We will fling the winding sheet
> O'er the despot at our feet,
> And dye it deep in the gore he has pour'd.
>
> Though black as his heart its hue,
> Since his veins are corrupted to mud,
> Yet this is the dew
> Which the tree shall renew
> Of Liberty, planted by Ludd![56]

This section of the chapter will consider the background to this act of ventriloquial sedition. Byron's 'Ludd' is a force for violent revolutionary change, a virtuous and righteous reawakening of sans-culotte republicanism. History is written 'in the gore' of vanquished despots. Byron imagines the unimaginable: this is not the mindless and anarchic violence of the spectacular mob, but a disciplined and high-minded vision of a plebeian insurrection.[57] This does not mean that Byron was actively recommending such a course of action, but his intervention into the Luddite controversy is an excellent opportunity to study an 'engaged' Romantic response to national-popular violence.

When Byron returned from his Eastern travels in July 1811, he found himself at the centre of industrial conflict. He had some problems with his own mines in Rochdale, 'contested coal-pits' as he called them,[58] but he also resided in an epicenter of Luddism. According to E. P. Thompson, a 'major phase of Luddism' took place in Nottinghamshire between March 1811 and February 1812. The scale of the violence can be gauged by the fact that about 1000 frames were destroyed in this period.[59] A correspondent to a Nottingham newspaper commented that 'The insurrectional state to which this country has been reduced for the last month has no parallel in history, since the troubled days of Charles the First'.[60] In early 1812, the government responded to this militancy with a new law which made frame-breaking a capital offence. Like many other liberals and radicals, Byron was outraged by the severity of this measure. His determination to oppose the Bill in parliament launched his political career. In February 1812, Byron attacked the Bill in his maiden speech in the House of Lords. He also published 'An Ode: To the Framers of the Frame Bill' in the *Morning Chronicle*. These interventions coincided almost exactly with Byron's explosion onto the literary scene with the publication of the first Cantos of *Childe Harolde's Pilgrimage*. Without pushing the point too far, it is possible to see the Luddite moment in 1812 as providing two different 'frames' for the relation between Romanticism and politics: on the one hand, the literary, subjectivised radicalism of the Byronic cult of alienation, celebrity and transgression; on the other hand, the overt, direct intervention into politics through the medium of literary propaganda, public harangue and popular print culture. The stakes of Byron's intervention on behalf of the Luddites could not have been higher, as Byron was literally writing and speaking to save lives, to preserve the bodies or 'frames' of the rioters. In order to rebut the new law, Byron made the exchange of inanimate and animate frames one of his central tropes. He also framed this obscene exchange within the larger, determining institutions and agencies of economic and political power. Unfortunately for the Luddites, it was the 'mythic' violence of the spectacular mob which went forward into the nineteenth-century literary imagination. If the literary teleology of the Gordon riots was *Barnaby Rudge*, the equivalent 'novelization' of Luddism (in Bakhtinian terms) was Charlotte Bronte's *Shirley*, a text in which the Luddites are presented through female eyes as a 'famished and furious mass of the operative class'.[61]

Byron only had to read local Nottingham newspapers to appreciate that Luddism was not a knee-jerk response to new technology. The Luddites were not, like Cobbett, nostalgic for a pre-modern, pre-industrialized mode of production. Their complaint, exacerbated by a poor harvest and Napoleonic blockades, was about the speed and manner in which new capitalist relations of production were being imposed on the community. The frames represented a new means of production which was being used to undermine the moral economy and destroy traditional legal and paternalist safeguards, 'breaking down working customs and disrupting a settled way of life', in E. P. Thompson's words.[62] The frames were targeted, as they were both a real threat (an industrial Trojan horse) and a symbol of the future. One Luddite notice demanded 'an Act to put down all Machinery hurtful to Commonality'.[63] The Luddites saw a bleak future of industrial dehumanization and social degradation. This message is clear in the 'Address from the Framework-knitters to the Gentleman Hosiers of the Town of Nottingham', published in the Whiggish *Nottingham Review* in November 1811. Byron could well have read this Address, as the newspaper was later to publish his Luddite Ode.

> On account of the great rise in the necessaries of life, a man that has full employ, with all his industry, and a woman, with all her care and economy, can by no means support a family with any degree of comfort. If this be the case (which it really is) how deplorable must the situation of those be, that have but a small portion of employ, and at very low rates; but still worse, what must the situation of those that have none at all ... We wish to live peaceably and honestly by our Labour, and to train up our children in the paths of virtue and rectitude, but we cannot accomplish our wishes. Our children, instead of being trained up by a regular course of education, for social life, virtuous employments, and all the reciprocal advantages of mutual enjoyment, are scarce one remove from the brute, are left to all the dangerous evils attendant on an uncultivated mind, and often fall dreadful victims to that guilt, which ignorance is the parent of.[64]

There is whole social, even national narrative of decline in this plea for economic justice. The Address disproves at a stroke the idea that the Luddites were irresponsible industrial thugs and philistines. Luddism only became what E. P. Thompson calls a 'quasi-insurrectionary movement'[65] when this respectable plebeian discourse of artisan radicalism was refused legitimacy in the public sphere. Rather than engage in a dialogue, the government response to artisan power was to mobilize the repressive state apparatus. About 12,000 troops were deployed nationally to suppress the Luddites, which was a greater force than Wellington commanded in the Peninsular campaign. Byron would have seen at first hand the social effects of the 3000 troops billeted in Nottingham. As he put it sarcastically in his 'Ode: To the Framers of the Frame Bill',

> Justice is now in pursuit of the wretches,
> Grenadiers, Volunteers, Bow-Street Police,
> Twenty-two regiments, a score of Jack Ketches.

Byron's speech in the House of Lords exposed State power as an interlocking machinery of economic coercion, militarism and phony patriotism:

> The rejected workmen, in the blindness of their ignorance, instead of rejoicing at these improvements in arts so beneficial to mankind, conceived themselves to be sacrificed to improvements in mechanism.[66]

Byron uses his cosmopolitan credentials to take a swipe at Britain's imperial pretensions:

> I have traversed the seat of the Peninsula, I have been in some of the most oppressed provinces of Turkey, but never under the most despotic of infidel governments did I behold such squalid wretchedness as I have seen since my return in the very heart of a Christian country. (394)

He is also damning about the use of military power, which is presented as a *de facto* state of civil war, and he makes another jibe at the patriotic cachet of the war against Napoleon:

> All the cities you have taken, all the armies which have retreated before your leaders, are but paltry subjects of self-congratulation, if your land divides against itself, and your dragoons and your executioners must be let loose against your fellow-citizens . . . Do not forget, that a mob too often speaks the sentiments of the people. (393)

Byron frames Luddism within a liberal-radical analysis of corruption: political economy is being enforced by a militarized state and bloody penal code. Justice for the Luddites comprises 'twelve butchers for a jury, and a Jeffreys for a judge!' (395).

The House of Lords speech was only one arm of Byron's intervention into the Luddite controversy. While the Bill was still being debated in Parliament, Byron's 'An Ode: To the Framers of the Frame Bill' appeared anonymously in the *Morning Chronicle* on 2 March 1812. It was then reprinted four days later in the *Nottingham Review*. Though some real names were blanked out, the poem's appearance in a local Nottingham paper may well have given it added impact.[67] The poem is a merciless ventriloquism of Tory heartlessness and bigotry:

> The rascals, perhaps, may betake them to robbing,
> The dogs to be sure have got nothing to eat –
> So if we can hang them for breaking a bobbin,
> 'Twill save all the Government's money and meat.
>
> Men are made more easily than Machinery,
> Stockings will fetch higher prices than lives;
> Gibbets on Sherwood will heighten the scenery,
> Shewing how Commerce, how Liberty thrives...
>
> Some folks for certain have thought it was shocking,
> When famine appeals, and when poverty groans;
> That life should be valued at less than a stocking,
> And breaking of frames, lead to breaking of bones.

In the last stanza of the poem, the satirical mask is partially removed:

> If it should prove so, I trust by this token,
> (And who will refuse to partake in the hope,)
> That the frames of the fools, may be first to be broken,
> Who when ask'd for a remedy, sent down a rope. (Binfield,
> *Writings of the Luddites*, 115–16)

Note that alliteration is crucial to the satirical success of the poem. The truculent 'b' of Luddite violence – 'breaking a bobbin' – contrasts with the more emollient 'm' of the masters' system of 'money and meat', but in fact the real power relations are the reverse. It is government violence which is literally and metaphorically breaking the frame(s) of the English moral economy. Unmasked, the meta-violence of the frame-makers or policy 'framers' is simply legalized vengeance, the class tyranny of an unreformed government protecting a system of 'money and meat' in which (with the alliterative ghost of Malthus lurking) 'men are made more easily than Machinery'. This is not a Foucauldian regime of regulation, but rather the brute force of commodification and judicial Terror.

Coincidentally, 1812 also saw the publication of Shelley's first great literary intervention into politics, *Queen Mab*. Shelley is vitriolic about the psycho-social effects of capitalism: 'The harmony and happiness of man / Yields to the wealth of nations', leaving 'nothing but the sordid lust of self, / The grovelling hope of interest and gold' (V: 79–80, 90–91).[68] This is more than a traditional attack on the evils of luxury. The phrase 'wealth of nations' signifies the entry of Adam Smith into radical demonology. Shelley's acerbic lines reflected a wider radical consciousness about the darker side of political economy. In Luddite discourse, Smith and his 'disciples' are class enemies: 'We have only Dr A. Smiths Disciples to contend with whose principles are execrated all over the kingdom' wrote Gravener Henson, leader of the Luddite Committee which presented a petition to parliament in June 1812.[69] In Byron's Ode and the later 'Song for the Luddites', the reader has the satisfaction of seeing this 'execration' transformed into a 'quasi-insurrectionary' plea to break the frames of the framing fools.

But in order to fully appreciate Byron's contribution to Luddite resistance, it is surely necessary to 'frame' his Ode within the fugitive subculture of Luddite songs and poems. As already indicated, Luddism was a movement of skilled artisans, traditionally the most educated sector of the working class. So it can be assumed that Luddite poems and songs, however populist in their tone and format, demonstrate a degree of literary sophistication. As it is only possible to look at a modest selection of these texts, the appropriate place to begin is with the most famous Luddite song, 'General Ludd's Triumph', composed in early 1812.

> The guilty may fear, but no vengeance he aims
> At honest man's life or Estate
> His wrath is entirely confined to wide frames
> And to those that old prices abate
> These engines of mischief were sentenced to die
> By unanimous vote of the Trade
> And Ludd who can all opposition defy
> Was the grand Executioner made. (Binfield, *Writings of the Luddites*, 99)

The precariously reassuring message is that the 'honest man' is safe for now, though the 'wide frame' of wrath undoubtedly has spare capacity. The song inverts the State's immoral trading of human frames for machine frames. In a carnivalesque imitation of the judicial process, 'These engines of mischief were sentenced to die'. The literary circumlocution 'engines of mischief' performs a considerable degree of poetical and ideological work. The phrase recalls the diabolical military technology of Spenser's and Milton's epics, but it also alludes to and neutralizes anti-Jacobin attacks on the radical press. In 1816, the year of Byron's 'Song for the Luddites', the backsliding Southey used this exact phrase to malign radical periodicals:

> Of all the engines of mischief which were ever yet employed for the destruction of mankind, the press is the most formidable, when perverted in its uses, as it was by the Revolutionists in France, and is at this time by the Revolutionists in England.[70]

For General Ludd, however, it was the State which was intent on bringing about 'the destruction of mankind'. In Luddite self-representation, violent acts such as machine breaking and intimidation were the righteous, defensive or retaliatory measures of the victimized. In February 1812, just before Byron's Ode appeared, General Ludd sent a threat-letter to Spencer Perceval, the British Prime Minister:

> The Bill for Punish.g with death has only to be viewd. with contempt & oppos.d by measure equally strong; & the Gentleman who framd. it will have to repent the act: for if one man's life is Sacrificed, ! Blood for !blood. (Binfield, *Writings of the Luddites*, 113)

Such threats may have been deliberately exaggerated, though Byron worried that the 'effect of the present bill' would be to 'drive' the Luddites 'into actual rebellion'.[71] A Nottingham broadside of May 1812 might have confirmed Byron's worst fears:

> Welcome Ned Ludd, your case is good,
> Make Perceval your aim;
> For by this Bill, 'tis understood
> It's death to brake a Frame – . . .
>
> You might as well be hung for death
> As breaking a machine –
> So now my Lad, your sword unsheathe
> And make it sharp and keen –
>
> We are ready now your cause to join
> Whenever you may call;
> So make foul blood, run clear & fine
> Of *Tyrants great and small*! (Binfield,
> *Writings of the Luddites*, 132)

Some bizarre historical coincidences frame this text. Only a few days after it appeared, Perceval was assassinated on the steps of the parliament building. His assassin, a bankrupt Liverpool timber merchant called Bellingham, was not a Luddite, but he was a victim of capitalist failure. E. P. Thompson notes that there was widespread rejoicing at the news of the Prime Minister's death, and many people hoped – mistakenly, as it turned out – that a more radical government would be elected.[72] Byron took a window seat to watch the execution of Bellingham at Newgate.[73] Byron may have been remembering this moment when he 'framed' his highly inflammatory 'Song for the Luddites' in 1816, a period of renewed Luddite agitation. The sanguinary imagery of Byron's final stanza may owe a debt to the closing lines of the Nottingham broadside. Even if there was no direct literary influence, it is still possible that Byron was picking up on the 'bloody' aspects of Luddite rhetoric. This does not mean that Luddite songs can be regarded as a direct reflection of historical events, though Luddism did become more violent in 1812, particularly in the north of England, where pitched battles took place at mills and factories (Charlotte Bronte made the attack on Rawdons mill in the Spen valley the basis for her novel *Shirley*). It is more productive to consider the trope of bloodiness as part of a collective radical poetic lexicon. The closing image of the Nottingham broadside conveys lucidly the idea of the republican purging of the rotten body politic. There is even a hint of alchemical transformation – 'make foul blood, run clear & fine'. This anticipates the imagery of natural renewal in Byron's poem – 'Since his veins are corrupted to mud/Yet this is the dew/Which the tree shall renew/Of Liberty, planted by Ludd!' – and it also prefigures Shelley's definition of princes in his 'Peterloo' sonnet 'England in 1819': 'mud from a muddy spring'. The medicinal metaphor of bleeding is a refinement on the more primitive, retributive popular justice of 'blood for blood'. In a Luddite threat letter issued in the wake of the Middleton disturbances of May 1812 (in which 10 Luddites were shot dead), the national plebeian mood is described alliteratively as 'blood or bread'. A short poem attached to the letter concludes,

> The poor cry aloud for bread
> Prince Regent shall lose his head. (Binfield, *Writings of the Luddites*, 183)

This is perhaps the ultimate, regicidal appropriation of the government's tyrannical inversion of the economy of frames: 'Blood for blood' is now a lost head for lost bread. In Byronic terms, the frame of the greatest fool is fit to be broken: 'We will fling the winding sheet/Over the despot at our feet'.

But history had other designs. After the Peterloo massacre of August 1819, the arch-fool himself congratulated the Manchester authorities for their 'prompt, decisive and efficient measures for the preservation of the public tranquillity'.[74] For the Prince Regent, the spectacular mob had been kept at bay.

'Extraordinary riot and conspiracy': Walter Scott, *The Heart of Mid-Lothian* (1818)

The years 1816–20 saw a remarkable resurgence of popular radicalism in Britain. The end of the long war against France inspired many Britons to demand what we would now call a 'peace dividend'. In the radical analysis of corruption, economic justice would be achieved by political reform. A truly accountable government, elected by universal male suffrage, would abolish the onerous system of national debt which existed to serve the parasitical interests of political hangers-on and warmongers. This reform would in turn mean that taxation could be reduced and wealth redistributed, though property would not be expropriated. In order to pressure the unreformed government, the postwar years witnessed a prolific expansion of the radical press and the revival of the 'monster' or mass meeting. The highlights of this campaign are well known: in 1816, the phenomenal success of Cobbett's cheap *Weekly Political Register*; in 1816–17, the three Spa Fields meetings in London, the government crackdown on the press, Cobbett's flight to America, and the Pentridge 'rebellion' of 1817; in 1819, the Peterloo massacre and the Six Acts; in 1820, the Cato Street conspiracy and the Queen Caroline affair. In E. P. Thompson's words, these four years marked 'the heroic age of popular Radicalism'.[75] Unsurprisingly, the forces of anti-radicalism responded with a renewed propaganda offensive. Hannah More came out of retirement in order to lampoon radical leaders as swindlers and hypocrites, while Southey smeared plebeian politics as 'pot-house' demagoguery.[76] As in the 1790s, the character of the radical 'mob' was a fiercely contested political issue.

It was during this 'heroic age' of mass radical agitation that Walter Scott explored the theme of popular violence in his historical novel *The Heart of Mid-Lothian* (1818).[77] The first seven chapters of the novel are a detailed account of the Edinburgh 'Porteous' riot of 1736. This title of the riot comes from John Porteous, a commander of the City Guard, who had been sentenced to death for ordering his men to fire on a crowd who were protesting about the hanging of a popular robber named Wilson. When news arrived that Porteous had been reprieved, an angry crowd broke into the Tollbooth prison (nick-named 'Heart of Mid-Lothian'), extracted Porteous and hanged him. In a footnote, Scott summarized the violence as a combination of 'extraordinary riot and conspiracy' (85n.). The ambiguity of these words suggests that Scott may have been attracted to this riot precisely because of its unclassifiable character. The summary execution of a class enemy was clearly an act of popular justice, but the discipline and focus of the action did not conform to the licentiousness and self-destructiveness of the spectacular mob. As David Lodge has noted, Scott departed from anti-Jacobin conventions by presenting a crowd who were 'disciplined, orderly and responsible' and 'uncontaminated by criminal and anti-social elements'.[78] In fact, as we shall see, Scott's crowd is an unstable representation which fluctuates between spectacular mob and 'disciplined' paramilitary 'order'. This instability reflects Scott's ambivalent attitude towards popular democracy. In 1816, Scott told Lockhart that he could not contribute to the *Edinburgh Annual Register* as he was 'sickened' by 'the prospect of having no events to write but radical riots'.[79] In 1819, Scott noted the 'very alarming aspect of things in our manufacturing districts' and considered raising a militia of Border Sharpshooters.[80] His response to Peterloo was to agree with the government that the radical threat had to be 'counteracted by moral and physical means . . . And you may depend on it that a little intimidation at the first saves an ocean of blood in the long run'.[81] But in his fiction, where these anxieties are displaced onto moments of historical crisis, popular violence is seen as both 'alarming' and impressively effective.

The first point to note about the structure of the Porteous riot is that it comprises two execution scenes: the first is the hanging of Wilson; the second is the hanging of Porteous. The first incident is like a rehearsal for the second: the failed attempt by the crowd to release Wilson from the scaffold is counter-pointed by the lynching of Porteous. The decision by Porteous to fire on the crowd is the catalyst for the outbreak of popular justice, and in this sense he is the author of his own demise, but the intervention of the mob is mediated by the failure of the State to carry out proper judicial process. If the reprieve is also included in the narrative equation, there are actually three executions at work in the riot scene. For the purposes of analysis, a structuralist methodology can be adopted. The three executions are (A) Wilson (disrupted by the crowd and enforced excessively by Porteous); (B) Porteous (disrupted by the reprieve); and (C) Porteous (inflicted by the crowd). This triangular scheme produces a complex and illuminating commentary on the pattern of power relations between the State and the people. For example, take the issue of leniency. It is refused in A, granted in B, and refused in C. C is the carnivalesque appropriation of A, which exposes the double standard of B. Or consider the idea of excessive or abusive power. This is present in all three scenes: in A there is both crowd power and brutal repression; in B the State operates remotely; in C the crowd makes Porteous's body the symbolic target of a politicized anger which is both class-conscious and nationalistic. Finally, consider the vital question of spectacle. In A the crowd is both spectator and victim; in B the spectacle of punishment is forestalled; and in C the agent of A is made the subject of the spectacle. There is no easy resolution of these shifting and conflicting relations: the effect of the interplay between the three positions is to keep the issues open for debate. Moreover, this debate revolves around the gallows, one of the starkest symbols of legal Terror.

In each of the three scenes, the narrative demonstrates an uneasy and muddled sympathy for the crowd's actions. The execution of Wilson is a 'melancholy spectacle' which attracts a 'great number of spectators' who flock to such 'unpleasant exhibitions' (30). The erection of the gallows is like 'the production of some foul demon'. The evoking of the discourse of Gothic Terror seems like a clear condemnation of public execution, but the reader is not allowed to reach this liberal conclusion, as there is an immediate change of tone. The narrator intervenes to question the validity of legal reforms such as the abolition of the carting of the condemned. He asks

> whether, in abridging the melancholy ceremony, we have not in part diminished that appalling effect upon the spectators which is the useful end of all such inflictions. (31)

Yet the credibility of this view is immediately undermined by the 'appalling effect upon the spectators' of Porteous's brutal reprisals. Porteous is clearly a villain, a man of 'of profligate habits, an unnatural son, and a brutal bastard' with a 'hot and surly temper, always too ready to come to blows and violence' (37, 39). Fearing a rescue attempt by the crowd, Porteous makes the 'diabolical' mistake of placing Wilson in manacles and gloating over his 'exquisite torture' (40–1). Porteous is a sadistic torturer, a familiar figure in the discourse of spectacular violence. Wilson's last words to Porteous carry the Foucauldian authority of the condemned man: he remarks ominously that 'your cruelty is great', and prophesies that Porteous will 'soon' be exchanging places (41). These words strike home with the crowd, though any possibility of crowd power is immediately checked by the narrator. We are reminded that 'the common people had some real, and many imaginary causes of complaint' (41). However, none of these 'imaginary causes' are specified. Instead, the moral and political authority of the crowd is strengthened by their nationalist credentials. As Wilson faces the fatal drop, many of the crowd show 'an indignant expression' which evokes 'the ancient Cameronians' who 'glorified the Covenant' and who were executed on 'the same spot' (41), an allusion which links this novel to *Old Mortality* (see Chapter 3). Porteous is therefore both a class enemy and a national enemy. We are reminded that the Riot Act was introduced in 1715 as a response to the first major Jacobite rebellion. But just as we catch sight of this revolutionary crowd, it is obscured by a key feature of the spectacular mob. When Porteous's troops kill some people of 'better rank' who are watching the execution 'at a distance' (42–3), this detail suggests that the crowd may have some genteel admirers. But this notion is soon quashed, as we are told that respectable middle-class citizens 'could not of course belong to the rioters' (48).

The same fluctuating image of the crowd occurs when Porteous is thrown in jail. On the one hand, the assembled crowd is an emblem of nationalist resistance:

> The mob of Edinburgh, when thoroughly excited, had been at all times one of the fiercest which could be found in Europe; and of late years they had risen repeatedly against the government, and sometimes not without temporary success. (45)

On the other hand, the crowd is a sinister mass, a 'dark lake or sea of human heads' (44). When it hears the news of the reprieve, the 'roar of indignation' is like a 'tiger from whom his meal has been rent by the keeper' (47).

This unstable juxtaposition of the spectacular and nationalist mob can be traced throughout the description of the attack on the prison and the execution of Porteous. In an echo of Parisian sans-culottism, the riot begins in a suburb 'inhabited by the lower order of citizens and mechanics' (63), though it quickly expands to include anyone who answers the call for 'all true Scotsmen to join them' (65). The scenes of violence are heightened by the fact that the riot takes place at night. The rioters are 'insurgents', a 'singular mob' (64), and their actions constitute a 'formidable insurrection' (66). There is even 'one stout Amazon' called Madge Wildfire, who is capable of overpowering and disarming a soldier (65–6). But despite this 'unnatural' contravention of the rules of gender, the crowd is scrupulous in protecting the polite classes and particularly women from violence, even to the extent of escorting them home. There is an eerie echo of Jacobin terror in the way that insurgent patrols turn back anyone 'in the garb of a gentleman', but we are reassured that 'terrified females' are not treated as might 'have been expected from the videttes [sentries] of a mob so desperate'. Scott lightens the tone at this point by inserting a class joke: 'many a quadrille table was spoiled that memorable evening'. But the discipline and restraint of the rioters is not benign. The point of patrolling their unrespectable fringes is to repel any 'casual' renegades who 'might disgrace their systematic and determined plan of vengeance' (68).

Like Newgate, the gates of the Tollbooth are burned down. The fire 'illuminates the ferocious and wild gestures of the rioters' (70), but there is no sympathy for the drunken Porteous. Madge Wildfire retorts that 'This sacrifice will lose half its savour if we do not offer it at the very horns of the altar', but Porteous is provided with a priest in order to ensure that the mob does not 'kill both his soul and body' (73). On the cusp of the lynching, the narrator sums up the contradictory qualities of the violence as a 'cruel and vengeful action with a show of justice and moderation' (74). Despite the crowd baying that 'Blood must have blood' (76), the rope maker who prepares the noose is paid for his work.

The description of Porteous's execution emphasizes its shocking quality. This stems from its illegality as well as its brutality. The spectators at nearby windows can be taken as representatives of the novel's readership. They 'muttered accents of encouragement; but in general they were so much appalled by a sight so strange and audacious, that they looked on with a sort of stupefied astonishment' (77). The last glimpse of Porteous is by the novel's appalled hero Butler. He flees from the scene, but 'cast back a terrified glance'. He sees 'a figure wavering and struggling', and 'men striking at it with their Lochabar axes and partisans' (78). Once they are 'completely satiated' by this orgy of violence, the crowd disperses with no 'further excesses' (79).

But it is not so easy for the reader, who, like Butler, is left with the problem of popular violence, 'a figure wavering and struggling'. The figure of the hanging corpse carried considerable political charge in the postwar period. Like the French guillotine, the gallows was a hallmark of State power, and the nemesis of popular violence. In Vic Gatrell's words, hangings also had an 'intensely visualized particularity'.[82] George Cruikshank's 1817 print 'Liberty Suspended!' is a good example of this. Cruikshank defended freedom of expression by showing the hanging of a gagged young woman who represents Liberty. But as Foucault noted, the moment of public execution also offered the condemned criminal a unique moment of political authority: the victim became the 'inverted figure of the king'.[83] It was for this reason that the authorities tried to prevent the crowd hearing the speeches of condemned radicals such as the Cato Street conspirators of 1820.[84] On such occasions, the public execution was a restive, unstable compound of spectacle and potential uprising.

It was these tensions which Scott explored in *The Heart of Mid-Lothian*. It is also worth noting that Scott returned to the gallows motif a few years later in his novel *Quentin Durward* (1823).[85] The novel is set in late-fifteenth-century France and deals with the internecine conflicts between the king and the nobility. The first significant historical fact pointed out by the narrator is that atrocity is a routine feature of aristocratic rule. The 'petty tyrants' ranged against the king have 'perpetrated with impunity the wildest excesses of fantastic oppression and cruelty' on the population, including 'incest, murder, and rapine' (35). But the king is little better; he is 'by nature vindictive and cruel, even to the extent of finding pleasure in the frequent executions which he commanded' (37). It is one of these 'frequent executions' which the rookie Scots soldier Quentin Durward stumbles across at the beginning of the novel. His sees the 'ghastly spectacle' of a bohemian or gypsy hanging from a tree, 'convulsed by the last agony' (91). Though he learns later that corpses of gypsies litter the countryside 'like grapes on every tree' (99), Quentin instinctively cuts the man down, unaware that he is breaking the law. His artless excuse, 'I went to cut him down out of mere humanity' (99), is met with derision, and he is immediately arrested and sentenced to death. His captors take 'a kind of pleasure in the discharge of their horrid office', as if sadism was a requirement of the job. But Scott points the finger of blame at the political culture of arbitrary power: 'under a tyranny, whether despotic or popular, the character of the hangman becomes a subject of great importance' (96). It is hard not to see some contemporaneous relevance in this foregrounding of the iconic figure of the hangman. *Quentin Durward* appeared only three years after the Cato Street conspirators were publicly decapitated.

Near the end of the novel, Quentin witnesses another hanging. This time he sees a French soldier executed for a trivial offence. After the soldier is hanged from the stanchions of a hall window, the effect of the moonlight on his corpse is to cast 'an uncertain shadow' over the scene (279). This image is like a grisly motto for Scott's engagement with the 'uncertain shadow' of popular violence. But the trope also has an uncanny topicality: the next major 'disturbance' in Britain took its name from its mythic leader, 'Captain Swing'.

'Rural war': The Swing riots

The agricultural disturbances known as the Swing riots of 1830 marked the beginning of several years of political turmoil in Britain. In November 1830 a Whig government came to power in England after being out of office for over 40 years. Inspired by the French and Belgian revolutions, the British people had high hopes that Whigs would introduce universal suffrage. In the event, it took almost two years for a watered-down Reform Bill to secure parliamentary assent. As we shall see, the rejection of the Bill in 1831 sparked serious riots in several major cities. It is not an exaggeration to regard the heated political temperature of the period 1830–32 as pre-revolutionary in character.[86] The pamphleteer Edward Gibbon Wakefield hoped that public opinion would prevent the government launching an 'exterminating war' of the type used in Russia and 'our own West Indies'.[87]

The Swing riots erupted in the south of England in 1830.[88] Unlike the disturbances looked at so far in this chapter, Swing was an exclusively rural phenomenon. Motivated by economic rather than political grievances, it comprised organized bands who systematically burned hayricks and intimidated farmers with threat letters. Within months, the unrest had spread across the agricultural counties of southern and eastern England. Cobbett estimated that 26 counties were caught up in the 'great *commotion*'.[89] He made this calculation in a special issue of the *Political Register* entitled 'Rural War'. The title of the pamphlet was provocative, though in fact Cobbett laboured incessantly to bring about a peaceful resolution of the dispute. He understood that the violence was a desperate measure involving impoverished farmers and small producers, the yeomanry class which Cobbett regarded as the social backbone of the moral economy and the guardians of the freeborn Englishmen's traditional rights. Cobbett counselled against the use of violence, though this did not prevent his enemies smearing him as a firebrand. In the fictitious 'Confession of Thomas Goodman', a working-class man claims to have heard Cobbett recommend arming: 'he said it would be verrey Propper for everrey man to keep a gun espesealey young men'.[90] The title page of a loyalist pamphlet called *Imposture Unmasked* (1832) shows Cobbett consorting with a ragged rioter while the countryside blazes in the background. The imagery is a distortion of Cobbett's intentions, but its apocalyptic flavour conveys the revolutionary potential of this 'rural war'. As Ian Dyck has argued, Cobbett was in a unique position to forge a 'radical nexus between town and country' and to 'unite all English workers in a common radical vocabulary'. It was Cobbett's failure to 'exploit these opportunities to their full potential' which explains what Dyck calls 'the missing or lost revolution of 1830–31'.[91] The threat of this 'lost revolution' may explain the Whig government's harsh response to Swing. When the Whigs took office, there were almost 2000 rioters awaiting trial. Special Commissions were appointed and punishments were severe: 252 people were given capital sentences, 19 were hanged, and around 500 were transported to Australia – John Stevenson calls the latter figure 'exceptional'. These losses scarred rural communities for generations.[92]

Clearly, Swing was a major social and political event. But it was the propaganda wars sparked by the riots which turned Swing into a spectacular cultural event. Metropolitan radicals were quick off the mark. At the Rotunda, a London venue of politics and entertainment run by Richard Carlile, Swing was turned quite literally into a stage spectacle. In early 1831 the maverick preacher 'Dr' Taylor performed a 'politico-monological tragedy' called *Swing! Or Who are the Incendiaries?* In this flagrantly seditious republican fantasy, the Swings are a respectable family whose eldest son John worships the 'Genius of Reason'. John converts his brother Frank to poaching and incendiarism as justified responses to the economic misery of rural communities. When Frank is hanged on forged evidence, John becomes 'king' Swing, hoisting a tricolour flag and swearing vengeance and insurrection. He leads a 'People's Revolution' and is crowned the new 'Citizen-King', only to immediately resign and return, 'a British Cincinnatus, to the plough'.[93] In an audacious display of self-promotion, Swing's success is attributed to the Rotunda, the 'Centre of Reason'. Carlile's publications are described by the government as follows:

> Like nitrate of silver
> Which being made up
> In balls of clay, the but dropping one of them
> Within fifty yards of a corn-rick, is more than enough
> To set the whole on fire. (14)

The trope literalizes the loyalist metaphor of 'incendiary' radical writing. The Rotunda's enthusiastic support for the Swing riots is a sensational illustration of what Dyck calls 'the radical nexus between town and country'. 'Swing is the hero that has accelerated Reform in this country, and he deserves to be canonized', declared Carlile in his periodical the *Prompter*.[94] Carlile responded with gusto when the 'rural war' erupted into print. His *Life and History of Swing, the Kent Rick Burner. Written by Himself* contributed to the growing number of fictitious biographies which claimed to give the 'authentic' insight into the mysterious Swing's background. Like Taylor's *Swing!*, Carlile's story explains the riots as the outcome of a long process of economic and social injustice. Swing is a respectable farmer who is ruined by a series of calamities: he is evicted so that his land can be turned into a foxing course; he is wrongly arrested for poaching; and an increase in rent and church tithes forces Swing and his family into destitution. When the local parson refuses charity (he prefers to give a cake to his dog), he is sent a threatening note. Swing's wife dies, leaving father and son sleeping rough in a barn. The son accidentally starts a fire, and the Swing legend is born. Swing becomes a reluctant leader, but he is convinced that 'in a very short time, Reform or Revolution must release me'.[95]

Loyalist ripostes to Carlile's and Taylor's 'canonization' of Swing placed the blame for the violence firmly on the shoulders of radicals. In *A Short Account of the Life and Death of Swing, the Rick Burner, Written by One Well Acquainted With Him*, Swing is a drunken farmer led astray by an agitator. When Swing is caught and jailed, his narrator-friend visits him and reminds him of the horrors of civil war:

> You never yet saw civil war! You have never seen the streets stream with blood; – brothers armed against brothers, fathers against sons, neighbours against neighbours! You have only *heard* of wives and maidens being violated, of children massacred, of murder in open day, of riot lording it over this fair land.[96]

In a similar vein, Mary Mitford's tale 'The Incendiary' (1832) recalled the invasion fears and atrocity fantasies of the 1790s, as well as the activities of the Luddites. In an anticipation of *Shirley*, the violence is witnessed by a genteel woman who is simultaneously fascinated and appalled by the rioters' actions:

> their day-light marches on the high road, regular and orderly as those of an army, or their midnight visits to lonely houses, lawless and terrific as the descent of pirates, or the incursions of banditti; – all brought us close to a state of things which we never thought to have witnessed in peaceful and happy England. In the sister island, indeed, we had read of such horrors, but now they were brought home to our very household hearths.[97]

The demonization of Swing reached a playful climax in a pamphlet called *The Genuine Life of Mr Francis Swing*. In this Gothic variation on the biographical theme, the Swing brothers John and Francis sell their souls to the devil. Swing becomes the ultimate 'infidel' threat, a reincarnation of the atheistic, republican Jacobins.

The competing cultural appropriations of the Swing riots fed off and fed into the highly-charged political climate of the Reform Bill crisis. For diehard Tories, the violence could be interpreted as evidence of the incorrigible savagery and backwardness of the lower classes. For liberals and most radicals, Swing was a warning to the government: blocking reform risked a revolution. When the Reform Bill was rejected by the House of Lords in 1831, it seemed that this warning had been willfully ignored. The response of reformers was a series of disturbances, culminating in a devastating riot in Bristol. With the dust of Swing barely settled, the spectacular mob was once again on the centre stage.

'The three days of the Bristol riots'

The historian Edward Royle has summed up the state of Britain at the end of 1831:

> not only had large parts of the south and east of England been engulfed by riots, but Merthyr Tydfil, in south Wales, had fallen to an insurrection which lasted three days; Bristol had suffered major destruction of property; Nottingham castle had been burnt down; middle-class political unions had prepared to form their own National Guard, and working-class political unions had again talked of arming and revolution.[98]

This situation had been brought about by the exasperation of reformers at the slow pace of political change. The French revolution of July 1830 and the election of a Whig government in November of the same year raised expectations that the long campaign for electoral reform was finally coming to fruition. Political unions with mixed working- and middle-class membership were established to keep up the pressure on the government. In the north of England, the election of the veteran radical orator Henry Hunt to a political union was celebrated with the hoisting of tricolour flags and the parading of banners inscribed with the mottoes 'Bread or Blood' and 'Liberty or Death', a clear allusion to Peterloo.[99] In April 1831, the Reform Bill was approved by the House of Commons by the slenderest of margins (1 vote), but in October a revised version of the Bill was rejected by the House of Lords. This was the final straw for many reformers, and riots broke out in Derby, Nottingham, Leicester, Tiverton, Yeovil, Exeter, Worcester, London and Bristol. In London, the windows of the Duke of Wellington's house were broken and the Duke was attacked in the street. But the most devastating of the riots took place in Bristol at the end of October 1831. The violence was sparked by the visit to the city of Sir Charles Wetherell, Bristol's recorder or senior judge and a well-known opponent of the Reform Bill. Over the next three days of rioting, many public buildings were burned down, including several prisons, the Mansion House, the Custom House, and the Bishop's palace and its library (the Bishop had voted against the Bill). Around 6000 books may have been destroyed.[100] The 'ferocious suppression' of the violence by the authorities drew considerable criticism, as up to 250 people were killed or wounded.[101] There were 31 capital convictions, and 4 men were hanged.[102] Political factions blamed the riots on each other: Tories blamed Whig and radical demagoguery; Whigs cited the Priestley riots as evidence of the involvement of Tory *agent provocateurs*; and radicals smelled a Whig plot to discredit them in advance of the government jettisoning universal male suffrage.

Contemporary prints capture the apocalyptic *frisson* of the burning city (Figures 21 and 22). The spectacular mob was back with a vengeance. Charles Kingsley witnessed the riots as a schoolboy:

Figure 21 'The City of Bristol' (1831)

he most violent way, not confining hemselves to menaces, but proceed- ng to other acts—destroying the 3ridewell of the town, & afterwards ransferring the same violence to the ʒaol. Whether their conduct pro- been from first to last an active leader, and did much serious mischief in ex- citing others. With regard to all the other prisoners, he did not know that they would be affected by evi- dence of the same description : but

Figure 22 James Catnach, 'View of the Dreadful Fires at Bristol' (1831)

It was an afternoon of sullen autumn rain. The fog hung thick over the docks and lowlands. Glaring through that fog I saw a bright mass of flame – almost like a half-risen sun . . . The fog rolled slowly upward. Dark figures, even at that great distance, were flitting to and fro across what seemed the mouth of the pit. The flame increased – multiplied – at one point after another; till by ten o'clock that night I seemed to be looking down upon Dante's inferno, and to hear the multitudinous moan and wail of the lost spirits surging to and fro amid that sea of fire.

Right behind Brandon Hill, how can I ever forget it? – rose the central mass of fire; till the little mound seemed converted into a volcano, from the peak of which the flame streamed up, not red alone, but delicately green and blue, pale rose and pearly white, while crimson sparks leapt and fell again in the midst of that rainbow, not of hope, but of despair; and dull explosions down below mingled with the roar of the mob, and the infernal hiss and crackle of the flame.[103]

E. P. Thompson thought that the Bristol violence carried just 'a whiff of the Gordon and Priestley riots', but this is an understatement.[104] The *Annual Register* noted that 1780 was the last time Britain 'had exhibited such scenes', and Craik made the same comparison.[105] Reportage and pamphlets constructed the riots as the triumph of popular misrule. The *Annual Register*, which characterized the national mood of 1831 as an 'unexpected Saturnalia' (151), declared dramatically that 'the rioters were masters of the city; the government of the mob had begun' (294). As the following excerpts will show, the Bristol riots exhibit many carnivalesque features. The epicenter of violence in Queen Square fits particularly neatly into the Bakhtinian definition of carnival. According to Bakhtin, the public square is 'the main arena for carnival acts' such as 'free familiar contact' and the 'communal performance of crowning and decrowning.'[106] Queen Square was a location in which the crowd had 'undisputed control' over a highly symbolic space.[107] The statue of William III was 'decrowned' (it was topped with a Cap of Liberty), French-style barricades were erected, and around 10,000 people took possession of the area. In the reportage, however, the carnival elements of 'free familiar contact' are all portrayed negatively. Queen Square becomes a visual emblem of the grotesque 'government of the mob', a sight simultaneously terrifying and ludicrous (Figure 23). *The Times* (3 November) reported that the Square

presented sights most exasperating to the citizens, and most revolting to human nature. Men stretched in drunken stupor besides puncheons of rum; women in loathsome shapes, bearing the outward marks of the sex, were in the same state of beastly degradation.

Figure 23 Queen Square on the Night of October 30th, 1831

This is a purely negative version of Bakhtin's idea of 'grotesque realism', an aesthetic of the subversive, 'degraded' body which transgresses the rules of 'classical' form:

> The essential principle of grotesque realism is degradation, that is, the lowering of all that is high... the emphasis is on the apertures or the convexities, or on various ramifications and offshoots: the open mouth, the genital organs, the breasts, the phallus, the potbelly, the nose.[108]

W. H. Somerton, editor of the *Bristol Mercury*, added a sensational, cannibalistic motif to his description of the bibulous mob:

> Without waiting to draw the corks, the necks of the bottles were broken off; and blood was not infrequently seen to flow from the lacerated mouth of many a wretched being, while he drank the maddening draught... At one spot, three of the incendiaries, who seemed exhausted with their fatigues, were joined by two females, and, seating themselves in chairs, the whole group gave themselves up for a while to refreshment. Whilst they were eating, and drinking wine, each one from a separate bottle, they reveled in delight at the scene before them.[109]

Another pamphlet went even further, evoking the Gothic Eucharist trope of anti-slavery writing:

> in the centre of the Square, by the equestrian statue of William the Third, surmounted with a cap of liberty, were costly tables spread, and the revel of a plundered feast, with yell and imprecation, and wine and blood, was held to celebrate this first Sabbath of Reform – of Revolution... these are the horrors which characterised the second of the Three Days of the Bristol riots.[110]

Amazonian women are everywhere: 'the lower orders of females were particularly vociferous, frequently charging the men with cowardice and want of spirit'.[111] The disregard for high culture and tradition is epitomized by the attack on the Palace library: 'A sacrilegious ruffian knelt on the book as he tore out the leaves, and then with horrible execrations threw it into the blazing fire of the Palace'.[112] The climax of the violence is promiscuous, insensate, intemperate self-destruction:

> [The cellars of the Mansion House] were next plundered, and to the common violence of a lawless mob was now added the reckless and brutal fury of intoxication... All ages, of both sexes, were to be seen greedily swallowing the intoxicating licquors, while upon the ground scores were to be found dead with drunkenness. (*Annual Register* (1831), 293, Chronicle, 174)

> A considerable number of them suffered the just retribution of their crimes, by being burnt in the fires which they themselves had kindled, or buried in the ruins of the buildings which they had pulled down... At the Custom-House... three men (I feel as if I profaned the word) were entombed in the glowing mass. Two leaped from the roof, and were dashed to pieces; and two boys, who attempted a similar mode of escape, were, I was assured, actually seen frying in the molten lead that streamed upon the pavement. (*Times*, 3 November)

This pathetic fecklessness is contrasted with the phallic heroism of the authorities:

> A very powerful man at the end of Castle-street had been actively cheering the mob, urging them to keep their ground, at the same time pelting the troops; he was singled out by a private, who with a back-handed blow cut off his head. (Ibid., 145)

This scene was captured in a broadside issued by James Catnach, the 'doyen of street printers' (Figure 24).[113] The stylized and unrealistic visual composition of the print is a reminder that violence was a favourite

Figure 24   James Catnach, 'Riots at Bristol' (1831)

topic of popular spectacle in the circus, pantomime and the 'illegitimate' theatre.[114]

The account of the Bristol riots in *Blackwood's* is worth quoting at some length, as it provides clear evidence of the fascination which the spectacular mob held for the bourgeois imagination. The passage is a disingenuous disavowal of sensationalism:

> It is not our purpose to follow the outbreaking through all its horrid and disgusting scenes of insult, revolutionary organization, and subsequent drunkenness, rapine, sack, and burning. We have little pleasure in dwelling on either the bloodshed, or the howlings of intoxicated demons, dropping into the furnaces of the blazing ruins of the mansions and homes of the ejected and destitute citizens; nor will our eye follow them in their passages over the molten lead, like the 'damned' of the poet driving over 'the burning marl'; nor shall our pen attempt to picture to the life the infuriate revellers below, at the magnificent and costly tables of a mayoralty house, loaded with feast, and wine, and plunder, around the equestrian statue of William III (surmounted with a cap of liberty prepared for the occasion, and in honour to their beloved Reforming king, another William, alone left uninjured). We will not describe their maniacal waste and wassail; their cries of insult, or triumph; their savage sport and laughter even at the peril of the less fortunate wretches of their gangs, dropping from the beams and rafters, from parapets, roofs, and windows, into the mass of roaring flames beneath them. Moved by an

> instinct averse to revolution, we shrink from the description of blood and conflagration. If we feel compelled occasionally to plunge into the fiery vortex of these infernal regions of Reform, it will be with disgust and reluctance. (471–2)

Such writing is clear evidence of the significance of the Bristol riots in reviv-ifying and consolidating the idea of the spectacular mob.

However, it is important to recognize that the spectacular riot had another target besides anarchic 'intoxicated demons': the role of the genteel or polite interloper. Craik's distinction between the genteel-led rebellion and the plebeian-led riot is realized in terms of a sartorial code which isolates 'well-dressed' figures. In the demonized spectacular riot there is no acceptable role for the middle-classes as participants, so their presence is exposed as irresponsible interference or negligent passivity. The constant recurrence of these figures, however, raises an anxiety about the mere possibility of collu-sion or sympathy – as Lord Loughborough commented in 1792, 'the Lookers on make the mob'.[115]

The trope first occurs in the Gordon riots. Holcroft singles out 'a well-dressed decent-looking man' who refused to call the military (29). The minor dramatist Frederick Reynolds observed 'persons decently dressed, who appeared to be incited to extravagance by a species of fanatical phrenzy'.[116] More extravagantly, the Archbishop of York stated that 'No mob acted without a number of well-dressed men to direct them. Two were this day dug out of the ruins of a house... one had ruffles, with a large diamond at his shirt pocket, the other very well dressed with a plan of London in his pocket.'[117] As Castro notes sardonically, ruffles and maps would surely have been 'combustible'.[118] Moving on to the Priestley riots, two witnesses claimed to have seen 'well-dressed men' acting as leaders.[119] In the Reform Bill disturbances, an eyewitness of one of the numerous window-breaking attacks on Duke of Wellington's house observed that 'One individual there was whom he could identify as giving orders. This individual was a remark-ably well-dressed man' (*Annual Register* (1831), 288–9). Returning to the Bristol riots, *Blackwood's* berated the fact that

> a very great mass of citizens, of a rank even above ten pound renters, looked upon the excesses with a worse feeling than apathy; so thor-oughly had the poison from the reservoirs of the press, and the stores of their local demagogues, infected their minds. (*Blackwood's* (March 1832), 471–2)

Another report was similarly outraged: 'during these disgraceful proceedings, numerous respectably dressed persons... took no notice of the conduct of the mob', while 'two respectably dressed men were very active in giving directions'.[120] Behind these vignettes is the implication that the 'ill-dressed' are not fit to act independently in the political public sphere. Put another way, no spectacular riot can have an enlightened political goal. A Royal Proclamation of November 1831 referred to the Bristol rioters simply as 'lawless multitudes' (*Annual Register* (1831), Chronicle, 178).

Once the saturnalian orgy of destruction and licentiousness is over, the spectacular riot succumbs to the 'last sad scenes' of trial and execution.[121] The punishment of the Bristol rioters was a particularly 'sad' affair (Figure 25). Christopher Davis, for example, was damned for his verbal damning. He is reported to have shouted 'This is the end of your d–d magistrates and bishops, and we'll send them all to hell', followed by 'This is the blaze of liberty' (*Annual Register* (1832), Chronicle, 4, 7).[122] The perceived injustice of the sentences led to an effective boycott of the public executions which took place in January 1832: only 7000 of the regular 20,000 spectators attended.[123] The *Annual Register* completed its report of the execution with these words: 'The criminals struggled, but not violently, for five minutes' (*Annual Register* (1832), Chronicle, 18). The qualifying phrase is both chilling and poignant. Even on the gallows, the violent energy of the spectacular mob remained a symbolic threat.

Figure 25   James Catnach, 'Trials and Execution of the Unhappy Rioters at Bristol' (1832)

Conclusion

If the combination of literary and historical analysis in this book has achieved its aim, it will have persuaded the reader that spectacular violence must be taken into account in any assessment of the composition of Romantic print culture, Romantic literature and the Romantic imagination. I am not claiming that spectacular violence is the most important context for Romanticism, but it requires more attention than has previously been given. I have shown that the Romantic reader was exposed to an astonishing amount of hyperbolic violence, a fact which challenges the idea that Romanticism was essentially a turning away from or internalization of the nightmare of history. Seen from the 'bottom up', Romantic print culture overvalued rather than undervalued the bloody vignette. Spectacular violence took the redemptive aesthetics of both sensibility and the sublime to an extreme: just how much suffering was it possible to represent in a 'pleasing' (acceptable and effective) manner? The word 'much' in that question refers intentionally to both quantity and quality: the driving force behind spectacular violence was the need to represent both the magnitude and the nature of extreme violence. The bloody vignette was both a synecdoche and a critique of the systems and institutions of power which produced and sustained violent regimes on a global scale. The bloody vignette can be regarded as the *ne plus ultra* of all scenes of distress and suffering in Romantic literature, the point at which sympathy is a barely credible response to the horrors being depicted. Bloody Romanticism is an intentionally disconcerting concept, as it both consolidates and questions the ability of literary texts to say and do something meaningful about the 'real' world of power, suffering and pain. If there are no easy answers, there are still many questions.

Notes

The place of publication is London unless otherwise noted.

Introduction: Romantic agonies

1. E. B. Murray, ed., *The Prose Works of Percy Bysshe Shelley. Volume 1* (Oxford: Clarendon Press, 1993), 71.
2. Dorothy Wordsworth, *The Grasmere and Alfoxden Journals*, Pamela Woof, ed. (Oxford: Oxford University Press, 2002), 78–9.
3. The incident is cited by Joan Baum to illustrate the fact that most families knew someone who served at sea at this time (Joan Baum, *Mind Forg'd Manacles: Slavery and the English Romantic Poets* (North Haven, Connecticut: Archon Books, 1994), 52).
4. Marcus Wood, *Blind Memory: Visual Representations of Slavery in England and America 1780–1865* (Manchester: Manchester University Press, 2000); Marcus Wood, *Slavery, Empathy and Pornography* (Oxford: Oxford University Press, 2002).
5. Jean Paul Sartre, Preface to Frantz Fanon, *The Wretched of the Earth* (1961; Penguin 1985), 17.
6. Luke Gibbons, *Edmund Burke and Ireland: Aesthetics, Politics and the Colonial Sublime* (Cambridge: Cambridge University Press, 2003), xi–xiii.
7. David Hume, *An Enquiry Concerning the Principles of Morals* (Oxford: Clarendon Press, 1983), 220n.
8. Janet Todd, *Sensibility: An Introduction* (London: Methuen, 1986), 27.
9. Adam Smith, *The Theory of Moral Sentiments* (1759), in D. D. Raphael, ed., *British Moralists 1650–1800*, 2 vols (Clarendon Press, 1969), 2: 202.
10. Wood, *Slavery, Empathy and Pornography*, 103.
11. Edmund Burke, *A Philosophical Enquiry into the Origin of our Ideas of the Sublime and Beautiful* (Oxford: Oxford University Press, 1998), 36–7.
12. Josephine McDonagh, *Child Murder and British Culture, 1720–1900* (Cambridge: Cambridge University Press, 2003), 36–7, 55–7.
13. Michel Foucault, *Discipline and Punish: The Birth of the Prison* (1975; Penguin, 1991), 8, 15.
14. Cesare Beccaria, 'On Crimes and Punishments', in *On Crimes and Punishments and Other Writings*, Richard Bellamy, ed., trans. Richard Davies (Cambridge: Cambridge University Press, 1995), 70.
15. Thomas Paine, *The Rights of Man* (Penguin, 1984), 57–8.
16. Wood, *Blind Memory*, 15. To try to answer this point, Wood cites Hazlitt's description of the effect of reading about the horrors of slavery: 'it very properly carries away the feelings, and (if you will) overpowers the judgment, because it is a mass of evil so monstrous and warranted as not to be endured, even in thought'. As Wood observes, Hazlitt is in a 'terrible bind', as the successful imagining of atrocity creates an unthinkable 'mass of evil'.
17. *SAE*, 1: xiii.
18. Debbie Lee, *Slavery and the Romantic Imagination* (Philadelphia: University of Pennsylvania Press, 2002), 1.

19. Simon Schama, *Citizens: A Chronicle of the French Revolution* (Penguin, 1989), xv.
20. Mary Favret, 'Coming Home: The Public Spaces of Romantic War', *Studies in Romanticism*, 33 (1994), 539–48, 539.
21. Betty T. Bennett, *British War Poetry in the Age of Romanticism: 1793–1815* (New York and London: Garland Publishing, 1976), 6; Simon Bainbridge, *British Poetry and the Revolutionary and Napoleonic Wars: Visions of Conflict* (Oxford: Oxford University Press, 2003), 30–1.
22. I am indebted to Tim Fulford for allowing me to read chapters of his book *Romantic Indians* (Oxford: Oxford University Press, 2006) in manuscript.
23. Mario Praz, *Romantic Agony* (1951; Oxford: Oxford University Press, 1970), 118.
24. The Phrase 'atrocities of democracy' comes from *Annual Register* (1792), viii.

1 'Beneath the bloody scourge laid bare the man': Slavery and violence

1. Cited in Wylie Sypher, *Guinea's Captive Kings: British Anti-Slavery Literature of the XVIIIth Century* (1942; New York: Octagon Books, 1969), 100.
2. Cited in Thomas Clarkson, *The History of the Rise, Progress, and Accomplishment of the Abolition of the African Slave-Trade by The British Parliament*, 2 vols (Longman, Hurst, Rees and Orme, 1808), 1: 100.
3. Brycchan Carey, *British Abolitionism and the Rhetoric of Sensibility* (Basingstoke: Palgrave, 2005), 20.
4. Josephine McDonagh, *Child Murder and British Culture, 1720–1900* (Cambridge: Cambridge University Press, 2003), 55.
5. Markman Ellis, *The Politics of Sensibility: Race, Gender and Commerce in the Sentimental Novel* (Cambridge: Cambridge University Press, 1996), 55.
6. Anne K. Mellor argues that 'the violation of familial relationships as the fundamental evil of slavery' was a particular preoccupation of female anti-slavery writers, though my own researches suggest that the trope was universal. See Anne K. Mellor, '"Am I not a Woman and a Sister?": Slavery, Romanticism, and Gender', in Alan Richardson and Sonia Hofkosh, eds, *Romanticism, Race, and Imperial Culture, 1780–1834* (Bloomington and Indianapolis: Indiana University Press, 1996), 311–29, 316.
7. Linda Colley, *Captives: Britain, Empire and the World, 1600–1850* (Jonathan Cape, 2002), 63–4.
8. Marcus Wood, *Slavery, Empathy and Pornography* (Oxford: Oxford University Press, 2002), 101–3. Wood argues that such scenes function essentially as a covert form of self-indulgent voyeurism or 'extreme psychic masochism'.
9. Peter J. Kitson, 'Races, places, peoples, 1785–1800', in Tim Fulford and Peter J. Kitson, eds, *Romanticism and Colonialism: Writing and Empire, 1780–1830* (Cambridge: Cambridge University Press, 1998), 22. There were earlier works in which the horrors of slavery were vividly depicted. According to Wylie Sypher, the first 'museum of horrors' was Hans Sloane's *Voyage to the Islands of Madeira, Barbadoes, Nieves, S. Christophers and Jamaica* (1707), which described forms of violence including burning alive, gelding, and applying salt and pepper to wounds of whipping (Sypher, *Guinea's Captive Kings*, 39–40). But it was unquestionably the anti-slavery movement which bombarded the reading public with such 'horrors'.
10. See Olaudah Equiano, *The Interesting Narrative of the Life of Olaudah Equiano, or Gustavus Vassa, The African*, Vincent Caretta, ed. (Penguin, 1995), Notes, 287–8.

11. Adam Smith, *The Theory of Moral Sentiments* (1759), in D. D. Raphael, ed., *British Moralists 1650–1800*, 2 vols (Clarendon Press, 1969), 2: 219–20.
12. Claude Rawson, *God, Gulliver and Genocide: Barbarism and the European Imagination* (Oxford: Oxford University Press, 2001), Chapter 1.
13. [James Stephen], *England Enslaved by Her Own Slave Colonies. To the Electors and People of the United Kingdom* (1826), *SAE*, 3: 278.
14. Montesquieu, *L'Esprit des Lois* (1748); cited in Roger Anstey, *The Atlantic Slave Trade and British Abolition 1760–1810* (Macmillan, 1975), 103.
15. Clarkson, *History of the Rise, Progress, and Accomplishment of the Abolition of the African Slave*, 1: 519–20.
16. Henry Louis Gates, Jr, *The Signifying Monkey* (Oxford and New York: Oxford University Press, 1988), 4; cited in Marcus Wood, *Blind Memory: Visual Representations of Slavery in England and America 1780–1865* (Manchester: Manchester University Press, 2000), 19.
17. Wood, *Blind Memory*, 23.
18. Robin Blackburn, *The Making of New World Slavery: From the Baroque to the Modern 1492–1800* (Verso, 1997), 385.
19. Wood, *Blind Memory*, 22–3. See also Marcus Wood, 'Black Bodies and Satiric Limits in the Long Eighteenth Century', in Steven E. Jones, ed., *Forms of Satire in the Romantic Period* (Basingstoke: Palgrave Macmillan, 2003), 56–7.
20. Moira Ferguson, *Subject to Others: British Women Writers and Colonial Slavery, 1670–1834* (New York and London: Routledge, 1992), 220.
21. Burke's utilitarian answer to the problem of 'unlawful communication' was a system of fines: £5 for an officer and £2 for a seaman (Edmund Burke, *Sketch of a Negro Code* (1792), *SAE*, 2: 191–2).
22. Equiano, *The Interesting Narrative of the Life of Olaudah Equiano*, 5.
23. The review appeared in Joseph Johnson's *Analytical Review* (May 1789) and is cited by Caretta, Introduction to Equiano, *The Interesting Narrative of the Life of Olaudah Equiano*, xxvi. Compare David Dabydeen's preference for the 'mass of grouty, teary incidentals' in black writing of the eighteenth century, which Dabydeen regards as 'far more poignant and affecting than the descriptions of being transported across the Atlantic or of the subsequent terrors and harrassments' (*SAE*, 1: liv, lv). This may indeed be the case for Dabydeen and many other contemporary readers, but Wollstonecraft's comments indicate that 'terrors and harrassments' were equally if not more 'affecting' for the eighteenth-century reader. Wollstonecraft's lukewarm response to the spiritual autobiographical elements of the book is also against the grain of modern criticism: see Helen Thomas, *Romanticism and Slave Narratives: Transatlantic Testimonies* (Cambridge: Cambridge University Press, 2000).
24. Helen Thomas locates a tension between this scene and Equiano's experience as a slave trader during which he witnessed (if not presided over) such atrocities himself (Thomas, *Romanticism and Slave Narratives*, 239–41).
25. Letter to Lady Hesketh, cited by Alan Richardson, *SAE*, 4: 74.
26. Clarkson, *History of the Rise, Progress, and Accomplishment of the Abolition of the African Slave-Trade*, 2: 190.
27. J. Hector St. John Crevecoeur, *Letters from an American Farmer* [1782] and *Sketches of Eighteenth-Century America* [1925] (Penguin, 1987), 178.
28. See Bryan Edwards, *The History, Civil and Commercial, of the British Colonies in the West Indies*, 4th edition, 3 vols (1793; John Stockdale, 1797), 2: 268–71. For further information on Tacky's rebellion, see Michael Craton, *Testing the Chains: Resistance*

to Slavery in the British West Indies (Ithaca and London: Cornell University Press, 1982), Chapter 11.

29. Michel Foucault, *Discipline and Punish: The Birth of the Prison* (1975; Penguin, 1991), 29.

30. Peter Linebaugh and Marcus Rediker, *The Many-Headed Hydra: Sailors, Slaves, Commoners, and the Hidden History of the Revolutionary Atlantic* (Verso, 2000), Chapters 4 and 6.

31. Wood, *Blind Memory*, Chapter 5.

32. 'Epistle to William Wilberforce, Esq., on the Rejection of the Bill for Abolishing the Slave Trade' (1792), in Duncan Wu, ed., *Romanticism: An Anthology* (Oxford: Blackwell, 1994), 20–2.

33. Jennifer Breen, *Women Romantic Poets 1785–1832: An Anthology* (J. M. Dent, 1992), 10–20. The title of the poem was later changed to 'The Black Slave Trade' (*SAE*, 4: 103).

34. Breen, *Women Romantic Poets 1785–1832*, 16.

35. See Angela Keane, *Women Writers and the English Nation in the 1790s* (Cambridge: Cambridge University Press, 2000), 154.

36. Alan Richardson suggests that this poem was a collaboration between More and the obscure poet Eaglesfield Smith, and that More probably added the conversion scene; see *SAE*, 4: 224.

37. William Fox, *An Address to the People of Great Britain, on the Propriety of Abstaining from West India Sugar and Rum* (1791), *SAE*, 2: 156. According to William St. Clair, there may have been 100,000 copies of this pamphlet in circulation in the 1790s (William St. Clair, *The Reading Nation in the Romantic Period* (Cambridge: Cambridge University Press, 1994), 561).

38. See Joan Baum, *Mind Forg'd Manacles: Slavery and the English Romantic Poets* (North Haven, Connecticut: Archon Books, 1994), 18.

39. 'On Sugar', *Manchester Herald*, 17 April 1792, in Michael Scrivener, ed., *Poetry and Reform: Periodical Verse from the English Democratic Press 1792–1824* (Detroit: Wayne State University Press, 1992), 47–8.

40. See Timothy Morton, 'Blood Sugar', in Fulford and Kitson, eds, *Romanticism and Colonialism*, 100.

41. See Deidre Coleman, 'Post-colonialism', in Nicholas Roe, ed., *Romanticism: An Oxford Guide* (Oxford: Oxford University Press, 2005), 237–56.

42. In 1803 Coleridge wrote to Sir George and Lady Beaumont regretting that this 'turbid Stream of wild Eloquence' was 'alas! a faithful specimen of too many of my Declamations of that Time / fortunately for me, the Government, I suppose, knew that both Southey & I were utterly unconnected with any party or club or society'. See *Collected Letters of Samuel Taylor Coleridge*, Earl Leslie Griggs, ed. (Oxford: Oxford University Press, 1956), 2: 1000–01; cited in *The Collected Works of Samuel Taylor Coleridge. 1: Lectures 1795 on Politics and Religion*, Lewis Patton and Peter Mann, eds (Routledge and Kegan Paul, 1971), xxix. For further discussion of Coleridge's use of the cannibalistic metaphor, see Peter J. Kitson, 'Romantic Displacements: Representing Cannibalism', in Peter J. Kitson, ed., *Placing and Displacing Romanticism* (Aldershot: Ashgate, 2001), 209–14.

43. Jacqueline Pearson, *Women's Reading in Britain, 1750–1835* (Cambridge: Cambridge University Press, 1999), 43.

44. According to Patrick J. Keane, Coleridge never abandoned his moral repugnance of slavery, though he later became a committed adherent of the emerging scientific racism which placed blacks on the lowest rungs of the ladder of intelligence and

civilization (Patrick J. Keane, *Coleridge's Submerged Politics* (Columbia and London: University of Missouri Press, 1994), Chapter 1).

45. Cited in *SAE*, 4: 249.

46. See Herbert Aptheker, *American Negro Slave Revolts* (New York: Columbia University Press, 1944), 173.

47. Craton, *Testing the* Chains, 100.

48. W. E. B. Du Bois, 'The souls of black folk', in *Three Negro Classics* (New York: Avon Books, 1999), 244.

49. Michael Craton argues that 'slave unrest as much influenced metropolitan ideas and actions as vice versa' ('Slave Culture, Resistance and the Achievement of Emancipation in the British West Indies, 1783–1838', in James Walvin, ed., *Slavery and British Society 1776–1846* (Macmillan, 1982), 102).

50. C. L. R. James, *The Black Jacobins: Toussaint L'Ouverture and the San Domingo Revolution* (1938; Penguin, 2001), 45.

51. David Geggus, *Slavery, War, and Revolution: The British Occupation of Saint Domingue 1793–1798* (Oxford: Clarendon Press, 1982), 188.

52. David Geggus, 'British Opinion and the Emergence of Haiti, 1791–1805', in Walvin, ed., *Slavery and British Society*, 128.

53. Thomas Clarkson, *Thoughts on the Necessity of Improving the Condition of the Slaves in the British Colonies, with a View to Their Ultimate Emancipation* (1823), *SAE*, 3: 112–13.

54. Cited in Geggus, 'British Opinion and the Emergence of Haiti, 1791–1805', 138.

55. On Grenada, see: [Gordon Turnbull], *A Narrative of the Revolt and Insurrection of the French Inhabitants in the Island of Grenada. By an Eye-Witness* (Edinburgh: Constable, 1795). The book is dedicated to the families of the British who died in 'the horrid and unnatural Rebellion'. Julius Fedon was a free mulatto who embraced French republicanism and declared the island a republic. For further information on the spate of 'republican' slave uprisings in the Caribbean at this time, see Craton, *Testing the Chains*, Chapters 15–17.

56. Robin Blackburn, *The Overthrow of Colonial Slavery 1776–1848* (Verso, 1988), 232.

57. Bryan Edwards, *An Historical Survey of the French Colony in the Island of St. Domingo* (John Stockdale, 1797).

58. Clarkson, *Thoughts on the Necessity of Improving the Condition of the Slaves in the British Colonies*, *SAE*, 3: 113n.

59. See Nigel Leask, *Curiosity and the Aesthetics of Travel Writing, 1770–1840* (Oxford: Oxford University Press, 2002), 3; cited in Deirdre Coleman, *Romantic Colonization and British Anti-Slavery* (Cambridge: Cambridge University Press, 2005), 20.

60. Edwards, *The History, Civil and Commercial, of the British Colonies in the West Indies*, 1: 559.

61. The success of this scene as a piece of anti-French propaganda can be measured by the fact that it is cited in a British anti-Napoleonic pamphlet in 1803 as evidence of 'the horrid manner in which those White Savages put their prisoners to death'. See [James Stephen], *Buonaparte in the West Indies* (1803), 4.

62. Edwards, *The History, Civil and Commercial, of the British Colonies in the West Indies*, 1: 104.

63. John Gabriel Stedman, *Narrative of a Five Years' Expedition against the Revolted Negroes of Surinam in Guinea on the Wild Coast of South America; from the Year 1772 to 1777* (Joseph Johnson, 1796).

64. See Richard Price and Sally Price, eds, *Stedman's Narrative . . . from the Original 1790 Manuscript* (Baltimore: John Hopkins University Press, 1988); Thomas, *Romanticism and Slave Narratives*, 128–9.

65. Thomas, *Romanticism and Slave Narratives*, Chapter 4; Lee, *Slavery and the Romantic Imagination*, Chapter 4.
66. See Wood, *Blind Memory*, 234–9; Wood, *Slavery, Empathy and Pornography*, Chapter 2.
67. See Wood, *Slavery, Empathy and Pornography*, 21, 86.
68. Marcus Wood denies that there is a positive carnivalesque power in the scene. For Wood, the 'nihilistic buffoonery' of the dying slave is disqualified from the Foucauldian paradigm by 'a hyperbolic insensateness' which is 'an involved parody of the controlled violence of European torture' (Wood, *Blind Memory*, 232). Wood's analysis ignores the way in which the scene is constructed as a specific challenge to the insidious smugness of Stedman's interlocutor.
69. Lee, *Slavery and the Romantic Imagination*, 66.
70. For example, in Wood, *Slavery, Empathy and Pornography*, 106–14.
71. As Marcus Wood notes, Neptune's 'self-constructed comedic commodity fetishism' is a skit on 'the ultimate model for the tortured and fetishized body as cannibalistic ritual – Jesus'. But the idea that the text is 'inviting us to enter into a perverse and erotic world of cannibalism' is to confuse theme and affect (ibid., 106, 113).
72. Wood, *Blind Memory*, 236–7. The problem of Blake's image, argues Wood, is 'the confusion of suffering with desirability', though Blake is accorded a degree of explicit irony not granted to the lesser genius of Stedman: 'it is hard to know what to think – maybe that is Blake's point. Blake's image teeters on the edge of pornography in order to confront us with our own corruptibility'. On the theme of whipping as pornography, see also Mary Favret, 'Flogging: The anti-slavery movement writes pornography', in Anne Janowitz, ed., *Romanticism and Gender* (English Association, 1998).
73. See Angela Carter, *The Sadeian Woman: An Exercise in Cultural History* (1979; Virago, 1987), 78–115.
74. See Peter Hulme, *Colonial Encounters: Europe and the Native Caribbean 1492–1797* (1986; Routledge, 1992), Chapter 6.
75. Wood, *Slavery, Empathy and Pornography*, 131; Thomas, *Romanticism and Slave Narratives*, Chapter 4.
76. Again, Marcus Wood remains unconvinced by this apologia, and reads the image as yet more pornography, a lesbian 'reward' for reaching the end of the book (Wood, *Slavery, Empathy and Pornography*, 131–40).
77. Marcus Wood's survey of British writing on slavery in this period is the most complete coverage; see *Slavery, Empathy and Pornography*, Chapters 4–5.
78. Clarkson, *Thoughts on the Necessity of Improving the Condition of the Slaves*, SAE, 3: 36–7.
79. See Ian Haywood, *The Revolution in Popular Literature: Print, Politics and the People, 1790–1860* (Cambridge: Cambridge University Press, 2004), 85.
80. I have used the 1822 text which is reprinted in *SAE*, 6. The story is credited to William Earle and originally appeared in 1800 in epistolary form with authenticating footnotes.
81. My account is based primarily on Cecil Northcott, *Slavery's Martyr: John Smith of Demerara and the Emancipation Movement* (Epworth Press, 1976). See also Craton, *Testing the Chains*, Chapter 21.
82. Northcott, *Slavery's Martyr*, 60; Craton, *Testing the Chains*, 287.
83. Kate Teltscher, 'Empire and Race', in Zachary Leader and Ian Haywood, eds, *Romantic Period Writings 1798–1832: An Anthology* (Routledge, 1998), 94.

84. Elizabeth Heyrick, *Immediate, not Gradual Abolition, or An Inquiry into the Shortest, Safest, and Most Effectual Means of Getting Rid of West Indian Slavery* (1824), in Teltscher, 'Empire and Race', 103.
85. Cited in Northcott, *Slavery's Martyr*, 110–12.
86. George Canning, *The Speech of the Rt Hon. George Canning, in the House of Commons, on the 16th Day of March, 1824, SAE*, 3: 239–40.
87. Chris Baldick, *In Frankenstein's Shadow: Myth, Monstrosity and Nineteenth-Century Writing* (Oxford: Clarendon Press, 1987).
88. William Wilberforce, *An Appeal to the Religion, Justice and Humanity of the Inhabitants of the British Empire, in behalf of the Negro Slaves in the West Indies* (1823), *SAE*, 3: 18.
89. Clarkson, *Thoughts on the Necessity of Improving the Condition of the Slaves, SAE*, 3: 84.
90. The persistence of planter fictions of slave insensibility could also draw on historiography. John Hay's *A Narrative of the Insurrection in the Island of Grenada* was published in 1823, possibly to aid the planter cause in the Demerara conflict. Hay claims that the rebel leader Julius Fedon 'began the bloody massacre in the presence of his wife and daughters, who remained there, unfeeling spectators of his horrid barbarity' (76).
91. Mary Prince, *The History of Mary Prince, a West Indian Slave, Related by Herself* (London 1831), in *SAE*, volume 1.
92. See Ferguson, *Subject to Others*, Chapter 13. See also Sara Salih, 'The History of Mary Prince, the black subject, and the black canon', in Brygchan Carey, Markman Ellis and Sara Salih, eds, *Discourses of Slavery and Abolition* (Basingstoke: Palgrave, 2004).
93. James Walvin, 'The propaganda of anti-slavery', in Walvin, ed., *Slavery and British Society*, 52–3, 60.
94. See Aptheker, *American Negro Slave Revolts*, Chapter XII.
95. [Nat Turner], *The Confessions of Nat Turner, The Leader of the Late Insurrection in Southampton, VA. As fully and voluntarily made to Thomas R. Gray, In the prison where he was confined, and acknowledged by him to be such when read before the Court of Southampton; with the certificate, under seal of the Court, convened at Jerusalem, Nov. 5, 1831, for his trial. Also, an Authentic Account of the whole insurrection. With lists of the whites who were murdered. And of the Negroes brought before the Court of Southampton, and there sentenced* (Baltimore: Thomas R. Gray, 1831); rptd in Herbert Aptheker, *Nat Turner's Slave Rebellion* (New York: Humanities Press, 1975).
96. Herbert Aptheker, 'The event', in Kenneth S. Greenberg, ed., *Nat Turner: A Rebellion in History and Memory* (Oxford: Oxford University Press, 2003), 57.
97. David F. Allmendinger, Jr, 'The construction of *The Confessions of Nat Turner*', in Greenberg, ed., *Nat Turner*, 37; Herbert Aptheker, *American Negro Slave Revolts* (New York: Columbia University Press, 1944), 381. According to some oral traditions, Turner was decapitated and his body skinned and turned into a purse (Kenneth S. Greenberg, 'Name, face, body', in Greenberg, ed., *Nat Turner*, 19).
98. Greenberg, 'Name, face, body', 8; Allmendinger, 'The Construction of *The Confessions of Nat Turner*', 32, 38.
99. Linebaugh and Rediker, *The Many-Headed Hydra*, 247; see also Chapter 6.
100. See Allmendinger, 'The construction of *The Confessions of Nat Turner*' 41–2.
101. Aptheker, *The Confessions of Nat Turner*, 38–47.
102. Cited in ibid., 1.

103. Cited in ibid., 3.
104. Craton, *Testing the Chains*, Chapter 22.
105. Henry Bleby, *Death Struggles of Slavery: Being a Narrative of Facts and Incidents which Occurred in a British Colony, During the Two Years Immediately Preceding Negro Emancipation* (Hamilton, Adams and Co., 1853).
106. Henry Whitely, *Three Months in Jamaica, in 1832; Comprising a Residence of Seven Weeks on a Sugar Plantation* (J. Hatchard and Son, 1832).
107. See E. Royston Pike, ed., *Human Documents of the Industrial Revolution* (1966; George Allen and Unwin, 1970), 134.

2   'Disturbed imagination': The French revolution

1. Cited in Gregory Dart, *Rousseau, Robespierre and English Romanticism* (Cambridge: Cambridge University Press, 1999), 68.
2. *Shelley: Poetical Works*, Thomas Hutchinson, ed. (Oxford: Oxford University Press, 1991), 607.
3. Alan Liu, *Wordsworth: The Sense of History* (1989; Stanford: Stanford University Press, 2000), 136.
4. Nicolas Roe's post-Levinsonian excavation of submerged historical allusions in 'Tintern Abbey' shows the continuing critical fascination with the 'hidden Wordsworth', though Roe himself is ambivalent about the methodology. See Nicolas Roe, 'Politics, history and Wordsworth's poems', in Stephen Gill, ed., *The Cambridge Companion to Wordsworth* (Cambridge: Cambridge University Press, 2003), particularly 209–10.
5. See Ian Haywood, ' "The renovating fury": Southey, republicanism and sensationalism', *Romanticism on the Net*, 36 (2004).
6. Luke Gibbons, *Edmund Burke and Ireland: Aesthetics, Politics and the Colonial Sublime* (Cambridge: Cambridge University Press, 2003), xi–xii.
7. *The Writings and Speeches of Edmund Burke. Volume VI: The Launching of the Hastings Impeachment 1786–1788*, P. J. Marshall, ed. (Oxford: Clarendon Press, 1991), 420–1.
8. Michael J. Franklin, 'Accessing India: Orientalism, anti-"Indianism" and the rhetoric of Jones and Burke', in Tim Fulford and Peter J. Kitson, eds, *Romanticism and Colonialism: Writing and Empire, 1780–1830* (Cambridge: Cambridge University Press, 1998), 54–5.
9. Cited in Franklin, 'Accessing India', 53. Franklin observes perceptively that the allusion to a 'disproportioned member' is 'ominously ithyphallic' (55).
10. Richard Price, *Political Writings*, D. O. Thomas, ed. (Cambridge: Cambridge University Press, 1991), 195.
11. For the 'revolution controversy' texts, see in particular two anthologies: Marilyn Butler, ed., *Burke, Paine, Godwin and the Revolution Controversy* (Cambridge: Cambridge University Press, 1984); Gregory Claeys, ed., *Political Writings of the 1790s*, 8 vols (William Pickering, 1995).
12. See for example Gillray's *Smelling out a Rat; or the Athestical Revolutionist Disturbed at his Midnight Calculations* (1790), in which Burke rather than Price is lampooned; the cartoon is discussed in Ronald Paulson, *Representations of Revolution (1789–1820)* (New Haven and London: Yale University Press, 1983), 183–4.
13. James T. Boulton, *The Language of Politics in the Age of Wilkes and Burke* (Routledge and Kegan Paul, 1963), 98.

14. Edmund Burke, *Reflections on the revolution in France, and on the proceedings in certain societies in London relative to that event. In a letter intended to have been sent to a Gentleman in Paris,* in *The Writings and Speeches of Edmund Burke. Volume VIII. The French Revolution 1790–94,* L. G. Mitchell, ed. (Oxford: Clarendon Press, 1989), 117.

15. Tom Furniss, 'Gender in revolution: Edmund Burke and Mary Wollstonecraft', in Kelvin Everest, ed., *Revolution in Writing: British Literary Responses to the French Revolution* (Oxford: Oxford University Press, 1991), 79; see also Furniss's book *Edmund Burke's Aesthetic Ideology: Language, Gender, and Political Economy in Revolution* (Cambridge: Cambridge University Press, 1993), Chapters 5 and 6, and his essay, 'Cementing the nation: Burke's *Reflections* on nationalism and national identity', in John Whale, ed., *Edmund Burke's Reflections on the Revolution in France: New Interdisciplinary Essays* (Manchester: Manchester University Press, 2000). Ronald Paulson brings out the scene's Oedipal connotations: see *Representations of Revolution,* Chapter 3. On this theme see also Lynn Hunt, *The Family Romance of the French Revolution* (Routledge, 1992); Dorinda Outram, *The Body and the French Revolution: Sex, Class and Political Culture* (New Haven and London: Yale University Press, 1989), Chapter 8. For an assessment of the scene's accuracy, see F. P. Lock, 'Rhetoric and representation in Burke's *Reflections*', in Whale, ed., *Edmund Burke's Reflections on the Revolution in France,* 28 and 35n. Marilyn Butler is critical of the over-reliance of critics of the revolution debate on Burke, Wollstonecraft and Godwin, all of whom are 'literal and elitist' in their stereotypical polarization of public figures ('leading actors') and plebeian 'chorus' ('Telling it like a story: The French revolution as narrative', *Studies in Romanticism,* 28 (1989), 345–64, 351). At least Paine (discussed below) breaks the mould by refusing to be unsympathetic towards the crowd at Versailles.

16. Thomas Paine, *The Rights of Man* (Penguin, 1984), 51.

17. I have taken this term from Rousseau, who notes that democracy degenerates into ochlocracy, just as monarchy degenerates into despotism, and aristocracy into oligarchy (Jean-Jacques Rousseau, *The Social Contract: or, Principles of Political Right* (1762; Penguin, 1968), 133).

18. See David Bindman, *The Shadow of the Guillotine: Britain and the French Revolution* (British Museum, 1989); Paulson, *Representations of Revolution,* Chapter 2; John Brewer, *The Common People and Politics 1750–1790s* (Chadwick-Healey, 1986). George Rudé notes Burke's influence on nineteenth-century historians of revolution like Taine and Carlyle (*The Crowd in History: A Study of Popular Disturbances in France and England 1730–1848* (John Wiley, 1964), 7–9).

19. Paine, *The Rights of Man,* 49–50.

20. See Steven Blakemore, *Crisis in Representation: Thomas Paine, Mary Wollstonecraft, Helen Maria Williams and the Rewriting of the French Revolution* (Madison and London: Fairleigh Dickinson University Press, 1997).

21. Don Herzog points out that in his private letters Burke was scathing about the fecklessness of the royal couple (Don Herzog, *Poisoning the Minds of the Lower Orders* (1998; Princeton, New Jersey: Princeton University Press, 2000), 27).

22. Charlotte Smith, *Desmond,* Antje Blank and Janet Todd, eds (William Pickering, 1997), 155.

23. Claeys, ed., *Political Writings of the 1790s,* 1: 56.

24. Mary Wollstonecraft, *Vindication of the Rights of Women* (Penguin, 1975), 179.

25. Janet Todd and Marilyn Butler, eds, *The Works of Mary Wollstonecraft,* 7 vols (William Pickering, 1989), 6: 47.

26. Feminist critics are divided about the success of Wollstonecraft's conspiratorial plotting. Adriana Craciun notes that Wollstonecraft's poissards are 'unwitting dupes of conspiratorial (male) agitation', while Vivien Jones sees the women as the Duke of Orlean's seraglio. See Adriana Craciun, *Fatal Women of Romanticism* (Cambridge: Cambridge University Press, 2003), 72, 76–7; Vivien Jones, 'Women writing revolution: Narratives of history and sexuality in Wollstonecraft and Williams', in Stephen Copley and John Whale, eds, *Beyond Romanticism: New Approaches to Texts and Contexts 1780–1832* (London and New York: Routledge, 1992), 185–8.

27. Catherine Macaulay, *Observations on the Reflections of the Right Hon. Edmund Burke* (1790), in Claeys, ed., *Political Writings of the 1790s*, 1: 138.

28. Joseph Towers, *Thoughts on the Commencement of a New Parliament* (1791), in Claeys, ed., *Political Writings of the 1790s*, 1: 97.

29. Radicals commonly blamed the excesses of popular violence in the French revolution on the dehumanising effects of the *ancien régime*. Charles James Fox, for example, asserted that 'Men bred in the school of the house of Bourbon could not be expected to act otherwise' (cited by Claeys, ed., *Political Writings of the 1790s*, 1: xlv). In general, however, this view tended to lead to moderate, Whiggish demands for gradual political reform. As Fox's colleague Richard Brinsley Sheridan noted, the French people were 'on the first recovery of their rights, unfit for the exertion of them' (cited in ibid.).

30. James Mackintosh, *Vindiciæ Gallicæ: Defence of the French revolution and its English admirers against the accusations of the right Hon. Edmund Burke (1791)*, in Claeys, ed., *Political Writings of the 1790s*, 1: 273.

31. John Moore, *A Journal During a Residence in France, from the Beginning of August, to the Middle of December, 1792. To Which is Added, An Account of the Most Remarkable Events Which Happened at Paris from that Time to the Death of the Late King of France*, 2 vols (G. G. and J. Robinson, 1793).

32. Matthew Lewis, *The Monk* (Oxford: Oxford University Press), 356.

33. Liu, *Wordsworth: The Sense of History*, 151.

34. Janet Todd comments that Williams's *Letters* were 'much read' (*Sensibility*, 130); Angela Keane notes 'the readiness with which extracts' of the *Letters* were 'reprinted in periodicals and newspapers' (Keane, *Women Writers and the English*, 75), and Adriana Craciun calls the *Letters* 'among the most influential British accounts of the French Revolution' (Adriana Craciun, *British Women Writers and the French Revolution: Citizens of the World* (Basingstoke: Palgrave, 2005), 98).

35. Helen Maria Williams, *LWF*, Neil Fraistat and Susan Lanser, eds (Ontario: Broadview Press, 2001), 194–203.

36. Ibid., 207–12.

37. See Bindman, *The Shadow of the Guillotine*, 39.

38. See also her poem 'The Bastille: A Vision', *LWF*, 203–6.

39. Fred Botting, *Gothic* (1996; London and New York: Routledge, 1999), 88–9.

40. Breen, ed., *Women Romantic Poets*, 86–93, 91.

41. *The Poems of Alexander Pope*, John Butt, ed. (1963; Methuen, 1975), 800.

42. Claeys, ed., *Political Writings of the 1790s*, 1: 323.

43. Gary Kelly, *Women, Writing, and Revolution 1790–1827* (Oxford: Clarendon Press, 1993), 64–5.

44. For an account of the Vendée pacification, see Simon Schama, *Citizens: A Chronicle of the French Revolution* (Penguin, 1989), 779–92.

45. See Chris Jones, *Radical Sensibility: Literature and Ideas in the 1790s* (London and New York: Routledge, 1993), 145.

46. Lynne Hunt has shown that in fact the Jacobins tried to replace Marianne with Hercules as the national emblem (Lynne Hunt, *Politics, Culture and Class in the French Revolution* (Berkeley, Los Angeles and London: University of California Press, 1984), 94–119).

47. Jones, 'Women Writing Revolution', 189.

48. It is worth noting that Wollstonecraft also imagined the ghosts of the victims of Terror 'fleeing from the despotism of licentious freedom' (*Works of Mary Wollstonecraft*, 6: 85).

49. See Williams, *LWF*, 189.

50. Todd and Butler, eds, *Works of Mary Wollstonecraft*, 6: 235.

51. For an unembarrassed radical deployment of the surgical metaphor, see 'The Goitre', a satirical poem which was published in Daniel Isaac Eaton's *Politics for the People* in 1794. 'Sir Goitre' is 'lopped' by a '*French surgeon*', who 'whipping out his knife, / Made an incision to the quick', leaving Goitre 'a wither'd lifeless lump, / While the disburthen'd body vigorous grew and plump' (ll. 67–8). The poem is reprinted in Scrivener, *Poetry and Reform*, 79–81.

52. William Wordsworth, *The Prelude: A Parallel Text*, J. C. Maxwell, ed. (Penguin, 1976).

53. The text was first published in America in 1796. I have used the edition published by J. Wright in London 1797.

54. The quotation comes from Lewis Melville, ed., *The Life and Letters of William Cobbett in England and America*, 2 vols (John Lane, 1913), 1: 101.

55. Both pamphlets are reprinted in *William Cobbett: Selected Writings*, Leonora Nattrass, ed., 5 vols (Pickering and Chatto, 1998), volume 1, *Early Writings*.

56. Raymond Williams, *Cobbett* (Oxford: Oxford University Press, 1983), 8.

57. Edward Smith states that the pamphlet had 'a great sale both in America and England', though no sources are cited (Edward Smith, ed., *William Cobbett: A Biography*, 2 vols (Sampson Low, Marston, Searle and Rivingham, 1878), 1: 149). The more authoritative George Spater notes that 'a great number of editions' were sold in America and England, and the work was reprinted in Pennslyvania as late as 1823 (George Spater, *William Cobbett: The Poor Man's Friend*, 2 vols (Cambridge: Cambridge University Press, 1982), 1: 64).

58. Cobbett mentions the following sources (I have added some publishing details): Abbe Barruel, *The History of the French Clergy* [1794]; *The Relation of the Cruelties, committed in the Lyonnese*; *Histoire de La Conjuration de Robespierre* [1795]; *Trials of the Members of the Revolutionary Committee at Nantes*; Auguste Danican, *Banditti Unmasked* [ed. John Gifford (1797)]; and *A Residence in France, during the Years 1792, 1793, 1794, and 1795, described in a Series of Letters from an English Lady* [ed. John Gifford (1797)].

59. Raymond Williams describes the Peter Porcupine anti-Jacobin pamphlets as 'relatively carefully documented' (*Cobbett*, 9).

60. The tract has received little critical attention. Cobbett's admirers, most of whom have been and continue to be on the political left, clearly regard the work as vulgar populism. G. D. H. Cole recognized the pamphlet's 'full-frontal attack' on the French revolution, but concluded that the work was 'rightly forgotten' (G. D. H. Cole, *The Life of William Cobbett* (W. Collins, 1925), 59–60; and G. D. H. Cole, ed., *Letters from William Cobbett to Edward Thornton Written in the Years 1797–1800* (Oxford: Oxford University Press,

1937), xlvi). In a rare recent assessment, David Simpson calls the text a 'catalogue of right-wing pornography published under the name of one who still subsists in English literary history as some sort of populist hero' (David Simpson, *Romanticism, Nationalism, and the Revolt Against Theory* (Chicago and London: University of Chicago Press, 1993), 117). I hope I have shown in chapter 1 that the label 'pornography' in this context is reductive, unhelpful and unhistorical.

61. Abbé Barruel, *The History of the Clergy During the French Revolution. A Work Dedicated to the English Nation* (Dublin: N. Fitzpatrick, 1794), 294. One of Cobbett's earliest biographers derided the reliance on Barruel, 'a man steeped to the very eyes in fanaticism, bigotry, superstition, and prejudice' and therefore a 'fallacious authority' (Robert Huish, *Memoirs of the Late William Cobbett*, 2 vols (John Saunders, 1836), 1: 143).

62. See Craciun, *British Women Writers and the French Revolution*, 128–9.

63. To think of spectacular violence as a body-count is not necessarily demeaning, simplistic or reductive. Consider, for example, the mobilization of casualty statistics in the opposition to the 2003 American-led invasion and occupation of Iraq. One important website, which compiles details of casualties, is called 'Iraq Body-count'.

64. H. T. Dickinson, 'Popular conservatism and militant loyalism 1789–1815', in H. T. Dickinson, ed., *Britain and the French Revolution 1789–1815* (Basingstoke: Macmillan, 1989), 124–5.

65. See Paulson, *Representations of Revolution*, 183–202; Brewer, *The Common People and Politics*, 46; Bindman, *In the Shadow of the Guillotine*, 61–2.

66. *William Cobbett: Selected Writings*, 2: 10.

67. The very wide distribution of the pamphlet is confirmed by Spater, *William Cobbett: Selected Writings*, 1: 127–8.

68. See Leonora Nattrass, *William Cobbett: The Politics of Style* (Cambridge: Cambridge University Press, 1995), 85.

69. See Duncan Wu, *Romanticism: An Anthology*, 518–20.

70. For an overview of Napoleon's reputation in Britain in the Romantic period, see Simon Bainbridge, *British Poetry and the Revolutionary and Napoleonic Wars: Visions of Conflict* (Oxford: Oxford University Press, 2003).

71. T. F. J. Klingberg and S. B. Hustvedt, eds, *The Warning Drum. The British Home Front Faces Napoleon. Broadsides of 1803* (Berkeley and Los Angeles: University of California Press, 1944), 64.

72. See Betty T. Bennett, *British War Poetry in the Age of Romanticism: 1793–1815* (New York and London: Garland Publishing, 1976); Bainbridge, *British Poetry and the Revolutionary and Napoleonic Wars*; J. R. Watson, *Romanticism and War: A Study of British Romantic Period Writers and the Napoleonic Wars* (Basingstoke: Palgrave, 2003), 33–8.

73. The 'Declaration of Rights' was appended to Shelley's Irish pamphlet, 'Proposals for an Association' (1812). See E. B. Murray, ed., *The Prose Works of Percy Bysshe Shelley. Volume 1* (Oxford: Clarendon Press, 1993), 58.

74. See Haywood, ' "The renovating fury" '.

75. *The Collected Works of Samuel Taylor Coleridge. Volume 2: The Watchman*, Lewis Patton, ed. (Routledge and Kegan Paul, 1970). The articles appeared in numbers VII and VIII (April 1796).

76. See Philip Shaw, 'Introduction' to Philip Shaw, ed., *Romantic Wars: Studies in Culture and Conflict, 1793–1822* (Aldershot: Ashgate, 2000), 3.

77. See Samuel Taylor Coleridge, *Complete Works*, 2 vols, Ernest Hartley Coleridge, ed. (1912; Oxford: Clarendon Press, 1968), Vol. 1, *Poems*. In a further recycling, the vignette went into *The Destiny of Nations* (published in *Sybilline Leaves*, 1817), ll. 209–17.
78. *Complete Works*, 1: 162n.
79. See Wu, ed., *Romanticism*, 521–6.
80. Mark Rawlinson, 'Invasion! Coleridge, the defence of Britain and the cultivation of the public's fear', in Shaw, ed., *Romantic Wars*, 120.
81. Bainbridge, *British Poetry and the Revolutionary and Napoleonic Wars*, 67–79.
82. Jerome Christenson reads this scene as an 'imagined invasion and a rape or primal fantasy' (Jerome Christenson, *Romanticism and the End of History* (Baltimore and London: John Hopkins University Press, 2000), 85).
83. Stephen Gill, ed., *William Wordsworth* (Oxford: Oxford University Press, 1984), 599.
84. See Debbie Lee, *Slavery and the Romantic Imagination* (Philadelphia: University of Pennsylvania Press, 2002), Chapter 3.
85. See Josephine McDonough, *Child Murder and British Culture 1720–1900* (Cambridge: Cambridge University Press, 2003), 72–80.
86. See Coleridge, *Complete Works*, Vol. 1.
87. On the poem's seditious qualities, see John Barrell, 'Fire, famine and slaughter', *Huntingdon Library Quarterly*, Vol. 63, No. 3, 2000, 277–98.
88. Coleridge, *Complete Works*, 2: 1100.
89. Robert Maniquis argues that Coleridge actually 'enjoyed participating' in the imagining of 'virtuous terror', despite this later renunciation (Robert M. Maniquis, 'Filling up and emptying out the sublime: Terror in British radical culture', *Huntingdon Library Quarterly*, Vol. 63, No. 3, 2000, 369–405, 377). See also Maniquis's 'Holy savagery and wild justice: English romanticism and the terror', *Studies in Romanticism*, 28 (Fall 1989), 365–95, 391–4.
90. See Philip Shaw, *Waterloo and the Romantic Imagination* (Basingstoke: Palgrave, 2002).
91. *Byron: Poetical Works*, Frederick Page, ed. (1904; Oxford: Oxford University Press, 1991), 188.
92. For a thorough discussion of Goya's images, see Paulson, *Representations of Revolution*, Chapter 9.
93. Lord Byron, *Don Juan*, T. G. Steffan, E. Steffan and W. W. Pratt, eds (Penguin, 1977).
94. Simon Bainbridge, ' "Of war and taking towns": Byron's siege poems', in Shaw, ed., *Romantic Wars*, 176.
95. Byron to Tom Moore, 19 September 1818. Cited in *The Selected Poetry and Prose of Byron*, W. H. Auden, ed. (Signet, 1966), 168.
96. Bainbridge, *British War Poetry in the Age of Romanticism*, 182.

3 'The most distressful country': The Irish rebellion of 1798

1. E. B. Murray, ed., *The Prose Works of Percy Bysshe Shelley. Volume 1* (Oxford: Clarendon Press, 1993), 36.
2. Ruan O'Donnell, 'Rebellion of 1798', in Iain McCalman, ed., *An Oxford Companion to the Romantic Age: British Culture 1776–1832* (1999; Oxford: Oxford University Press, 2001), 670.

3. William T. W. Tone, 'The third and last expedition for the liberation of Ireland, and the capture, trial and death of Theobald Wolfe Tone [1826]', in *Life of Theobald Wolfe Tone. Compiled and arranged by William Theobald Wolfe Tone*, Thomas Bartlett, ed. (Dublin: The Lilliput Press, 1998), 877.

4. For a very useful survey of the historiography of the Irish rebellion, see Tom Dunne, *Rebellions: Memoir, Memory and 1798* (Dublin: The Lilliput Press, 2004), Chapter 6.

5. Roy Foster, *Modern Ireland 1600–1972* (Penguin, 1989), 280. Foster also states that the rebellion 'was a campaign marked by horrific and unforgotten atrocities on both sides' (279). W. A. Maguire calls the rebellion 'the bloody climax of a violent period' (W. A. Maguire, *The 1798 Rebellion in Ireland: A Bicentenary Exhibition* (Ulster Museum, 1998), xv).

6. The term 'religious war' is used by Daniel Gahan, 'The rebellion of 1798 in south Leinster', in Thomas Bartlett, David Dickson, Dáire Keogh, Kevin Whelan, eds, *1798: A Bicentenary Perspective* (Dublin: Four Courts Press, 2003), 120.

7. Jim Smyth has noted the effectiveness of this 'propagandist creation' of a 'sectarian bloodbath' in Wexford. See Jim Smyth, *The Men of No Property: Irish Radicals and Popular Politics in the Late Eighteenth Century* (1992; Houndmills: Macmillan, 1998), 181.

8. Ina Ferris, *The Romantic National Tale and the Question of Ireland* (Cambridge: Cambridge University Press, 2002).

9. *Report from the Committee of Secrecy, of the House of Lords in Ireland, 30 August 1798* (J. Debrett, 1798), 14.

10. Cited in R. B. McDowell, 'Burke and Ireland', in David Dickson, Dáire Keogh and Kevin Whelan, eds, *The United Irishmen: Republicanism, Radicalism and Rebellion* (Dublin: Lilliput Press, 1993), 112.

11. See Kevin Whelan, 'Reinterpreting the 1798 rebellion in County Wexford', in Dáire Keogh and Nicholas Furlong, eds, *The Mighty Wave: The 1798 Rebellion in Wexford* (Dublin, Four Courts Press, 1996), 20. Clive Emsley agrees that the repression in Ireland 'might justifiably be given the name "terror"'. See 'The impact of the French revolution', in Ceri Crossley and Ian Small, eds, *The French Revolution and British Culture* (Oxford: Oxford University Press, 1989), 31–62, 58–9.

12. James Gordon, *History of the Rebellion in Ireland in the Year 1798* (Dublin: William Porter, 1801), 214, 212, 209.

13. William Hazlitt, *Life of Napoleon* (1828–30); cited in Robert M. Maniquis, 'Holy savagery and wild justice: English romanticism and the terror', *Studies in Romanticism*, 28 (Fall 1989), 365–95, 378.

14. According to David Cairns and Shaun Richards, the Irish figured increasingly in the nineteenth-century imagination as 'a race of covert blacks' (David Cairns and Shaun Richards, *Writing Ireland: Colonialism, Nationalism and Culture* (Manchester: Manchester University Press, 1988), 48).

15. See James Kelly, '"We were all to have been massacred": Irish Protestants and the experience of rebellion', in Bartlett, Dickson, Keogh, Whelan, eds, *1798: A Bicentenary Perspective*, 326–8.

16. Thomas Moore, *Memoirs of Captain Rock the Celebrated Irish Chieftain, with Some Account of his Ancestors* (Longman, 1824). The quotation forms the heading for the chapter '1649'.

17. As an example of this absence, there are no images of the rebellion in Fintan Cullen's otherwise very interesting book, *Visual Politics: The Representation of Ireland 1750–1930* (Cork: Cork University Press, 1997). The best sources for visual

representations of the rebellion are the hard-to-obtain catalogues of the two bicentenary exhibitions held in Ireland and Northern Ireland in 1998. See Kevin Whelan, ed., *The Fellowship of Freedom: Companion Volume to the Bicentenary Exhibition by the National Library and National Museum at Collins Barracks, Dublin 1998* (Cork: Cork University Press, 1998), and Maguire, *The 1798 Rebellion in Ireland*.

18. Thomas Bartlett, Kevin Dawson and Dáire Keogh, *Rebellion: A Television History of 1798* (Dublin: Gill and Macmillan, 1998), 121.

19. 'The address of the United Britons to the United Irishmen', January 1798, in *Report from the Committee of Secrecy*, Appendix II, 29.

20. *Paddy's Resource, or the Harp of Erin, Attuned to Freedom; Being a Collection of Patriotic Songs, Selected for Paddy's Amusement* (Dublin: np, nd [1795]). A handwritten note in the British Library edition which I consulted states that the printer was executed in the rebellion. For a harsh assessment of the songbook's sentimentalism, see Tom Dunne, 'Popular ballads, revolutionary rhetoric and politicisation', in Hugh Gough and David Dickson, eds, *Ireland and the French Revolution* (Dublin: Irish Academic Press, 1990).

21. *William Wordsworth*, Stephen Gill, ed. (1984; Oxford: Oxford University Press, 1990), 31–43.

22. This term is coined by Luke Gibbons in his excellent book *Edmund Burke and Ireland: Aesthetics, Politics and the Colonial Sublime* (Cambridge: Cambridge University Press, 2003). Gibbons speculates that Burke derived his hatred of colonial violence from his Irish background (see Chapters 1 and 3). Burke's family may have been implicated in Whiteboy violence which resulted in the 'judicial murder' of its alleged organizer Father Sheehey in 1766. Sheehey's head was spiked on Clonmel jail for 20 years until it was recovered by his sister, who was married to Burke's cousin (37).

23. *Memoirs of Myles Byrne*, 3 vols (Paris and New York: Gustave Bossange, 1863), 1: 35.

24. Marianne Elliot, *Partners in Revolution: The United Irishmen and France* (New Haven and London: Yale University Press, 1982), 196–7.

25. Moore, *Memoirs of Captain Rock*, 361. Tadgh O'Sullivan argues that conservatives and loyalists were justified in attacking Moore for playing down 'the reality of agrarian insurgency' which was such an 'endemic' feature of Irish history, though O'Sullivan also seems to overlook Moore's overt references to rebel violence. See Tadgh O'Sullivan, ' "The violence of a servile war": three narratives of Irish rural insurgency post-1798', in Laurence M. Geary, ed., *Rebellion and Remembrance in Modern Ireland* (Dublin: Four Courts Press, 2001), 85, 91–2.

26. Cited in Foster, *Modern Ireland*, 276.

27. In a recent discussion of the rebel massacres, Charles Dixon asks for an 'equal condemnation' of the 'much more numerous murders of defenceless people' committed by 'the forces of law and order' (*The Wexford Rising in 1798: Its Causes and Its Course* (1955; London: Constable, 1997), 153).

28. Musgrave states that 184 were killed inside and 37 shot outside the barn (Richard Musgrave, *Memoirs of The Different Rebellions in Ireland*, 3rd edition, 2 vols (1801; Dublin and London, 1803), 1: 525).

29. Thomas Pakenham agrees that Scullabogue 'left an indelible mark on Irish history'. See Thomas Pakenham, *The Year of Liberty: The Story of the Great Irish Rebellion of 1798* (1969; Weidenfeld and Nicholson, 1997), 198.

30. For a contemporary example of what Dunne calls 'distortion' at work, see Edward Hay, *History of the Insurrection in the County of Wexford* (1803). For Hay, who was a

member of the council of the Wexford republic, Scullabogue was a 'characteristic' example of the 'precipitate' and 'indiscriminate... deeds of outrage' of 'popular commotion' (165). He insists that 'no person of superior condition' was involved (164), and that Catholics were also killed. Dunne challenges the latter point, claiming that the murdered Catholics were chosen because of their Protestant connections (*Rebellions*, 253, 262–3). More recently, see Kevin Whelan, who argues that the Wexford rebellion 'issued from politicisation' ('Reinterpreting the 1798 Rebellion in County Wexford', 20–1). For the debate about whether a republic of Wexford actually existed, see Dunne, *Rebellions*, 118–23.

31. Marianne Elliott agrees, blaming the 'totally uncoordinated' United Irish tactics for producing a 'bloodbath of their worst dreams' (Marianne Elliott, 'Ireland and the French Revolution', in H. T. Dickinson, ed., *Britain and the French Revolution 1789–1815* (Basingstoke: Macmillan, 1989), 99).

32. Dunne's target here is probably Whelan, who asks historians to 'relinquish our obsession with the military aspects of 1798, with pikes and deaths, murder, mayhem and martyrdom... the gory details of the campaign can only distract us from the enduring legacy of '98" ' ('Reinterpreting the 1798 rebellion in County Wexford', 35).

33. Gordon, *History of the Rebellion in Ireland*, 148, 73.

34. Roy Foster, 'Ascendancy and union', in Roy Foster, ed., *The Oxford History of Ireland* (Oxford: Oxford University Press, 1989), 152–3.

35. Musgrave puts the figure at around 500 (*Memoirs of The Different Rebellions in Ireland*, 1: 461).

36. The document is included in Gordon, *History of the Rebellion in Ireland in the Year 1798*, Appendix, 4–5.

37. Charles Tilly notes that priests marched in the rebel armies in the Vendée (Charles Tilly, *The Vendée* (Cambridge, Massachusetts and London: Harvard University Press, 1976), 321).

38. Musgrave, *Memoirs of The Different Rebellions in Ireland*, 1: 461–2.

39. Musgrave, *Memoirs of The Different Rebellions in Ireland*, 1: 529. Musgrave's book was the 'political bible' of loyalists, according to its modern editor David Dickson. Dickson is cited in Dáire Keogh, 'Sectarianism in the rebellion of 1798', in Keogh and Furlong, eds, *The Mighty Wave*, 46.

40. *A Narrative of the Sufferings and Escape of Charles Jackson, Late resident at Wexford, in Ireland, including an Account, by way of Journal, of several Barbarous Atrocities committed, in June, 1798, by the Irish Rebels in that Town, while it was in their Possession, to the Greater Part of which he was an Eye-Witness* (Printed for the Author, 1798), 22.

41. Dunne, *Rebellions*, 252–3.

42. *A Narrative of the Sufferings and Escape of Charles Jackson*, 25–6.

43. Myles Byrne concurred with Gordon's defence of rebel restraint: see *Memoirs of Myles Byrne*, 1: 257–8.

44. See Dáire Keogh, 'The women of 1798: Explaining the silence', in Bartlett, Dickson, Keogh, Whelan, eds, *1798: A Bicentenary Perspective*.

45. *A Narrative of the Sufferings and Escape of Charles Jackson*, 68, 180.

46. The incident is reported in Daniel Gahan, *The People's Rising: Wexford 1798* (Dublin, Gill and MacMillan, 1995), 255.

47. Thomas Bartlett, 'Clemency and compensation: the treatment of defeated rebels and suffering loyalists after the 1798 rebellion', in Jim Smyth, ed. *Revolution, Counter-revolution and Union: Ireland in the 1790s* (Cambridge: Cambridge

University Press, 2000), 108. The most complete source of eye-witness accounts of loyalist atrocities is Rev. Myles V. Ronan, ed., *Insurgent Wicklow 1798. The story as written by Rev. Bro. Luke Cullen, O. D. C. (1793–1859). With additional Material from other MSS* (Dublin: Clonmore and Reynolds, 1948). Cullen claimed to have gathered testimony from survivors and veterans of the rebellion. In one incident, a man and wife are shot dead in their bed, and 'an infant was found striving to suck the breast of its dead mother' (21). This scene resembles closely the vignette of 'denatalization' used by Coleridge in his anti-war journalism.

48. Cited in Terence Folley, ed., *Eyewitness to 1798* (Cork: Mercier Press, 1996), 25, 60.
49. Ibid., 38.
50. Gordon, *History of the Rebellion in Ireland in the Year 1798*, 212.
51. Cited in Folley, ed., *Eyewitness to 1798*, 88.
52. James Alexander, *Some Account of the First Apparent Symptoms of the late Rebellion in the County of Kildare and in the County of Wexford* (Dublin: John Jones, 1800), 65–6.
53. [Anon.], *Narrative of a Private Soldier, in one of his majesty's Regiment of Foot. Written by Himself* (Glasgow: Young, Gallie and Co., 1819), 17–18. I am grateful to Neil Ramsey for this reference.
54. The soldier could have been remembering 'Bloody Friday', a massacre which took place on 22 June 1798 (see *Memoirs of Myles Byrne*, 1: 254).
55. *Ierne: An Elegy* (London: Wm. Clark; Dublin: G. Burnet, 1798). I am grateful to Markman Ellis for alerting me to this poem.
56. See: http://www.linuxlots.com/~dunne/ireland/Croppies_lie_down.html.
57. J. Aikin and A. L. Aikin, *Miscellaneous Pieces, in Prose* (J[oseph] Johnson, 1775), 196.
58. Terry Eagleton, *Heathcliff and the Great Hunger: Studies in Irish Culture* (Verso, 1995), 165.
59. Cited in Janet Todd, *Rebel Daughters: Ireland in Conflict 1798* (Viking, 2003), 182.
60. *Memoirs of Richard Lovell Edgeworth, Esq. Begun by Himself and Concluded by his Daughter, Maria Edgeworth*, 2 vols (R. Hunter, 1820), 2: 222–3; Marilyn Butler, 'Introduction' to Maria Edgeworth, *Castle Rackrent and Ennui* (Penguin, 1992). All page references are from this edition of the novel.
61. Cited in Brian Hollingworth, *Maria Edgeworth's Irish Writing: Language, History, Politics* (Basingstoke: Macmillan, 1997), 40.
62. The phrase is used by Maria Edgeworth in a letter cited by Hollingworth, *Maria Edgeworth's Irish Writing*, 41.
63. Butler, 'Introduction', 49.
64. Sigmund Freud, *Case Histories 1, The Penguin Freud Library. Volume 8* (Penguin, 1990, 44).
65. Tom Dunne, 'Representations of Rebellion: 1798 in Literature', in F. B. Smith, ed., *Ireland, England and Australia: Essays in Honour of Oliver Macdonagh* (Cork and Canberra: Cork University Press, 1990), 17; Hollingworth, *Maria Edgeworth's Irish Writing*, 142, 132.
66. The phrase 'magical realism' is used by Marilyn Butler, 'General Introduction' to *The Novels and Selected Works of Maria Edgeworth*, 12 vols (Pickering and Chatto, 1999–2003), 1: xlix.
67. [Charles Maturin], *The Milesian Chief. A Romance*, 4 vols (Henry Colburn, 1812).
68. Eagleton, *Heathcliff and the Great Hunger*, 187.
69. Ferris confirms that the rebellion is fictional (*The Romantic National Tale*, 103).

70. Ferris, *The Romantic National Tale*, 118.
71. Shelley, 'An address, to the Irish people', in Murray, ed., *The Prose Works of Percy Bysshe Shelley*, 12, 23.
72. Katie Trumpener, *Bardic Nationalism: The Romantic Novel and the British Empire* (Princeton, New Jersey: Princeton University Press, 1997), 148.
73. Eagleton, *Heathcliff and the Great Hunger*, 183, 148–54.
74. [Michael Banim], *The Croppy: A Tale of 1798*, 3 vols (Henry Colburn, 1828). Michael Banim is credited with the authorship of the novel in the British Library catalogue, and by Mark D. Hawthorne, *John and Michael Banim (The 'O'Hara Brothers'): A Study in the Early Development of the Anglo-Irish Novel* (Salzburg: Institut Fur Englische Sprache und Literatur, 1975), though the original 1828 edition attributed both John and Michael Banim under their pseudonym the 'O'Hara' brothers.
75. The quotations are from Dunne, 'Representations of Rebellion', 15; and Eagleton, *Heathcliff and the Great Hunger*, 200. For a reading of the novel's use of Gothic scenes, see Hawthorne, *John and Michael Banim*, 136–42.
76. See Dunne, 'Representations of Rebellion', 36–40. Ferris points out that Catholic Irish writers were attacked for their political bias: 'writing supplements to the newspapers', according to the *Atheneum* in 1828 (*The Romantic National* Tale, 131).
77. Cited in Eagleton, *Heathcliff and the Great Hunger*, 202.
78. W. J. McCormack, *Ascendancy and Tradition in Anglo-Irish Literary History from 1789 to 1939* (Oxford: Clarendon Press, 1985), 170. Kevin Whelan calls Banim a 'Kilkenny O'Connellite' who used the novel to 'distance respectable middle-class Catholics from any complicity in the rising'. See Kevin Whelan, ed., *The Fellowship of Freedom*, 131.
79. Jon Mee, *Enthusiasm and Regulation: Poetics and the Policing of Culture in the Romantic Period* (Oxford: Oxford University Press, 2003), Chapters 1–2.
80. Ferris's reading of this intervention is that 'enlightenment becomes incomprehension' (*The Romantic National* Tale, 133), but 'incomprehension' seems to me a vague way to describe the resort to spectacular violence.
81. On this identification, see Thomas Flanagan, *The Irish Novelists 1800–1850* (New York: Columbia University Press, 1959), 200.
82. Ferris, *The Romantic National Tale*, 136.
83. Banim may have been encouraging his readers to look at *Memoirs of Captain Rock*, published just a few years earlier in 1824. Moore blamed the Scullabogue massacre on 'the panic which the severities of the Government had diffused' (361).
84. Dunne, *Rebellion*, Chapters 11, 12, 14.
85. Dunne, 'Representations of Rebellion', 36.
86. 'Plant, Plant the Tree', in *Paddy's Resource*, 18–19.
87. Banim could have found this document in Gordon, *History of the Rebellion in Ireland in the Year 1798*, Appendix, 5. Banim regarded Gordon's book as more accurate than either Musgrave or Taylor (see Banim's Preface to the 1865 edition of the novel published in Dublin by James Duffy).
88. Whelan, 'Reinterpreting the 1798 rebellion in County Wexford', 9. See also Banim's notes to the 1865 reprint, 430–1.
89. John Sutherland, *The Life of Walter Scott* (1995; Oxford: Blackwell, 1997), 198–9.
90. *Memoirs of The Different Rebellions in Ireland*, 1: 459.
91. Robert M. Maniquis, 'Filling up and emptying out the sublime: Terror in British radical culture', *Huntingdon Library Quarterly*, Vol. 63, No. 3, 2000, 369–405, 378.

92. The most obvious connection between Ireland and the Waverley novels is of course Scott's acknowledged debt to Maria Edgeworth: 'she may be truly said to have done more towards completing the Union than perhaps all the legislative enactments by which it has been followed up'. Scott's professed aim in imitating Edgeworth was to cast the Scots in a similar 'favourable light' and 'to procure sympathy for their virtues and indulgence for their foibles' ('General Preface' (1829), in Walter Scott, *Waverley* (Penguin, 1980), 523). Recent criticism has questioned Scott's optimistic gloss on Scottish and Irish history. For Luke Gibbons, Scott's real indebtedness to Irish history was 'an aesthetics of terror and disintegration' (Gibbons, *Edmund Burke and Ireland*, 84). In an illuminating discussion of *Waverley*, Saree Makdisi sees a parallel between Scott's portrayal in *Waverley* of the crushing of Jacobitism in 1745 and the defeat of the Irish in 1798 (Saree Makdisi, *Romantic Imperialism: Universal Empire and the Culture of Modernity* (Cambridge: Cambridge University Press, 1998), 77–81; 112–14; 204–5, 24n.). Some parallels can also be drawn between the 'enthusiastic' Biblical discourse of Scottish Covenanters and Irish Defenders. According to Jim Smyth, Defender passwords and catechisms were 'an explosive blend of Biblical, Jacobite, Jacobin and Masonic symbolism' (Jim Smyth, 'Introduction: The 1798 rebellion in its eighteenth-century contexts', in Smyth, ed., *Revolution, Counter-revolution and Union*, 9). See also Julie Kipp, 'Back to the future: Walter Scott on the politics of radical reform in Ireland and Scotland', *European Romantic Review*, Vol 16, No. 2, 2005, 231–42, 233–4.
93. Walter Scott, *Old Mortality* (Penguin, 1980), 386.
94. For a more detailed discussion of the significance of 'well-dressed' figures at scenes of violence, see Chapter 5.
95. Trumpener, *Bardic Nationalism*, 273.
96. *Narrative of the Life of Walter Scott, Bart. Begun by Himself and Continued by J. G. Lockhart* (London and Toronto: Dent, 1922), 318.
97. *Narrative of the Life of Walter Scott*, 297.

4 American 'savagery'

1. William Blake, *America: A Prophecy (1793)*, 'Preludium', l. 30, in *The Poems of William Blake*, W. H. Stevenson and David V. Erdman, eds (Longman, 1975), 190.
2. Alexis de Tocqueville, *Democracy in America*, 2 vols (Collins, 1968), 1: 410.
3. Letter to Southey, October 1794; cited by Nigel Leask, 'Pantisocracy', in Iain McCalman, ed., *An Oxford Companion to the Romantic Age* (Oxford: Oxford University Press, 1999), 635. The topic of Pantisocracy has been well covered by Romantic scholars: see J. R. MacGillivray, 'The pantisocracy scheme and its immediate background', in *Studies in English by Members of University College* [Toronto], M. W. Wallace, ed. (Toronto, 1931), 131–69; Nicholas Roe, *Wordsworth and Coleridge: The Radical Years* (Oxford: Oxford University Press, 1988), 113–15, 211–12; James C. McKusick, ' "Wisely forgetful": Coleridge and the politics of pantisocracy', in Tim Fulford and Peter J. Kitson, eds, *Romanticism and Colonialism: Writing and Empire, 1780–1830* (Cambridge: Cambridge University Press, 1998).
4. The poem can be found in *The Collected Letters of Samuel Taylor Coleridge*, Earl L. Griggs, ed., 6 vols (Oxford: Oxford University Press, 1956–71), 1: 104.
5. See Kenneth Curry, *Southey* (Routledge and Kegan Paul, 1975), 21–9. When Southey's aunt, with whom he was lodging, discovered his plans, the self-styled 'Apostle of Pantisocracy' was promptly evicted (29).

6. I have used the text in Duncan Wu, ed., *Romanticism: An Anthology* (Oxford: Blackwell, 1994), 191–7.

7. Cited in ibid., 194n.

8. The phrase 'national contentment' is used by David Bindman, *The Shadow of the Guillotine* (British Museum, 1989), 63. See also Ian Haywood, *The Revolution in Popular Literature: Print, Politics and the People, 1790–1860* (Cambridge: Cambridge University Press, 2004), Chapters 2–4.

9. Wu, ed., *Romanticism*, 237–9.

10. Ibid., 237.

11. See Tim Fulford's intriguing study of the influence of Hearne's book on Coleridge's *The Rime of the Ancient Mariner* (Tim Fulford, *Romantic Indians* (Oxford: Oxford University Press, 2006), Chapter 9).

12. I. S. McLaren, 'Samuel Hearne's Accounts of the massacre at Bloody Fall, 17 July 1771', *Ariel: A Review of International Literature*, 22: 1 (1991), 25–51, 46n.; cited in Kevin D. Hutchings, 'Writing commerce and cultural progress in Samuel Hearne's *A journey . . . to the Northern Ocean*', *Ariel: A Review of International English Literature*, 28: 2 (1997), 49–78, 56.

13. See *TEE*, 3: 70.

14. J. Hector St. John Crevecoeur, *Letters from an American Farmer* [1782] and *Sketches of Eighteenth-Century America* [1925] (Penguin, 1987).

15. *TEE*, 1: 21.

16. Ian K. Steele, *Betrayals: Fort William Henry and the 'Massacre'* (Oxford: Oxford University Press, 1990), vii.

17. *New York Mercury*, 22 August 1757; cited in Steele, *Betrayals*, 117.

18. See Lewis Leary, Introduction to Michel René Hilliard d'Auberteuil, *Miss McCrea: A Novel of the American Revolution*, trans. Eric LaGuardia (Gainesville, Florida: Scholars Facsimiles and Reprints, 1958), 14.

19. Hoffman Nickerson, *The Turning Point of the Revolution: or Burgoyne in America* (Boston and New York: Houghton Mifflin Company, 1928), 185.

20. Ibid., 288.

21. Colin Galloway, *The American Revolution in Indian Country: Crisis and Diversity in Native American Communities* (Cambridge: Cambridge University Press), 295.

22. See Ray Raphael, *The American Revolution: A People's History* (2001; Profile Books, 2002), 201–2; Barbara Graymont, *The Iroquois in the American Revolution* (Syracuse, New York: Syracuse University Press, 1972), 168–74.

23. *Conciones ad Populam* (1795), in *The Collected Works of Samuel Taylor Coleridge. 1: Lectures 1795 on Politics and Religion*, Lewis Patton and Peter Mann, eds (Routledge and Kegan Paul, 1971), 53.

24. For a full reading of the poem, see Fulford, *Romantic Indians*, Chapter 11.

25. Jean Paul Sartre, Preface to Frantz Fanon, *The Wretched of the Earth* (1961; Penguin, 1985), 16–17.

26. David Hume, 'Of the original contract', in *Essays Moral, Political and Literary* T. H. Green and T. H. Grose, eds (Longmans Green and Co, 1898).

27. De Tocqueville, *Democracy in America*, 1: 421.

28. Tzvetan Todorov, *The Conquest of America: The Question of the Other*, trans. Richard Howard (HarperPerennial, 1984) 133, 144–5.

29. [Bartoleme Las Casas], *The Tears of the Indians: Being An Historical and True Account of the Cruel Massacres and Slaughters of above Twenty Millions of Innocent People; Committed by the Spaniards in the Islands of Hispaniola, Cuba, Jamaica, etc. As also in the Continent of Mexico, Peru, and Other Places of the West Indies, to the Total*

Destruction of those Countries. Written in Spanish by Casas, an Eye Witness of Those Things (1656).

30. For a brief overview of the importance of this book, see Claude Rawson, *God, Gulliver and Genocide: Barbarism and the European Imagination* (Oxford: Oxford University Press, 2001), 18–20.
31. Samuel Johnson, 'Idler 81', in *The Yale Edition of the Works of Samuel Johnson*, W. J. Bate, John M. Bullitt, L. F. Powell, eds (New Haven and London: Yale University Press, 1963), 252–3.
32. William Robertson, *The History of America*, 2 vols (Edinburgh, W. Strahan and T. Cadell, 1777), 1: 218, 1: 225–6.
33. Helen Maria Williams, *Peru: A Poem* (T. Cadell, 1784).
34. Alan Richardson, 'Epic ambivalence: Imperial politics and romantic deflection in Williams's *Peru* and Landor's *Gebir*', in *Romanticism, Race, and Imperial Culture, 1780–1834*, Alan Richardson and Sonia Hofkosh, eds (Bloomington and Indianapolis: Indiana University Press, 1996), 265–82, 271.
35. Richard Brinsley Sheridan, *Pizarro: A Tragedy*, 7th edition (James Ridgway, 1799).
36. For a useful discussion of the play's implied audience, see Gillian Russell, *Theatres of War: Performance, Politics and Society 1793–1815* (Oxford: Clarendon Press, 1995), 54–9.
37. Bryan Edwards, *The History, Civil and Commercial, of the British Colonies in the West Indies*, 4th edition, 3 vols (1793; John Stockdale, 1797), 1: 110–11n.
38. For a survey of the atrocities committed on both sides in the American revolutionary war, see Raphael, *The American Revolution*, Chapters 2–5. Linda Colley claims that American atrocity propaganda was more effective than its British equivalent: see Linda Colley, *Captives: Britain, Empire, and the World 1600–1850* (Jonathan Cape, 2002), 216–31.
39. Alfred Grant, *Our American Brethren: A History of Letters in the British Press During the American Revolution, 1775–1781* (Jefferson, North Carolina, and London: McFarland and Company, 1967), 25.
40. Ibid., 26, 34–7.
41. Raphael, *The American Revolution*, 71, 368, 220n., 82.
42. See John C. Dann, *The Revolution Remembered: Eyewitness Accounts of the War of Independence* (London and Chicago: University of Chicago Press, 1980), 202–3.
43. Cited in Raphael, *The American Revolution*, 133.
44. Cited in Charlotte Smith, *The Old Manor House*, Jacqueline M. Labbe, ed. (Ontario: Broadview press, 2002), Appendix, 576.
45. Thomas Paine, 'Common Sense' (January 1776), in *The Thomas Paine Reader*, Michael Foot and Isaac Kramnick, eds (Penguin, 1987), 67.
46. On Paine's use of Oedipal metaphors, see Ronald Paulson, *Representations of Revolution 1789–1820* (New Haven and London: Yale University Press, 1983) 73–9.
47. Thomas Day, *Ode for the New Year 1776* (J. Almon, 1776), VII, 4–5.
48. See Richard D. Brown, *Major Problems in the Era of the American Revolution, 1760–1791* (1992); cited in Smith, *The Old Manor House*, Appendix, 578, 580.
49. Cited in Raphael, *The American Revolution*, 196.
50. Thomas Day, *The Desolation of America* (G. Kearsley, 1777).
51. *Gentleman's Magazine*, xlviii (1777), 122–3.
52. Cited in Michelle Burnham, *Captivity and Sentiment: Cultural Exchange in American Literature, 1682–1861* (Hanover and London: University Press of New England, 1997), 75.

53. Edmund Burke, 'Draft petition on the use of Indians', in *The Writings and Speeches of Edmund Burke. Volume III: Party, Parliament, and the American War 1774–1780*, W. M. Elofson and John A. Woods, eds (Oxford: Clarendon Press, 1996), 179–81.

54. See Raphael, *The American Revolution*, Chapter 6.

55. See the report of the speech in the *Annual Register* (1778), 'History of Europe', 110–14.

56. Burke, *The Writings and Speeches of Edmund Burke. Volume III*, 356.

57. See Luke Gibbons, *Edmund Burke and Ireland: Aesthetics, Politics and the Colonial Sublime* (Cambridge: Cambridge University Press, 2003), Chapter 7. Burke compares the Versailles mob to 'a procession of American savages, entering into Onondaga, after some of their murders called victories, and leading into hovels hung round with scalps, their captives, overpowered with the scoffs and buffets of women as ferocious as themselves'.

58. Michel René Hilliard d'Auberteuil, *Miss McCrea: A Novel of the American Revolution*, trans. Eric LaGuardia (1784 in French; rptd Gainesville, Florida: Scholars Facsimiles and Reprints, 1958). Introduction by Lewis Leary.

59. See June Namias, *White Captives: Gender and Ethnicity on the American Frontier* (Chapel Hill and London: University of North Carolina Press, 1993), Chapter 4.

60. Ibid., 123–40.

61. Cited by Leary, 'Introduction', 9.

62. One of the most detached Romantic views of Indian stoicism under torture is Joanna Baillie's in the *Introductory Discourse* to *A Series of Plays: In which it is Attempted to Delineate the Stronger Passions of the Mind* (1798; rptd Oxford and New York: Woodstock, 1990). She argues that Indian torture is a 'national custom' deriving from the universal human desire to 'behold man in every situation, putting forth his strength against the current of adversity, scorning all bodily anguish'. As the function of this 'grand and terrible game' is to test 'the fortitude of the soul' only 'the excess of cruelty exercised upon their miserable victim' will achieve this goal, and every male Indian is potentially a 'savage tormentor' and 'haughty victim' (7–8).

63. *TEE*, 1: xxxvii; Fulford, *Romantic Indians*, Chapter 6.

64. See Annette Kolodny, *The Land Before Her: Fantasy and Experience of the American Frontiers, 1630–1860* (Chapel Hill and London: University of North Carolina Press, 1984), Chapters 1–4; Burnham, *Captivity and Sentiment*, Chapter 3; Colley, *Captives*, Chapters 5–7.

65. Katherine Zabelle Derounian-Stodola, ed., *Women's Indian Captivity Narratives* (Penguin, 1998), Introduction, xiv.

66. *French and Indian cruelty; exemplified in the life and various vicissitudes of fortune of Peter Williamson*, Michael Fry, ed. (Bristol: Thoemmes Press, 1996).

67. Colley, *Captives*, 190.

68. Williamson's text can be compared with Henry Grace, *The History of the Life and Sufferings of Henry Grace* (Basingstoke: Printed for the Author, 1764), another popular captivity narrative. Grace does not provide any explanatory framework for Indian atrocities, though he is rescued at one point by a squaw (21).

69. David Hume, *An Enquiry Concerning the Principles of Morals* (1751) (Oxford: Clarendon Press, 1983), 191.

70. On the Romantic fascination with the death song, see: Helen Carr, *Inventing the American Primitive: Politics, Gender and the Representation of Native American Literary Traditions, 1789–1936* (Cork: Cork University Press, 1996), Chapter 2; Fulford, *Romantic Indians*, Chapter 8.

71. James Fenimore Cooper, *The Last of the Mohicans* (Oxford: Oxford University Press, 1998). Introduction, essays and Notes by John McWilliams.

72. Terence Martin, 'From atrocity to requiem: History in *The Last of the Mohicans*', in *New Essays on The Last of the Mohicans*, H. Daniel Peck, ed. (Cambridge: Cambridge University Press, 1992), 47.

73. Steele, *Betrayals*, vii.

74. John McWilliams, 'The historical contexts of *The Last of the Mohicans*', in *The Last of the Mohicans*, 400.

75. Steele, *Betrayals*, 169–70, 160. For an analysis of the novel's historical accuracy, see David P. French, 'James Fenimore Cooper and Fort William Henry', *American Literature*, 32 (1960), 28–38; Thomas Philbrick, 'The sources of Cooper's knowledge of Fort William Henry', *American Literature*, 36 (1964), 209–14; Robert Lawson-Peebles, 'The lesson of the massacre at Fort William Henry', in Peck, ed., *New Essays on the Last of the Mohicans*.

76. Mary Jemison, *A Narrative of the Life of Mrs. Mary Jemison*, in *Women's Indian Captivity Narratives*, Derounian-Stodola, ed., 187. Derounian-Stodola confirms that this atrocity was 'a standard narrative icon and propagandist ploy to stress victimization and to rationalize the woman captive's ensuing vengefulness' (Introduction, xxii). See also Kolodny, *The Land Before Her*, 81.

77. For a discussion of the novel as a series of increasingly contrived captivity narratives, see Louise K. Barnett, *The Ignoble Savage: American Literary Racism, 1790–1860* (Westport, Connecticut and London: Greenwood Press, 1975), 62–4.

78. See Michael Paul Rogin, *Fathers and Children: Andrew Jackson and the Subjugation of the American Indian* (New York: Alfred A. Knopf, 1975), Chapter 7.

79. De Tocqueville, *Democracy in America*, 1: 397.

80. See: Lucy Maddox, *Removals: Nineteenth-Century American Literature and the Politics of Indian Affairs* (New York and Oxford: Oxford University Press, 1991), 44–6; John McWilliams, *The Last of the Mohicans: Civil Savagery and Savage Civility* (Toronto: Twayne Publishers, 1995), 17; Richard Slotkin, 'Introduction' to James Fenimore Cooper, *The Last of the Mohicans* (Penguin, 1986), xii.

81. Slotkin, 'Introduction', xx–xxvii; Jane Tompkins, *Sensational Designs: The Cultural Work of American Fiction 1790–1860* (New York and Oxford: Oxford University Press, 1985), Chapter 4.

82. For an overview of Cooper's 'Leatherstocking myth', see Richard Slotkin, *Regeneration through Violence: The Mythology of the American Frontier* (Norman: University of Oklahoma Press, 1973), Chapter 13. See also Robert F. Berkhofer, *The White Man's Indian: Images of the American Indian from Columbus to the Present* (New York: Alfred A. Knopf, 1978), 91–3. D. H. Lawrence and other critics observed that Cooper's imaginative investment in this homosocial masculine fantasy was also a way to overcome the effeminizing power of the genteel, female-dominated literary market. See D. H. Lawrence, *Studies in Classic American Literature*, Ezra Greenspan, Lindeth Vasey and John Worthen, eds (Cambridge: Cambridge University Press, 2003), 58–62; Slotkin, 'Introduction', xi.

83. See Slotkin, *Regeneration through Violence*, 21 and Chapter 9.

84. Joel Barlow, *The Columbiad* (Philadelphia: Fry and Kammerer, 1807).

85. See Slotkin, *Regeneration through Violence*, 342–4; John P. McWilliams, *The American Epic: Transforming a Genre, 1770–1860* (Cambridge: Cambridge University Press, 1989), 53–66.

86. Ethan Allen, *A Narrative of Colonel Ethan Allen's Captivity* (New York: Corinth Books, 1961).

87. Colley, *Captives*, 225.
88. De Tocqueville, *Democracy in America*, 1: 447, 426.

5 Unruly people: The spectacular riot

1. *The Political Magazine* (June 1780), 1: 441.
2. *Annual Register* (1831), 294.
3. The quotations are from: Robert Shoemaker, *The London Mob: Violence and Disorder in Eighteenth-Century England* (London and New York: Hambledon and London, 2004), 151; John Plotz, *The Crowd: British Literature and Public Politics* (Berkeley and Los Angeles: University of California Press, 2000), 5.
4. Mark Philp, ed., *The Political and Philosophical Writings of William Godwin*, 7 vols (William Pickering 1993), 3: 279.
5. Saree Makdisi, *William Blake and the Impossible History of the 1790s* (Chicago and London: Chicago University Press, 2003), 49.
6. Ronald Paulson, *Representations of Revolution (1789–1820)* (New Haven and London: Yale University Press, 1983), 45.
7. *Annual Register* (1780), Appendix to the Chronicle, 261–2.
8. Cited in the entry for Lord George Gordon, *Oxford Dictionary of National Biography* (Oxford: Oxford University Press, 2004), 22: 896.
9. Nathaniel Wraxall, *Historical Memoirs of My Own Time* (1815); cited in Thomas Jackson Rice, *Barnaby Rudge: An Annotated Bibliography* (New York and London: Garland Publishing, 1987), 95.
10. John Stevenson, *Popular Disturbances in England 1700–1832*, 2nd edition (London and New York: Longman, 1992), 83; Shoemaker, *The London Mob*, 147.
11. Stevenson, *Popular Disturbances in England 1700–1832*, 76; Shoemaker, *The London Mob*, 21, 142.
12. Edmund Burke, *The Writings and Speeches of Edmund Burke Volume III: Party, Parliament, and the American War 1774–1780*, W. M. Elofson and John A. Woods, eds (Oxford: Clarendon Press, 1996), 425.
13. Peter Linebaugh, *The London Hanged: Crime and Civil Society in the Eighteenth Century* (Allen Lane, 1991), Chapter 10. Linebaugh points out that some of the blacks involved, including some leaders, were veterans of the American war (346–56), and that the attack on Lord Mansfield's house was condemned in the loyal press as a 'republican phrenzy' (cited 358). See also Iain McCalman, 'Controlling the riots: Dickens, *Barnaby Rudge* and romantic revolution', in *Radicalism and Revolution in Britain, 1775–1848: Essays in Honour of Malcolm I. Thomis*, Michael T. Davis, ed. (Basingstoke: Palgrave Macmillan, 2000), 207–27. An anti-republican conspiracy has been proposed by Simon Maccoby, who makes the point that the riots coincided with the introduction of a parliamentary Bill for universal suffrage (Simon Maccoby, *English Radicalism 1762–1835* (1955), 305–25).
14. Dickens to Forster, 11 and 18 September 1841, in *Dickens: The Critical Heritage*, Philip Collins, ed. (Routledge and Kegan Paul, 1971), 101–2.
15. William Vincent [Thomas Holcroft], *A Plain and Succint Narrative of the Late Riots and Disturbances in the Cities of London and Westminster, and Borough of Southwark*, Garland Harvey Smith, ed. (1780; Atlanta, Georgia: Emory University Library, 1944), 29.
16. George Lillie Craik, *Sketches of Popular Tumults; Illustrative of the Evils of Social Ignorance* (London: C. Knight and Co., 1837), 78.
17. Charles Dickens, *Barnaby Rudge* (Penguin, 1973), 616–17.

18. Stevenson, *Popular Disturbances*, 83–90; Shoemaker, *The London Mob*, 130.
19. For the social composition of the rioters, see George Rudé, *Paris and London in the Eighteenth Century: Studies in Popular Protest* (1952; Collins, 1970), 268–92, 289. See also Shoemaker, *The London Mob*, 137–9.
20. Cited in J. Paul de Castro, *The Gordon Riots* (Oxford: Oxford University Press, 1926), 91.
21. For a comprehensive and unrivalled study of the cultural experience of hanging in Britain, see Vic Gatrell, *The Hanging Tree: Execution and the English People 1770–1868* (Oxford: Oxford University Press, 1994).
22. Cited in E. P. Thompson, *The Making of the English Working Class* (Penguin, 1977), 78.
23. 'Some thoughts on the approaching executions' (10 July 1780) and 'Additional reflexions on the executions' (18 July 1780), *The Writings and Speeches of Edmund Burke. Volume III*, 611–17, 614.
24. Rudé, *Paris and London in the Eighteenth Century*, 289.
25. *Annual Register* (1780), 276.
26. Thompson, *The Making of the English Working Class*, 75, 78.
27. Shoemaker, *The London Mob*, 142.
28. Stevenson, *Popular Disturbances in England 1700–1832*, 90.
29. David Bindman, *The Shadow of the Guillotine: Britain and the French Revolution* (British Museum, 1989), 45. See also Diana Donald, *The Age of Caricature: Satirical Prints in the Age of George III* (New Haven and London: Yale University Press, 1996), 129.
30. See Mark Philp, 'Vulgar conservatism, 1792–3', *English Historical Review* (1995), 42–69; Ian Haywood, *The Revolution in Popular Literature: Print, Politics and the People, 1790–1860* (Cambridge: Cambridge University Press, 2004), Chapters 2–3.
31. William Blackstone, *Commentaries on the Laws of England*, 4 vols (W. Strahan, T. Cadell, 1783), 1: 144.
32. See: Roger Wells, 'English society and revolutionary politics in the 1790s: The case for insurrection', in Roger Wells and Mick Reed, eds, *Class, Conflict and Protest in the English Countryside 1700–1880* (Cass, 1990); Edward Royle, *Revolutionary Britannia? Reflections on the threat of revolution in Britain, 1789–1848* (Manchester: Manchester University Press, 2000), Chapter 4.
33. Thompson, *The Making of the English Working Class*, 135.
34. Jon Mee, *Romanticism, Enthusiasm and Regulation: Poetics and the Policing of Culture in the Romantic Period* (Oxford: Oxford University Press, 2003), 48–9.
35. See Haywood, *The Revolution in Popular Literature*, 39–42, for a longer discussion of this breach between Godwin and plebeian radicals.
36. Harold Bloom, ed. *The Selected Poetry of Coleridge* (New York and Ontario: New English Library, 1972), 128–9.
37. Robert Bage, *Hermsprong: Or Man as He is Not* (Oxford: Oxford University Press, 1974), 225–6.
38. The source is a handbill, cited in Haywood, *The Revolution in Popular Literature*, 64–5.
39. Saree Makdisi, *William Blake and the Impossible History of the 1790s* (Chicago and London: Chicago University Press, 2003), Chapter 1.
40. See Bindman, *The Shadow of the Guillotine*, 198–203.
41. See Mark Philp, 'The fragmented ideology of reform', in *The French Revolution and British Popular Politics*, Mark Philp, ed. (Cambridge: Cambridge University Press,

1991), 70–72; John Barrell, *Imagining the King's Death: Figurative Treason, Fantasies of Regicide 1793–1796* (Oxford: Oxford University Press, 2000), 120–4.

42. See, Gregory Claeys, ed. *The Politics of English Jacobinism: Writings of John Thelwall* (University Park: Pennsylvania University Press, 1995), 130–1. The incident is also mentioned by Mary Wollstonecraft: see Janet Todd and Marilyn Butler, eds, *The Works of Mary Wollstonecraft*, 7 vols (William Pickering, 1989), 6: 129.

43. John Stevenson, 'Popular radicalism and popular protest 1789–1815', in *Britain and the French Revolution 1789–1815*, H. T. Dickinson, ed. (Basingstoke: Macmillan, 1989), 74.

44. See: R. B. Rose, 'The Priestley riots of 1791', *Past and Present*, No. 18, 1960, 68–88; Thompson, *The Making of the English Working Class*, 79–80; Stevenson, *Popular Disturbances in England 1700–1870*, 137–42; Jenny Uglow, The *Lunar Men: The Friends who made the Future 1730–1810* (Faber and Faber, 2002), Chapter 37.

45. Cited in Uglow, The *Lunar Men*, 438.

46. Rose, 'The Priestley riots of 1791', 81–2; Uglow, *The Lunar Men*, 446.

47. *An Authentic Account of the Dreadful Riots in Birmingham*, (Birmingham, 1791), rptd in *The Riots at Birmingham, July 1791* (Birmingham: Arthur Bache Matthews, 1863), 2.

48. Cited in George Rudé, *The Crowd in History: A Study of Popular Disturbances in France and England 1730–1848* (John Wiley, 1964), 142. See also Craik, *Sketches of Popular Tumults*, 133.

49. Joseph Priestley, *An Appeal to the Public on the Subject of the Riots in Birmingham* (J. Thompson, 1791), 24.

50. Vivian Bird, *The Priestley Riots, 1791, and the Lunar Society* (Birmingham: Birmingham and Midland Institute, [n.d.]), 47.

51. Rose, 'The Priestley riots of 1791', 76.

52. The word 'fickle' is from Rudé, *The Crowd in History*, 147.

53. Cited in Rose, 'The Priestley Riots of 1791', 77.

54. Thompson, *The Making of the English Working Class*, 80.

55. George Walker, *The Vagabond: A Novel*, W. M. Verhoeven, ed. (Ontario: Broadview Press, 2004), 53–4.

56. Frederick Page, ed., *Byron: Poetical Works* (1904; Oxford: Oxford University Press, 1991), 101.

57. For a summary of the historical debate about the revolutionary potential of the Luddites, see Royle, *Revolutionary Britannia?*, 35–42.

58. Cited in Peter Quennell, *Byron: A Self-Portrait* (Oxford: Oxford University Press, 1990), 13–14.

59. Thompson, *The Making of the English Working Class*, 585.

60. Cited in Royle, *Revolutionary Britannia?*, 37.

61. Charlotte Bronte, *Shirley* (Penguin, 1978), 335.

62. Thompson, *The Making of the English Working Class*, 577.

63. Cited in ibid., 579.

64. Cited in Kevin Binfield, *The Writings of the Luddites* (Baltimore: John Hopkins University Press, 2004), 77–8.

65. Thompson, *The Making of the English Working Class*, 604.

66. Cited in Christopher Hampton, *A Radical Reader: The Struggle for Change in England, 1381–1914* (Penguin, 1984), 392.

67. See Tom Mole, 'Byron's "Ode to the framers of the frame bill": The embarrassment of industrial culture', *Keats-Shelley Journal*, 52, 2003, 111–29. Mole argues that the

deletion of names emasculated the poem, though I doubt that the device fooled the reader.

68. *Shelley: Poetical* Works, Thomas Hutchinson, ed. (1905; Oxford: Oxford University Press, 1991), 780.
69. Cited in Thompson, *The Making of the English Working Class*, 589.
70. Robert Southey, 'On the state of public opinion and the political reformers' (1816), in *Essays, Moral and Political*, 3 vols (John Murray, 1832), 1: 415.
71. Cited in Quennell, *Byron*, 135.
72. Thompson, *The Making of the English Working Class*, 623.
73. See Quennell, *Byron*, 93–4.
74. Cited in Ian Haywood, 'Radical journalism', in *Romantic Period Writings: An Anthology*, Zachary leader and Ian Haywood, eds (Routledge, 1998), 11.
75. Thompson, *The Making of the English Working Class*, 660.
76. See Haywood, *The Revolution in Popular Literature*, Chapter 4.
77. Walter Scott, *The Heart of Mid-Lothian* (Everyman, 1970).
78. David Lodge, 'The French revolution and the condition of England: Crowds and power in the early Victorian novel', in *The French Revolution and British Culture*, Ceri Crossley and Ian Small, eds, (Oxford: Oxford University Press, 1989), 138.
79. *Narrative of the Life of Walter Scott, Bart. Begun by Himself and Continued by J. G. Lockhart* (London and Toronto: Dent), 316.
80. Ibid., 363–4.
81. Cited in Julie Kipp, 'Back to the future: Walter Scott on the politics of radical reform in Ireland and Scotland', *European Romantic Review*, Vol. 16, No. 2, 2005, 231–42, 239, 234.
82. Gatrell, *The Hanging Tree*, 6. See also Chapter 5.
83. Michel Foucault, *Discipline and Punish: The Birth of the Prison* (1975; Penguin, 1991), 29.
84. On Cato Street, see: David Worrall, *Radical Culture: Discourse, Resistance and Surveillance 1790–1820* (Brighton: Harvester Wheatsheaf, 1992), 187–202; Gatrell, *The Hanging Tree*, Chapter 11.
85. Walter Scott, *Quentin Durward* (Everyman, 1969).
86. See Royle, *Revolutionary Britannia?*, Chapter 2; Ian Dyck, ' "Rural war" and the missing revolution in early nineteenth-century England', in *Radicalism and Revolution in Britain*, Davis, ed.
87. Edward Gibbon Wakefield, *Swing Unmasked; or, the Causes of Rural Incendiarism* (Effingham Wilson, 1831), 43–4.
88. See E. J. Hobsbawm and George Rudé, *Captain Swing* (Lawrence and Wishart, 1969), particularly Chapters 3–4.
89. William Cobbett, *The Collected Social and Political Writings of William Cobbett*, Noel Thomson and David Eastwood, eds, 17 vols (Routledge/Thoemmes Press), 10: 578.
90. 'Confession of Thomas Goodman', Appendix to *A Short Account of the Life and Death of Swing, the Rick-Burner, Written by One Well-Acquainted With Him* (Effingham Wilson [1830]), 25.
91. Dyck, ' "Rural war" and the missing revolution in early nineteenth-century England', 185–7. See also Ian Dyck, *William Cobbett and Rural Popular Culture* (Cambridge: Cambridge University Press, 1992).
92. Hobsbawm and Rudé, *Captain Swing*, 257; Stevenson, *Popular Disturbances in England 1700–1870*, 268.

93. 'Reverend' Robert Taylor, *Swing: or, Who are the Incendiaries? A Tragedy, founded on late circumstances, and as performed at The Rotunda* (Richard Carlile, 1831), 47.
94. *Prompter* (1830), 41, 336, 120.
95. Richard Carlile, *Life and History of Swing, the Kent Rick Burner. Written by Himself* (R. Carlile, 1830), 24.
96. *A Short Account of the Life and Death of Swing, the Rick Burner, Written by One Well Acquainted With Him*, 24.
97. Mary Mitford, 'The Incendiary. A country tale', in *Our Village*, 3 vols (London: Whittaker and Co, 1835), 3: 282. The 'Farewell' at end of volume 3 is dated April 1832. For an interesting discussion of Mitford's story, see Elizabeth K. Helsinger, *Rural Scenes and National Representation: Britain, 1815–1850* (Princeton, N.J.: Princeton University Press, 1997), Chapter 3.
98. Royle, *Revolutionary Britannia?*, 67.
99. Stevenson, *Popular Disturbances in Britain 1700–1870*, 289.
100. George Amey, *City Under Fire: The Bristol Riots and their Aftermath* (Lutterworth Press, 1979), 69.
101. Mark Harrison, *Crowds and History: Mass Phenomena in English Towns, 1790–1835* (Cambridge: Cambridge University Press, 1988), 299.
102. Stevenson, *Popular Disturbances in England 1700–1832*, 292.
103. Charles Kingsley, 'Great cities and their influence for good and evil' (1857), in *Sanitary and Social Essays* (1882; Macmillan, 1895), 188.
104. Thompson, *The Making of the English Working Class*, 88.
105. *Annual Register* (1831), 295; Craik, *Sketches of Popular Tumults*, 55.
106. Mikhail Bakhtin, *Problems of Dostoyevsky's Poetics*, Carl Emerson, ed. (Manchester: Manchester University Press, 1984), 128. See also Harrison, *Crowds and History*, 309.
107. Harrison, *Crowds and History*, 298.
108. Mikhail Bakhtin, *Rabelais and his World* (1965; Bloomington: Indiana University Press, 1984), 26.
109. [W. H. Somerton], *A Full Report of the Trials of the Bristol Rioters* (Bristol, 1832), 30–1.
110. *The Bristol Riots, Their Causes, Progress and Consequences. By a Citizen* (Bristol, 1832), 134–5.
111. *Annual Register* (1831), Chronicle, 172.
112. *The Bristol Riots, Their Causes, Progress and Consequences*, 119.
113. See Victor E. Neuberg, *Popular Literature: A History and Guide* (Penguin, 1977), 140.
114. See Jane Moody, *Illegitimate Theatre in London, 1770–1840* (Cambridge: Cambridge University Press, 2000), 27–8.
115. Cited in Clive Emsley, 'The impact of the French revolution', in *The French Revolution and British Culture*, Crossley and Small, eds, 39.
116. Cited in Castro, *The Gordon Riots*, 34.
117. Cited in ibid., 217.
118. Cited in ibid., 221.
119. Cited in Rose, 'The Priestley riots of 1791', 79.
120. *The Bristol Riots, Their Causes, Progress and Consequences*, 72, 111.
121. Craik, *Sketches of Popular Tumults*, 318.
122. See also Thompson, *The Making of the English Working Class*, 81.
123. Harrison, *Crowds and History*, 311.

Bibliography

The place of publication is London unless otherwise specified.

Primary sources

Aikin, J. and A. L. Aikin, *Miscellaneous Pieces, in Prose* (J[oseph] Johnson, 1775).

Alexander, James, *Some Account of the First Apparent Symptoms of the Late Rebellion in the County of Kildare and in the County of Wexford* (Dublin: John Jones, 1800).

Allen, Ethan, *A Narrative of Colonel Ethan Allen's Captivity* (New York: Corinth Books, 1961).

Annual Register.

[Anon.], *Narrative of a Private Soldier, in One of His Majesty's Regiment of Foot. Written by Himself* (Glasgow: Young, Gallie and Co., 1819).

An Authentic Account of the Dreadful Riots in Birmingham (Birmingham, 1791), rptd in *The Riots at Birmingham, July 1791* (Birmingham: Arthur Bache Matthews, 1863).

Bage, Robert, *Hermsprong: Or Man as He is Not* (Oxford: Oxford University Press, 1974).

Baillie, Joanna, *A Series of Plays: In Which it is Attempted to Delineate the Stronger Passions of the Mind* (1798; rptd Oxford and New York: Woodstock, 1990).

[Banim, Michael], *The Croppy: A Tale of 1798*, 3 vols (Henry Colburn, 1828).

Barlow, Joel, *The Columbiad* (Philadelphia: Fry and Kammerer, 1807).

Barruel, Abbe, *The History of the Clergy During the French Revolution. A Work Dedicated to the English Nation* (Dublin: N. Fitzpatrick, 1794).

Beccaria, Cesare, 'On Crimes and Punishments', in *On Crimes and Punishments and Other Writings*, Richard Bellamy, ed., trans. Richard Davies (Cambridge: Cambridge University Press, 1995).

Bennett, Betty, T., ed., *British War Poetry in the Age of Romanticism: 1793–1815* (New York and London: Garland Publishing, 1976).

Binfield, Kevin, *The Writings of the Luddites* (Baltimore: John Hopkins University Press, 2004).

Blackstone, William, *Commentaries on the Laws of England*, 4 vols (W. Strahan, T. Cadell, 1783).

Blake, William, *The Poems of William Blake*, W. H. Stevenson and David V. Erdman, eds (Longman, 1975).

Bleby, Henry, *Death Struggles of Slavery: Being a Narrative of Facts and Incidents Which Occurred in a British Colony, During the Two Years Immediately Preceding Negro Emancipation* (Hamilton, Adams and Co., 1853).

Breen, Jennifer, *Women Romantic Poets 1785–1832: An Anthology* (J. M. Dent, 1992).

The Bristol Riots, Their Causes, Progress and Consequences. By a Citizen (Bristol, 1832).

Bronte, Charlotte, *Shirley* (Penguin, 1978).

Burke, Edmund, *Sketch of a Negro Code* (1792), in *SAE*, 2.

——, *Reflections on the Revolution in France, and on the Proceedings in Certain Societies in London Relative to that Event. In a Letter intended to have been sent to a Gentleman in Paris*, in *The Writings and Speeches of Edmund Burke. Volume VIII. The French Revolution 1790–94*, L. G. Mitchell, ed. (Oxford: Clarendon Press, 1989).

——, *The Writings and Speeches of Edmund Burke. Volume VI: The Launching of the Hastings Impeachment 1786–1788*, P. J. Marshall, ed. (Oxford: Clarendon Press, 1991).

——, *The Writings and Speeches of Edmund Burke. Volume III: Party, Parliament, and the American War 1774–1780*, W. M. Elofson and John A. Woods, eds (Oxford: Clarendon Press, 1996).

——, *A Philosophical Enquiry into the Origin of our Ideas of the Sublime and Beautiful* (Oxford: Oxford University Press, 1998).

Butler, Marilyn, ed., *Burke, Paine, Godwin and the Revolution Controversy* (Cambridge: Cambridge University Press, 1984).

Byron, George Gordon, *The Selected Poetry and Prose of Byron*, W. H. Auden, ed. (Signet, 1966).

——, *Don Juan*, T. G. Steffan, E. Steffan and W. W. Pratt, eds (Penguin, 1977).

——, *Byron: Poetical Works*, Frederick Page, ed. (1904; Oxford: Oxford University Press, 1991).

Canning, George, *The Speech of the Rt Hon. George Canning, in the House of Commons, on the 16th Day of March, 1824*, in *SAE*, 3.

Carlile, Richard, *Life and History of Swing, the Kent Rick Burner. Written by Himself* (R. Carlile, 1830).

Claeys, Gregory, ed., *Political Writings of the 1790s*, 8 vols (William Pickering, 1995).

Clarkson, Thomas, *The History of the Rise, Progress, and Accomplishment of the Abolition of the African Slave-Trade by The British Parliament*, 2 vols (Longman, Hurst, Rees and Orme, 1808).

——, *Thoughts on the Necessity of Improving the Condition of the Slaves in the British Colonies, with a View to Their Ultimate Emancipation* (1823), in *SAE*, 3.

Cobbett, William, *The Collected Social and Political Writings of William Cobbett*, Noel Thomson and David Eastwood, eds, 17 vols (Routledge/Thoemmes Press, 1998).

——, *William Cobbett: Selected Writings*, Leonora Nattrass, ed., 5 vols (Pickering and Chatto, 1998).

Coleridge, Samuel Taylor, *The Collected Letters of Samuel Taylor Coleridge*, Earl L. Griggs, ed., 6 vols (Oxford: Oxford University Press, 1956–71).

——, *The Collected Works of Samuel Taylor Coleridge. 1: Lectures 1795 on Politics and Religion*, Lewis Patton and Peter Mann, eds (Routledge and Kegan Paul, 1971).

——, *The Selected Poetry of Coleridge*, Harold Bloom, ed. (New York and Ontario: New English Library, 1972).

Cooper, James Fenimore, *The Last of the Mohicans* (Oxford: Oxford University Press, 1998).

Craik, George Lillie, *Sketches of Popular Tumults; Illustrative of the Evils of Social Ignorance* (London: C. Knight and Co., 1837).

Crevecoeur, J. Hector St. John, *Letters from an American Farmer* [1782] and *Sketches of Eighteenth-Century America* [1925] (Penguin, 1987).

D'Auberteuil, Michel René Hilliard, *Miss McCrea: A Novel of the American Revolution*, trans. Eric LaGuardia (Gainesville, Florida: Scholars Facsimiles and Reprints, 1958).

Day, Thomas, *Ode for the New Year 1776* (J. Almon, 1776).

——, *The Desolation of America* (G. Kearsley, 1777).

De Tocqueville, Alexis, *Democracy in America*, 2 vols (Collins, 1968).

Dickens, Charles, *Barnaby Rudge* (Penguin, 1973).

Edwards, Bryan, *An Historical Survey of the French Colony in the Island of St. Domingo* (John Stockdale, 1797).

——, *The History, Civil and Commercial, of the British Colonies in the West Indies*, 4th edition, 3 vols (1793; John Stockdale, 1797).

Equiano, Olaudah, *The Interesting Narrative of the Life of Olaudah Equiano, or Gustavus Vassa, The African*, Vincent Caretta, ed. (Penguin, 1995).

Fanon, Frantz, *The Wretched of the Earth* (1961; Penguin, 1985).

Folley, Terence, ed., *Eyewitness to 1798* (Cork: Mercier Press, 1996).

Fox, William, *An Address to the People of Great Britain, on the Propriety of Abstaining from West India Sugar and Rum* (1791), in *SAE*, 2.

Gentleman's Magazine.

Godwin, William, *The Political and Philosophical Writings of William Godwin*, Mark Philp, ed., 7 vols (William Pickering, 1993).

Gordon, James, *History of the Rebellion in Ireland in the Year 1798* (Dublin: William Porter, 1801).

Grace, Henry, *The History of the Life and Sufferings of Henry Grace* (Basingstoke: Printed for the Author, 1764).

Hampton, Christopher, *A Radical Reader: The Struggle for Change in England, 1381–1914* (Penguin, 1984).

Hay, Edward, *History of the Insurrection in the County of Wexford* (1803) (Dublin: J. Stockdale).

Holcroft, Thomas ['William Vincent'], *A Plain and Succint Narrative of the Late Riots and Disturbances in the Cities of London and Westminster, and Borough of Southwark*, Garland Harvey Smith, ed. (1780; rptd Atlanta, Georgia: Emory University Library, 1944).

Hume, David, 'Of the original contract', in *Essays Moral, Political and Literary*, T. H. Green and T. H. Grose, eds (Longmans Green and Co, 1898).

——, *An Enquiry Concerning the Principles of Morals* (Oxford: Clarendon Press, 1983).

Ierne: An Elegy (London: Wm. Clark; Dublin: G. Burnet, 1798).

[Jackson, Charles], *A Narrative of the Sufferings and Escape of Charles Jackson, Late resident at Wexford, in Ireland, including an Account, by way of Journal, of several Barbarous Atrocities committed, in June, 1798, by the Irish Rebels in that Town, while it was in their Possession, to the Greater Part of which he was an Eye-Witness* (Printed for the Author, 1798).

Jemison, Mary, *A Narrative of the Life of Mrs. Mary Jemison (1824)*, in *Women's Indian Captivity Narratives*, Katherine Zabelle Derounian-Stodola, ed. (Penguin, 1998).

Johnson, Samuel, *The Yale Edition of the Works of Samuel Johnson*, W. J. Bate, John M. Bullitt, L. F. Powell, eds (New Haven and London: Yale University Press, 1963).

Klingberg, T. F. J. and S. B. Hustvedt, eds, *The Warning Drum. The British Home Front Faces Napoleon. Broadsides of 1803* (Berkeley and Los Angeles: University of California Press, 1944).

[Las Casas, Bartoleme], *The Tears of the Indians: Being An Historical and True Account of the Cruel Massacres and Slaughters of above Twenty Millions of Innocent People; Committed by the Spaniards in the Islands of Hispaniola, Cuba, Jamaica, etc. As also in the Continent of Mexico, Peru, and Other Places of the West Indies, to the Total Destruction of those Countries. Written in Spanish by Casaus, an Eye Witness of Those Things* (1656).

Lewis, Matthew, *The Monk* (Oxford: Oxford University Press, 1990).

Macaulay, Catherine, 'Observations on the Reflections of the Right Hon. Edmund Burke (1790)', in Claeys, *Political Writings of the 1790s*, 1.

Mackintosh, James, *Vindicæ Gallicæ: Defence of the French Revolution and its English Admirers Against the Accusations of the Right Hon. Edmund Burke (1791)*, in *Political Writings of the 1790s*, G. Claeys, ed., 1.

[Maturin, Charles], *The Milesian Chief. A Romance*, 4 vols (Henry Colburn, 1812).

Memoirs of Richard Lovell Edgeworth, Esq. Begun by Himself and Concluded by his Daughter, Maria Edgeworth, 2 vols (R. Hunter, 1820).

Mitford, Mary, 'The incendiary. A country tale', in *Our Village*, 3 vols (London: Whittaker and Co, 1835).

Moore, John, *A Journal During a Residence in France, from the Beginning of August, to the Middle of December, 1792*, 2 vols (G. G. and J. Robinson, 1793).

Moore, Thomas, *Memoirs of Captain Rock the Celebrated Irish Chieftain, with Some Account of his Ancestors* (Longman, 1824).

Musgrave, Richard, *Memoirs of The Different Rebellions in Ireland*, 3rd edition, 2 vols (1801; Dublin and London, 1803).

Myles Byrne, *Memoirs of Myles Byrne*, 3 vols (Paris and New York: Gustave Bossange, 1863).

Northcott, Cecil, *Slavery's Martyr: John Smith of Demerara and the Emancipation Movement* (Epworth Press, 1976).

Paddy's Resource, or the Harp of Erin, Attuned to Freedom; Being a Collection of Patriotic Songs, Selected for Paddy's Amusement (Dublin: np, nd [1795]).

Paine, Thomas, *The Rights of Man* (Penguin, 1984).

——, *The Thomas Paine Reader*, Michael Foot and Isaac Kramnick, eds (Penguin, 1987).

Pike, E. Royston, ed., *Human Documents of the Industrial Revolution* (1966; George Allen and Unwin, 1970).

Political Magazine.

Price, Richard, *Political Writings*, D. O. Thomas, ed. (Cambridge: Cambridge University Press, 1991).

Priestley, Joseph, *An Appeal to the Public on the Subject of the Riots in Birmingham* (J. Thompson, 1791).

Prince, Mary, *The History of Mary Prince, a West Indian Slave, Related by Herself* (1831), in *SAE*, 1.

Prompter.

Report from the Committee of Secrecy, of the House of Lords in Ireland, 30 August 1798 (J. Debrett, 1798).

Robertson, William, *The History of America*, 2 vols (Edinburgh: W. Strahan and T. Cadell, 1777).

Ronan, Rev. Myles V., ed., *Insurgent Wicklow 1798. The story as written by Rev. Bro. Luke Cullen, O. D. C. (1793–1859). With additional Material from other MSS* (Dublin: Clonmore and Reynolds, 1948).

Rousseau, Jean-Jacques, *The Social Contract: or, Principles of Political Right* (Penguin, 1968).

Scott, Walter, *Narrative of the Life of Walter Scott, Bart. Begun by Himself and Continued by J. G. Lockhart* (London and Toronto: Dent, 1922).

——, *The Heart of Mid-Lothian* (Everyman, 1970).

——, *Old Mortality* (Penguin, 1974).

Scrivener, Michael, *Poetry and Reform: Periodical Verse from the English Democratic Press 1792–1824* (Detroit: Wayne State University Press, 1992).

Shelley, Percy Bysshe, *Shelley: Poetical Works*, Thomas Hutchinson, ed. (Oxford: Oxford University Press, 1991).

——, *The Prose Works of Percy Bysshe Shelley. Volume 1*, E. B. Murray, ed. (Oxford: Clarendon Press, 1993).

Sheridan, Richard Brinsley, *Pizarro: A Tragedy*, 7th edition (James Ridgway, 1799).

A Short Account of the Life and Death of Swing, the Rick-Burner, Written by One Well-Acquainted With Him (Effingham Wilson [1830]).

Smith, Adam, *The Theory of Moral Sentiments* (1759), in *British Moralists 1650–1800*, D. D. Raphael, ed., 2 vols (Clarendon Press, 1969).

Smith, Charlotte, *Desmond*, Antje Blank and Janet Todd, eds (William Pickering, 1997).

——, *The Old Manor House*, Jacqueline M. Labbe, ed. (Ontario: Broadview Press, 2002).

[Somerton, W. H.], *A Full Report of the Trials of the Bristol Rioters* (Bristol, 1832).

Southey, Robert, 'On the state of public opinion and the political reformers' (1816), in *Essays, Moral and Political*, 3 vols (John Murray, 1832).

[Stephen, James], *Buonaparte in the West Indies* (1803).

——, *England Enslaved by Her Own Slave Colonies. To the Electors and People of the United Kingdom* (1826), *SAE*, 3.

Taylor, Robert, *Swing: or, Who are the Incendiaries? A Tragedy, Founded on Late Circumstances, and as Performed at The Rotunda* (Richard Carlile, 1831).

Thelwall, John, *The Politics of English Jacobinism: Writings of John Thelwall*, Gregory Claeys, ed. (University Park: Pennsylvania University Press, 1995).

Tone, William T. W., 'The third and last expedition for the liberation of Ireland, and the Capture, Trial and Death of Theobald Wolfe Tone [1826]', in *Life of Theobald Wolfe Tone. Compiled and arranged by William Theobald Wolfe Tone*, Thomas Bartlett, ed. (Dublin: The Lilliput Press, 1998).

Towers, Joseph, *Thoughts on the commencement of a new Parliament* (1791), in *Political Writings of the 1790s*, Claeys, ed., 1.

[Turnbull, Gordon], *A Narrative of the Revolt and Insurrection of the French Inhabitants in the Island of Grenada. By an Eye-Witness* (Edinburgh: Constable, 1795).

[Turner, Nat], *The Confessions of Nat Turner* (1831). Reprinted in Herbert Aptheker, *Nat Turner's Slave Rebellion* (New York: Humanities Press, 1975).

Wakefield, Edward Gibbon, *Swing Unmasked; or, the Causes of Rural Incendiarism* (Effingham Wilson, 1831).

Walker, George, *The Vagabond: A Novel*, W. M. Verhoeven, ed. (Ontario: Broadview Press, 2004).

Whitely, Henry, *Three Months in Jamaica, in 1832; Comprising a Residence of Seven Weeks on a Sugar Plantation* (J. Hatchard and Son, 1832).

Wilberforce, William, *An Appeal to the Religion, Justice and Humanity of the Inhabitants of the British Empire, in Behalf of the Negro Slaves in the West Indies* (1823), in *SAE*, 3.

Williams, Helen Maria, *Peru: A Poem* (T. Cadell, 1784).

——, *Letters from France; Containing a Great Variety of Original Information Concerning the Most Important Events that have Occurred in that Country in the Years 1790, 1791, 1792, and 1793*, 2 vols (Dublin: J Chambers, 1794).

——, *Letters Containing a Sketch of the Politics of France from the Thirty-First of May 1793, till the Twenty-Eighth of July 1794, and of the Scenes which have passed in the prisons of Paris*, 2 vols (G. G. and J. Robinson, 1795).

——, *Letters Written in France*, Neil Fraistat and Susan Lanser, eds (Ontario: Broadview Press, 2001).

Williamson, Peter, *French and Indian Cruelty; Exemplified in the Life and Various Vicissitudes of Fortune of Peter Williamson*, Michael Fry, ed. (Bristol: Thoemmes Press, 1996).

Wollstonecraft, Mary, *Vindication of the Rights of Women* (Penguin, 1975).

——, *Works of Mary Wollstonecraft*, Janet Todd and Marilyn Butler, eds, 7 vols (William Pickering, 1989).

Wordsworth, Dorothy, *The Grasmere and Alfoxden Journals*, Pamela Woof, ed. (Oxford: Oxford University Press, 2002).

Wordsworth, William, *The Prelude: A Parallel Text*, J. C. Maxwell, ed. (Penguin, 1976).

——, *William Wordsworth*, Stephen Gill, ed. (Oxford: Oxford University Press, 1984).

Wu, Duncan, ed., *Romanticism: An Anthology* (Oxford: Blackwell, 1994).

Zabelle Derounian-Stodola, Katherine, ed., *Women's Indian Captivity Narratives* (Penguin, 1998).

Secondary sources

Allmendinger, David F. Jr, 'The construction of *The Confessions of Nat Turner*', in *Nat Turner: A Rebellion in History and Memory*, Kenneth S. Greenberg, ed. (Oxford: Oxford University Press, 2003).

Amey, George, *City Under Fire: The Bristol Riots and their Aftermath* (Lutterworth Press, 1979).

Anstey, Roger, *The Atlantic Slave Trade and British Abolition 1760–1810* (Macmillan, 1975).

Aptheker, Herbert, *American Negro Slave Revolts* (New York: Columbia University Press, 1944).

——, 'The event', in *Nat Turner: A Rebellion in History and Memory*, Kenneth S. Greenberg, ed. (Oxford: Oxford University Press, 2003).

Bainbridge, Simon, *British Poetry and the Revolutionary and Napoleonic Wars: Visions of Conflict* (Oxford: Oxford University Press, 2003).

Bakhtin, Mikhail, *Problems of Dostoyevsky's Poetics*, Carl Emerson, ed. (Manchester: Manchester University Press, 1984).

Baldick, Chris, *In Frankenstein's Shadow: Myth, Monstrosity and Nineteenth-Century Writing* (Oxford: Clarendon Press, 1987).

Barnett, Louise K., *The Ignoble Savage: American Literary Racism, 1790–1860* (Westport, Connecticut and London: Greenwood Press, 1975).

Barrell, John, 'Fire, famine and slaughter', *Huntingdon Library Quarterly*, Vol. 63, No. 3, 2000, 277–98.

——, *Imagining the King's Death: Figurative Treason, Fantasies of Regicide 1793–1796* (Oxford: Oxford University Press, 2000).

Bartlett, Thomas, 'Clemency and compensation: The treatment of defeated rebels and suffering loyalists after the 1798 rebellion', in *Revolution, Counter-revolution and Union: Ireland in the 1790s*, Jim Smyth, ed. (Cambridge: Cambridge University Press, 2000).

Bartlett, Thomas, Kevin Dawson and Dáire Keogh, *Rebellion: A Television History of 1798* (Dublin: Gill and Macmillan, 1998).

Bartlett, Thomas, David Dickson, Dáire Keogh and Kevin Whelan, eds, *1798: A Bicentenary Perspective* (Dublin: Four Courts Press, 2003).

Baum, Joan, *Mind Forg'd Manacles: Slavery and the English Romantic Poets* (North Haven Connecticut: Archon Books, 1994).

Berkhofer, Robert F., *The White Man's Indian: Images of the American Indian from Columbus to the Present* (New York: Alfred A. Knopf, 1978).

Bindman, David, *The Shadow of the Guillotine: Britain and the French Revolution* (British Museum, 1989).

Bird, Vivian, *The Priestley Riots, 1791, and the Lunar Society* (Birmingham: Birmingham and Midland Institute, [n.d.]).

Blackburn, Robin, *The Overthrow of Colonial Slavery 1776–1848* (Verso, 1988).

——, *The Making of New World Slavery: From the Baroque to the Modern 1492–1800* (Verso, 1997).

Blakemore, Steven, *Crisis in Representation: Thomas Paine, Mary Wollstonecraft, Helen Maria Williams and the Rewriting of the French Revolution* (Madison and London: Fairleigh Dickinson University Press, 1997).

Botting, Fred, *Gothic* (1996; London and New York: Routledge, 1999).

Boulton, James T., *The Language of Politics in the Age of Wilkes and Burke* (Routledge and Kegan Paul, 1963).

Brewer, John, *The Common People and Politics 1750–1790s* (Chadwick-Healey, 1986).

Burnham, Michelle, *Captivity and Sentiment: Cultural Exchange in American Literature, 1682–1861* (Hanover and London: University Press of New England, 1997).

Butler, Marilyn, 'Telling it like a story: The French revolution as narrative', in *Studies in Romanticism*, 28, 1989, 345–64.

——, 'General introduction' to *The Novels and Selected Works of Maria Edgeworth*, 12 vols (Pickering and Chatto, 1999–2003).

Cairns, David and Shaun Richards, *Writing Ireland: Colonialism, Nationalism and Culture* (Manchester: Manchester University Press, 1988).

Carey, Brycchan, *British Abolitionism and the Rhetoric of Sensibility* (Basingstoke: Palgrave, 2005).

Carr, Helen, *Inventing the American Primitive: Politics, Gender and the Representation of Native American Literary Traditions, 1789–1936* (Cork: Cork University Press, 1996).

Carter, Angela, *The Sadeian Woman: An Exercise in Cultural History* (1979; Virago, 1987).

Christenson, Jerome, *Romanticism and the End of History* (Baltimore and London: John Hopkins University Press, 2000).

Clair, William St., *The Reading Nation in the Romantic Period* (Cambridge: Cambridge University Press, 1994).

Cole, G. D. H., *The Life of William Cobbett* (W. Collins, 1925).

——, ed., *Letters from William Cobbett to Edward Thornton Written in the Years 1797–1800* (Oxford: Oxford University Press, 1937).

Coleman, Deirdre, *Romantic Colonization and British Anti-Slavery* (Cambridge: Cambridge University Press, 2005).

Colley, Linda, *Captives: Britain, Empire and the World, 1600–1850* (Jonathan Cape, 2002).

Collins, Philip, ed., *Dickens: The Critical Heritage* (Routledge and Kegan Paul, 1971).

Craciun, Adriana, *Fatal Women of Romanticism* (Cambridge: Cambridge University Press, 2003).

Craton, Michael, 'Slave culture, resistance and the achievement of emancipation in the British West Indies, 1783–1838', in *Slavery and British Society 1776–1846*, James Walvin, ed. (Macmillan, 1982).

——, *Testing the Chains: Resistance to Slavery in the British West Indies* (Ithaca and London: Cornell University Press, 1982).

Cullen, Fintan, *Visual Politics: The Representation of Ireland 1750–1930* (Cork: Cork University Press, 1997).

Curry, Kenneth, *Southey* (Routledge and Kegan Paul, 1975).

Dann, John C., *The Revolution Remembered: Eyewitness Accounts of the War of Independence* (London and Chicago: University of Chicago Press, 1980).

Dart, Gregory, *Rousseau, Robespierre and English Romanticism* (Cambridge: Cambridge University Press, 1999).

De Castro, J. Paul, *The Gordon Riots* (Oxford: Oxford University Press, 1926).

Dickinson, H. T., 'Popular conservatism and militant loyalism 1789–1815', in *Britain and the French Revolution 1789–1815*, H. T. Dickinson, ed. (Basingstoke: Macmillan, 1989).

Dixon, Charles, *The Wexford Rising in 1798: Its Causes and Its Course* (1955; London: Constable, 1997).

Donald, Diana, *The Age of Caricature: Satirical Prints in the Age of George III* (New Haven and London: Yale University Press, 1996).

Du Bois, W. E. B., 'The souls of black folk', in *Three Negro Classics* (1965; New York: Avon Books, 1999).

Dunne, Tom, 'Popular ballads, revolutionary rhetoric and politicisation', in *Ireland and the French Revolution*, Hugh Gough and David Dickson, eds (Dublin: Irish Academic Press, 1990).

——, 'Representations of rebellion: 1798 in literature', in *Ireland, England and Australia: Essays in Honour of Oliver Macdonagh*, F. B. Smith, ed. (Cork and Canberra: Cork University Press, 1990).

——, *Rebellions: Memoir, Memory and 1798* (Dublin: The Lilliput Press, 2004).

Dyck, Ian, *William Cobbett and Rural Popular Culture* (Cambridge: Cambridge University Press, 1992).

——, '"Rural war" and the missing revolution in early nineteenth-century England', in *Radicalism and Revolution in Britain, 1775–1848: Essays in Honour of Malcolm I. Thomis*, Michael T. Davis, ed. (Basingstoke: Palgrave Macmillan, 2000).

Eagleton, Terry, *Heathcliff and the Great Hunger: Studies in Irish Culture* (Verso, 1995).

Elliot, Marianne, *Partners in Revolution: The United Irishmen and France* (New Haven and London: Yale University Press, 1982).

——, 'Ireland and the French revolution', in *Britain and the French Revolution 1789–1815*, H. T. Dickinson, ed. (Basingstoke: Macmillan, 1989).

Ellis, Markman, *The Politics of Sensibility: Race, Gender and Commerce in the Sentimental Novel* (Cambridge: Cambridge University Press, 1996).

Emsley, Clive, 'The impact of the French revolution', in *The French Revolution and British Culture*, Ceri Crossley and Ian Small, eds (Oxford: Oxford University Press, 1989).

Favret, Mary, 'Coming home: The public spaces of romantic war', in *Studies in Romanticism*, 33, 1994, 539–48.

——, 'Flogging: The anti-slavery movement writes pornography', in *Romanticism and Gender*, Anne Janowitz, ed. (English Association, 1998).

Ferguson, Moira, *Subject to Others: British Women Writers and Colonial Slavery, 1670–1834* (New York and London: Routledge, 1992).

Ferris, Ina, *The Romantic National Tale and the Question of Ireland* (Cambridge: Cambridge University Press, 2002).

Flanagan, Thomas, *The Irish Novelists 1800–1850* (New York: Columbia University Press, 1959).

Foster, Roy, 'Ascendancy and union', in *The Oxford History of Ireland*, Roy Foster, ed. (Oxford: Oxford University Press, 1989).

——, *Modern Ireland 1600–1972* (Penguin, 1989).

Foucault, Michel, *Discipline and Punish: The Birth of the Prison* (1975; Penguin, 1991).

Franklin, Michael J., 'Accessing India: Orientalism, anti-"Indianism" and the rhetoric of Jones and Burke', in *Romanticism and Colonialism: Writing and Empire, 1780–1830*, Tim Fulford and Peter J. Kitson, eds (Cambridge: Cambridge University Press, 1998).

French, David P., 'James Fenimore Cooper and Fort William Henry', *American Literature*, 32, 1960, 28–38.

Fulford, Tim, *Romantic Indians* (Oxford: Oxford University Press, 2006).

Furniss, Tom, 'Gender in revolution: Edmund Burke and Mary Wollstonecraft', in *Revolution in Writing: British Literary Responses to the French Revolution*, Kelvin Everest, ed. (Oxford: Oxford University Press, 1991).

——, *Edmund Burke's Aesthetic Ideology: Language, Gender, and Political Economy in Revolution* (Cambridge: Cambridge University Press, 1993).

——, 'Cementing the nation: Burke's *Reflections* on nationalism and national identity', in *Edmund Burke's Reflections on the Revolution in France: New Interdisciplinary Essays*, John Whale, ed. (Manchester: Manchester University Press, 2000).

Gahan, Daniel, *The People's Rising: Wexford 1798* (Dublin, Gill and MacMillan, 1995).

——, 'The rebellion of 1798 in south Leinster', in *1798: A Bicentenary Perspective*, Thomas Bartlett, David Dickson, Dáire Keogh, Kevin Whelan, eds (Dublin: Four Courts Press, 2003).

Galloway, Colin, *The American Revolution in Indian Country: Crisis and Diversity in Native American Communities* (Cambridge: Cambridge University Press).

Gatrell, Vic, *The Hanging Tree: Execution and the English People 1770–1868* (Oxford: Oxford University Press, 1994).

Geggus, David, *Slavery, War, and Revolution: The British Occupation of Saint Domingue 1793–1798* (Oxford: Clarendon Press, 1982).

——, 'British opinion and the emergence of Haiti, 1791–1805', in *Slavery and British Society 1776–1846*, James Walvin, ed. (Macmillan, 1982).

Gibbons, Luke, *Edmund Burke and Ireland: Aesthetics, Politics and the Colonial Sublime* (Cambridge: Cambridge University Press, 2003).

Grant, Alfred, *Our American Brethren: A History of Letters in the British Press During the American Revolution, 1775–1781* (Jefferson, North Carolina, and London: McFarland and Company, 1967).

Graymont, Barbara, *The Iroquois in the American Revolution* (Syracuse, New York: Syracuse University Press, 1972).

Harrison, Mark, *Crowds and History: Mass Phenomena in English Towns, 1790–1835* (Cambridge: Cambridge University Press, 1988).

Hawthorne, Mark D., *John and Michael Banim (The 'O'Hara Brothers'): A Study in the Early Development of the Anglo-Irish Novel* (Salzburg: Institut Fur Englische Sprache und Literatur, 1975).

Haywood, Ian, 'Radical journalism', in *Romantic Period Writings: An Anthology*, Zachary leader and Ian Haywood, eds (Routledge, 1998).

——, *The Revolution in Popular Literature: Print, Politics and the People, 1790–1860* (Cambridge: Cambridge University Press, 2004).

——, ' "The renovating fury": Southey, republicanism and sensationalism', *Romanticism on the Net*, 36, 2004.

Helsinger, Elizabeth K., *Rural Scenes and National Representation: Britain, 1815–1850* (Princeton, N.J.: Princeton University Press, 1997).

Herzog, Don, *Poisoning the Minds of the Lower Orders* (1998; Princeton, New Jersey: Princeton University Press, 2000).

Hobsbawm, E. J. and George Rudé, *Captain Swing* (Lawrence and Wishart, 1969).

Hollingworth, Brian, *Maria Edgeworth's Irish Writing: Language, History, Politics* (Basingstoke: Macmillan, 1997).

Huish, Robert, *Memoirs of the Late William Cobbett*, 2 vols (John Saunders, 1836).

Hulme, Peter, *Colonial Encounters: Europe and the Native Caribbean 1492–1797* (1986; Routledge, 1992).

Hunt, Lynn, *Politics, Culture and Class in the French Revolution* (Berkeley, Los Angeles and London: University of California Press, 1984).

——, *The Family Romance of the French Revolution* (Routledge, 1992).

Hutchings, Kevin D., 'Writing commerce and cultural progress in Samuel Hearne's *A Journey . . . to the Northern Ocean*', in *Ariel: A Review of International English Literature*, Vol. 28, No. 2, 1997, 49–78.

James, C. L. R., *The Black Jacobins: Toussaint L'Ouverture and the San Domingo Revolution* (1938; Penguin, 2001).

Jones, Chris, *Radical Sensibility: Literature and Ideas in the 1790s* (London and New York: Routledge, 1993).

Jones, Vivien, 'Women writing revolution: Narratives of history and sexuality in Wollstonecraft and Williams', in *Beyond Romanticism: New Approaches to Texts and Contexts 1780–1832*, Stephen Copley and John Whale, eds (London and New York: Routledge, 1992).

Keane, Angela, *Women Writers and the English Nation in the 1790s* (Cambridge: Cambridge University Press, 2000).

Keane, Patrick J., *Coleridge's Submerged Politics* (Columbia and London: University of Missouri Press, 1994).

Kelly, Gary, *Women, Writing, and Revolution 1790–1827* (Oxford: Clarendon Press, 1993).

Kelly, James, ' "We were all to have been massacred": Irish protestants and the experience of rebellion', in *1798: A Bicentenary Perspective*, Thomas Bartlett, David Dickson, Dáire Keogh, Kevin Whelan, eds (Dublin: Four Courts Press, 2003).

Keogh, Dáire, 'The women of 1798: Explaining the silence', in *1798: A Bicentenary Perspective*, Thomas Bartlett, David Dickson, Dáire Keogh, Kevin Whelan, eds (Dublin: Four Courts Press, 2003).

Kipp, Julie, 'Back to the future: Walter Scott on the politics of radical reform in Ireland and Scotland', in *European Romantic Review*, Vol. 16, No. 2, 2005, 231–42.

Kitson, Peter J., 'Races, places, peoples, 1785–1800', in *Romanticism and Colonialism: Writing and Empire, 1780–1830*, Tim Fulford and Peter J. Kitson, eds (Cambridge: Cambridge University Press, 1998).

——, 'Romantic displacements: Representing cannibalism', in *Placing and Displacing Romanticism*, Peter J. Kitson, ed. (Aldershot: Ashgate, 2001).

Kolodny, Annette, *The Land Before Her: Fantasy and Experience of the American Frontiers, 1630–1860* (Chapel Hill and London: University of North Carolina Press, 1984).

Lawrence, D. H., *Studies in Classic American Literature*, Ezra Greenspan, Lindeth Vasey and John Worthen, eds (Cambridge: Cambridge University Press, 2003).

Lawson-Peebles, Robert, 'The lesson of the massacre at Fort William Henry', in *New Essays on The Last of the Mohicans*, H. Daniel Peck, ed. (Cambridge: Cambridge University Press, 1992).

Leary, Lewis, 'Introduction' to Michel René Hilliard d'Auberteuil, in *Miss McCrea: A Novel of the American Revolution*, trans. Eric LaGuardia (Gainesville, Florida: Scholars Facsimiles and Reprints, 1958).

Leask, Nigel, 'Pantisocracy', in *An Oxford Companion to the Romantic Age*, Iain McCalman, ed. (Oxford: Oxford University Press, 1999).

Lee, Debbie, *Slavery and the Romantic Imagination* (Philadelphia: University of Pennsylvania Press, 2002).

Linebaugh, Peter, *The London Hanged: Crime and Civil Society in the Eighteenth Century* (Allen Lane, 1991).

Linebaugh, Peter and Marcus Rediker, *The Many-Headed Hydra: Sailors, Slaves, Commoners, and the Hidden History of the Revolutionary Atlantic* (Verso, 2000).

Liu, Alan, *Wordsworth: The Sense of History* (1989; Stanford: Stanford University Press, 2000).

Lock, F. P., 'Rhetoric and representation in Burke's *Reflections*', in *Edmund Burke's Reflections on the Revolution in France: New Interdisciplinary Essays*, JohnWhale, ed. (Manchester: Manchester University Press, 2000).

Lodge, David, 'The French revolution and the condition of England: Crowds and power in the early victorian novel', in *The French Revolution and British Culture*, Ceri Crossley and Ian Small, eds (Oxford: Oxford University Press, 1989).

MacGillivray, J. R., 'The pantisocracy scheme and its immediate background', in *Studies in English by Members of University College* [Toronto], M. W. Wallace, ed. (Toronto, 1931).

Maddox, Lucy, *Removals: Nineteenth-Century American Literature and the Politics of Indian Affairs* (New York and Oxford: Oxford University Press, 1991).

Maguire, W. A., *The 1798 Rebellion in Ireland: A Bicentenary Exhibition* (Belfast: Ulster Museum, 1998).

Makdisi, Saree, *Romantic Imperialism: Universal Empire and the Culture of Modernity* (Cambridge: Cambridge University Press, 1998).

——, *William Blake and the Impossible History of the 1790s* (Chicago and London: Chicago University Press, 2003).

Maniquis, Robert M., 'Holy savagery and wild justice: English romanticism and the terror', *Studies in Romanticism*, 28 (Fall 1989), 365–95.

——, 'Filling up and emptying out the sublime: Terror in British radical culture', *Huntingdon Library Quarterly*, Vol. 63, No. 3, 2000, 369–405.

Martin, Terence, 'From atrocity to requiem: History in *The Last of the Mohicans*', in *New Essays on The Last of the Mohicans*, H. Daniel Peck, ed. (Cambridge: Cambridge University Press, 1992).

McCalman, Iain, 'Controlling the riots: Dickens, *Barnaby Rudge* and romantic Revolution', in *Radicalism and Revolution in Britain, 1775–1848: Essays in Honour of Malcolm I. Thomis*, Michael T. Davis, ed. (Basingstoke: Palgrave Macmillan, 2000).

——, ed., *An Oxford Companion to the Romantic Age: British Culture 1776–1832* (1999; Oxford: Oxford University Press, 2001).

McCormack, W. J., *Ascendancy and Tradition in Anglo-Irish Literary History from 1789 to 1939* (Oxford: Clarendon Press, 1985).

McDonagh, Josephine, *Child Murder and British Culture, 1720–1900* (Cambridge: Cambridge University Press, 2003).

McDowell, R. B., 'Burke and Ireland', in *The United Irishmen: Republicanism, Radicalism and Rebellion*, David Dickson, Dáire Keogh and Kevin Whelan, eds (Dublin: Lilliput Press, 1993).

McKusick, James C., ' "Wisely forgetful": Coleridge and the politics of pantisocracy', in *Romanticism and Colonialism: Writing and Empire, 1780–1830*, Tim Fulford and Peter J. Kitson, eds (Cambridge: Cambridge University Press, 1998).

McWilliams, John P., *The American Epic: Transforming a Genre, 1770–1860* (Cambridge: Cambridge University Press, 1989).

——, *The Last of the Mohicans: Civil Savagery and Savage Civility* (Toronto: Twayne Publishers, 1995).

——, 'The historical contexts of *The Last of the Mohicans*', in James Fenimore Cooper, ed. *The Last of the Mohicans* (Oxford: Oxford University Press, 1998).

Mee, Jon, *Enthusiasm and Regulation: Poetics and the Policing of Culture in the Romantic Period* (Oxford: Oxford University Press, 2003).

Mellor, Anne K., ' "Am I not a Woman and a Sister?": Slavery, romanticism, and gender', in *Romanticism, Race, and Imperial Culture, 1780–1834*, Alan Richardson and Sonia Hofkosh, eds (Bloomington and Indianapolis: Indiana University Press, 1996).

Melville, Lewis, ed., *The Life and Letters of William Cobbett in England and America*, 2 vols (John Lane, 1913).

Mole, Tom, 'Byron's "Ode to the Framers of the Frame Bill": The embarrassment of industrial culture', *Keats-Shelley Journal*, 52, 2003, 111–29.

Moody, Jane, *Illegitimate Theatre in London, 1770–1840* (Cambridge: Cambridge University Press, 2000).

Morton, Timothy, 'Blood sugar', in *Romanticism and Colonialism: Writing and Empire, 1780–1830*, Tim Fulford and Peter J. Kitson, eds (Cambridge: Cambridge University Press, 1998).

Namias, June, *White Captives: Gender and Ethnicity on the American Frontier* (Chapel Hill and London: University of North Carolina Press, 1993).

Nattrass, Leonora, *William Cobbett: The Politics of Style* (Cambridge: Cambridge University Press, 1995).

Neuberg, Victor E., *Popular Literature: A History and Guide* (Penguin, 1977).

Nickerson, Hoffman, *The Turning Point of the Revolution: or Burgoyne in America* (Boston and New York: Houghton Mifflin Company, 1928).

O'Donnell, Ruan, 'Rebellion of 1798', in *An Oxford Companion to the Romantic Age: British Culture 1776–1832*, Iain McCalman, ed. (1999; Oxford: Oxford University Press, 2001).

O'Sullivan, Tadgh, ' "The violence of a servile war": three narratives of Irish rural insurgency post-1798', in *Rebellion and Remembrance in Modern Ireland*, Laurence M. Geary, ed. (Dublin: Four Courts Press, 2001).

Outram, Dorinda, *The Body and the French Revolution: Sex, Class and Political Culture* (New Haven and London: Yale University Press, 1989).

Pakenham, Thomas, *The Year of Liberty: The Story of the Great Irish Rebellion of 1798* (1969; Weidenfeld and Nicholson, 1997).

Paulson, Ronald, *Representations of Revolution 1789–1820* (New Haven and London: Yale University Press, 1983).

Pearson, Jacqueline, *Women's Reading in Britain, 1750–1835* (Cambridge: Cambridge University Press, 1999).

Peck, H. Daniel, ed., *New Essays on The Last of the Mohicans* (Cambridge: Cambridge University Press, 1992).

Philbrick, Thomas, 'The sources of Cooper's knowledge of Fort William Henry', *American Literature*, 36, 1964, 209–14.

Philp, Mark, 'The fragmented ideology of reform', in *The French Revolution and British Popular Politics*, Mark Philp, ed. (Cambridge: Cambridge University Press, 1991).

——, 'Vulgar conservatism, 1792–3', *English Historical Review* (1995), 42–69.

Plotz, John, *The Crowd: British Literature and Public Politics* (Berkeley and Los Angeles: University of California Press, 2000).

Praz, Mario, *Romantic Agony* (1951; Oxford: Oxford University Press, 1970).

Price, Richard and Sally Price, eds, *Stedman's Narrative . . . from the Original 1790 Manuscript* (Baltimore: John Hopkins University Press, 1988).

Quennell, Peter, *Byron: A Self-Portrait* (Oxford: Oxford University Press, 1990).

Raphael, Ray, *The American Revolution: A People's History* (2001; Profile Books, 2002).

Rawlinson, Mark, 'Invasion! Coleridge, the defence of Britain and the cultivation of the public's fear', in *Romantic Wars: Studies in Culture and Conflict, 1793–1822*, Philip Shaw, ed. (Aldershot: Ashgate, 2000).

Rawson, Claude, *God, Gulliver and Genocide: Barbarism and the European Imagination* (Oxford: Oxford University Press, 2001).

Rice, Thomas Jackson, *Barnaby Rudge: An Annotated Bibliography* (New York and London: Garland Publishing, 1987).

Richardson, Alan, 'Epic ambivalence: Imperial politics and romantic deflection in Williams's *Peru* and Landor's *Gebir*', in *Romanticism, Race, and Imperial Culture, 1780–1834*, Alan Richardson and Sonia Hofkosh, eds (Bloomington and Indianapolis: Indiana University Press, 1996).

Roe, Nicholas, *Wordsworth and Coleridge: The Radical Years* (Oxford: Oxford University Press, 1988).

——, 'Politics, history and Wordsworth's poems', in *The Cambridge Companion to Wordsworth*, Stephen Gill, ed. (Cambridge: Cambridge University Press, 2003).

Rogin, Michael Paul, *Fathers and Children: Andrew Jackson and the Subjugation of the American Indian* (New York: Alfred A. Knopf, 1975).

Rose, R. B., 'The Priestley riots of 1791', *Past and Present*, 18, 1960, 68–88.

Royle, Edward, *Revolutionary Britannia? Reflections on the Threat of Revolution in Britain, 1789–1848* (Manchester: Manchester University Press, 2000).

Rudé, George, *The Crowd in History: A Study of Popular Disturbances in France and England 1730–1848* (John Wiley, 1964).

——, *Paris and London in the Eighteenth Century: Studies in Popular Protest* (1952; Collins, 1970).

Russell, Gillian, *Theatres of War: Performance, Politics and Society 1793–1815* (Oxford: Clarendon Press, 1995).

Salih, Sara, 'The History of Mary Prince, the black subject, and the black canon', in *Discourses of Slavery and Abolition*, Brycchan Carey, Markman Ellis and Sara Salih, eds (Basingstoke: Palgrave, 2004).

Schama, Simon, *Citizens: A Chronicle of the French Revolution* (Penguin, 1989).

Shaw, Philip, ed., *Romantic Wars: Studies in Culture and Conflict, 1793–1822* (Aldershot: Ashgate, 2000).

——, *Waterloo and the Romantic Imagination* (Basingstoke: Palgrave, 2002).

Shoemaker, Robert, *The London Mob: Violence and Disorder in Eighteenth-Century England* (London and New York: Hambledon and London, 2004).

Simpson, David, *Romanticism, Nationalism, and the Revolt Against Theory* (Chicago and London: University of Chicago Press, 1993).

Slotkin, Richard, *Regeneration through Violence: The Mythology of the American Frontier* (Norman: University of Oklahoma Press, 1973).

Smith, Edward, ed., *William Cobbett; A Biography*, 2 vols (Sampson Low, Marston, Searle and Rivingham, 1878).

Smyth, Jim, *The Men of No Property: Irish Radicals and Popular Politics in the Late Eighteenth Century* (1992; Houndmills: Macmillan, 1998).

Spater, George, *William Cobbett: The Poor Man's Friend*, 2 vols (Cambridge: Cambridge University Press, 1982).

Steele, Ian K., *Betrayals: Fort William Henry and the 'Massacre'* (Oxford: Oxford University Press, 1990).

Stevenson, John, 'Popular radicalism and popular protest 1789–1815', in *Britain and the French Revolution 1789–1815*, H. T. Dickinson, ed. (Basingstoke: Macmillan, 1989).

——, *Popular Disturbances in England 1700–1832*, 2nd edition (London and New York: Longman, 1992).

Sutherland, John, *The Life of Walter Scott* (1995; Oxford: Blackwell, 1997).

Sypher, Wylie, *Guinea's Captive Kings: British Anti-Slavery Literature of the XVIIIth Century* (1942; New York: Octagon Books, 1969).

Teltscher, Kate, 'Empire and race', in *Romantic Period Writings 1798–1832: An Anthology*, Zachary Leader and Ian Haywood, eds (Routledge, 1998).

Thomas, Helen, *Romanticism and Slave Narratives: Transatlantic Testimonies* (Cambridge: Cambridge University Press, 2000).

Thompson, E. P., *The Making of the English Working Class* (1963; Penguin, 1977).

Tilly, Charles, *The Vendée* (Cambridge, Massachusetts and London: Harvard University Press, 1976).

Todd, Janet, *Sensibility: An Introduction* (London: Methuen, 1986).

——, *Rebel Daughters: Ireland in Conflict 1798* (Viking, 2003).

Todorov, Tzvetan, *The Conquest of America: The Question of the Other*, trans. Richard Howard (HarperPerennial, 1984).

Trumpener, Katie, *Bardic Nationalism: The Romantic Novel and the British Empire* (Princeton, New Jersey: Princeton University Press, 1997).

Uglow, Jenny, *The Lunar Men: The Friends who made the Future 1730–1810* (Faber and Faber, 2002).

Watson, J. R., *Romanticism and War: A Study of British Romantic Period Writers and the Napoleonic Wars* (Basingstoke: Palgrave, 2003).

Wells, Roger, 'English society and revolutionary politics in the 1790s: The case for insurrection', in *Class, Conflict and Protest in the English Countryside 1700–1880*, Roger Wells and Mick Reed, eds (Cass, 1990).

Whelan, Kevin, 'Reinterpreting the 1798 rebellion in County Wexford', in *The Mighty Wave: The 1798 Rebellion in Wexford*, Dáire Keogh and Nicholas Furlong, eds (Dublin, Four Courts Press, 1996).

——, ed., *The Fellowship of Freedom: Companion Volume to the Bicentenary Exhibition by the National Library and National Museum at Collins Barracks, Dublin 1998* (Cork: Cork University Press, 1998).

Williams, Raymond, *Cobbett* (Oxford: Oxford University Press, 1983).

Wood, Marcus, *Blind Memory: Visual Representations of Slavery in England and America 1780–1865* (Manchester: Manchester University Press, 2000).

——, *Slavery, Empathy and Pornography* (Oxford: Oxford University Press, 2002).

——, 'Black bodies and satiric limits in the long eighteenth century', in *Forms of Satire in the Romantic Period*, Steven E. Jones, ed. (Basingstoke: Palgrave Macmillan, 2003).

Worrall, David, *Radical Culture: Discourse, Resistance and Surveillance 1790–1820* (Brighton: Harvester Wheatsheaf, 1992).

Index

August-2006   MAC/BRM   Page-265   1403_94282X_13_ind01

Printed in the United States
105219LV00003B/42/A